Reading in America

Reading in America

Literature & Social History

Edited by Cathy N. Davidson

The Johns Hopkins University Press

Baltimore / London

© 1989 The Johns Hopkins University Press
All rights reserved
Printed in the United States of America

The Johns Hopkins University Press, 701 West 40th Street, Baltimore,
Maryland 21211
The Johns Hopkins Press Ltd., London

The paper used in this publication meets the minimum requirements of
American National Standard for Information Sciences—Permanence of
Paper for Printed Library Materials, ANSI Z39.48-1984.

Library of Congress Cataloging-in-Publication Data

Reading in America.

  Bibliography: p.
  1. Books and reading—United States—History. 2. Literature and
society—United States—History. 3. Books and reading—Social
aspects—United States. 4. United States—Intellectual life. 5. United
States—Popular culture. 6. United States—Social conditions.
I. Davidson, Cathy N.
Z1003.2.R424 1989   028'.9'0973   88-35821
ISBN 0-8018-3799-5 (alk. paper)
ISBN 0-8018-3800-2 (pbk. : alk. paper)

Contents

Acknowledgments

The editor is pleased to acknowledge generous support from the American Council of Learned Societies, the John Simon Guggenheim Memorial Foundation, Michigan State University, and Princeton University (and especially the chairpersons at those universities, Victor Paananen and Emory Elliott). Much of the final editing of the volume was done in Japan while I was a visiting professor at Kobe Jogakuin Daigaku (Kobe College). Administrators at Kobe College—especially Michio Okamoto, Kosaku Yamaguchi, and Yukihito Hijiya—helped to make trans-Pacific editing possible, as did the editorial staff at the Johns Hopkins University Press and my exemplary research assistants, Rod Phillips and Deborah Barker.

Reading in America

Introduction

Toward a History of Books and Readers

Cathy N. Davidson

Book, either numerous sheets of white paper that have been stitched together in such a way that they can be filled with writing; or, a highly useful and convenient instrument constructed of printed sheets variously bound in cardboard, paper, vellum, leather, etc. for presenting the truth to another in such a way that it can be conveniently read and recognized. Many people work on this ware before it is complete and becomes an actual book in this sense. The scholar and the writer, the papermaker, the type founder, the typesetter and the printer, the proofreader, the publisher, the book binder, sometimes even the gilder and the brass-worker, etc. Thus many mouths are fed by this branch of manufacture.

> *Allgemeines Oeconomisches Lexicon,* 1753

The History of Books

Georg Heinrich Zinck's multileveled eighteenth-century definition emphasizes that a book exists, simultaneously, as a physical object, a sign system, the end product of diverse arts and labors, and the starting point for intercultural and intracultural communication. Moreover, because a book is both meaning ("truth," to use Zinck's term) and the vehicle by which meaning is conveyed (the object of various enterprises of production, distribution, and consumption), just what it is under one of these headings necessarily influences what it is under the others. Or as the eminent bibliographer G. Thomas Tanselle has observed, "What a text says is forever linked to the mundane realities underlying the physical product that gives the text a material embodiment."[1]

Those interested in the history of books must, accordingly, be sensitive to the "material embodiment" of books and to the material reasons for that embodiment. Yet such "mundane realities" are often ignored by literary critics who for the most part have been trained to explicate complex meanings in subtle texts, texts that until recently came packaged mostly as nondescript paperbound books specifically designed for the classroom trade. (Recall, for example, the covers on the old Penguin, Modern Library, or Riverside editions, each volume virtually indistinguishable from others in the series and all as solidly reassuring and conventional as, say, the cover of *PMLA*.) The historian of books would not find this homogeneous presentation accidental. On the contrary, these classroom editions support Tanselle's assertion about the relationship between the physical book and its meaning. By printing tastefully understated series of classics, publishers implicitly endorsed a certain notion of what went on within the literature class-room and—again, like the issues of *PMLA*—what went onto the library shelves. Reading, in that classroom, was a specialized activity, an elite academic enterprise not to be confused with ordinary acts of reading by those who did not attend college. Specialized academic publishers eschewed the gaudier competition of the open market in favor of the university classroom, where a select body of required texts would be elucidated by a trained scholar (the professor as hiero-phant expounding on mysteries hidden to the uninitiated). The acolyte who might later wish to pursue on his or her own the kind of reading learned in the classroom could then proceed to other Great Books, designated as such by the familiar covers.

Many of the same titles elucidated in the classroom were also marketed with considerably more sensational covers by companies such as Pocket Books that aimed at a wider audience. (What terrible sin marked Hester's breast with the scarlet letter? What passionate obsession drove Ahab to his watery grave?) The book historian well might wonder how such dramatic differences in presentation and, implicitly, audience also influence the understanding of what is read or what divisions in the society are marked by these different read-ings. A field of study that makes the book its focus constantly moves between material, aesthetic, and ideological planes, and assumes that a book, like meaning itself, is created within a specific historical context. Or to cite a more contemporary example, a book historian, noting how much the physical appearance of classroom texts has changed of late, could assess the massive changes that have occurred during the past twenty years both in publishing (takeovers by mega-corporations with no previous publishing interests, mergers among the major and minor publishing houses, and then subsequent de-mergers) and in academe (an expanding and contracting student population, a devaluing of a liberal arts education, and decanonization within the humanities).

Zinck's early definition underscores the need to examine just how books work in the society in which they are written and read, how books themselves are manufactured. Not surprisingly, the history of books as a field of study departs from text-based models of literary criticism—whether New Critical or deconstructionist—to consider a constellation of problems surrounding the production of books as well as the production of meaning by those who read books. A historian interested in the late eighteenth century might begin with physical features of books such as binding techniques or whether the paper is handmade or the type hand-set, then further inquire about the operations of the printing shop, and from there proceed to investigate the terms of apprenticeship, the division of labor, or the degree of artisanship, specialization, or mechanization required for the manufacture of a book, all important aspects of working-class history and industrial development. Or the historian might investigate the financial arrangements among printers, authors, and readers. Obviously questions about the economics of publishing have direct bearing on who can afford to be a writer or a reader in a given society and, ultimately, on what kinds of literature are available (or popular) at any one time. Could the apprentice who trod the pelts or sorted the type in an eighteenth-century printer's shop afford to purchase his own copy of Charles Brockden Brown's *Wieland* (1798)? For that matter, could Brown afford novels written by his contemporaries? Could he support himself by writing fiction? Could his publisher support himself by selling Brown's novels? In short, how much does literature cost? And what is the social cost of that particular financial requirement?

The large question of how books work in society can be posed and approached in various ways. Some book historians, for example, trace out the distribution of books among various subgroups (regional, racial, religious, sexual, or economic); some search for evidence of the ways in which readers responded to the books they read; some juxtapose such past readings with the historians' own interpretation or valuation of the text; some chart the rise and fall of particular titles and types of literature. Aesthetic criteria, as book historians frequently note, change radically from one period to another, and one century's bestseller—Jean-Jacques Rousseau's *Julie, ou la nouvelle Héloïse*, Susanna Rowson's *Charlotte Temple*, or T. S. Arthur's *Ten Nights in a Barroom*—can be unread or even unreadable in another era. Yet changing aesthetics—the vicissitudes of taste—are of particular interest to book historians because they provide an important point of intersection between studies of the book and other aspects of social or intellectual history.

Although the separate aspects of books and book production have been studied seriously at least since the Renaissance, only recently have scholars conjoined their research on the discrete dimensions of the book to found a comprehensive discipline. Originating in France as *l'histoire du livre* and carried on energetically in Germany (where it is known as *Geschichte des Buchwesens*), the field has different parameters and emphases in different countries but is based on certain fundamental assumptions about the importance of the printed word. In the formulation of Robert Darnton, one of its foremost theorists and practitioners, the history of the book is concerned with nothing less than the "social and cultural history of communication by print, . . . how ideas were transmitted through print and how exposure to the printed word affected the thought and behavior of mankind during the last five hundred years."[2] More recently, historians have expanded even this wide definition by emphasizing continuities (rather than disjunctions) between the age of the manuscript and the post-Gutenberg print world, a practice that pushes back the history of books in the West to at least the second or third century of the Christian era.[3]

Given such an enormous subject matter, fragmentation and specialization within the field are necessary and inevitable. Yet as Darnton suggests in the first essay in this collection, all books, no matter what their period or place of origin, are part of a "communications circuit" that remains more or less constant. Focusing on Voltaire's *Questions sur l'Encyclopédie*, Darnton describes a circuit that encompasses author and publisher, as well as printers, compositors, editors, and press workers (or their computer-age equivalents); suppliers of paper, ink, and type; distributors (from literary agents to smugglers), booksellers, and librarians; and, finally, readers (professional readers such as censors, reviewers, and academic critics as well as general readers).

The main goals and possibilities of the history of the book were originally outlined in the landmark *L'Apparition du livre* (1958) by Lucien Febvre and Henri-Jean Martin, which, as its English subtitle attests, analyzes "The Impact of Printing 1450–1800."[4] Febvre and Martin address one crucial and comprehensive question: How did the advent of printing change the shape of culture? Other scholars, primarily European, continue to investigate this same matter, often by integrating the key questions of book history with the socioeconomic methodologies of the *"Annales* school" of French history. Three major studies written by American scholars in the 1970s—Natalie Zemon Davis's *Society and Culture in Early Modern France* (1975), Robert Darnton's *The Business of Enlightenment: A Publishing History of the Encyclopédie, 1775–1800* (1979), and Elizabeth L. Eisenstein's *The Printing Press as an Agent of Change* (1979)—also examine the extensive European history of the book and pose, along with the Continental studies, crucial questions regarding that history. How were books produced? By whom? And for whom? What relationships existed between authors and publishers? How did national or religious ideologies (especially with respect to censorship or propaganda) affect what books were printed and how ideas would be disseminated? What relationships existed between the legalities (such as copyright laws) and the economics of authorship and publishing? How much did books cost? Were books the province only of some citizens, or could the ideas set forth (if not the actual books themselves) be transmitted throughout the populace, regardless of readers' class, region, political or religious affiliation, ethnic background, or gender? How were books distributed to readers, and what were the circumstances by which these readers acquired sufficient literacy to allow them to participate in print culture? To what degree did cultural authorities such as political leaders, educators, clergy, and reviewers control access to books, both indirectly (by distributing praise and blame) and directly (by enforcing censorship)? What books are canonized (elevated to the special status of literature), and how, why, and to what end?

The implicit political import of these questions—essentially questions about the power and authority of the printed word—is made more explicit in a number of British studies such as Richard Altick's and Robert Webb's investigations of working-class readers, or Raymond Williams's Marxist analysis of the "long revolution," the technological and social march into the modern world.[5] Other sociological analysts of reading, from Robert Escarpit to Pierre Bourdieu, focus especially on the politics of book distribution and the cultural determination of taste.[6] In America, these questions have been effectively (and differently) addressed by literary critics—especially feminist and Marxist critics—such as Nina Baym, Fredric Jameson, Annette Kolodny, Susan Koppelman, Paul Lauter, Richard Ohmann, Janice A. Radway, Barbara Herrnstein Smith, Jane Tompkins, and Alan Wald.[7] One particularly American concern is the definition and vagaries of "value," especially the contingencies that influence the fluctuating evaluations of given authors or works and the mechanisms by which literature is brought before the reading public. Poststructuralist literary theory and German-inspired reception theory have also prompted historians of the book to examine the power relationships inherent in the structure of communication.[8] Similarly, the New Historicism currently generating excitement (and controversy) in American universities almost inevitably connects literary history and the history of the book.[9]

A major concern of book historians has been the relationship between the dissemination of books and the larger institutional structures of a society. It should be noted that book historians too work within such structures, and in America at least some of the interest in book history must be attributed to two important programs for book research. In 1979 the Library of Congress established its Center for the Book. Hosting conferences as well as publishing numerous books and pamphlets on subjects ranging from copyright law to the history of literacy, this center serves as a locus for scholarly activity. It also operates as a public outreach facility, designed, in the words of Daniel Boorstin, "to organize, focus, and dramatize our nation's interest and attention on the book, to marshal the nation's support—spiritual, physical, and fiscal—for the book."[10] To foster both goals, the Library of Congress recently published Alice D. Shreyer's *The History of Books: A Guide to Selected Resources in the Library of Congress* (1987) and also declared 1987 the "Year of the Reader," a project intended to increase public awareness of the importance of literacy and reading.

One year later, in 1980, the American Antiquarian Society established its Program in the History of the Book in American Culture. Chaired by historian David D. Hall, the program effectively utilizes the society's extensive holdings for the first two and a half centuries of American history (the period before 1877), and sponsors lectures (including the annual James Russell Wiggins Lecture in the History of the Book in American Culture), workshops, and seminars, as well as a residential fellowship program. The society also publishes numerous books and pamphlets in the field and a thrice-yearly newsletter, *The Book*, which includes abstracts of work in progress, reviews of scholarship in the area of the book, and announcements of various events of interest to historians of the book.[11]

Thanks partly to these two programs, the history of books is already well established in America and promises to become even more so because of the remarkable ingenuity of its practitioners in appropriating and drawing together the concerns and methodologies of various disciplines. The present collection serves as a sampler of the kinds of approaches that are available, of the diverse methodologies used by book historians, of the controversies in this field of study, and, explicitly, of the range of critical stances that can be brought to bear on the subject of the book in history. The essays range from traditional historical, material, and enumerative bibliographical studies to more theoretical and even polemical pieces. As Darnton concludes in his overview essay, books "do not respect limits, either linguistic or national," and thus "neither history nor literature nor economics nor sociology nor bibliography can do justice to all the aspects of the life of a book." The same, as these essays attest, is also true of the history of books.

The essays have been arranged chronologically by subject (from the seventeenth century to the present), yet certain key issues recur in the different studies, just as they have done throughout the history of books. For example, the collection ends much as it begins, with a study of literacy. These two essays employ different tactics to discuss the crucial problem of the nature, meaning, and distribution of reading and writing skills within society, important ideological as well as intellectual issues whether we address American society in 1690 or 1990. Other issues also recur: the relationship between the material study of books (bibliography) and social history; the controversial notion of a nineteenth-century "reading revolution" that changed the readership, if not the very nature, of reading; and the problems in what might be termed the sociology of readership (including, methodologically, the ways in which different reading communities can be isolated and studied).

Bibliography and Social History

All good book history—including the most speculative and theoretical—begins with sound bibliography. Thus virtually every study of early American culture is indebted to Charles Evans's monumental *American Bibliography* (1903–34). Not surprisingly, both the Library of Congress and the American Antiquarian Society (AAS) have energetically championed a broadly interdisciplinary and international approach to the history of books while also continuing their basic work in bibliography. Currently, AAS bibliographers are working on the North American Imprints Program (NAIP), which updates and corrects Evans and also supplements his pioneering work in other important ways. Responding to an increasing scholarly interest in the question of readership, the NAIP bibliographers have cited inscribers' names in AAS volumes, a first step toward partially documenting who actually read given titles in early America. Furthermore, NAIP is computerized, so this invaluable bibliographical resource will be readily available throughout the country.

Two essays in the present collection provide the basic bibliographical information that is the foundation for a social history of books in America and also illustrate diverse methods used by historical bibliographers. In "Chapbooks in America: Reconstructing the Popular Reading of Early America," the distinguished British bibliographer and social historian Victor Neuburg addresses the fundamental problem of how we can understand the intellectual life of predominantly poor or working-class readers, when these readers left behind virtually no evidence of their own reading in the form of letters or diaries. Paper was far too costly for the poor to use indiscriminately, and little was written about poor or even average citizens (except in novels or in the occasional sensationalized "last confessions of a dying sinner"). Nor can we extrapolate "implied readers" from extant cheap books. Precisely because they were inexpensively produced and widely circulated (and, it should be added, rarely collected by early American libraries), many once-popular books no longer exist. Most chapbooks, the cheapest volumes available in colonial America, were literally "read to pieces."

The book historian who would attempt to reconstruct popular colonial reading habits must work from such evidence as booksellers' catalogues (themselves both unreliable and fragmentary), newspaper advertisements, shipping invoices, auction records, and the sparse anecdotal testimony found in letters, diaries, or memoirs. A literary detective, the historical bibliographer must piece together a composite picture of the early American print world from such fragments as do remain. Thus Neuburg conjoins lists of the chapbooks and other "ephemeral, throwaway literature" that he has discovered with portraits of some of the people who published, sold, read, or collected this same material—characters such as Chapman Whitcomb, a colorful, sometimes eccentric late-eighteenth-century teacher, ragpicker (in the eighteenth century there was a chronic shortage of the rags needed for papermaking), traveling bookseller, and publisher of chapbooks. Neuburg's essay also illustrates how, for historians of the book, traditional bibliography merges with and becomes indistinguishable from social history.

Victor Neuburg's essay helps to flesh out our ideas of American reading, as, in a different way, does "Reflections on the Changing Publishing Objectives of Secular Black Book Publishers, 1900–1986," by librarian and book historian Donald Franklin Joyce. Like Neuburg, Joyce must employ unconventional sources and methods even to find the publishers who are the subject of his study. Often operating on a small scale, with extremely limited capital, and against almost impossible odds, many of the black publishers Joyce describes are missing from standard bibliographical sources. But through two important reference works, *The Catalog of the Arthur B. Spingarn Collection of Negro Authors* (1971) and *Black American Writers, 1773–1949: A Bibliography and Union List* (1975), and by searching for book advertisements in primarily black periodicals and journals, Joyce located and studied sixty-eight black-owned book publishers active in the United States before 1976. He also conducted a survey in which he located and questioned contemporary black publishers to ascertain not only what they are publishing but why. In this study, bibliography again merges with social history. We can note, for example, that the Reverend Sutton E. Griggs established his Orion Publishing Company in Nashville in 1901 to publish his protest novels against the ways blacks were being treated by white southerners. We can note too that the exemplary moral and social purpose behind Griggs's careers as writer and publisher is representative of early black publishers but is not totally removed from the concerns of contemporary black book publishers either.

Literacy

Anyone interested in the ways in which the printed word may have influenced thought and behavior in any particular place and time must address basic questions of literacy. Who could read? Who could write? What was the personal and social meaning of literacy? What was the relationship between mass education and book culture? At what point does a nation consider itself to be sufficiently literate or well educated? How does one define levels of literacy, and how does the concept of literacy, in the fullest sense of the term, bear on a nation's estimation of itself? John Adams, for example, liked to boast that "a native American who cannot read and write is as rare as a comet or an earthquake." Yet slaves in Adams's America were explicitly forbidden literacy, and even the exceptionally articulate Abigail Adams lamented the state of women's literacy and education in her era.[12] Obviously the term "literate," as applied to either individuals or a society, can be elastic. And just as obviously there can be varying levels of literacy within the same society, and part of any educational agenda is to establish which segments of the society should be educated and how.

The whole matter of who should learn what has (in America as elsewhere) a long and troubled history. The Company of the Massachusetts Bay established guidelines for the education of its young (specifically, its young men) even before leaving England. And in 1987, with two pedagogical works on the bestseller lists (Allan Bloom's vitriolic *The Closing of the American Mind: How Higher*

Education Has Failed Democracy and Impoverished the Souls of Today's Students and E. D. Hirsch, Jr.'s, *Cultural Literacy: What Every American Needs to Know*), we are no closer to a satisfactory national consensus.[13] Indeed, these two volumes aptly illustrate some of the most persistent contradictions in American theories of education and literacy. In a democracy, should one evaluate the success of the educational system by how well how many can read? Or should the nation particularly concern itself with providing an excellent education for a ruling elite—the best for the brightest? And are these different agendas really mutually exclusive?

Despite the use of "democracy" in his subtitle, Bloom is not concerned with mass education or mass literacy. There is no place for the *demos* or "common people" in his ideal university, which would be dedicated to educating an elite now slighted, Bloom would have it, by contemporary "egalitarian" (a dirty word for Bloom) educational principles and practices. To remedy this situation, he seeks to reinstate philosophy (especially classical philosophy) at the core of his curriculum. His is, as Martha Nussbaum has amply documented, a limited and limiting *paideia*. Not only does he want to restrict who receives the best education and just what goes into that education; he also wants to restrict the interpretation of those classical philosophers at the core of his agenda to his own consistently eccentric readings— readings that, tautologically, justify his educational program in the first place.[14] Moreover, and again despite the implication of his title and subtitle, Bloom obviously believes that the American mind has always been closed. He acknowledges no influences by American thinkers other than negative ones. He also is unequivocally condemnatory about the concepts "equality," "historicism," "psychology," and "relativism" (the latter term consistently misused by Bloom).[15] Only Great Books (defined largely as works of classical philosophy and European high culture) can ostensibly open American minds (defined—and this is a subtext running through Bloom's book—as the minds of, essentially, white men, as if no other minds could either warrant or repay the effort to educate them into an awareness of their own proclaimed primary place in the culture).

Bloom's arguments, as procedure and policy, are dubiously circular. They are also substantially based on a nostalgic reconstruction of the 1950s. Bloom even extols the McCarthy era as "one of the great periods of the American university."[16] In this respect, he is simply the most recent in a long line of middle-aged commentators who do not see in their children, students, or younger colleagues any signs of the same rigorous education ("standards") that they themselves received in their youth. The abandonment of the study of Greek and Latin as the basis for American education in the early national period occa-sioned precisely the same dire warnings of an impending crisis in American education that would have adverse consequences for the fiber and character of the entire society.

Bloom, at his most hysterical, postulates a two-thousand-year phil-osophical tradition destroyed in less than two generations by maraud-ing hordes of postadolescent hippies. It is sometimes difficult to take him seriously. One must, however, take seriously the popularity of his book and of Hirsch's *Cultural Literacy*, for it is not often that ped-agogical studies make the nation's bestseller lists. Yet this too is an American tradition, the concern with education and its relationship to society as a whole (a concern, incidentally, that would seem to belie Bloom's thesis about the closed American mind). In some respects, Hirsch's concern with the same issue seems more considered than Bloom's. For example, his educational program evinces less overt ra-cial and gender prejudice, and his recommendations for educational reform are both different from Bloom's and far more specific. While Bloom is concerned with the best students at the best universities, Hirsch's focus is America's primary and secondary schools, and his objective is to encourage a minimal level of "cultural literacy," by which he seems to mean a basic syllabus in the three R's taught through standardized texts that also encourage nationalistic and mor-alistic civic virtues.

The specter of Japanese superiority haunts Hirsch's book (and is, no doubt, one of the subliminal reasons for the popularity of both of these books). But Hirsch makes two dubious assumptions about that presumed superiority. First, he implies, on the first page of his study, that the Japanese educational system—almost exclusively dependent on rote learning and on the passing of brutal standardized tests—is responsible for Japan's "economic miracle." However, he in no way examines this alternative system, nor does he note, as do many in-creasingly alarmed Japanese educators, the social problems (national and international) occasioned by this extremely competitive system, a system that well may be more the *product* than the *producer* of Japan's current economic success. Second, like Bloom's, Hirsch's study is too much rooted in nostalgia, but now the nostalgia centers on a time (pre–John Dewey) when America was unquestionably su-preme in the world and society was as "orderly" and "standardized" as the curriculum. There is even a certain nostalgia for humble text-books such as McGuffey's reader, hardly the speculative stuff of phi-losophy. One wonders if matriculation from Hirsch's ideal high school would gain one admittance into Bloom's university.

Whereas Bloom eschews American contributions to contemporary thought, Hirsch praises the contributions of past American thinkers and relies heavily on American ideas for his prescriptive syllabus for the schools. He insists that American education (and society) can be saved only through "shared knowledge" cultivated throughout the school years, only through a body of collective allusions that all citizens, regardless of gender or race, will share. However, the long list of what "every American needs to know" with which his book concludes is itself clearly biased, and Hirsch's envisioned "every American" turns out to be suspiciously white, masculine, middle class, and, one must add, middle-aged (Elvis Presley makes the list but not the Rolling Stones, thalidomide but not AIDS)—none of which is particularly surprising. A syllabus necessarily excludes far more than it includes, which brings me to my other and main criticism of Hirsch's listings. He wants to believe that fewer options—a more rigorous, content-based, standardized national educational agenda—will better serve all. Yet what are the implications here? Do courses that also include Afro-American history actually deprive Afro-Americans of their share of the American pie and also handicap white students so that they cannot begin to compete in the world economy anymore? Like Bloom, Hirsch seems to assume that including in the curriculum information by and about women or minorities has somehow irreparably damaged American education and thus American society, whereas in the past the exclusion of these topics (in favor of a homogeneous "cultural literacy") actually served everyone, including women and minorities.

As both books attest, questions of literacy are always charged and political. Three essays in this volume, although not directly related to these best-selling tracts, do raise the same kinds of questions. For example, while using different theoretical procedures, all of these essays underscore a basic contention that literacy is never simply a "rate" that can be quantitatively measured, but is an exceptionally complicated social process as well as the embodiment of significant social ideals.[17] They show too that even though "cultural literacy" can be an ideal, it can also embody a limiting and even debilitating ideology and, similarly, that education does not automatically confer upon its recipients (in any era) social elevation, monetary reward, or even a drive toward social change.

In "Literacy Instruction and Gender in Colonial New England," E. Jennifer Monaghan assesses a number of important literacy studies, scrutinizing the theoretical assumptions that inform their conclusions. Her topic is the crucial matter of the relationship between ideologies of gender and the resources a society uses to educate its female inhabitants. As she notes, early Puritan school laws provided

specifically for boys, not for girls, and there was a concomitant disparity in the level of educational abilities between the sexes. But, Monaghan wonders, how well could colonial girls read, even given the fact
that many of them received only a minimal education? Were there
girls, for example who could read at an elementary level but could not
write? And, if so, what are the implications (social, intellectual) of
that discrepancy? By examining private and public documents, Monaghan assesses not just questions of literacy but how social assumptions influence educational principles and procedures. Although her
study focuses primarily on the seventeenth century, many of her
assumptions about the relationship between social inequities and
illiteracy are as true today as they were in early America.[18]

Dana Nelson Salvino also surveys the interrelationships between
social agendas and educational motives in "The Word in Black and
White: Ideologies of Race and Literacy in Antebellum America."
Briefly, from the beginning educators have advocated improved education and higher levels of literacy to foster two partly contradictory
programs. On the one hand, education has been seen as a form of
empowerment (sometimes the further empowerment, as Bloom advocates, of a group already socially recognized as elite, and sometimes
the very different matter of empowering new immigrants or the hitherto disenfranchised such as women and minorities). On the other
hand, education has been advocated as a social leveler, as a way to
blend together both the individuals and the ideals that compose the
nation (rather like the program Hirsch advocates). Salvino shows how
both agendas were at work, sometimes simultaneously, in early writings on Afro-American literacy and emphasizes the "reciprocal relation of literacy and culture." She examines the ways in which white
attitudes toward mass literacy and education for whites carried over
to white institutional stances toward black literacy in the antebellum
period. Most notably, the official attempt to deny literacy to slaves is a
compelling testimonial to the ideal of literacy as a form of empowerment. Salvino notes too the ways in which the slave community
accepted the notion of empowerment and used it for its own subversive purposes. However, she also cautions that even advanced literacy
skills could not in themselves free blacks, after manumission, from
racism, poverty, and low social status. The ideology of an empowering
"cultural literacy" works only insofar as the possessors of that advanced literacy can negotiate a society's power structures. For most
nonwhite citizens in the past century, that transaction was simply
not allowed, and the rhetoric of literacy ultimately failed to bring the
social and material rewards that the rhetoric promised.

In the last essay in this collection, "Literacy and Mass Media: The

Political Implications," Donald Lazere assesses the relationship between oral and written culture in our own hyperliterate, highly technological era, in which literacy is nonetheless still not universal or literacy levels uniformly high. Like Bloom and Hirsch, Lazere critiques contemporary media-saturated culture, but he does so more from a leftist than a rightist political perspective. His concern is that "the low level of cognitive development to which the discourse of American mass media and politics is presently geared is woefully inadequate for the effective functioning of a democracy." Lazere does not find a pronounced leftist bias in American media (the lament of many conservative watchdog groups) but rather sees the media as inducing the kind of "one-dimensional society" Herbert Marcuse described, a limited and limiting society in which "the capacity to imagine alternatives to the status quo . . . has been systematically destroyed." In this polemical closing essay, Lazere wonders, essentially, if the book is not now threatened by the pervasiveness of an oral media that undermines the very cognitive, imaginative, and interpretive skills that reading requires. Are books, he wonders, already on the verge of irrelevancy and even extinction?

The "Reading Revolution"

Lazere's study has substantial historical antecedents. New technologies and new forms of mass culture have always evoked the concern of social philosophers, both conservative and progressive. Many in the early American Republic, for example, feared that the diffusion of print—newspapers, sensational crime or captivity narratives, and, especially, novels—would lead not to increased literacy but to a range of social evils from anti-intellectualism to anarchy. Any determination of whether or not their most dire predictions were realized depends, of course, partly on the ideology of the historian investigating the period; but, unarguably, the late eighteenth and early nineteenth centuries saw dramatic changes in the number of titles being published as well as the number of copies of books being printed. Moreover, as the French historian Roger Chartier has noted, with the diffusion of print in the latter parts of the eighteenth century (so that more people read more books than ever before), many elite critics felt a certain anxiety at the loss of their status as the "literate" and thus created new status distinctions.[19] As basic literacy and even book ownership became more commonplace, it became necessary to enhance one's status by differentiating a proclaimed elite from lower and less worthy mass forms of literate culture.

Contemporary critical discourse is still clogged by this imprecise and ultimately indefensible dichotomy between elite and popular (mass) literature that evolved partly from dramatic changes in literary distribution and education in the early national period. The meaning of this change is itself one of the most controversial and fertile questions investigated by book historians. How were changes in publishing practices and reading habits *facilitated* or *caused* (that difference in wording is part of the controversy) by the advent of new papermaking and printing techniques as well as by improved transportation systems (especially the new railroads) that expedited book distribution? Numerous historians have argued that the technological innovations of the early nineteenth century were as momentous as Gutenberg's invention of movable type, and that the increasing literacy, expanding mass education, and developing technologies that characterize this era constitute a veritable "reading revolution."

Ronald J. Zboray's essay "Antebellum Reading and the Ironies of Technological Innovation" situates itself at the center of this debate over the changes in readership wrought by the technological changes of the early nineteenth century. The well-chosen word "ironies" in Zboray's title signals his departure from two standard earlier views— the contention that the new printing methods promoted a beneficial "diffusion of knowledge" among all of America's citizens, and the countering claim that nineteenth-century industrialism, emblematized by printing technologies, forever alienated and fragmented American society. Zboray shows how the same technologies that could make more books available than ever before to *some* Americans also displaced another class of readers—primarily the artisans in the older printing shop. He explores the relationships between the technological aspects of book production (printing, publishing) and the life of the mind, but also shows that technological innovation can have dramatically different impact on different social groups or classes or in different regions of the nation.

Zboray, by pointing out that the nineteenth century saw changes in printing and publishing that were unevenly distributed and of mixed social value, refines the more sweeping notion of a reading revolution as posited by historian Rolf Engelsing, who promoted the term *Leserevolution*.[20] Engelsing's thesis is that changes were so momentous that the nature of reading itself—as individual action and community interaction—was transformed as a result of the new availability of books. In an earlier, more restricted print world, Engelsing maintains, readers read "intensively," rereading over the course of a lifetime the same few precious books and incorporating those books into their most intimate and important moments and activities (as seen, for example, in the recording of births, christenings, marriages, and deaths on the endleaves of the family Bible, one of the few books that an average family might own in preindustrial society). By contrast, in the modern world of mass production, readers are deemed to read "extensively," rapidly consuming more and more books while according decreasing significance to any particular book they chance to peruse. There are moral and social implications embedded in Engelsing's vivid contrast. More is definitely less; books, in postindustrial society, dwindle to commodities; formerly engaged readers become passive consumers.

Other scholars (and I must include myself among their number) have sought to modify this model of a reading revolution on a number of counts. First, Engelsing's model, when applied to colonial America, too much romanticizes the preindustrial world. The hierarchies of Puritan theocracy hardly represent a Golden Age of American culture. As Raymond Williams has cautioned, it is mere nostalgia to posit some egalitarian time before the advent of capitalism and modernization.[21] Second, do books really decrease in value as they become more accessible? Books have always been available to the wealthy but did not suffer thereby—witness the common aristocratic valuing of a good library. Why, then, are books somehow diminished when they come more and more into the hands of middle-class or even poor citizens? Certain books, moreover, clearly were read intensively, even in settings in which books had become abundant. Susanna Rowson's *Charlotte Temple*, to cite one example, was published in preindustrial America, but continued to be widely read and individually cherished until well into the twentieth century, and enjoyed popularity among both an elite and a mass audience.

One other general cavil to the reading revolution hypothesis can be noted. Michel de Certeau has written eloquently of "everyday creativity," the ways in which the very act of reading a text transforms and enhances the meaning of that text. This active intellectual and emotional engagement renders suspect any model of reading in which the reader is relegated to a merely passive, receptive role.[22] By examining the ways in which the Hamilton family actively incorporated their reading into their lives and their familial interaction, Barbara Sicherman's essay in this volume provides an excellent case study in postindustrial intensive reading. In this particular family (and there is little reason to see them as totally idiosyncratic), such ostensibly "preindustrial" practices as group reading and reading aloud had persisted longer than the reading revolution theory required. Conversely, despite the prevalence of books, the majority of Americans still do not read many books in the course of a year and certainly cannot be accused of consuming books as frequently (or as programmatically) as they do, say, tubes of toothpaste or television shows.[23] As Zboray has shown, the reading revolution was not universal in America. It did not, by any means, encompass all potential readers.

Books, in whatever era, have performed many different functions for different readers and different functions for the same reader at different times. Similarly, within one society (pre- or postindustrial) there can exist many different and often overlapping reading communities and many kinds of readers. An individual can participate in more than one reading community and can have different strategies and purposes in different situations (a professional paleographer, for example, well might also be a detective mystery addict, a literary critic who writes on the late novels of Henry James might also be a closet reader of Harlequin romances). Nor do the dubiously dichotomizing terms "elite" (serious) and "mass" (popular) culture help to clarify the issues. Too often it is simply assumed that readers of elite books (however one determines just what books qualify for the category) are somehow free of the socioeconomic imperatives that govern those who read popular works. This is an arrogant and even a pernicious assumption. It posits a simplistic demarcation that masks other distinctions—what Chartier calls "cleavages" between "men and women, between urban and rural citizens, between Catholics and members of the Reformed faith, but also between generations, professions, and neighborhoods."[24] That the elite-versus-popular polarity has persisted in academic discourse may well be a factor of the academic's own desire to identify with elite values rather than any objective assessment of cultural production or consumption. Many recent analyses of taste and canonization have attempted to arrive at more sophisticated differentiations of the varieties of literature and a less circular description of the relationships between class attitudes and reading choices.

Another loaded term in all of this debate is "consumer," a word employed with some frequency by both Marxist and non-Marxist historians as a synonym for "reader of popular books." Janice A. Radway, however, has persuasively countered this metaphor of reading as commodity consumption by pointing out that it reduces a complex interaction between a reader and a text to a simple, passive process. As Radway observes, "By focusing on social process—that is, on what people do with texts and objects rather than on those texts and objects themselves—we should begin to see that people do not ingest mass culture whole but often remake it into something they can use."[25]

The reading revolution thesis stresses the impact of technological changes on society as a whole and on individual readers. This one-way reading of that "revolution" does not sufficiently acknowledge interactions in the opposite direction. John P. Feather and other historians suggest that the implementation of a new printing technology is not necessarily a first cause but can often itself be seen as a response to preexisting political processes and social needs (real or perceived). Gutenberg, Feather notes,

> was not only the first printer, he was also the first printer to go bankrupt. It was not until the 1480s that printing was established on a sound commercial and financial basis. Printing was ultimately successful not simply because it represented a technical advance on copying by scribes, but because it became available at a time and in a place where it was economically, socially, and political desirable. . . . The printing press was an agent of change because it was to play an important role in the society in which it was invented and from whose needs it had been developed.[26]

As has been often argued, the Reformation was as responsible for inventing the printed book as was Gutenberg, even though the Reformation was also, in one sense, invented by Gutenberg's printed book. Feather's comments do not minimize the importance of technological changes but place them within a larger context of social and political process.

The Sociology of Reading Communities

The matter of who, at any particular time, could or could not read is crucial to any understanding of the role books played during that time, and so is the question of specifically who *did* read given works. One of the classic techniques of *l'histoire du livre* is to examine such surviving evidence as purchase orders, account books, lending library rosters, and subscription lists in order to identify the actual readers of a given work. Once identified, these readers are then grouped by class, gender, nationality, race, profession, region, neighborhood, or religion in order to ascertain a sociological profile of a given book's readership. This is precisely the method used by François Furet and Jacques Ozouf in their influential *Reading and Writing: Literacy in France from Calvin to Jules Ferry* (1977). With similarly meticulous historical sleuthing, David Paul Nord has tracked down the class, occupation, and address of actual late eighteenth-century readers of the *New-York Magazine*. His conclusions about readership provide a valuable corrective to purely text-based projections of "implied readers" (a useful construct but one that sometimes obscures the existence of real readers). Thus, a simple content analysis could well suggest that the *New-York Magazine* was a thoroughly traditional periodical intended only for an elite audience. Nord, however, has identified a surprising number of readers belonging to the working class.[27]

Nord's essay also addresses some of the theoretical issues central to other essays in this volume. Why did working-class men and women subscribe to a magazine that seemed intended for their social betters? Were they reading to rise in the world (advanced literacy, once again, seen as social empowerment)? And just how did they read—that is, did they really encounter the same text as did their middle-class counterparts? Except for surviving chance observations and marginal comments in the works themselves, it is virtually impossible to know how past readers evaluated and understood particular books. Yet this always difficult topic is what Barbara Sicherman assays in "Sense and Sensibility: A Case Study of Women's Reading in Late-Victorian America." Sicherman documents the intensive and communal nature of the reading of the Hamilton women, how they read both elite and popular literature with attention and respect, how they read aloud to one another, how they used literary allusions as a kind of symbolic code and a shorthand for shared experiences, and how they took the characters in the books they read as models of behavior. Clearly these women—a number of whom went on to distinction— were exceptional; but it is not at all clear that their reading was untypical compared with that of other middle-class Victorian women. More work in this area of the history of the book will determine just how representative the Hamiltons were. But as Sicherman concludes, in the lives of the Hamilton family reading had both more positive and more practical consequences for women than has previously been assumed.

The Hamiltons were not only great readers—they were also good critics. They judged the books they read and passed on their evaluations to other members of their family. In "Becoming Noncanonical: The Case against Willa Cather," Sharon O'Brien discusses more official forms of literary criticism in order to understand how the critical reception of a literary work can promote its success or hasten its failure. What role do cultural authorities play in the shaping of what we think of as "literature," something that is part of the nation's accomplishment and thus a record to be saved? O'Brien focuses on the declining literary stock of Willa Cather to show how changing political climates and evolving academic structures—leftist 1930s intellectuals and the establishment of American literature as an academic discipline—also change the criterion whereby official judgment is rendered. As O'Brien also argues, covert subjective assumptions about gender are inextricably implicated in overt and ostensibly objective critical judgment. Aesthetic questions, even when formulated

by authoritative arbiters of cultural taste, are not always purely aesthetic but are partly grounded in the other interests of those who pose
them. O'Brien, like the other contributors to this volume, dispenses
with a monolithic idea of "the reader" and acknowledges that there
can be different communities of readers within a culture—within,
indeed, a very narrow segment of that culture—and even for a given
book. Whose reading counts and why? Cather, incidentally, believed
strongly that her most important readers were neither critics nor
academics, but those frequenters of bookshops and libraries who happened to pick up one of her novels and find it good.

The essays by David Paul Nord, Barbara Sicherman, and Sharon
O'Brien emphasize that authors and publishers are not the only participants in the communications circuit. Readers (both general and
professional) play a crucial role as judges who, on some level, also help
to determine what kinds of books will be published. One of the most
extraordinary recent examples of the force exerted by professional
readers is the surprising bestseller status of Bloom's *The Closing of
the American Mind*. As even the publisher acknowledges, this is a
"reviewer's book" that was "made" a bestseller by enthusiastic early
reviews such as those appearing in the *New York Times* and the
Washington Post. Curiously, when the book first made its appearance
on the *Times* and *Post* bestseller lists, only ten thousand copies were
in print and only seven thousand of those had been distributed to
bookstores. No one, in retrospect, quite understands how a title could
be listed as a bestseller when there were not enough copies in print to
qualify it for that status. Nevertheless, Simon and Schuster happily
responded to this publishing incongruity by reprinting the book and
shipping copies immediately to the bookstores even as they also
waged an aggressive and provocative advertising campaign ("Why Are
So Many People Rushing To Buy This Infuriating Book?"). As the sales
director at Simon and Schuster notes, "If we had expected a bestseller,
we would have initially printed more than 10,000 copies."[28]

The case of the Bloom book is unusual but, as a bestseller anticipated by neither its author nor its publisher, it is hardly unique. So far,
no one has yet been able to predict precisely which books will sell
because readers do not operate according to prescribed rules. As
William Charvat, a book historian before there was such a field, has
cogently argued, so far as the book trade is concerned, we need to
replace the diadic model of producer and consumer (the traditional
capitalistic model) with a triadic and interactive model of print
culture: "The book trade is acted upon by both writer and reader, and
in receiving their influence the book trade interprets and therefore

transmutes it. Correspondingly, the writer and reader dictate to and are dictated to by the book trade."[29]

Readers, of course, do make choices. One might argue that the spectrum of choices available to a reader at any particular time is not sufficiently wide or, as some members of the Frankfurt School would insist, that choice itself is an illusion since it overlooks the ways in which capitalism arouses desire without satisfying it. Nevertheless, individual readers, for whatever reasons, do decide what books they are going to read and also determine how they are going to interpret and use what they read. In her *Reading the Romance: Women, Patriarchy, and Popular Literature,* Janice A. Radway documents some of the uses to which a community of women put their reading and demonstrates how that process is much more complicated and multifaceted than previous models allowed. In her essay for this volume, she looks at the publishing process from a different perspective and uses ethnographic methods to analyze the ways in which books are selected by the influential Book-of-the-Month Club. We see the complex and often highly individualistic or even idiosyncratic procedures by which the club makes its selections, anticipating, responding to, and sometimes consciously directing the tastes of its readers. While new polling and other data-collecting procedures well may change the selection processes used, at this point the club still mirrors much of the American publishing industry. In both cases, an editorial hunch is a major marketing principle.

Radway's essay helps to demystify one aspect of the publishing business while suggesting other questions that will become even more relevant as the book trade itself evolves. Do sophisticated market research techniques serve the reading public? Do they really reflect the wishes of the public—and *which* public? Can one quantify taste? Will there ever be a reliable way to predict or create a bestseller? If so, how will this affect the production and publication of other kinds of books, including specialized, experimental, or politically radical titles? Once again we are at a juncture with new technologies having a major impact on the history of the book and, conversely and concomitantly, with different books promoting or protesting new technologies.

What is a book? As these essays (like Zinck's early definition) indicate, the question is multifaceted and can be approached in diverse ways, all rich with historical, literary, and theoretical possibilities. Books cannot be understood apart from the society that creates them, and, conversely, no literate society can be understood without some study of the books it produces. At least since Gutenberg, "books" and "history" have been inseparably intertwined. Although relatively new as a distinct field of study, the history of the book explores that long-standing double complicity.

Notes

An earlier version of this essay appeared in *American Quarterly* 40, no. 1 (March 1988).

Epigraph: Georg Heinrich Zinck, *Allgemeines Oeconomisches Lexicon,* trans. and quoted in Martha Woodmansee, "The Genius and the Copyright: Economic and Legal Conditions of the Emergence of the 'Author,'" *Eighteenth-Century Studies* 17 (Summer 1984): 425.

1. G. Thomas Tanselle, "The Bibliography and Textual Study of American Books," *Proceedings of the American Antiquarian Society* 95, no. 2 (October 1985): 113.

2. Quoted from the first essay in this volume. See also Robert Darnton, "First Steps toward a History of Reading," *Australian Journal of French Studies* 23 (January–April 1986): 5–30, and "Reading, Writing, and Publishing in Eighteenth-Century France: A Case Study in the Sociology of Literature," *Daedalus* 100 (Winter 1971): 214–56. For other overviews of the history of the book, see Raymond Birn, "*Livre et société* after Ten Years: Formation of a Discipline," *Studies on Voltaire and the Eighteenth Century* 151 (1976): 287–312, and the special issue of *Eighteenth-Century Studies* 17 (Summer 1984) edited by Birn. Other important contributions to the history of the book are Kenneth E. Carpenter, ed., *Books and Society in History* (New York, 1983); Roger Chartier, "Intellectual History or Sociocultural History? The French Trajectories," in *Modern European Intellectual History: Reappraisals and New Perspectives,* ed. Dominick La Capra and Steven L. Kaplan (Ithaca, N.Y., 1982), 13–46; John P. Feather and David McKitterick, *The History of Books and Libraries: Two Views* (Washington, D.C., 1986); Feather, "Cross-Channel Currents: Historical Bibliography and *l'Histoire du livre,*" *Library* 6th ser., 2 (1980): 1–15; David D. Hall, *On Native Ground: From the History of Printing to the History of the Book* (Worcester, Mass., 1984) and "A Report on the 1984 Conference on Needs and Opportunities in the History of the Book in American Culture," *Proceedings of the American Antiquarian Society* 95, no. 1 (1985): 101–12; and G. Thomas Tanselle, *The History of Books as a Field of Study* (Chapel Hill, N.C., 1981).

3. Roger Chartier, "Frenchness in the History of the Book: From the History of Publishing to the History of Reading," *Proceedings of the American Antiquarian Society* 97, no. 2 (1988): 310–15. See also M. T. Clancy, *From Memory to Written Record, England 1066–1307* (London, 1979); Sandra Hindman and James Douglas Farquhar, *Pen to Press: Illustrated Manuscripts and Printed Books in the First Century of Printing* (Baltimore, Md.,

1977); Bernard M. W. Knox, "Silent Reading in Antiquity," *Greek, Roman and Byzantine Studies* 9 (1968): 421–35; and Paul Saenger, "Silent Reading: Its Impact on Late Medieval Script and Society," *Viator, Medieval and Renaissance Studies* 13 (1982): 367–414.

4. Lucien Febvre and Henri-Jean Martin, *The Coming of the Book: The Impact of Printing 1450–1800*, trans. David Gerard, ed. Geoffrey Nowell-Smith and David Wootton (1976; rept. London, 1984).

5. Richard D. Altick, *The English Common Reader: A Social History of the Mass Reading Public, 1800–1900* (Chicago, 1957); Robert K. Webb, *The British Working Class Reader* (London, 1955); and Raymond Williams, *The Long Revolution* (New York, 1961), *Marxism and Literature* (Oxford, 1977), and *The Sociology of Culture* (New York, 1982).

6. Robert Escarpit, *Sociology of Literature*, trans. Ernest Pick, 2d ed. (London, 1971); and Pierre Bourdieu, *Distinction: A Social Critique of the Judgement of Taste*, trans. Richard Nice (Cambridge, Mass., 1984).

7. Nina Baym, *Novels, Readers, and Reviewers: Responses to Fiction in Antebellum America* (Ithaca, N.Y., 1984); Fredric Jameson, *The Political Unconscious: Narrative as a Socially Symbolic Act* (Ithaca, N.Y., 1981) and "Reification and Utopia in Mass Culture," *Social Text* 1 (Winter 1979): 130–48; Annette Kolodny, "The Integrity of Memory: Creating a New Literary History of the United States," *American Literature* 57 (May 1985): 291–307; Susan Koppelman, Introduction, *Old Maids: Short Stories by Nineteenth-Century U.S. Women Writers* (New York, 1984); Paul Lauter, "Race and Gender in the Shaping of the American Literary Canon: A Case Study from the Twenties," *Feminist Studies* 9 (Fall 1983): 435–63; Richard Ohmann, "The Shaping of a Canon: U.S. Fiction, 1960–75," *Critical Inquiry* 10 (September 1983): 199–221; Janice A. Radway, *Reading the Romance; Women, Patriarchy, and Popular Literature* (Chapel Hill, N.C., 1984); Barbara Herrnstein Smith, "Contingencies of Value," in *Canons*, ed. Robert von Hallberg (Chicago, 1984), 5–40; Jane Tompkins, *Sensational Designs: The Cultural Work of American Fiction, 1790–1860* (New York, 1985); and Alan Wald, "Hegemony and Literary Tradition in America," *Humanities in Society* (Fall 1981): 419–30.

8. See, for example, Roger Chartier, "Du Livre au lire," in *Pratiques de la lecture*, ed. Roger Chartier (Paris, 1985), 62–87; Cathy N. Davidson, *Revolution and the Word: The Rise of the Novel in America* (New York, 1986), ch. 1; and Walter J. Ong, "The Writer's Audience Is Always a Fiction," *PMLA* 90 (1975): 9–21.

9. See, for example, Richard Brodhead, *The School of Hawthorne* (New York, 1986); and Michael Denning, *Mechanic Accents: Dime Novels and Working-Class Culture in America* (London and New York, 1987). For a perceptive overview, see Michael Warner, "Literary Studies and the History of the Book," *Book* 12 (July 1987): 3–9.

10. Quoted in Robert A. Carter, "The Center for the Book: Seeking Outreach," *Publishers Weekly* (January 4, 1985).

11. Of special interest to readers of this volume are two American Antiquarian Society collections of essays: David D. Hall and John B. Hench, eds.,

Needs and Opportunities in the History of the Book: America, 1639–1876 (Worcester, Mass., 1987); and William L. Joyce et al., eds., *Printing and Society in Early America* (Worcester, Mass., 1983). In the second volume, see especially the excellent introduction by David D. Hall, "The Uses of Literacy in New England, 1600–1850," 2–47.

12. Charles Frances Adams, ed., *The Works of John Adams*, 10 vols. (Boston, 1850–56), 3:456, and *Letters of Mrs. Adams, the Wife of John Adams*, 3d ed., 2 vols. (Boston, 1841), 2:79.

13. Allan Bloom, *The Closing of the American Mind: How Higher Education Has Failed Democracy and Impoverished the Souls of Today's Students* (New York, 1987); and E. D. Hirsch, Jr., *Cultural Literacy: What Every American Needs To Know* (Boston, 1987).

14. Martha Nussbaum, "Undemocratic Vistas," *New York Review of Books*, 34 (November 5, 1987): 20–26. See also Alexander Nehamas's apt observation in "Swallowing Goldfish," *London Review of Books* 9 (December 10, 1987), 13, that Bloom "does not give any serious arguments to support the views he attributes to Plato, his greatest hero. He simply refers to him consistently as a 'great', 'true' or 'real' philosopher. But this is not a call to reason. It is an exhortation to accept a particular set of views with little to recommend them apart from Bloom's intense commitment to them. Though the book is devoted to the defense of reason, it relies not on argument but on passion."

15. For other critiques of Bloom (from various ideological viewpoints), see especially Robert Gorham Davis, "Thus Spake Bloom," *New Leader* 70 (June 29, 1987): 17–18; Alfie Kohn, "The Conservation of Old Values," *Psychology Today* 21, no. 8 (August 1987): 70–71; Myron A. Marty, "Saving the Soul of Higher Education," *Christian Century* 104 (July 29, 1987): 659–62; Louis Menand, "Mr. Bloom's Planet," *New Republic* 196 (May 25, 1987): 38–41; and Robert Pattison, "On the Finn Syndrome and the Shakespeare Paradox," *Nation* 244 (May 30, 1987): 710–20.

16. Bloom, *Closing of the American Mind*, 322. Bloom also notes, "Another aspect of the mythology is that McCarthyism had an extremely negative impact on the universities. Actually the McCarthy period was the last time the university had any sense of community, defined by a common enemy. . . . In major universities [McCarthy and his supporters] had no effect whatsoever on curriculum or appointments. The range of thought and speech that took place within them was unaffected. Academic freedom had for that last moment more than an abstract meaning" (p. 324).

17. For a survey of recent literacy studies, see Carl F. Kaestle, "The History of Literacy and the History of Readers," in *Review of Research in Education*, vol. 12, ed. Edmund W. Gordon (Washington, D.C., 1985). See also William J. Gilmore's *Elementary Literacy on the Eve of the Industrial Revolution: Trends in Rural New England, 1760–1830* (Worcester, Mass., 1982) and his forthcoming *Reading Becomes a "Necessity of Life": Material and Cultural Life in Rural New England, 1780–1830* (Knoxville, Tenn., 1989).

18. For a provocative discussion of contemporary issues in literacy, see Kenneth Levine, *The Social Context of Literacy* (London, 1986).

19. Roger Chartier, *The Cultural Uses of Print in Early Modern France,* trans. Lydia G. Cochrane (Princeton, N.J., 1987), 238.

20. Rolf Engelsing, *Analphabetentum und Lektüre. Zur Sozial-geschichte des Lesens in Deutschland zwischen feudaler und industrieller Gesellschaft* (Stuttgart, 1973); "Die Perioden der Lesergeschichte in der Neuzeit," in *Zur Sozialgeschichte deutscher Mittel- und Unterschichten* (Göttingen, 1973), 112–54; and *Der Bürger als Leser. Lesergeschichte in Deutschland 1500–1800* (Stuttgart, 1974). For critiques of Engelsing's position, see Darnton, *The Great Cat Massacre and Other Episodes in French Cultural History* (New York, 1984), 249–52; Davidson, *Revolution and the Word,* 69–79; and Reinhart Siegert, *Aufklärung und Volkslektüre exemplarisch dargestellt an Rudolph Zacharias Becker und seinem "Noth- und Hülfsbüchlein" mit einer Bibliographie zum Gesamtthema* (Frankfurt am Main, 1978).

21. Raymond Williams, *The Country and the City* (New York, 1973), 83. For an excellent discussion of the ways in which numerous contemporary historians romanticize the *communitas* of preindustrial America, see Joyce Appleby, "Value and Society," in *Colonial British America: Essays in the New History of the Early Modern Era,* ed. Jack P. Greene and J. R. Pole (Baltimore, Md., 1984), 290–316.

22. Michel de Certeau, *L'Invention du quotidien* (Paris, 1980). See also his *La Culture au pluriel* (Paris, 1974) and "Une Culture très ordinaire," *Esprit* 10 (1978): 3–26.

23. For discussions of variable literacy skills and reading habits within a society, see especially Harvey J. Graff, *The Legacies of Literacy: Continuities and Contradictions in Western Culture and Society* (Bloomington, Ind., 1987) and *The Literacy Myth: Literacy and Social Structure in the Nine-teenth-Century City* (New York, 1979); Joseph F. Kett and Patricia A. Mc-Clung, "Book Culture in Post-Revolutionary Virginia," *Proceedings of the American Antiquarian Society* 94 (1984): 97–138; and Ian Watt and Jack Goody, "The Consequences of Literacy," in *Literacy in Traditional Societies,* ed. Jack Goody (Cambridge, 1968).

24. Chartier, "Frenchness in the History of the Book," 325.

25. Janice A. Radway, "Reading Is Not Eating: Mass-Produced Literature and the Theoretical, Methodological, and Political Consequences of a Metaphor," *Book Research Quarterly* 2 (1986): 26. For another discussion of the imprecise uses of "popular" culture, see David Grimsted, "Books and Culture: Canned, Canonized, and Neglected," in *Needs and Opportunities in the History of the Book,* pp. 187–232.

26. John P. Feather, "The Book in History and the History of the Book," in *History of Books and Libraries,* 6.

27. For other discussions of actual readers and reading communities, see Darnton, "Readers Respond to Rousseau," in *Great Cat Massacre;* Elizabeth Long, "Women, Reading, and Cultural Authority: Some Implications of the

Audience Perspective in Cultural Studies," *American Quarterly* 38 (Fall 1986): 606–10; and David Paul Nord, "Working-Class Readers: Family, Community, and Reading in Late Nineteenth-Century America," *Communication Research* 13 (April 1986): 156–81.

28. William Goldstein, "Story Behind the Bestseller: Allan Bloom's 'The Closing of the American Mind,'" *Publishers Weekly* 231 (July 3, 1987): 25–27.

29. William Charvat, "Literary Economics and Literary History," in *English Institute Essays*, ed. Alan S. Downer (1949; rept. New York, 1965), 74–75.

Chapter One **What Is the History of Books?**

Robert Darnton

Histoire du livre in France, *Geschichte des Buchwesens* in Germany, "history of books" or "of the book" in English-speaking countries— its name varies from place to place, but everywhere it is being recognized as an important new discipline. It might even be called the social and cultural history of communication by print, if that were not such a mouthful, because its purpose is to understand how ideas were transmitted through print and how exposure to the printed word affected the thought and behavior of mankind during the last five hundred years. Some book historians pursue their subject deep into the period before the invention of movable type. Some students of printing concentrate on newspapers, broadsides, and other forms besides the book. The field can be extended and expanded in many ways; but for the most part, it concerns books since the time of Gutenberg, an area of research that has developed so rapidly during the last few years that it seems likely to win a place alongside fields like the history of science and the history of art in the canon of scholarly disciplines.

Whatever the history of books may become in the future, its past shows how a field of knowledge can take on a distinct scholarly identity. It arose from the convergence of several disciplines on a common set of problems, all of them having to do with the process of communication. Initially, the problems took the form of concrete questions in unrelated branches of scholarship: What were Shakespeare's original texts? What caused the French Revolution? What is the connection between culture and social stratification? In pursuing those questions, scholars found themselves crossing paths in a no man's land located at the intersection of a half-dozen fields of study. They decided to constitute a field of their own and to invite in historians, literary scholars, sociologists, librarians, and anyone else who wanted to understand the book as a force in history. The history of books began to acquire its own journals, research centers, conferences, and lecture circuits. It accumulated tribal elders as well as Young Turks. And although it has not yet developed passwords or secret handshakes or its own population of Ph.D.'s, its adherents can recognize one another by the glint in their eyes. They belong to a common cause, one of the few sectors in the human sciences where there is a mood of expansion and a flurry of fresh ideas.

To be sure, the history of the history of books did not begin yesterday. It stretches back to the scholarship of the Renaissance, if not beyond; and it began in earnest during the nineteenth century, when the study of books as material objects led to the rise of analytical bibliography in England. But the current work represents a departure from the established strains of scholarship, which may be traced to their nineteenth-century origins through back issues of the *Library* and *Börsenblatt für den Deutschen Buchhandel* or theses in the Ecole des Chartes. The new strain developed during the 1960s in France, where it took root in institutions like the Ecole Pratique des Hautes Etudes and spread through publications like *L'Apparition du livre* (1958), by Lucien Febvre and Henri-Jean Martin, and *Livre et société dans la France du XVIIIe siècle* (two volumes 1965 and 1970) by a group connected with the sixth section of the Ecole Pratique des Hautes Etudes.

The new book historians brought the subject within the range of themes studied by the *"Annales* school" of socioeconomic history. Instead of dwelling on fine points of bibliography, they tried to uncover the general pattern of book production and consumption over long stretches of time. They compiled statistics from requests for *privilèges* (a kind of copyright), analyzed the contents of private libraries, and traced ideological currents through neglected genres like the *bibliothèque bleue* (primitive paperbacks). Rare books and fine editions had no interest for them; they concentrated instead on the most ordinary sort of books, because they wanted to discover the literary experience of ordinary readers. They put familiar phenomena like the Counter Reformation and the Enlightenment in an unfamiliar light by showing how much traditional culture outweighed the avant-garde in the literary fare of the entire society. Although they did not come up with a firm set of conclusions, they demonstrated the importance of asking new questions, using new methods, and tapping new sources.[1]

Their example spread throughout Europe and the United States, reinforcing indigenous traditions, such as reception studies in Germany and printing history in Britain. Drawn together by their commitment to a common enterprise, and animated by enthusiasm for new ideas, book historians began to meet, first in cafés, then in conferences. They created new journals—*Publishing History, Bibliography Newsletter, Nouvelles du livre ancien, Revue française d'histoire du livre* (new series), *Buchhandelsgeschichte,* and *Wolfenbütteler Notizen zur Buchgeschichte.* They founded new centers—the Institut d'Etude du Livre in Paris, the Arbeitskreis für Geschichte des Buchwesens in Wolfenbüttel, the Center for the Book in the Library of Congress. Special colloquia—in Geneva, Paris, Boston, Worcester, Wolfenbüttel, and Athens, to name only a few that took place in the late 1970s—disseminated their research on an international scale. In the brief span of two decades, the history of books had become a rich and varied field of study.

So rich did it prove, in fact, that it now looks less like a field than a tropical rain forest. The explorer can hardly make his way across it. At every stop he becomes entangled in a luxuriant undergrowth of journal articles and disoriented by the crisscrossing of disciplines—analytical bibliography pointing in this direction, the sociology of knowledge in that, while history, English, and comparative literature stake out overlapping territories. He is beset by claims to newness—*la nouvelle bibliographie matérielle,* "the new literary history"—and bewildered by competing methodologies, which would have him collating editions, compiling statistics, decoding copyright law, wading through reams of manuscript, heaving at the bar of a reconstructed common press, and psychoanalyzing the mental processes of readers. The history of books has become so crowded with ancillary disciplines that one can no longer see its general contours. How can the book historian neglect the history of libraries, of publishing, of paper, type, and reading? But how can he master their technologies, especially when they appear in imposing foreign formulations, like *Geschichte der Appellstruktur* and *Bibliométrie bibliologique?* It is enough to make one want to retire to a rare book room and count watermarks.

To get some distance from interdisciplinarity run riot, and to see the subject as a whole, it might be useful to propose a general model for analyzing the way books come into being and spread through society. To be sure, conditions have varied so much from place to place and from time to time since the invention of movable type that it would be vain to expect the biography of every book to conform to the same pattern. But printed books generally pass through roughly the same life cycle. It could be described as a communications circuit that runs from the author to the publisher (if the bookseller does not assume that role), the printer, the shipper, the bookseller, and the reader. The reader completes the circuit, because he influences the author both before and after the act of composition. Authors are readers themselves. By reading and associating with other readers and writers, they form notions of genre and style and a general sense of the literary enterprise, which affects their texts, whether they are composing Shakespearean sonnets or directions for assembling radio kits. A writer may respond in his writing to criticisms of his previous work or anticipate reactions that his text will elicit. He addresses implicit readers and hears from explicit reviewers. So the circuit runs full cycle. It transmits messages, transforming them en route, as they pass from thought to writing to printed characters and back to thought again. Book history concerns each phase of this process and the process as a whole, in all its variations over space and time and in all its relations with other systems, economic, social, political, and cultural, in the surrounding environment.

That is a large undertaking. To keep their task within manageable proportions, book historians generally cut into one segment of the communications circuit and analyze it according to the procedures of a single discipline—printing, for example, which they study by means of analytical bibliography. But the parts do not take on their full significance unless they are related to the whole, and some holistic view of the book as a means of communication seems necessary if book history is to avoid being fragmented into esoteric specializations, cut off from each other by arcane techniques and mutual misunderstanding. The model shown in Figure 1.1 provides a way of envisaging the entire communication process. With minor adjustments, it should apply to all periods in the history of the printed book (manuscript books and book illustrations will have to be considered elsewhere), but I would like to discuss it in connection with the period I know best, the eighteenth century, and to take it up phase by phase, showing how each phase is related to (1) other activities that a given person has under way at a given point in the circuit, (2) other persons at the same point in other circuits, (3) other persons at other points in the same circuit, and (4) other elements in society. The first three considerations bear directly on the transmission of a text, while the last concerns outside influences, which could vary endlessly. For the sake of simplicity, I have reduced the latter to the three general categories in the center of the diagram.

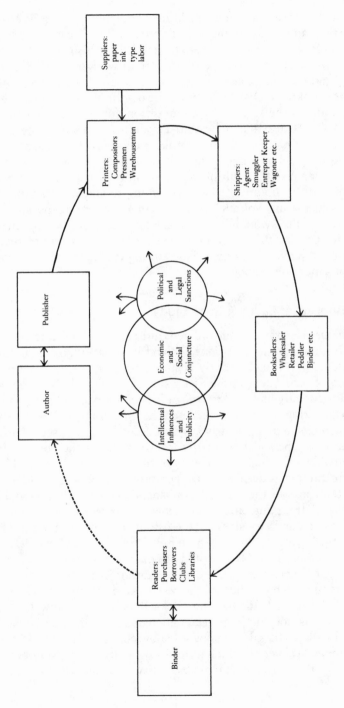

Figure 1.1. The Communications Circuit

Models have a way of freezing human beings out of history. To put
some flesh and blood on this one, and to show how it can make sense
of an actual case, I will apply it to the publishing history of Voltaire's
Questions sur l'Encyclopédie, an important work of The Enlightenment, and one that touched the lives of a great many eighteenth-
century bookmen. One could study the circuit of its transmission at
any point—at the stage of its composition, for example, when Voltaire shaped its text and orchestrated its diffusion in order to promote
his campaign against religious intolerance, as his biographers have
shown; or at its printing, a stage in which bibliographical analysis
helps to establish the multiplication of editions; or at the point of its
assimilation in libraries, where, according to statistical studies by
literary historians, Voltaire's works occupied an impressive share of
shelf space.[2] But I would like to consider the least familiar link in the
diffusion process, the role of the bookseller, taking Isaac-Pierre Rigaud
of Montpellier as an example, and working through the four considerations mentioned above.[3]

The Bookseller Link—A Case Study

On August 16, 1770, Rigaud ordered thirty copies of the nine-volume
octavo edition of the *Questions*, which the Société typographique de
Neuchâtel (STN) had recently begun to print in the Prussian prin-
cipality of Neuchâtel on the Swiss side of the French-Swiss border.
Rigaud generally preferred to read at least a few pages of a new book
before stocking it, but he considered the *Questions* such a good bet
that he risked making a fairly large order for it, sight unseen. He did
not have any personal sympathy for Voltaire. On the contrary, he
deplored the philosophe's tendency to tinker with his books, adding
and amending passages while cooperating with pirated editions behind the backs of the original publishers. Such practices produced
complaints from customers, who objected to receiving inferior (or
insufficiently audacious) texts. "It is astonishing that at the end of his
career M. de Voltaire cannot refrain from duping booksellers," Rigaud
complained to the STN. "It would not matter if all these little ruses,
frauds, and deceits were blamed on the author. But unfortunately the
printers and still more the retail booksellers are usually held responsible."[4] Voltaire made life hard for booksellers, but he sold well.

There was nothing Voltairean about most of the other books in
Rigaud's shop. His sales catalogues show that he specialized somewhat in medical books, which were always in demand in Montpellier,
thanks to the university's famous faculty of medicine. Rigaud also

kept a discreet line of Protestant works, because Montpellier lay in Huguenot territory. And when the authorities looked the other way, he brought in a few shipments of forbidden books.[5] But he generally supplied his customers with books of all kinds, which he drew from an inventory worth at least forty-five thousand livres, the largest in Montpellier and probably in all Languedoc, according to a report from the intendant's *subdélégué*.[6]

Rigaud's way of ordering from the STN illustrates the character of his business. Unlike other large provincial dealers, who speculated on a hundred or more copies of a book when they smelled a bestseller, he rarely ordered more than a half-dozen copies of a single work. He read widely, consulted his customers, took soundings by means of his commercial correspondence, and studied the catalogues that the STN and his other suppliers sent to him (by 1785 the STN's catalogue included 750 titles). Then he chose about ten titles and ordered just enough copies of them to make up a crate of fifty pounds, the minimum weight for shipment at the cheapest rate charged by the wagoners. If the books sold well, he reordered them; but he usually kept his orders rather small, and made four or five of them a year. In this way, he conserved capital, minimized risks, and built up such a large and varied stock that his shop became a clearinghouse for literary demand of every kind in the region.

The pattern of Rigaud's orders, which stands out clearly from the STN's account books, shows that he offered his customers a little of everything—travel books, histories, novels, religious works, and the occasional scientific or philosophical treatise. Instead of following his own preferences, he seemed to transmit demand fairly accurately and to live according to the accepted wisdom of the book trade, which one of the STN's other customers summarized as follows: "The best book for a bookseller is a book that sells."[7] Given his cautious style of business, Rigaud's decision to place an advance order for thirty nine-volume sets of the *Questions sur l'Encyclopédie* seems especially significant. He would not have put so much money on a single work if he had not felt certain of the demand—and his later orders show that he had calculated correctly. On June 19, 1772, soon after receiving the last shipment of the last volume, Rigaud ordered another dozen sets; and he ordered two more two years later, although by then the STN had exhausted its stock. It had printed a huge edition, twenty-five hundred copies, approximately twice its usual press run, and the booksellers had fallen all over themselves in the rush to purchase it. So Rigaud's purchase was no aberration. It expressed a current of Voltaireanism that had spread far and wide among the reading public of the Old Regime.

How does the purchase of the *Questions* look when examined from the perspective of Rigaud's relations with the other booksellers of Montpellier? A book trade almanac listed nine of them in 1777:[8]

Printer-Booksellers: Aug. Franç. Rochard
                       Jean Martel

Booksellers: Isaac-Pierre Rigaud
               J. B. Faure
               Albert Pons
               Tournel
               Bascon
               Cézary
               Fontanel

But according to a report from a traveling salesman of the STN, there were only seven.[9] Rigaud and Pons had merged and completely dominated the local trade; Cézary and Faure scraped along in the middle ranks; and the rest teetered on the brink of bankruptcy in precarious boutiques. The occasional binder and under-the-cloak peddler also provided a few books, most of them illegal, to the more adventuresome readers of the city. For example, the demoiselle Bringand, known as the "students' mother," stocked some forbidden fruit "under the bed in the room to the right on the second floor," according to the report of a raid that was engineered by the established booksellers.[10] The trade in most provincial cities fell into the same pattern, which can be envisaged as a series of concentric circles: at the center, one or two firms tried to monopolize the market; around the margin, a few small dealers survived by specializing in chapbooks and old volumes, by setting up reading clubs (*cabinets littéraires*) and binderies, or by peddling their wares in the back country; and beyond the fringe of legality, adventurers moved in and out of the market, selling forbidden literature.

When he ordered his shipment of the *Questions*, Rigaud was consolidating his position at the center of the local trade. His merger with Pons in 1770 provided him with enough capital and assets to ride out the mishaps—delayed shipments, defaulting debtors, liquidity crises—that often upset smaller businesses. Also, he played rough. When Cézary, one of the middling dealers, failed to meet some of his payments in 1781, Rigaud drove him out of business by organizing a cabal of his creditors. They refused to let him reschedule the payments, had him thrown into prison for debt, and forced him to sell off his stock at an auction, where they kept down the prices and gobbled up the books. By dispensing patronage, Rigaud controlled most of Montpellier's binderies; and by exerting pressure on the binders, he produced delays and snags in the affairs of the other booksellers. In

1789 only one of them remained, Abraham Fontanel, and he stayed solvent only by maintaining a *cabinet littéraire,* "which provokes terrible fits of jealousy by the sieur Rigaud, who wants to be the only one left and who shows his hatred of me every day,"[11] as Fontanel confided to the STN.

Rigaud did not eliminate his competitors simply by outdoing them in the dog-eat-dog style of commercial capitalism of early modern France. His letters, theirs, and the correspondence of many other booksellers show that the book trade contracted during the late 1770s and 1780s. In hard times, the big booksellers squeezed out the small, and the tough outlasted the tender. Rigaud had been a tough customer from the very beginning of his relations with the STN. He had ordered his copies of the *Questions* from Neuchâtel, where the STN was printing a pirated edition, rather than from Geneva, where Voltaire's regular printer, Gabriel Cramer, was producing the original, because he had extracted better terms. He also demanded better service, especially when the other booksellers in Montpellier, who had dealt with Cramer, received their copies first. The delay produced a volley of letters from Rigaud to the STN. Why couldn't the STN work faster? Didn't it know that it was making him lose customers to his competitors? He would have to order from Cramer in the future if it could not provide quicker shipments at a lower price. When volumes one through three finally arrived from Neuchâtel, volumes four through six from Geneva were already on sale in the other shops. Rigaud compared the texts, word for word, and found that the STN's edition contained none of the additional material that it had claimed to receive on the sly from Voltaire. So how could he push the theme of "additions and corrections" in his sales talk? The recriminations flew thick and fast in the mail between Montpellier and Neuchâtel, and they showed that Rigaud meant to exploit every inch of every advantage that he could gain on his competitors. More important, they also revealed that the *Questions* was being sold all over Montpellier, even though in principle it could not circulate legally in France. Far from being confined to the under-the-cloak trade of marginal characters like the "students' mother," Voltaire's work turned out to be a prize item in the scramble for profits at the very heart of the established book trade. When dealers like Rigaud scratched and clawed for their shipments of it, Voltaire could be sure that he was succeeding in his attempt to propel his ideas through the main lines of France's communications system.

The role of Voltaire and Cramer in the diffusion process raises the problem of how Rigaud's operation fit into the other stages in the life cycle of the *Questions*. Rigaud knew that he was not getting a first edition, the STN had sent a circular letter to him and its other main customers, explaining that it would reproduce Cramer's text, but with corrections and additions provided by the author himself, so that its version would be superior to the original. One of the STN's directors had visited Voltaire at Ferney in April 1770, and had returned with a promise that Voltaire would touch up the printed sheets he was to receive from Cramer and then would forward them to Neuchâtel for a pirated edition.[12] Voltaire often played such tricks. They provided a way to improve the quality and increase the quantity of his books, and therefore served his main purpose—which was not to make money, for he did not sell his prose to the printers, but to spread enlightenment. The profit motive kept the rest of the system going, however. So when Cramer got wind of the STN's attempt to raid his market, he protested to Voltaire, Voltaire retracted his promise to the STN, and the STN had to settle for a delayed version of the text, which it received from Ferney, but with only minimal additions and corrections.[13] In fact, this setback did not hurt its sales, because the market had plenty of room to absorb editions, not only the STN's but also one that Marc Michel Rey produced in Amsterdam, and probably others as well. The booksellers had their choice of suppliers, and they chose according to whatever marginal advantage they could obtain on matters of price, quality, speed, and reliability in delivery. Rigaud dealt regularly with publishers in Paris, Lyon, Rouen, Avignon, and Geneva. He played them off against each other, and sometimes ordered the same book from two or three of them so as to be certain of getting it before his competitors did. By working several circuits at the same time, he increased his room for maneuver. But in the case of the *Questions*, he was outmaneuvered and had to receive his goods from the circuitous Voltaire-Cramer-Voltaire-STN route.

That route merely took the copy from the author to the printer. For the printed sheets to reach Rigaud in Montpellier from the STN's shop in Neuchâtel, they had to wind their way through one of the most complex stages in the book's circuit. They could follow two main routes. One led from Neuchâtel to Geneva, Turin, Nice (which was not yet French), and Marseilles. It had the advantage of skirting French territory—and therefore the danger of confiscation—but it involved huge detours and expenses. The books had to be lugged over the Alps and pass through a whole army of middlemen—shipping agents, bargemen, wagoners, entrepôt keepers, ship captains, and dockers—before they arrived in Rigaud's storeroom. The best Swiss shippers claimed they could get a crate to Nice in a month for thirteen livres, eight sous, per hundredweight; but their estimates proved to be far too low. The direct route from Neuchâtel to Lyon and down the Rhône was fast, cheap, and easy—but dangerous. The crates had to be sealed at their point of entry into France and inspected by the booksellers' guild and the royal book inspector in Lyon, then reshipped and inspected once more in Montpellier.[14]

Always cautious, Rigaud asked the STN to ship the first volumes of the *Questions* by the roundabout route, because he knew he could rely on his agent in Marseilles, Joseph Coulomb, to get the books into France without mishap. They left on December 9, 1771, but did not arrive until after March, when the first three volumes of Cramer's edition were already being sold by Rigaud's competitors. The second and third volumes arrived in July, but loaded down with shipping charges and damaged by rough handling. "It seems that we are five or six thousand leagues apart," Rigaud complained, adding that he regretted he had not given his business to Cramer, whose shipments had already reached volume six.[15] By this time, the STN was worried enough about losing customers throughout southern France to set up a smuggling operation in Lyon. Their man, a marginal book dealer named Joseph-Louis Berthoud, got volumes four and five past the guild inspectors, but then his business collapsed in bankruptcy; and to make matters worse, the French government imposed a tax of sixty livres per hundredweight on all book imports. The STN fell back on the Alpine route, offering to get its shipments as far as Nice for fifteen livres per hundredweight if Rigaud would pay the rest of the expenses, including the import duty. But Rigaud considered the duty such a heavy blow to the international trade, that he suspended all his orders with foreign suppliers. The new tariff policy had made it prohibitively expensive to disguise illegal books as legal ones and to pass them through normal commercial channels.

In December, the STN's agent in Nice, Jacques Deandreis, somehow got a shipment of volume six of the *Questions* to Rigaud through the port of Sète, which was supposed to be closed to book imports. Then the French government, realizing that it had nearly destroyed the foreign book trade, lowered the tariff to twenty-six livres per hundredweight. Rigaud proposed sharing the cost with his foreign suppliers: he would pay one-third if they would pay two-thirds. This proposal suited the STN, but in the spring of 1772, Rigaud decided that the Nice route was too expensive to be used under any conditions. Having heard enough complaints from its other customers to reach the same conclusion, the STN dispatched one of its directors to Lyon, and he persuaded a more dependable Lyonnais dealer, J.-M. Barret, to clear its shipments through the local guild and forward them to its provincial clients. Thanks to this arrangement, the last three volumes of Rigaud's *Questions* arrived safely in the summer.

It had required continuous effort and considerable expense to get the entire order to Montpellier, and Rigaud and the STN did not stop realigning their supply routes once they had completed this transaction. Because economic and political pressures kept shifting, they had constantly to readjust their arrangements within the complex world of middlemen, who linked printing houses with bookshops and often determined, in the last analysis, what literature reached French readers.

How the readers assimilated their books cannot be determined. Bibliographical analysis of all the copies that can be located would show what varieties of the text were available. A study of notarial archives in Montpellier might indicate how many copies turned up in inheritances, and statistics drawn from auction catalogues might make it possible to estimate the number in substantial private libraries. But given the present state of documentation, one cannot know who Voltaire's readers were or how they responded to his text. Reading remains the most difficult stage to study in the circuit followed by books.

All stages were affected by the social, economic, political, and intellectual conditions of the time; but for Rigaud, these general influences made themselves felt within a local context. He sold books in a city of thirty-one thousand inhabitants. Despite an important textile industry, Montpellier was essentially an old-fashioned administrative and religious center, richly endowed with cultural institutions, including a university, an academy of sciences, twelve Masonic lodges, and sixteen monastic communities. And because it was a seat of the provincial estates of Languedoc and an intendancy, and had as well an array of courts, the city had a large population of lawyers and royal officials. If they resembled their counterparts in other provincial centers,[16] they probably provided Rigaud with a good many of his customers and probably had a taste for Enlightenment literature. He did not discuss their social background in his correspondence, but he noted that they clamored for the works of Voltaire, Rousseau, and Raynal. They subscribed heavily to the *Encyclopédie*, and even asked for atheistic treatises like *Système de la nature* and *Philosophie de la nature*. Montpellier was no intellectual backwater, and it was good book territory. "The book trade is quite extensive in this town," an observer remarked in 1768. "The booksellers have kept their shops well stocked ever since the inhabitants developed a taste for having libraries."[17]

These favorable conditions prevailed when Rigaud ordered his

Questions. But hard times set in during the early 1770s; and in the 1780s, Rigaud, like most booksellers, complained of a severe decline in his trade. The whole French economy contracted during those years, according to the standard account of C. E. Labrousse.[18] Certainly, the state's finances went into a tailspin: hence the disastrous book tariff of 1771, which belonged to Terray's unsuccessful attempt to reduce the deficit accumulated during the Seven Years' War. The government also tried to stamp out pirated and forbidden books, first by more severe police work in 1771–74, then by a general reform of the book trade in 1777. These measures eventually ruined Rigaud's commerce with the STN and with the other publishing houses that had grown up around France's borders during the prosperous midcentury years. The foreign publishers produced both original editions of books that could not pass the censorship in Paris and pirated editions of books put out by the Parisian publishers. Because the Parisians had acquired a virtual monopoly over the legal publishing industry, their rivals in the provinces formed alliances with the foreign houses and looked the other way when shipments from abroad arrived for inspection in the provincial guild halls (*chambres syndicales*). Under Louis XIV, the government had used the Parisian guild as an instrument to suppress the illegal trade; but under Louis XV, it became increasingly lax, until a new era of severity began with the fall of Choiseul's ministry (December 1770). Thus Rigaud's relations with the STN fit perfectly into an economic and political pattern that had prevailed in the book trade since the early eighteenth century and that began to fall apart just as the first crates of the *Questions* were making their way between Neuchâtel and Montpellier.

Other Schemata

Other patterns might show up in other research, for the model need not be applied in this manner, nor need it be applied at all. I am not arguing that book history should be written according to a standard formula, but trying to show how its disparate segments can be brought together within a single conceptual schema. Different book historians might prefer different schemata. They might concentrate on the book trade of all Languedoc, as Madeleine Ventre has done; or on the general bibliography of Voltaire, as Giles Barber, Jeroom Vercruysse, and others are doing; or on the overall pattern of book production in eighteenth-century France, in the manner of François Furet and Robert Estivals.[19] But however they define their subject, they will not draw out its full significance unless they relate it to all the elements that worked together as a circuit for transmitting texts.

To make the point clearer, I will go over the model circuit once more, noting questions that have been investigated successfully or that seem ripe for further research.

Authors. Despite the proliferation of biographies of great writers, the basic conditions of authorship remain obscure for most periods of history. At what point did writers free themselves from the patronage of wealthy noblemen and the state in order to live by their pens? What was the nature of a literary career, and how was it pursued? How did writers deal with publishers, printers, booksellers, reviewers, and one another? Until those questions are answered, we will not have a full understanding of the transmission of texts. Voltaire was able to manipulate secret alliances with pirate publishers because he did not depend on writing for a living. A century later, Zola proclaimed that a writer's independence came from selling his prose to the highest bidder.[20] How did this transformation take place? The work of John Lough begins to provide an answer, but more systematic research on the evolution of the republic of letters in France could be done from police records, literary almanacs, and bibliographies (*La France littéraire* gives the names and publications of 1,187 writers in 1757 and 3,089 in 1784). The situation in Germany is more obscure, owing to the fragmentation of the German states before 1871. But German scholars are beginning to tap sources like *Das gelehrte Teutschland*, which lists four thousand writers in 1779, and to trace the links among authors, publishers, and readers in regional and monographic studies.[21] Marino Berengo has shown how much can be discovered about author-publisher relations in Italy.[22] And the work of A. S. Collins still provides an excellent account of authorship in England, although it needs to be brought up to date and extended beyond the eighteenth century.[23]

Publishers. The key role of publishers is now becoming clearer, thanks to articles appearing in the *Journal of Publishing History* and monographs like Martin Lowry's *The World of Aldus Manutius*, Robert Patten's *Charles Dickens and His Publishers*, and Gary Stark's *Entrepreneurs of Ideology: Neoconservative Publishers in Germany, 1890–1933*. But the evolution of the publisher as a distinct figure in contrast to the master bookseller and the printer still needs systematic study. Historians have barely begun to tap the papers of publishers, although they are the richest of all sources for the history of books. The archives of the Cotta Verlag in Marbach, for example, contain at least one hundred fifty thousand documents, yet they have only been skimmed for references to Goethe, Schiller, and other famous writers. Further investigation almost certainly would turn up a great deal of information about the book as a force in nineteenth-century Germany. How did publishers draw up contracts with authors, build alliances with booksellers, negotiate with political authorities, and handle finances, supplies, shipments, and publicity? The answers to those questions would carry the history of books deep into the territory of social, economic, and political history, to their mutual benefit.

The Project for Historical Biobibliography at Newcastle upon Tyne and the Institut de Littérature et de Techniques Artistiques de Masse at Bordeaux illustrate the directions that such interdisciplinary work has already taken. The Bordeaux group has tried to trace books through different distribution systems in order to uncover the literary experience of different groups in contemporary France.[24] The researchers in Newcastle have studied the diffusion process through quantitative analysis of subscription lists, which were widely used in the sales campaigns of British publishers from the early seventeenth to the early nineteenth century.[25] Similar work could be done on publishers' catalogues and prospectuses, which have been collected in research centers like the Newberry Library. The whole subject of book advertising needs investigation. One could learn a great deal about attitudes toward books and the context of their use by studying the way they were presented—the strategy of the appeal, the values invoked by the phrasing—in all kinds of publicity, from journal notices to wall posters. American historians have used newspaper advertisements to map the spread of the printed word into the back reaches of colonial society.[26] By consulting the papers of publishers, they could make deeper inroads in the nineteenth and twentieth centuries.[27] Unfortunately, however, publishers usually treat their archives as garbage. Although they save the occasional letter from a famous author, they throw away account books and commercial correspondence, which usually are the most important sources of information for the book historian. The Center for the Book in the Library of Congress is now compiling a guide to publishers' archives. If they can be preserved and studied, they might provide a different perspective on the whole course of American history.

Printers. The printing shop is far better known than the other stages in the production and diffusion of books, because it has been a favorite subject of study in the field of analytical bibliography, whose purpose as defined by R. B. McKerrow and Philip Gaskell, is "to elucidate the transmission of texts by explaining the processes of book production."[28] Bibliographers have made important contributions to textual criticism, especially in Shakespearean scholarship, by building inferences backward from the structure of a book to the process of its printing and hence to an original text, such as the missing Shakespeare manuscripts. That line of reasoning has been undercut recently by D. F. McKenzie.[29] But even if they can never reconstruct an Ur-Shakespeare, bibliographers can demonstrate the existence of different editions of a text and of different states of an edition, a necessary skill in diffusion studies. Their techniques also make it possible to decipher the records of printers and so have opened up a new, archival phase in the history of printing. Thanks to the work of McKenzie, Leon Voet, Raymond de Roover, and Jacques Rychner, we now have a clear picture of how printing shops operated throughout the handpress period (roughly 1500–1800).[30] More work needs to be done on later periods, and new questions could be asked. How did printers calculate costs and organize production, especially after the spread of job printing and journalism? How did book budgets change after the introduction of machine-made paper in the first decade of the nineteenth century and Linotype in the 1880s? How did the technological changes affect the management of labor? And what part did journeymen printers, an unusually articulate and militant sector of the working class, play in labor history? Analytical bibliography may seem arcane to the outsider, but it could make a great contribution to social as well as literary history, especially if it were seasoned with a reading of printers' manuals and autobiographies, beginning with those of Thomas Platter, Thomas Gent, N. E. Restif de la Bretonne, Benjamin Franklin, and Charles Manby Smith.

Shippers.   Little is known about the way books reached bookstores from printing shops. The wagon, the canal barge, the merchant vessel, the post office, and the railroad may have influenced the history of literature more than one would suspect. Although transport facilities probably had little effect on the trade in great publishing centers like London and Paris, they sometimes determined the ebb and flow of business in remote areas. Before the nineteenth century, books were usually sent in sheets, so that the customer could have them bound according to his taste and his ability to pay. They traveled in large bales wrapped in heavy paper, and were easily damaged by rain and the friction of ropes. Compared with commodities like textiles, their intrinsic value was slight, yet their shipping costs were high, owing to the size and weight of the sheets. So shipping often took up a large proportion of a book's total cost and a large place in the marketing strategy of publishers. In many parts of Europe, printers could not count on getting shipments to booksellers in August and September, because wagoners abandoned their routes to work the harvests. The Baltic trade frequently ground to a halt after October, because ice closed the ports. Routes opened and shut everywhere in response to the pressures of war, politics, and even insurance rates. Unorthodox literature has traveled underground in huge quantities from the sixteenth century to the present, so its influence has varied according to the effectiveness of the smuggling industry. And other genres, like chapbooks and penny dreadfuls, circulated through special distributions systems, which need much more study, although book historians are now beginning to clear some of the ground.[31]

Booksellers. Thanks to some classic studies—H. S. Bennett on early modern England, L. C. Wroth on colonial America, H.-J. Martin on seventeenth-century France, and Johann Goldfriedrich on Germany—it is possible to piece together a general picture of the evolution of the book trade.[32] But more work needs to be done on the bookseller as a cultural agent, the middleman who mediated between supply and demand at their key point of contact. We still do not know enough about the social and intellectual world of men like Rigaud, about their values and tastes and the way they fit into their communities. They also operated within commercial networks, which expanded and collapsed like alliances in the diplomatic world. What laws governed the rise and fall of trade empires in publishing? A comparison of national histories could reveal some general tendencies, such as the centripetal force of great centers like London, Paris, Frankfurt, and Leipzig, which drew provincial houses into their orbits, and the countervailing trend toward alignments between provincial dealers and suppliers in independent enclaves like Liège, Bouillon, Neuchâtel, Geneva, and Avignon. But comparisons are difficult, because the trade operated through different institutions in different countries, which generated different kinds of archives. The records of the London Stationers' company, the Communauté des libraires et imprimeurs de Paris, and the Leipzig and Frankfurt book fairs have had a great deal to do with the different courses that book history has taken in England, France, and Germany.[33]

Nevertheless, books were sold as commodities everywhere. A more unabashedly economic study of them would provide a new perspective to the history of literature. James Barnes, John Tebbel, and Frédéric Barbier have demonstrated the importance of the economic element in the book trades of nineteenth-century England, America, and France.[34] But more work could be done—on credit mechanisms, for example, and the techniques of negotiating bills of exchange, of defense against suspensions of payment, and of exchanging printed sheets in lieu of payment in specie. The book trade, like other businesses during the Renaissance and early modern periods, was largely a confidence game, but we still do not know how it was played.

Readers. Despite a considerable literature on its psychology, phenomenology, textology, and sociology, reading remains mysterious. How do readers make sense of the signs on the printed page? What are the social effects of that experience? And how has it varied? Literary scholars like Wayne Booth, Wolfgang Iser, Stanley Fish, Walter Ong, and Jonathan Culler have made reading a central concern of textual criticism, because they understand literature as an activity, the construal of meaning within a system of communication, rather than a canon of texts.[35] The book historian could make use of their notions of fictitious audiences, implicit readers, and interpretive communities. But he may find their observations somewhat time-bound. Although the critics know their way around literary history (they are especially strong on seventeenth-century England), they seem to assume that texts have always worked on the sensibilities of readers in the same way. But a seventeenth-century London burgher inhabited a different mental universe from that of a twentieth-century American professor. Reading itself has changed over time. It was often done aloud and in groups, or in secret and with an intensity we may not be able to imagine today. Carlo Ginzburg has shown how much meaning a sixteenth century miller could infuse into a text, and Margaret Spufford has demonstrated that still humbler workmen fought their way to mastery over the printed word in the era of *Areopagitica*.[36] Everywhere in early modern Europe, from the ranks of Montaigne to those of Menocchio, readers wrung significance from books; they did not merely decipher them. Reading was a passion long before the *"Lesewut"* and the *"Wertherfieber"* of the romantic era; and there is *Sturm und Drang* in it yet, despite the vogue for speed-reading and the mechanistic view of literature as the encoding and decoding of messages.

But texts shape the response of readers, however active they may be. As Walter Ong has observed, the opening pages of *The Canter-*

bury Tales and *A Farewell to Arms* create a frame and cast the reader in a role, which he cannot avoid no matter what he thinks of pilgrimages and civil wars.[37] In fact, typography as well as style and syntax determine the ways in which texts convey meanings. McKenzie has shown that the bawdy, unruly Congreve of the early quarto editions settled down into the decorous neoclassicist of the *Works* of 1709 as a consequence of book design rather than bowd-lerization.[38] The history of reading will have to take account of the ways that texts constrain readers as well as the ways that readers take liberties with texts. The tension between those tendencies has existed wherever men confronted books, and it had produced some extraordinary results, as in Luther's reading of the Psalms, Rousseau's reading of *Le Misanthrope,* and Kierkegaard's reading of the sacrifice of Isaac.

If it is possible to recapture the great rereadings of the past, the inner experience of ordinary readers may always elude us. But we should at least be able to reconstruct a good deal of the social context of reading. The debate about silent reading during the Middle Ages has produced some impressive evidence about read-ing habits,[39] and studies of reading societies in Germany, where they proliferated to an extraordinary degree in the eighteenth and nineteenth centuries, have shown the importance of reading in the development of a distinct bourgeois cultural style.[40] German scholars have also done a great deal in the history of libraries and in reception studies of all kinds.[41] Following a notion of Rolf Engels-ing, they often maintain that reading habits became transformed at the end of the eighteenth century. Before this *Leserevolution,* readers tended to work laboriously through a small number of texts, especially the Bible, over and over again. Afterward, they raced through all kinds of material, seeking amusement rather than edification. The shift from intensive to extensive reading coincided with a desacralization of the printed word. The world began to be cluttered with reading matter, and texts began to be treated as commodities that could be discarded as casually as yes-terday's newspaper. This interpretation has recently been disputed by Reinhart Siegert, Martin Welke, and other young scholars, who have discovered "intensive" reading in the reception of fugitive works like almanacs and newspapers, notably the *Noth- und Hülfsbüchlein* of Rudolph Zacharias Becker, an extraordinary bestseller of the *Goethezeit.*[42] But whether or not the concept of a reading revolution will hold up, it has helped to align research on reading with general questions of social and cultural history.[43] The same can be said of research on literacy,[44] which has made it possi-

ble for scholars to detect the vague outline of diverse reading pub-
lics two and three centuries ago and to trace books to readers at
several levels of society. The lower the level, the more intense the
study. Popular literature has been a favorite topic of research during the last decade,[45] despite a growing tendency to question the
notion that cheap booklets like the *bibliothèque bleue* represented an autonomous culture of the common people or that one
can distinguish clearly between strains of "elite" and "popular"
culture. It now seems inadequate to view cultural change as a
linear, or trickle-down, movement of influences. Currents flowed
up as well as down, merging and blending as they went. Characters
like Gargantua, Cinderella, and Buscon moved back and forth
through oral traditions, chapbooks, and sophisticated literature,
changing in nationality as well as genre.[46] One could even trace the
metamorphoses of stock figures in almanacs. What does Poor Richard's reincarnation as *le Bonhomme Richard* reveal about literary
culture in America and France? And what can be learned about
German-French relations by following the Lame Messenger (*der
hinkende Bote, le messager boiteux*) through the traffic of almanacs across the Rhine?

Questions about who reads what, in what conditions, at what
time, and with what effect, link reading studies with sociology.
The book historian could learn how to pursue such questions from
the work of Douglas Waples, Bernard Berelson, Paul Lazarsfeld, and
Pierre Bourdieu. He could draw on the reading research that flour-
ished in the Graduate Library School of the University of Chicago
from 1930 to 1950, and that still turns up in the occasional Gallup
report.[47] And as an example of the sociological strain in historical
writing, he could consult the studies of reading (and nonreading) in
the English working class during the last two centuries by Richard
Altick, Robert Webb, and Richard Hoggart.[48] All this work opens
onto the larger problem of how exposure to the printed word affects
the way men think. Did the invention of movable type transform
man's mental universe? There may be no single satisfactory answer to that question, because it bears on so many different aspects
of life in early modern Europe, as Elizabeth Eisenstein has
shown.[49] But it should be possible to arrive at a firmer understanding of what books meant to people. Their use in the taking of oaths,
the exchanging of gifts, the awarding of prizes, and the bestowing
of legacies would provide clues to their significance within different societies. The iconography of books could indicate the weight
of their authority, even for illiterate laborers who sat in church
before pictures of the tablets of Moses. The place of books in

folklore, and of folk motifs in books, shows that influences ran both ways when oral traditions came into contact with printed texts, and that books need to be studied in relation to other media.[50] The lines of research could lead in many directions, but they all should issue ultimately in a larger understanding of how printing has shaped man's attempts to make sense of the human condition.

One can easily lose sight of the larger dimensions of the enterprise, because book historians often stray into esoteric byways and unconnected specializations. Their work can be so fragmented, even within the limits of the literature on a single country, that it may seem hopeless to conceive of book history as a single subject, to be studied from a comparative perspective across the whole range of historical disciplines. But books themselves do not respect limits, either linguistic or national. They have often been written by authors who belonged to an international republic of letters, composed by printers who did not work in their native tongue, sold by booksellers who operated across national boundaries, and read in one language by readers who spoke another. Books also refuse to be contained within the confines of a single discipline when treated as objects of study. Neither history nor literature nor economics nor sociology nor bibliography can do justice to all the aspects of the life of a book. By its very nature, therefore, the history of books must be international in scale and interdisciplinary in method. But it need not lack conceptual coherence, because books belong to circuits of communication that operate in consistent patterns, however complex they may be. By unearthing those circuits, historians can show that books do not merely recount history; they make it.

Notes

Reprinted from *Daedalus* 111, no. 3 (Summer 1982).

1. For examples of this work, see, in addition to the books named above, Henri-Jean Martin, *Livre, pouvoirs et société à Paris au XVIIe siècle (1598–1701)*, 2 vols. (Geneva, 1969); Jean Quéniart, *L'Imprimerie et la librairie à Rouen au XVIIIe siècle* (Paris, 1969); René Moulinas, *L'Imprimerie, la librairie et la presse à Avignon au XVIIIe siècle* (Grenoble, 1974); and Frédéric Barbier, *Trois cents ans de librairie et d'imprimerie: Berger-Levrault, 1676–*

1830 (Geneva, 1979), in the series "Histoire et civilisation du livre," which includes several monographs written along similar lines. Much of the French work has appeared as articles in the *Revue Française d'histoire du livre*. For a survey of the field by two of its most important contributors, see Roger Chartier and Daniel Roche, "Le Livre, un changement de perspective," *Faire de l'histoire* (Paris, 1974), 3:115–36; and Roger Chartier and Daniel Roche, "L'Histoire quantitative du livre," *Revue Française d'histoire du livre* no. 16 (1977): 3–27. For sympathetic assessments by two American fellow travelers, see Robert Darnton, "Reading, Writing, and Publishing in Eighteenth-Century France: A Case Study in the Sociology of Literature," *Daedalus* 100 (Winter 1971): 214–56; and Raymond Birn, "*Livre et société* after Ten Years: The Formation of a Discipline," *Studies on Voltaire and the Eighteenth Century* 151 (1976): 287–312.

2. As examples of these approaches, see Theodore Besterman, *Voltaire* (New York, 1969), 433–34; Daniel Mornet, "Les Enseignements des bibliothèques privées (1750–1780)," *Revue d'histoire littéraire de la France* 17 (1910): 449–92; and the bibliographical studies now being prepared under the direction of the Voltaire Foundation, which will replace the outdated bibliography by Georges Bengesco.

3. The following account is based on the ninety-nine letters in Rigaud's dossier in the papers of the Société typographique de Neuchâtel, Bibliothèque de la ville de Neuchâtel, Switzerland (henceforth referred to as STN), supplemented by other relevant material from the vast archives of the STN.

4. Rigaud to STN, July 27, 1771.

5. The pattern of Rigaud's orders is evident from his letters to the STN and the STN's Livres de Commission, where it tabulated its orders. Rigaud included catalogues of his major holdings in his letters of June 29, 1774, and May 23, 1777.

6. Madeleine Ventre, *L'Imprimerie et la librairie en Languedoc au dernier siècle de l'Ancien Régime* (Paris and The Hague, 1958), 227.

7. B. André to STN, August 22, 1784.

8. *Manuel de l'auteur et du libraire* (Paris, 1777), 67.

9. Jean-François Favarger to STN, August 29, 1778.

10. The procès-verbal of the raids is in the Bibliothèque nationale, Ms. français 22075, fol. 355.

11. Fontanel to STN, March 6, 1781.

12. STN to Gosse and Pinet, booksellers of The Hague, April 19, 1770.

13. STN to Voltaire, September 15, 1770.

14. This account is based on the STN's correspondence with intermediaries all along its routes, notably the shipping agents Nicole and Galliard of Nyon and Secrétan and De la Serve of Ouchy.

15. Rigaud to STN, August 28, 1771.

16. Robert Darnton, *The Business of Enlightenment: A Publishing History of the Encyclopédie, 1775–1800* (Cambridge, Mass., 1979), 273–99.

17. Anonymous, "Etat et description de la ville de Montpellier, fait en 1768," in *Montpellier en 1768 et en 1836 d'après deux manuscrits inédits,*

ed. J. Berthelé (Montpellier, 1909), 55. This rich contemporary description of Montpellier is the main source of the above account.

18. C. E. Labrousse, *La Crise de l'économie française à la fin de l'Ancien Régime et au début de la Révolution* (Paris, 1944).

19. Ventre, *L'Imprimerie et la librairie en Languedoc;* François Furet, "La 'Librairie' du royaume de France au 18e siècle," *Livre et société* 1 (1965): 3–32; and Robert Estivals, *La Statistique bibliographique de la France sous la monarchie au XVIIIe siècle* (Paris and The Hague, 1965). The bibliographical work will be published under the auspices of the Voltaire Foundation.

20. John Lough, *Writer and Public in France from the Middle Ages to the Present Day* (Oxford, 1978), 303.

21. For surveys and selections of recent German research, see Helmuth Kiesel and Paul Münch, *Gesellschaft und Literatur im 18. Jahrhundert. Voraussetzung und Entstehung des literarischen Marktes in Deutschland* (Munich, 1977); Franklin Kopitzsch, ed., *Aufklärung, Absolutismus und Bürgertum in Deutschland* (Munich, 1976); and Herbert G. Göpfert, *Vom Autor zum Leser* (Munich, 1978).

22. Marino Berengo, *Intellettuali e librai nella Milano della Restaurazione* (Turin, 1980). On the whole, however, the French version of *l' histoire du livre* has received a less enthusiastic reception in Italy than in Germany: see Furio Diaz, "Metodo quantitativo e storia delle idee," *Rivista storica italiana* 78 (1966): 932–47.

23. A. S. Collins, *Authorship in the Days of Johnson* (London, 1927); and A. S. Collins, *The Profession of Letters (1780–1832)* (London, 1928). For more recent work, see John Feather, "John Nourse and His Authors," *Studies in Bibliography* 34 (1981): 205–26.

24. Robert Escarpit, *Le Littéraire et le social. Eléments pour une sociologie de la littérature* (Paris, 1970).

25. Peter John Wallis, *The Social Index: A New Technique for Measuring Social Trends* (Newcastle upon Tyne, 1978).

26. William Gilmore is now completing an extensive research project on the diffusion of books in colonial New England. On the political and economic aspects of the colonial press, see Stephen Botein, "'Meer Mechanics' and an Open Press: The Business and Political Strategies of Colonial American Printers," *Perspectives in American History* 9 (1975): 127–225; and Bernard Bailyn and John B. Hench, eds., *The Press and the American Revolution* (Worcester, Mass., 1980), which contains ample references to work on the early history of the book in America.

27. For a general survey of work on the later history of books in the United States, see Hellmut Lehmann-Haupt, *The Book in America: A History of the Making, the Selling, and the Collecting of Books in the United States*, rev. ed. (New York, 1952).

28. Philip Gaskell, *A New Introduction to Bibliography* (New York and Oxford, 1972), preface. Gaskell's work provides an excellent general survey of the subject.

29. D. F. McKenzie, "Printers of the Mind: Some Notes on Bibli-

ographical Theories and Printing House Practices," *Studies in Bibliography* 22 (1969): 1–75.

30. D. F. McKenzie, *The Cambridge University Press 1696–1712*, 2 vols. (Cambridge, 1966); Leon Voet, *The Golden Compasses*, 2 vols. (Amsterdam, 1969 and 1972); Raymond de Roover, "The Business Organization of the Plantin Press in the Setting of Sixteenth-Century Antwerp," *De gulden passer* 24 (1956): 104–20; and Jacques Rychner, "A l'Ombre des Lumières: Coup d'oeil sur la main d'oeuvre de quelques imprimeries du XVIIIe siècle," *Studies on Voltaire and the Eighteenth Century* 155 (1976): 1925–55, and "Running a Printing House in Eighteenth-Century Switzerland: The Workshop of the Société typographique de Neuchâtel," *Library* 6th ser., 1 (1979): 1–24.

31. For example, see J.-P. Belin, *Le Commerce des livres prohibés à Paris de 1750 à 1789* (Paris, 1913); Jean-Jacques Darmon, *Le Colportage de librairie en France sous le second empire* (Paris, 1972); and Reinhart Siegert, *Aufklärung und Volkslektüre exemplarisch dargestellt an Rudolph Zacharias Becker und seinem "Noth- und Hülfsbüchlein" mit einer Bibliographie zum Gesamtthema* (Frankfurt am Main, 1978).

32. H. S. Bennett, *English Books & Readers 1475 to 1557* (Cambridge, 1952) and *English Books & Readers 1558–1603* (Cambridge, 1965); L. C. Wroth, *The Colonial Printer*, rev. ed. (Portland, Me., 1938); Martin, *Livre, pouvoirs et société*; and Johann Goldfriedrich and Friedrich Kapp, *Geschichte des deutschen Buchhandels*, 4 vols. (Leipzig, 1886–1913).

33. Compare Cyprian Blagden, *The Stationers' Company, A History, 1403–1959* (Cambridge, 1960); Martin, *Livre, pouvoirs et société*; and Rudolf Jentzsch, *Der deutschlateinische Büchermarkt nach den Leipziger Ostermesskatalogen von 1740, 1770 und 1800 in seiner Gliederung und Wandlung* (Leipzig, 1912).

34. James Barnes, *Free Trade in Books: A Study of the London Book Trade since 1800* (Oxford, 1964); John Tebbel, *A History of Book Publishing in the United States*, 4 vols. (New York, 1972–81); and Frédéric Barbier, *Trois cents ans de librairie et d'imprimerie.*

35. See, for example, Wolfgang Iser, *The Implied Reader: Patterns of Communication in Prose Fiction from Bunyan to Beckett* (Baltimore, Md., 1974); Stanley Fish, *Self-Consuming Artifacts: The Experience of Seventeenth-Century Literature* (Berkeley and Los Angeles, 1972) and *Is There a Text in This Class? The Authority of Interpretive Communities* (Cambridge, Mass., 1980); Walter J. Ong, "The Writer's Audience Is Always a Fiction," *PMLA* 90 (1975): 9–21; and, for a sampling of other variations on these themes, Susan R. Suleiman and Inge Crosman, eds., *The Reader in the Text: Essays on Audience and Interpretation* (Princeton, N.J., 1980).

36. Carlo Ginzburg, *The Cheese and the Worms: The Cosmos of a Sixteenth-Century Miller* (Baltimore, Md., 1980); and Margaret Spufford, "First Steps in Literacy: The Reading and Writing Experiences of the Humblest Seventeenth-Century Spiritual Autobiographers," *Social History* 4 (1979): 407–35.

37. Ong, "Writer's Audience" 9–21.

38. D. F. McKenzie, "Typography and Meaning: The Case of William Congreve," *Wolfenbütteler Schriften zur Geschichte des Buchwesens* 4 (1981): 81–125.

39. See Paul Saenger, "Silent Reading: Its Impact on Late Medieval Script and Society," Viator, *Medieval and Renaissance Studies* 13 (1982): 367–414.

40. See Otto Dann, ed., *Lesegesellschaften und bürgerliche Emanzipation: Ein europäischer Vergleich* (Munich: C. H. Beck, 1981), which has a thorough bibliography.

41. For examples of recent work, see Paul Raabe, ed., *Oeffentliche und private Bibliotheken im 17. und 18. Jahrhundert: Raritätenkammern, Forschungsinstrumente oder Bildungsstätten?* (Bremen and Wolfenbüttel, 1977). Much of the stimulus for recent reception studies has come from the theoretical work of Hans Robert Jauss, notably *Literaturgeschichte als Provokation* (Frankfurt am Main, 1970).

42. Rolf Engelsing, *Analphabetentum und Lektüre. Zur Sozialgeschichte des Lesens in Deutschland zwischen feudaler und industrieller Gesellschaft* (Stuttgart, 1973) and *Der Bürger als Leser. Lesergeschichte in Deutschland 1500–1800* (Stuttgart, 1974); Siegert, *Aufklärung und Volkslektüre*, and Martin Welke, "Gemeinsame Lektüre und frühe Formen von Gruppenbildungen im 17. und 18. Jahrhundert: Zeitungslesen in Deutschland," in *Lesegesellschaften und bürgerliche Emanzipation*, 29–53.

43. As an example of this alignment, see Rudolf Schenda, *Volk ohne Buch* (Frankfurt am Main, 1970); for examples of more recent work, see Rainer Gruenter, ed., *Leser und Lesen im achtzehntes Jahrhundert* (Heidelberg, 1977); and Herbert G. Göpfert, ed., *Lesen und Leben* (Frankfurt am Main, 1975).

44. See François Furet and Jacques Ozouf, *Lire et écrire: L'Alphabétisation des Français de Calvin à Jules Ferry* (Paris, 1978); Lawrence Stone, "Literacy and Education in England, 1640–1900," *Past and Present* 42 (1969): 69–139; David Cressy, *Literacy and the Social Order: Reading and Writing in Tudor and Stuart England* (Cambridge, 1980); Kenneth A. Lockridge, *Literacy in Colonial New England: An Enquiry into the Social Context of Literacy in the Early Modern West* (New York, 1974); and Carlo Cipolla, *Literacy and Development in the West* (Harmondsworth, 1969).

45. For a survey and a synthesis of this research, see Peter Burke, *Popular Culture in Early Modern Europe* (New York, 1978).

46. As an example of the older view in which the *bibliothèque bleue* serves as a key to the understanding of popular culture, see Robert Mandrou, *De la Culture populaire aux XVIIe et XVIIIe siècles. La Bibliothèque bleue de Troyes* (Paris, 1964). The more current view, which recognizes more nuances in the study of popular culture, is well represented by Roger Chartier, *Figures de la gueuserie* (Paris, 1982).

47. Douglas Waples, Bernard Berelson, and Franklyn Bradshaw, *What Reading Does to People* (Chicago, 1940); Bernard Berelson, *The Library's Public* (New York, 1949); Elihu Katz, "Communication Research and the Image of Society: The Convergence of Two Traditions," *American Journal of Sociology* 65 (1960): 435–40; and John Y. Cole and Carol S. Gold, eds.,

Reading in America 1978 (Washington, D.C., 1979). For the Gallup report, see American Library Association, *Book Reading and Library Usage: A Study of Habits and Perceptions* (Chicago, 1978). Much in this older variety of sociology still seems valid, and it can be studied in conjunction with the current work of Pierre Bourdieu; see especially Pierre Bourdieu, *La Distinction: Critique sociale du jugement* (Paris, 1979).

48. Richard D. Altick, *The English Common Reader: A social History of the Mass Reading Public, 1800–1900* (Chicago, 1957); Robert K. Webb, *The British Working Class Reader* (London, 1955); and Richard Hoggart, *The Uses of Literacy* (1957; rpt. Harmondsworth, 1960).

49. Elizabeth L. Eisenstein, *The Printing Press as an Agent of Change*, 2 vols. (Cambridge, 1979). For a discussion of Eisenstein's thesis, see Anthony T. Grafton, "The Importance of Being Printed," *Journal of Interdisciplinary History* 11 (1980): 265–86; Michael Hunter, "The Impact of Print," *Book Collector* 28 (1979): 335–52; and Roger Chartier, "L'Ancien Régime typographique: Réflexions sur quelques travaux récents," *Annales; Economies, sociétés, civilisations* 36 (1981): 191–209.

50. Some of these general themes are taken up in Eric Havelock, *Origins of Western Literacy* (Toronto, 1976); Jack Goody, ed., *Literacy in Traditional Societies* (Cambridge, 1968); Jack Goody, *The Domestication of the Savage Mind* (Cambridge, 1977); Walter J. Ong, *The Presence of the Word* (New Haven, Conn., 1967); and Natalie Z. Davis, *Society and Culture in Early Modern France* (Stanford, Calif., 1975).

Chapter Two   **Literacy Instruction and Gender in Colonial New England**

E. Jennifer Monaghan

Hanna Newberry, the most prominent mortgage-holder in Windsor, Connecticut, for most of the second quarter of the eighteenth century, was unable to sign the many documents to which she affixed her name. Instead, she subscribed her mark, the initials HN. Her case illustrates, according to Linda Auwers, "the widespread fact of female illiteracy among women born in the seventeenth century and the difficulty in relating literacy to social class."[1]

Literacy historians have used signatures and marks as indicators of, respectively, the literacy and illiteracy of ordinary people in the seventeenth and eighteenth centuries in Europe and America.[2] For colonial New England, the best-known study remains that by Kenneth Lockridge, who tabulated the signatures/marks made on over three thousand wills. He found that the proportion of males able to sign their own wills increased from 60 percent in the 1660s to 85 percent by 1760 and to almost 90 percent by 1790. Female signing rates were much lower throughout the entire period. Some 31 percent of the women signed their wills before 1670; this average increased, but only to 46 percent by the 1790s.[3] Three later studies have found a higher rate of signing than Lockridge did, in part by using deeds and other sources in addition to wills, so accessing a larger or less decrepit population.[4] One of these is the study cited above by Auwers, who allocated her signers/markers into birth cohorts and found that the proportion of women in Windsor who could sign their own names to deeds rose from 27 percent for the cohort born between 1650 and 1669 to 90 percent for the 1740–49 cohort.[5]

The equation of literacy possession with signing rests on the assumption that signing ability is roughly equivalent to fluent reading. As reading was taught before writing, the argument runs, the ability to write (as indicated by a signature) also indicates the ability to read. Carl Kaestle has recently summarized the arguments for and against this position, and—after warning us that the relationship between signing and reading may vary by gender, class, place, and period— finally suggests that signature counts indicate roughly the "minimum number of people who were minimally literate."[6]

Although scholars have varied in their interpretations of what a signature implies, there has been more general agreement about the mark: it has been viewed as a valid indicator of illiteracy. Lockridge's figures have therefore contributed to the widely held belief that in New England and elsewhere females were dramatically less literate than males throughout the colonial period, reaching roughly half the literacy level of males.

Several scholars, however, including Lockridge himself, have raised the possibility that some people—particularly women—could read but not write. Margaret Spufford and Victor Neuburg have provided examples of this in the context of seventeenth- and eighteenth-century England.[7] The thesis of the present study is that this was also true of colonial New England. When we examine the contexts in which literacy instruction was conducted, paying close attention to the role played by gender, it will become apparent that the mark cannot be considered an infallible indicator of illiteracy, particularly in the seventeenth century.

The evidence to be presented is qualitative in nature, scattered, and fragmentary; it is also skewed toward the seventeenth century. Further research will be necessary to see if the conclusions to be drawn will stand. Nonetheless, the bits and pieces of the puzzle seem to form a remarkably coherent picture across time and place. In order to support my contention, I first discuss how reading and writing were taught and by whom, then turn to examine how the colonists themselves viewed literacy from the legal and economic standpoints. Next follows an elaboration of the relationship between schooling and gender. Basic to the entire discussion is the concept that literacy was considered by the colonists to comprise a deliberately imparted set of skills, taught in ways that were both widely accepted and precise.

The Reading Curriculum

The colonial reading curriculum was, of course, brought over to the new continent, along with so much else, from England. The seventeenth-century curriculum followed the outline sketched by John Locke, who in 1693 characterized it as the "ordinary road of the Hornbook, Primer, Psalter, Testament, and Bible."[8]

There is plenty of evidence that the colonists followed this "ordinary road" in the early days of settlement and throughout the seventeenth century. The hornbook formed the novice's introduction to reading. Its name derived from its single page (originally covered with transparent protective horn), which was tacked onto a little wooden paddle. It presented the alphabet, the first few lines of the syllabarium (*ab eb ib ob ub*), and the Lord's Prayer. Often mentioned in the same context as primers, hornbooks turn up here and there in the sources over the course of the seventeenth century, and advertisements for primers and both gilt and plain hornbooks have been found in Philadelphia newspapers as late as 1760.[9] The hornbook was used in dame schools—private schools for small children run by a woman in her own home—as the child's first "text." Samuel Sewall mentioned one in just such a context. He recorded in his diary on April 27, 1691, that he had sent his little son Joseph, not yet three years old, to school (obviously for the first time). "This afternoon had Joseph to school to Capt. Townsend's Mother's, his cousin Jane accompanying him, carried his Horn-book."[10]

Hornbooks were apparently never manufactured on American soil, but were all imported.[11] Primers, the next step in the reading curriculum, were also imported into the colonies from very early on. They must have been a standard item in any village store. One example of their widespread availability is documented for New Haven, in 1645—only seven years after it was founded as a separate colony. That year, a Captain Turner was accused by Mistress Stolion before the New Haven Colony Court of having reneged on a deal in which he had promised to give her two cows in exchange for six yards of cloth. Not to be outdone, the captain accused Mrs. Stolion in turn of price gouging: he claimed that "she sold primmers at 9*d* [nine pence] apeece which cost but 4*d* here in New England."[12]

Primers were such essential texts for instruction in both reading and religion, however, that their publication on American presses is documented early in the colonial adventure. The oldest extant American primer was composed by John Eliot as part of his efforts to convert the Massachuset Indians. Written in the Massachuset dialect of the Algonquian language and published in 1669 on the Cambridge, Massachusetts, press, the primer admirably sums up, in its title, the dual role it, like the hornbook, played in both reading and religious instruction. The English version reads, *The Indian Primer; or, the Way of Training up of Our Indian Youth in the Good Knowledge of*

God, in the Knowledge of the Scriptures and in an Ability to Read.[13]

Primers as a genre became a publishing staple in New England and the middle states as presses increased in number. The *New England Primer,* the most famous of colonial textbooks, has a publishing history that runs from 1690, when it was already in its second impression, to long after the American Revolution. (Its sales up to 1830 have been estimated at between six million and eight million copies.) It contained several pages of instructional material, presenting the syllabarium and words of increasing length, from monosyllables to words of six syllables. Its popularity was enhanced by the inclusion of a catechism.[14] In addition to the *New England Primer,* there were numerous other primers in the marketplace.[15]

The next text in both the religious and reading curriculum was the Psalter (the Book of Psalms). Psalters too were extensively printed on American presses. They were generally published without the addition of any reading instructional material, but we do know of one 1760 Philadelphia edition that indicated that it had been "Improved by the addition of a variety of lessons in spelling. . . . Likewise, rules for reading. . . . The whole being a proper introduction, not only to learning, but to the training of children in the reading of the holy scriptures in particular."[16]

One incident that revealed the Psalter's status as a reading instructional text occurred in the context of writing instruction. John Proctor, master of the town-financed North Writing School in Boston from 1731 to 1743, was summoned in 1741 before the Boston selectmen to answer what seems to have been a parental complaint: he was accused of having refused to admit boys from "Families of low Circumstances" to his school. Proctor replied that he had "refus'd none of the Inhabitants Children, but such as could not Read in the Psalter."[17] Clearly, the Psalter was being used as a kind of minimum competency test of reading ability.

The final two stages in the reading curriculum consisted of mastering first the New Testament and then the entire Bible (both Old and New Testaments). Because it was illegal to print these on American presses (John Eliot's *Indian Bible* being a specialized exception), English Bibles were imported until after the American Revolution.

The use of the Scriptures as the climax of the reading curriculum is well known. Two seventeenth-century instances occur in the records of New Haven. The first illustrates the seventeenth-century assumption that reading instruction was supposed to have begun before a child entered the town school. The job description for a New Haven schoolmaster, hired in 1651, was to "perfect male chilldren in the English, after they can read in their Testament or Bible, and to learne them to wright," and to bring them on to Latin, if he could.[18] The second involved a school for girls. That same year, the daughter of a Captain How was brought before the New Haven Court and charged with misconduct that included speaking in a blasphemous way of the Scriptures. The girl's mother claimed that her daughter had picked up some of her bad habits at "Goodwife Wickams," where she went to school. Witnesses testified that they had seen the girl look in a Bible, turn over a leaf, and say that "it was not worth reading." It is not too far-fetched to assume that young Miss How had reached the stage of reading the Bible at her school.[19]

Not included in Locke's characterization of the "ordinary road" was the spelling book. In a major pedagogical shift that cannot be documented here in any detail, the spelling book was introduced into schools, perhaps fairly early in the eighteenth century, as an important beginning text for reading instruction.[20] In the rise of the speller we see the demands of religious content taking second place to the requirements of methodology, in a continuation of a process begun when the first alphabet was added to the primer.[21]

Spelling books as a genre appear at least as early as Edmund Coote's *The English Schoole-Maister*, published in London in 1596, and reprinted fifty-four times by 1737.[22] Moreover, spellers were printed very early on colonial presses: an unidentified speller came off Stephen Daye's press in Cambridge, in the Bay Colony, in about 1644.[23] It was not, however, until the eighteenth century that the speller's ascendancy as a school text began. An important clue to its popularity is the frequency with which English spellers were reprinted on American presses. (Unlike primers, some of which reflected colonial circumstances, American spellers were all reproduced verbatim from English copies until after the American Revolution.) When Benjamin Franklin in 1747 reprinted Thomas Dilworth's *A New Guide to the English Tongue*, he ushered onto the American scene a spelling book that would enjoy tremendous popularity in the second half of the eighteenth century ("the nurse of us all," as one user put it), until ousted by Noah Webster's speller after 1783.[24]

The name "spelling book" was a reflection of the prevailing methodology: spelling was the key to reading. After mastering the letters of the alphabet, the novice reader's next task was to spell out, orally, syllables and words (broken into syllables) from the printed page. Spelling books incorporated exactly the same methodology—the alphabetic method—as primers did. Although some spellers included secular content, a key difference between primers and spellers was that the latter presented the reading curriculum in a more elaborate and systematic fashion. The tables of words were greatly increased in number and were followed by "lessons"—reading material based in part on vocabulary already introduced.[25]

One key aspect of the alphabetic method was that reading instruction was conducted entirely orally, without requiring the child to write. Progress in learning to read could therefore be gauged simply by listening to the child's oral spelling. As Edmund Coote had put it in the 1596 preface to his speller, the purchaser of his book could sit at the loom or needle, "and neuer hinder thy worke, to heare thy scholers, after thou hast once made this little booke familiar vnto thee."[26]

Comprehension was virtually ignored, pedagogically speaking. It would probably be fairer to say that comprehension of the text was assumed. After all, the seventeenth-century reading curriculum was in essence a course in Christianity: the texts used were basic to the religion itself. Not until the spelling books of the eighteenth century would any reference be made to such matters as how easily a child could learn the material.

In sum, the task of the reading teacher throughout the entire colonial period was clearly laid out. Both methodology and content were agreed upon; the curriculum was, in effect, standardized. Moreover, no qualifications for teaching reading were necessary other than being able to read oneself. Not only did the child not write in the course of learning to read; the teacher did not need to know how to write either.

The Reading Teacher

Because the task of the reading teacher was so well defined and was considered, rightly or wrongly, to be easy, the teaching of reading was more often than not considered to be a female province. In the context of family education, it is significant that in those rare cases when we know who taught the child to read at home, it is the mother who is singled out. A pious mother was particularly motivated to teach her child to read. The Boston minister Increase Mather (father of Cotton Mather) was born in Dorchester, Massachusetts, in 1639, nine years after the town was founded. He wrote that he "learned to read of my mother" whom he described as a "very Holy praying woman." (Significantly, it was his father who taught him to *write*.) Richard Brown, born in 1675, also had a "pious and prudent" mother, who endeavored to instill in him "the principals of Religion and Holiness." After "she had caused me to read well at home, she sent me to school."[27]

It appears, however, that early in the colonial period children began attending a school to learn to read, either as well as, or instead of, learning from their mothers. Such schools were called dame schools or reading schools. The dame school is well documented for England in the seventeenth and eighteenth centuries.[28] A woman would take small children, both boys and girls, into her own home for a few hours. We even know of one two-year-old girl who drowned on her way to school.[29] While no doubt the dame's major contribution was to afford an overworked mother a few hours of respite from her three- and four-year-olds, ostensibly her purpose was to introduce her charges to reading. In fact, some dame schools taught a substantial amount of reading. John Barnard, born in 1681, recalled that when he was less than six years old his schoolmistress "made me a sort of usher, appointing me to teach some children that were older than myself, as well as smaller ones; and in which time I had read my Bible through thrice."[30]

The dame, or reading, school was not funded by the town, but was a private venture. It represented, of course, a most useful source of income for a woman. We meet women as paid teachers of reading in unexpected contexts. The Commissioners of the United Colonies of New England, who disbursed monies sent over from England for missionary work among the Indians, not only employed a woman to teach the Indians to read, but even gave her a raise. As their letter said, in 1653, "The wife of William Daniell of Dorchester hath for this three yeares last past bestowed much of her time in teaching severall Indians to Read and that shee hath onely Receiued the summe of six pounds towards her paines; [we] thought fitt to allow her nine pounds more for the time past."[31]

Women are notoriously invisible in colonial records. Even though most townships (Boston, for instance) required private schoolteachers to obtain permission from the town before they were allowed to teach, private women teachers do not appear in the Boston records until the 1730s. In the seventeenth century, therefore, most of our evidence comes from those rare cases in which women teachers were involved with the law, as happened to Goodwife Wickam of New Haven. One can only guess how many women must have earned a few pennies a week as private teachers of reading throughout that century. As we shall see, in the following century women would be called upon to ply their skills in the public arena as well.

Writing Instruction

Writing was defined, in the colonial context, as penmanship.[32] In only a few respects did writing instruction resemble reading instruction. Just as "good" reading was considered to be accurate oral reading, so "good" writing seemed to be viewed entirely in terms of fine letter formation. Composition seems rarely to have been discussed at all.

Similarly, mastery was to be attained by rote and repetition: by the careful reproduction by the learner of the "copy" set for him by the writing master. As was the case in reading instruction, mastery of the individual letters of the alphabet was the first step in the writing curriculum. Later the learner would copy, five or six times, pithy moral sentences, and then work up to copying poems or texts reproduced by the master from the traditional copybooks such as George Bickham's *The Universal Penman* (1743).[33]

In other respects, however, the contrast between the teaching of the two literacy skills could hardly have been greater. Writing was considered a craft, subject to all the limitations of access that that implied. The gender bias implicit in the term "penmanship" was not fortuitous: writing was largely a male domain. This was particularly true as it related to the gender of the instructor: men taught writing. The writing master, analogous to the scribe of earlier times, was the possessor of a fairly arcane skill. The most telling evidence that his knowledge was considered specialized was that he had usually had to attain it through the apprenticeship route.[34]

Moreover, unlike textbooks for reading instruction, which were early reproduced on American presses, the texts for writing instruction were, for technical reasons, not reprinted on American presses but imported. Although the successful reproduction of different kinds of "hands" (scripts) had been made much easier by the invention of copperplate engraving, engraving not only was costly but demanded a great deal of skill; in fact, the best engraving was undertaken by penmen themselves. (George Bickham, for instance, personally engraved the work of some twenty-five masters for his *Universal Penman*.) The closest Americans came to reproducing scripts was in a text like George Fisher's *The Instructor: or, Young Man's Best Companion*, which included a few pages of scripts in its American versions from 1748 on. Not until after the American Revolution would there be copy books penned by Americans and printed on American presses.[35]

Again unlike reading texts, which could be purchased in any colony for mere pennies and were probably in most households, copybooks were costly to purchase and the prized possessions of the writing master. It was clearly not to the best interests of the profession to encourage the notion that anyone could learn from a book, rather than from a person.[36] Writing, in short, unlike reading, was considered a specialized skill, and colonial access to instructional writing texts was far more limited than access to reading texts.

What penmanship was used for, however, was even more important, in terms of who would be taught to write, than its aspect as a specialized skill. Writing was a male job-related skill, a tool for ministers and shipping clerks alike. When the Boston town meeting voted in 1682 to open a town writing school, Bostonians were acknowledging the importance of Boston as a thriving commercial and mercantile center. Hundreds of boys a year passed through the three writing schools that Boston had established by 1720. They mastered the English round hand that had become the international script for commerce, routing the old secretary hand of the seventeenth century.[37] At a time when all clerical and bookkeeping work was a male stronghold, every young man with business aspirations needed to know how to form a legible script. Writing was also, of course, useful for rural concerns. Farmers who wanted to sell surplus produce needed to write in order to keep accounts. Penmanship was therefore both a hallmark of the well-educated and the servant of commerce.

Sequence of Instruction

The order, then, of the different components of the literacy curriculum followed the sequence implicit in the "three R's," a term still glossed today as "reading, 'riting, and 'rithmetic." There is nothing accidental about this universally agreed-upon phrase: its wording faithfully reflects the actual order of instruction during the colonial period. Reading instruction preceded, and was independent of, writing instruction. That this was possible was a function of its methodology—reading instruction was, as we have seen, conducted entirely orally. Arithmetic, which involved the endless writing of rules and examples, in turn presupposed the mastery of writing.[38]

It may be difficult for the modern reader/writer to believe reading instruction could be conducted without having the child write. A few examples will have to suffice. In 1660, a master in New Haven was asked whether he had seen to his apprentice's education, as he was legally obliged to do. He responded that the apprentice "could read pretty well, and that he was now learning to write." Two years later, one William Potter, who had been accused of (and was subsequently hanged for) the crime of bestiality, was asked by the New Haven Court if he had been educated. "He answered, well, and was taught to reade." Had he also been taught to write, he would undoubtedly have said so.[39]

A century later, in 1762, Samuel Giles of New York City advertised his private writing and arithmetic instruction at his evening school. After stating firmly that teaching small children the rudiments had taken up too much of his time, he said that "for the Future, no Children will be taken but such as have already been taught to Read, and are fit for Writing." Finally, there is an advertisement that appeared in a Boston newspaper in 1755. In it, the advertiser promised to teach "persons of both sexes from twelve to fifty years of age, who never wrote before, to write a good hand in five weeks, at one hour per day, at his house in Long Lane."[40]

Literacy and the Law

The Dissenters who had made their way over hazardous seas to settle in New England saw themselves as part of a literate culture. At a time when paper itself was precious and scarce, the meticulous records of the early town secretaries stand as a self-explanatory tribute to a new settlement's belief in the power of the written word to safeguard its new laws.

The greater importance placed by colonial Americans on the ability to read rather than to write is well exemplified by the legislation passed in 1642 by the colony of Massachusetts. Religious and political motives are explicit in this law; economic motives are implicit. The law empowered the colony's elected representatives, the selectmen, to inquire into the "calling and implyment" of all children, "especially of their ability to read and understand the principles of religion and the capitall lawes of this country." Children who were not being trained to a skill or taught to read were liable to be removed from their parents and apprenticed to someone else for such instruction.[41] While the provisions in the law for "putting out" indigent children to apprenticeship were borrowed from English precedents, the educational provisions were unique to the colonies. As Lawrence Cremin has put it, the statute was part of "a vigorous legislative effort to increase the political and economic self-sufficiency of the colony."[42]

The Massachusetts law that required that children be taught to read was quickly replicated by other colonies. Connecticut passed such a provision in 1650, New Haven (then a separate colony) in 1655, New York in 1665, Plymouth in 1671, and Pennsylvania in 1683.[43] The colony of New Haven was unusual in adding, in 1660, a writing requirement to the law. Significantly, only one of the sexes was to be taught this skill: "To the printed law, concerning the education of children, it is now added, that the sonnes of all the inhabitants within this jurisdiction, shall (vnder the same penalty) be learned to write a ledgible hand, so soone as they are capable of it."[44] The only other colony to require writing initially was Pennsylvania, which in its 1683 ordinance mandated that parents and guardians should ensure that children "may be able to read the Scriptures and to write" by the age of twelve.[45]

The 1642 law on reading was taken seriously by at least several Massachusetts townships. When the Dorchester selectmen called in Timothy Wales and his sons in 1672, they examined the boys and found that they were unable to read. The following year Salem conducted its own investigation, found several families in violation of the law, and initiated—although it may not have carried out—the process of finding persons to whom the children could be apprenticed.[46] Watertown, Massachusetts made a particularly consistent effort over successive decades to keep parents up to the mark. The first recorded Watertown inspection occurred in 1661. Upon surveying their fellow townsmen to see whether they fulfilled the law that required "the knowledg of God and excerising reading to the advancing of Catachising," the selectmen discovered that four families, with eighteen children among them, had failed in this respect. All the families were poor (so providing an early example of a correlation between poverty and illiteracy).[47]

Successive versions of what came to be called the Massachusetts Poor Laws continued to authorize the removal of children, without the consent of their parents, if the parents were considered unable to maintain them. A 1703 supplement to earlier acts reaffirmed the need to provide apprentices with an education by stipulating that the masters should provide "for the instructing of children so bound out, to read and write, if they be capable." Clearly, as both sexes could be apprenticed, both sexes were to be taught reading and writing. However, it turned out that the legislators had not intended this. In 1710, an amendment was passed that altered the order to, "males to read and write, females to read." The act was repeated in the same form once a decade until 1741, when the requirement of "cyphering" was added to the regulations for males. Finally, in 1771, the legislation was changed once again, and the legislation for children apprenticed under the Poor Laws now stipulated, "males, reading, writing, cyphering; females, reading, writing."[48]

In other words, it was not until 1771 that Massachusetts considered the ability to write to be a minimal educational necessity for girls. This is particularly significant because the whole purpose of apprenticing these children was to provide them with a skill with which they could eventually support themselves, so as not to be a burden on the town like their indigent parents. Boys needed to be able to write; girls did not.

Literacy and Employment

If legislation on involuntary apprenticeship reveals that children's gender made a difference to the kind of literacy instruction they were required to receive, so too do the terms of apprenticeship agreements that were completely voluntary. In a study of apprenticeship in seventeenth-century Massachusetts, Judith Walter identified 267 apprentices, of whom 32 were girls. For only 31 of all the apprentices was some kind of educational provision specified. For boys, the indenture usually stipulated that the boy be taught to read, write and cipher. James Chichester, for example, when apprenticed at the age of ten, was to be sent to school "until he can write a leagable hand." The 1658 indenture of Hopestill Chandler, who was being apprenticed to a blacksmith, required that he be taught to read the Bible and "to write enough to keep book for his trade." In contrast, the educational provisions made in 1674 for Sarah Joye of Salem were that she be taught her catechism, and "to read English, [and] the capital laws of the country," while Sarah Braibrok of Watertown was apprenticed in 1656 to a couple who were to teach her "to reade the English Tongue" and provide her with religious instruction. In not one case does Walter report finding a writing provision for female apprentices.[49]

The explanation lies in colonial perceptions of the function of writing. Writing was a job-related skill. Because girls were being trained not to hold jobs, but to be successful homemakers, penmanship was an irrelevant acquisition for them. The skill that corresponded, for girls, to what writing was for boys was the ability to sew. In the study just cited, Walter identified some forty different crafts and trades that the boys were to learn during their apprenticeships. There was no indication, however, that girls were to learn anything other than housewifery and, in two cases, sewing or knitting and spinning.[50]

Further evidence on the relationship between jobs and literacy comes from court rulings. In 1655, the Hartford Court ordered the administrators of Thomas Gridley's estate to educate his children, "learning the sons to read and write, and the daughters to read and sew well." The next year, the same court interpreted the provisions of Thomas Thomson's will that related to education as follows: "the sons shall have learning to write plainly and read distinctly in the Bible, and the daughters to read and sew sufficient for the making of their ordinary linen."[51]

More evidence of sewing as the advanced skill to be acquired by girls in lieu of writing is provided by contemporary records from across the Atlantic. They are particularly instructive because both sexes were being educated in the same institution. Orphaned or needy children between the ages of five and fifteen were admitted to the Great Yarmouth Children's Hospital, which was in effect a charitable workhouse. The master of the hospital was expected to see to the children's education, and kept a register of their educational attainments upon entering and leaving the hospital. David Cressy has tabulated the notes in the hospital register on 132 boys and 85 girls admitted to the hospital between 1698 and 1715. The register reveals that several boys were taught to write before they left the hospital. In contrast, "none of the girls reached the stage of writing," according to Cressy. Their "highest achievement was to sew well and to read in the testament or Bible."[52]

The fact that none of the girls was taught to write should, however, surely be interpreted differently. As eleven of the girls were already in either their Testament or Bible on entering the hospital, they were as ready as the thirty-six boys, similarly prepared, for further instruction. That not even these relatively accomplished readers were taught to write suggests that writing instruction was withheld from them because of their gender, not because they had not "reached the stage of writing." Mary Clark, for instance, had entered the hospital at the age of nine with the comment, "can't read at all." Four years later, she was characterized as reading "in her testament but indifferently and hath gone through her sampler."[53] If girls were to form letters, it would be through the medium of thread, not ink.

No wonder Anne Bradstreet, whose first book of poetry appeared in London in 1650, felt that she was incurring odium by stepping outside the role prescribed by society for women, in exchanging her needle for a pen:

> I am obnoxious to each carping tongue
> Who says my hand a needle better fits,
> A Poets pen all scorn I should thus wrong,
> For such despite they cast on female wits.[54]

Nor should gender restrictions on writing instruction be considered simply a seventeenth-century feature. Apprenticeship indentures for sixty poor children "put out" by the Newbury selectmen between 1743 and 1760 reveal precisely the same differentiation. Forty-nine boys were apprenticed to learn a range of skills from blacksmithing to making periwigs. The eleven girls, however, were to learn only "women's work" or "housewifery." All the apprentices were promised reading instruction, but only the boys were to be taught writing and arithmetic.[55]

There are several cases in which masters of apprentices were hauled into court for not fulfilling their educational obligations toward their apprentices. We have already noted the New Haven master who in 1660 was brought to court for his alleged failure to teach his apprentice his craft, and who was examined on how much literacy education his apprentice had received. A telling instance is provided about a century later by John Adams. In 1761, Adams remarked on the case of Daniel Prat, "a poor, fatherless Child" who was suing his master, Thomas Colson. The terms of the apprenticeship had required Colson to teach Prat to read, write, and cipher, and to teach him the trade of a weaver. He had done none of these. Adams felt strongly that Prat, as a child without a male parent, was to be favored in the case, "Because the English Law greatly favours Education. In every English Country, some sort of Education, some Acquaintance with Letters, is necessary, that a Man may fill any station whatever."[56]

From the earliest days of settlement, then, and throughout the colonial period, the colonists expected that all children ought to be able to read, no matter how low their station or how poor their circumstances.

Schooling and Gender

As we have seen, in 1642 the Bay Colony had legislated reading without any mention of either schools or writing. Five years later, in striking contrast, a new law mentioned writing and schoolmaster in the same breath: in 1647, Massachusetts passed its first schooling law. Every township of over fifty families was required to engage a master to "teach all such children as shall resort to him to write and reade," while towns of over a hundred families were to provide a (Latin) grammar school.[57]

The relationship between writing instruction and schooling is exemplified by Watertown, Massachusetts, which constructed its first schoolhouse in 1649 and soon thereafter hired Richard Norcross as its first schoolmaster. The job description spelled out that he was responsible "for the teaching of Chilldren to Reed and write and soe much of Lattin . . . as allso if any of the said towne, haue any maidens, that haue a desire to learne to write that the said Richard, should attend them for the Learning off them; as allso that he teac[h]e such as desire to Cast acompt."[58] The clear implication of this wording is that girls would attend the school only if they wished to learn writing and arithmetic. Obviously, they were supposed to have learned to read at home.

Norcross's contract is also an example of the ambiguity of the word "children." To modern ears, the word indicates children of both sexes.

In the colonial period, there was a strict separation of roles in the home and workplace by gender, and it was the males who held all the positions of responsibility and power.[59] Male children, therefore, were the prime targets of any town's educational efforts. As a result of this bias, the word "children" meant, in effect, male children, even though it always retained its broader meaning of children of both sexes. (In discussions of Boston schools, for example, the town records habitually refer to the students of their free schools as "children." Yet free schooling in the Boston system was restricted to males until 1789.)[60]

While "reading" is indeed included in Norcross's job description, as we saw earlier, children were supposed to have mastered initial reading before they reached the town school. The school was expected to "perfect" them in reading, not introduce them to it. Moreover, girls were often not admitted to town schools, particularly if such schools had any aspirations toward teaching Latin (the hallmark of the true grammar school). The rules and regulations of the Hopkins Grammar School, opened by New Haven in 1684, are a case in point. They insisted that "noe Boyes be admitted into the said Schoole for the learning of English Books, but such as have ben before taught to spell their letters well and begin to Read, thereby to perfect theire right Spelling, and Reading, or to learne to write, and Cypher . . . and that all others either too young and not instructed in letters and spelling, and all Girles be excluded as Improper and inconsistent with such a Grammer Schoole."[61]

Walter Small, in his study of some two hundred schools in the colonial period, reported finding only seven schools that definitely admitted girls, and another five that might have. The school in Rehoboth, Massachusetts, was among the seven. In 1699, Robert Dickson contracted with the Rehoboth selectmen "to do his utmost endeavor to teach *both sexes* of boys and girls to read English and write and cast accounts." Similarly, Deerfield, in northwestern Massachusetts, obviously allowed girls to enter its town school in 1698, because it warned parents that all heads of families with children between the ages of six and ten, whether male or female, should pay a poll tax to the school, "whether they send such children or not." Five years later the town made a similar motion, but this time changed the ages of admission. Families of "boys from four to eight, and girls from four to six years old," were to pay their proportion of ten pounds for the ensuing year.[62] (The shorter timespan for girls suggests that they were to leave school at the point when they were supposed to be able to read, having reached the age for the instruction in writing that they would not receive.)

The comparatively late dates at which these and similar provisions were enacted is significant: they suggest that on the boundaries of settlement, as the seventeenth century drew to a close, the town school had two characteristics. In the first place, it did not attempt any education fancier than the three R's, and in the second, it chose not to restrict its education to boys. Indeed the experience of the frontier settlement of Hatfield may prove, with further research, to be characteristic. From 1695 to 1699 there were no girls in Hatfield's town school; in 1700 there were four girls and forty-two boys during the winter term; nine years later there were sixteen girls in a total of sixty-four schoolchildren.[63]

Nevertheless, there were many towns that stood firm against the admission of girls to the master's school throughout the entire seventeenth and even the eighteenth century. Farmington, Connecticut, for example, voted in 1686 to devote twenty pounds to a town school, "for the instruction of all such children as shall be sent to it, to learn to read and write the English tongue." Some parents of daughters, it seems, interpreted this too broadly, for the following year the town issued a clarification: "*all* such children as shall be sent is to be understood only *male* children that are through their horning book [hornbook]." Small found many instances of town schools—Salem, Medford, Haverhill, Gloucester, Hingham, and Charlestown—that, shortly before or even well after the American Revolution, were only just beginning to open their doors to girls. And in these cases, the girls were being admitted only for a couple of hours a day (presumably for writing instruction). As one witness put it, remembering his schooling in Lynn, Massachusetts, "In all my school days which ended in 1801, I never saw but three females in public schools, and they were there only in the afternoon to learn to write."[64]

School Dames

A new feature in colonial town schooling can be detected as the seventeenth century drew to a close: the towns' formal sponsorship of women to teach reading. One presumes that private dame-school instruction had continued for decades in New England; after 1670, however, we see towns actively seeking female teachers to teach reading to small children. These women were paid a few pennies per week per child, and substantially less than their male colleagues.

Walter Small collected numerous references to such "school dames." Among Massachusetts towns, Woburn paid ten shillings to two women in 1673, and the same sum to another in 1686. Cambridge reported in 1680 that "For English, our school dame is Goodwife Healy; at present but nine scholars." Two years later, Springfield made an agreement with Goodwife Mirick that, in order to "encourage her in the good work of training up of children and teaching children to read," she should have three pence per child per week.[65]

After 1700, mention of school dames increases. Small found references to them in records running from 1700 to 1730 for, among others, Waterbury and Windsor in Connecticut, and for Weymouth, Lexington, Charlestown, Salem, and Falmouth, all in Massachusetts. A few of these, as was the case for Charlestown, only involved the town in paying women for the instruction of poor children who could not otherwise attend school. But increasingly, as the eighteenth century wore on, there seems to have been a definite shift in the direction of employing women to teach reading on a regular basis, in specific parts of town, with funds allocated for that purpose from the town treasury. Framingham had voted as early as 1713 to appoint selectmen to "settle school dames in each quarter of the town." Worcester in 1731 decided that, because small children could not walk to the school in the center of town, up to five school dames should be hired "for the teaching of small children to read" and placed in different parts of the town. Wenham, two years later, made an arrangement with its schoolmaster that permitted him to delegate some of his teaching responsibilities to others: he was to be "allowed to teach little children to read by suitable women, in the several parts of the town, that he shall agree with, by the approbation of the selectmen; also to teach to write by another man in another part of town."[66]

Marriage was no obstacle for a woman in teaching reading. In fact, there were those who taught for almost the whole of their adult lives. When Abigail Fowler died in Salem, Massachusetts, in 1771, her death was reported affectionately: "Widow Abigail Fowler, a noted school dame, finished her earthly labors. She was in her 68th year, and began to teach children before she was 18, and continued so to do till her decease, with the exception of a few years after she was married."[67]

The reason for the towns' new eagerness to employ women seems to have been the continuing failure of parents to carry out their legal responsibility to teach their children to read. For example, at the turn of the century Marblehead undertook a survey on the number of boys who could not read, and who could therefore not be admitted to the master's school. The town found a total of 122 such boys.[68]

Note that there were children who still read too poorly for the master's school despite the fact that standards for admission appear to have been lowered in many schools as the decades progressed. Whereas, formerly, schoolmasters had expected children to be in their Psalter or Bible (still the case in Boston's three elite writing schools, as the incident with John Proctor revealed), now the admission requirement was only, for the New Haven grammar school in 1684, to "have been taught to spell the letters well and begin to Read," or, for Farmington, Connecticut, two years later, that boys should be through their hornbook.

For many women, the chance to earn money from the town must have been most welcome. Others, as the eighteenth century lengthened, were able to use newspapers successfully to advertise their private literacy instruction.

Conclusion

The arguments made up to this point are as follows:

1. Reading was considered easy to teach, and reading instruction unaccompanied by writing instruction was the province of women, both at home and at school (private or town-sponsored). Texts for reading instruction were cheap and easy to obtain.

2. Writing was considered a craft, difficult to teach and taught by men. Texts for writing instruction were comparatively expensive and difficult to obtain.

3. Reading instruction preceded, and was independent of, writing instruction. Instruction in reading was conducted orally, by means of the oral alphabet method.

4. Because reading was considered to be important for religious, political, and economic reasons, legislation was passed that required it of all children.

5. Because writing was considered a job-related skill, society only required that it be taught to boys.

6. Writing was one of the key components of the curriculum of the town schools, which were taught by men and in many cases restricted to boys. Girls won access to some, but by no means all, of the masters' schools from the 1690s on.

7. Towns began to employ women (school dames) to teach reading to small children of both sexes from the 1680s on.

These statements generate further conclusions:

8. Because reading was required to be taught, and because people could and did learn to read without also learning to write, we cannot assume that all those—particularly women—who only marked documents were totally illiterate.

9. However, because educational standards in New England were raised over time, marks have to be interpreted in context.

In the seventeenth century, class, gender, and rural location all militated against obtaining writing instruction. In terms of class, the children whose apprenticeships have been mentioned above were at the bottom of the social heap, as were the orphans admitted to the Great Yarmouth Children's Hospital. Even at this low social level, it is clear that boys were offered both reading and writing instruction, but girls were only expected to know how to read and sew. If such girls could not sign when grown women, it was because no one had ever taught them to write.

Of course, then as now, low social class combined with poverty often correlated with illiteracy in reading as well as writing. It is surely no coincidence that the eighteen children found to be unable to read in Watertown in 1661 all came from impoverished families, and that the boys who could not read the Psalter, and who were therefore refused admittance to one of the Boston writing schools in 1741, were the children of "Families of low Circumstances."

As we would also expect, high social standing, when combined with an urban setting, was able to erase the restrictions on female access to writing instruction. In cities, the daughters of the higher ranks learned to write because their parents sent them off for private instruction. In Boston, for instance, even in the seventeenth century, girls were taught by private entrepreneurs like the writing master who taught Hannah Sewall (wife of Samuel Sewall) to write. In the eighteenth century, girls could also learn from publicly financed town masters who taught fee-paying female students "out of hours."[69] The fact that during the early colonial period rural women, even when wealthy, signed at a lower rate than urban women is surely to be explained by the exclusion of girls from the town school and the relative paucity of private male teachers in rural areas. But in cities, private teachers abounded: at least twenty private writing masters have been documented for Boston during the colonial period.[70]

It is the girls of modest social standing, however, who are of the most importance to my argument. Even in the seventeenth century, access to reading instructional materials was easy, and the teaching of reading was considered a female domain. There is every reason to believe that reading at some level was taught widely to girls by women, whereas writing, for a long time considered a male teaching preserve, was not.

Around the turn of the century, several strands were coming together, all of them favoring increasing education in general, and female education in particular. One that should not be ignored is domestic tranquility, bought at considerable cost to both whites and Indians. King Philip's short but bloody war, 1675 to 1676, spelled the end of the political and military power of the Indians. Slaughter and disease had thinned their ranks, and surviving Indian communities passed into obscurity.[71] The colonists were therefore freer to concentrate less on defense and more on such matters as education.

As we have seen, after 1680 women were increasingly incorporated into town educational systems, hired for their skill in teaching beginning reading. (Such women would have had to be taught to write, for they needed to be able to keep school records.) Girls were also winning access to some of the masters' town schools, and so to writing instruction.

There are several other factors that no doubt made their contribution, although proof of these lies beyond the scope of this essay. For instance, eighteenth-century instructional texts in reading improved, thanks to the advent of the spelling book. Similarly, the switch from the secretary hand of the seventeenth century to the eighteenth-century round hand would appear to have made penmanship easier. There were also political changes: some colonies began to put teeth into their education laws. The expansion during the course of the eighteenth century in the availability of secular reading material, including chapbooks and, at the end of the century, novels, was undoubtedly significant.

These speculations aside, it is still possible to take a fresh look at the supposed illiteracy of those who made marks instead of signatures. First, a comment on the mark itself. When we talk today about making a "mark" on a document, what springs to mind is the traditional X. That is not, however, how most colonists marked documents. When the information is available, marks often turn out to be initials, like the HN used by Hanna Newberry. These initials indicate, at the least, an acquaintance with the alphabet.[72]

We can now reinterpret some of the detailed information provided by Auwers for Windsor, Connecticut. What puzzled Auwers was that she found no correlation between social class and the signatures ("literacy") of Windsor women born before 1690: many rich women, like Hanna Newberry, only made marks. We can now explain this as a function of gender, which impeded access to writing instruction. Surely Hanna could read: her socioeconomic status alone makes it very unlikely that she would have been truly illiterate.

Windsor forms a useful example in other ways. In 1717 the town employed its first school dame: Sarah Stiles was hired to teach reading in the summer; schooling opportunities improved.[73] The dramatic

increase that Auwers found in the percentage of women able to sign
their names, as the decades passed, suggests that the right of girls to
write in Windsor had been permanently won by the 1740s.

And what of the female will-markers in Lockridge's study, cited so
often in defense of claims of massive female illiteracy in colonial New
England? The figures from these women are misleading, I believe, in
several respects. For one, as Lockridge is the first to point out, the
sample of females is small, representing under 15 percent of his total
sample and only 5 percent of the population he was investigating.[74]
Just as important is the fact that wills were Lockridge's only source.
Some women may have been able to sign but chose not to. People
often make their wills late in life, and when a mark was as legal as a
signature, initialing a will if you were old and ill may have seemed
more appealing than struggling to sign. Auwers's study, for instance,
identified thirty-one women who had affixed their names to both
deeds and wills. Eight of these (26 percent) signed their deeds but
marked their wills; only one did the reverse. (This could also be
interpreted, with Auwers, as evidence of the marginality of female
signing skill.)[75] We can speculate that no stigma would have attached
to a woman who chose not to sign her name. In contrast, because
society increasingly expected them to write, men by the early eighteenth century might have felt more deeply about the social cachet
attached to signing.[76] Even more important is the age at which a
person subscribed his or her will. A mark in the 1760s may represent
the absence of writing instruction as much as forty or fifty years
earlier.

Be that as it may, it is, in any case, likely that many of Lockridge's
female will-markers could read, at least to some extent. Further research, ideally using Linda Auwers's birth cohort approach, is likely to
produce evidence of higher female signing rates in the eighteenth
century similar to those found by Auwers and, later in the century,
William Gilmore.[77]

How well could someone read who could read but not write? The
colonists themselves were aware that there were differing levels of
literacy. Experience Mayhew, a pastor on Martha's Vineyard, discussed in 1727 the literacy of the Christian Indians who could read
books published in their own language; he said that such Indians read
and wrote only at the "rate that poor Men among the English are wont
to do."[78] The literacy of nonwriters fits the profile of "traditional
literacy" that David D. Hall has sketched, of readers who approached
print with reverential deliberation.[79] Probably, many nonwriters read
familiar material without too much trouble. This would have been
particularly true of the Scriptures: the advantage was that ministers,

heads of households, and other family members were constantly reading from them aloud. Nonwriters would also have been able to decipher writings such as the notes—like those asking for information on strayed animals—that were so often tacked onto the doors of meeting houses.[80] They surely could not, however, as Cathy N. Davidson points out, have been able to read the works of John Locke.[81]

On the other hand, we should not underestimate the pleasure that even a limited reading ability can bring. For a colonial woman, reading must have provided one of the very few sources of satisfaction that was not dependent upon others. In virtually all of the roles identified by Laurel Thatcher Ulrich, whether as housewife, deputy husband, consort, mother, mistress of servants, or neighbor, a woman was looking out for the welfare of others.[82] When she was reading, she was doing something for herself. Above all, if she were a Christian (another of the roles posited by Ulrich), her reading would have been an important and meaningful part of her private devotions.[83] For those who were called upon to teach reading to others, their reading ability transformed itself into a measure of independence. These were small treasures of the mind and spirit that we should not despise.

There is no reason to suppose that the conclusions drawn here for New England are very different from those to be drawn for other parts of colonial America—except, perhaps, for the South, where male tutors on plantations taught children of both genders to read and write. A poem penned by a judge in Philadelphia at the end of the seventeenth century shows that differentiation of schooling by gender was not exclusive to New England:

> Here are schools of divers sorts,
> To which our youth daily resorts,
> Good women, who do very well
> Bring little ones to read and spell,
> Which fits them for writing, and then,
> Here's men to bring them to their pen,
> And to instruct and make them quick
> In all sorts of arithmetick.[84]

Notes

An earlier version of this essay appeared in *American Quarterly* 40, no. 1 (March 1988).
This research was supported in part by grant no. 6-64048 from the PSC-CUNY Research Award Program of the City University of New York.

1. Linda Auwers, "Reading the Marks of the Past: Exploring Female Literacy in Colonial Windsor, Connecticut," *Historical Methods* 13 (1980): 209.

2. See Carl F. Kaestle's summary of literacy studies in "The History of Literacy and the History of Readers," in *Review of Research in Education*, vol. 12, ed. Edmund W. Gordon (Washington, D.C., 1985), 11–53.

3. Kenneth A. Lockridge, *Literacy in Colonial New England: An Enquiry into the Social Context of Literacy in the Early Modern West* (New York, 1974), 128 n. 4, 13, 38–42, 140 n. 57.

4. Auwers, "Reading the Marks of the Past"; and Ross W. Beales, Jr., "Studying Literacy at the Community Level: A Research Note," *Journal of Interdisciplinary History* 9 (1978): 93–102. The largest study to date is that by William Gilmore, who surveyed 10,467 documents dated between 1760 and 1830 from the Upper Connecticut Valley, and found almost universal male signing levels by the 1770s, while female signing began at two-thirds in the late 1770s and rose thereafter: William J. Gilmore, *Elementary Literacy on the Eve of the Industrial Revolution: Trends in Rural New England, 1760–1830* (Worcester, Mass. 1982), 98, 114.

5. Auwers, "Reading the Marks of the Past," 204–5.

6. Kaestle, "History of Literacy and the History of Readers," 21.

7. E.g. ibid., 21, 29; Margaret Spufford, *Small Books and Pleasant Histories: Popular Fiction and Its Readership in Seventeenth-Century England* (Cambridge, 1981), 22, 27, 29, 34–35; Victor E. Neuburg, *Popular Education in Eighteenth-Century England* (London, 1971), 55, 93; Geraldine Jonçich Clifford, "Buch und Lesen: Historical Perspectives on Literacy and Schooling," *Review of Educational Research* 54 (1984): 474–75 and Gerald F. Moran and Maris A. Vinovskis, "The Great Care of Godly Parents: Early Childhood in Puritan New England," in *History and Research in Child Development*, ed. Alice Boardman Smuts and John W. Hagen, *Monographs of the Society for Research in Child Development* 50, nos. 4–5 (1985): 34. Lockridge himself raises the possibility several times in *Literacy in Colonial New England*, 14, 109, 127, 134 n.26, but rejects it for the purpose of his analysis, 38.

8. James L. Axtell, ed., *The Educational Writings of John Locke: A Critical Edition with Introduction and Notes* (London, 1968), 260; and Lawrence A. Cremin, *American Education: The Colonial Experience, 1607–1783* (New York, 1970), 277. I would like to acknowledge here my indebtedness to Professor Cremin's bibliography.

9. George A. Plimpton, *The Hornbook and Its Use in America* (Worcester, Mass., 1916). Plain and gilt hornbooks were listed in the book inventories of a Boston bookseller in 1700: Worthington C. Ford, *The Boston Book Market, 1679–1700* (rpt. New York, 1972), 177–78.

10. Quoted in Andrew W. Tuer, *History of the Horn Book* (1897; rpt. New York, 1979), 133.

11. Plimpton, *Hornbook and Its Use in America*, 9.

12. Charles J. Hoadly, ed., *Records of the Colony and Plantation of New Haven, from 1638 to 1649* (Hartford, Conn., 1857), 176. For ease of reading, I have silently expanded all the abbreviations in this and other quotations (e.g., "ye," "yt," and "Testamt" appear as "the," "that," and "Testament"), but have preserved the spelling, punctuation, and capitalization of the originals.

13. John Eliot, *The Indian Primer* . . . (Cambridge, Mass., 1669).

14. Paul L. Ford, *The New-England Primer: A History of Its Origin and Development with a Reprint of the Unique Copy of the Earliest Known Edition* (New York, 1897); and Richard L. Venezky, "A History of the American Reading Textbook," *Elementary School Journal* 87, no. 3 (1987): 249. For a discussion of *The New England Primer* as the vehicle for a set of metaphors on Christian obedience, see David H. Watters, "'I Spake as a Child': Authority, Metaphor and *The New-England Primer*," *Early American Literature* 20 (1985–86): 193–213.

15. Charles F. Heartman, *American Primers, Indian Primers, Royal Primers, and Thirty-Seven Other Types of Non-New-England Primers Issued Prior to 1830* (Highland Park, N.J., 1935).

16. Quoted in Nila Banton Smith, *American Reading Instruction* (Newark, Del., 1965), 17–18.

17. Boston, Registry Department, *Records Relating to the Early History of Boston*, vol. 15, *A Report of the Record Commissioners of the City of Boston, Containing the Records of Boston Selectmen, 1736 to 1742* (Boston, 1886), 288.

18. Franklin B. Dexter, ed., *New Haven Town Records, 1649–1662* (New Haven, Conn., 1917), 97. Similarly, the Reverend Peter Thacher wrote of a new student in 1680 that he was "to perfect him in reading, and to teach him to write"; quoted in David D. Hall, "The Uses of Literacy in New England, 1600–1850," in *Printing and Society in Early America*, ed. William L. Joyce et al. (Worcester, Mass., 1983), 24.

19. Dexter, *New Haven Town Records*, 88.

20. For spelling books in Britain, see Neuburg, *Popular Education*, 64–91; R. C. Alston, *A Bibliography of the English Language from the Invention of Printing to the Year 1800*, vol. 4, *Spelling Books* (Bradford, England, 1967); and Ian Michael, *The Teaching of English: From the Sixteenth Century to 1870* (Cambridge, 1987). For spelling books in the American colonies, see Raoul N. Smith, "Interest in Language and Languages in Colonial and Federal America," *Proceedings of the American Philosophical Society* 123 (1979): 36–38.

21. Venezky, "History of the American Reading Textbook," 248.

22. William R. Hart, "*The English Schoole-Maister* (1596) by Edmund Coote: An Edition of the Text with Critical Notes and Introductions," diss., University of Michigan, 1963, 8.

23. Robert F. Roden, *The Cambridge Press, 1638–1692: A History of the*

First Printing Press Established in English America, Together with a Bibliographical List of the Issues of the Press (New York, 1905), 36.

24. E. Jennifer Monaghan, *A Common Heritage: Noah Webster's Blue-Back Speller* (Hamden, Conn., 1983), 31–34; quotation, 26. There were seventy-six editions of Dilworth by 1801, of which forty-three were printed before 1787: Smith, "Interest in Language and Languages," 36.

25. Monaghan, *Common Heritage,* 33–34; and Smith, *American Reading Instruction,* 25–31.

26. Edmund Coote, *The English Schoole-Maister* (London, 1596), A3; in Hart, "The English Schoole-Maister," 129.

27. M. G. Hall, ed., *The Autobiography of Increase Mather* (Worcester, Mass., 1962), 278; Richard Brown is quoted in James Axtell, *The School upon a Hill: Education and Society in Colonial New England* (New Haven, Conn., 1974), 174–75. Cf. Hall, "The Uses of Literacy," 25; and M. T. Clanchy, "Learning to Read in the Middle Ages and the Role of Mothers," *Studies in the History of Reading,* ed. Greg Brooks and A. K. Pugh (Reading, England, 1984), 33–39.

28. Spufford, *Small Books,* 35–36; J. H. Higginson, "Dame Schools," *British Journal of Educational Studies* 22, no. 2 (1974): 166–81; and D. P. Leinster-MacKay, "Dame Schools: A Need for Review," *British Journal of Educational Studies* 24, no. 1 (1976): 38–48; cited in Joan N. Burstyn, "Women in the History of Education," paper presented at the annual meeting of the American Educational Research Association, Montreal, April 1983.

29. Axtell, *School upon a Hill,* 176.

30. "Autobiography of the Rev. John Barnard," *Collections of the Massachusetts Historical Society* 3, no. 5 (1836): 178. Cf. "The Commonplace Book of Joseph Green," *Publications of the Colonial Society of Massachusetts* 34 (1943): 236.

31. David Pulsifer, ed., *Records of the Colony of New Plymouth, in New England. Acts of the Commissioners of the United Colonies of New England,* vol. 2, *1653–1679* (Boston, 1859), 106.

32. E. Jennifer Monaghan and E. Wendy Saul, "The Reader, the Scribe, the Thinker: A Critical Look at the History of American Reading and Writing Instruction," in *The Formation of School Subjects: The Struggle for Creating an American Institution,* ed. Thomas S. Popkewitz (New York, 1987), 88.

33. George Bickham, *The Universal Penman, Engraved by George Bickham, London 1743* (New York, 1954). For the writing curriculum, see E. Jennifer Monaghan, "Readers Writing: The Curriculum of the Writing Schools of Eighteenth-Century Boston," *Visible Language* 21, no. 2 (1987): 167–213.

34. Ray Nash, *American Writing Masters and Copybooks: History and Bibliography through Colonial Times* (Boston, 1959), 13.

35. George Fisher, *The Instructor; or, American Young Man's Best Companion,* 30th ed. (Worcester, Mass., n.d.); and Nash, *American Writing Masters and Copybooks,* 25–34.

36. At least one copybook, however, proclaimed (in 1656) that it was *Set*

forth for the benefit of poore Schollers, where the Master hath not time to set Copies: see Nash, *American Writing Masters and Copybooks,* 21–22.

37. Monaghan, "Readers Writing."

38. Cremin, *American Education,* 501–3; Patricia Cline Cohen, *A Calculating People: The Spread of Numeracy in Early America* (Chicago, 1982), 120–22.

39. Dexter, *New Haven Town Records,* 438; and Charles J. Hoadly, ed., *Records of the Colony or Jurisdiction of New Haven, from May 1653, to the Union, Together with the New Haven Code of 1656* (Hartford, Conn., 1858), 443.

40. Robert F. Seybolt, *The Evening School in Colonial America* (Urbana, Ill., 1925), 23; advertisement quoted in Walter H. Small, *Early New England Schools* (Boston, 1914), 317.

41. Nathaniel B. Shurtleff, ed., *Records of the Governor and Company of the Massachusetts Bay in New England,* vol. 2, *1642–1649* (Boston, 1853), 6–7.

42. Cremin, *American Education,* 125.

43. Ibid.

44. Hoadly, *Records of the Colony or Jurisdiction of New Haven, from May 1653, to the Union,* 376.

45. Quoted in Cremin, *American Education,* 125.

46. Dorchester Antiquarian and Historical Society, *History of the Town of Dorchester, Massachusetts* (Boston, 1859), 223–24; and Salem, Massachusetts, *Town Records of Salem, Massachusetts,* vol. 2, *1659–1680* (Salem, Mass., 1913), 180.

47. Watertown, Massachusetts, *Watertown Records Comprising the First and Second Books of Town Proceedings* (Watertown, Mass., 1894), 71. Subsequent inspections occurred in 1665, 1670, 1672, 1674, 1679, 1680, and later: ibid., 86, 104, 113, 121, 137, 145.

48. Robert F. Seybolt, *Apprenticeship and Apprenticeship Education in Colonial New England and New York* (New York, 1917), 46–47.

49. Judith Walter, "Apprenticeship Education and Family Structure in Seventeenth Century Massachusetts Bay," M.A. thesis, Bryn Mawr College, 1971, 33–34, 42–43.

50. Ibid., 34.

51. Walter H. Small, "Girls in Colonial Schools," *Education* 22 (1902): 534.

52. David Cressy, *Literacy and the Social Order: Reading and Writing in Tudor and Stuart England* (Cambridge, 1980), 30–34; quotation, 34.

53. Ibid., 34. For girls taught only reading and sewing in England, see Spufford, *Small Books,* 34–35.

54. Quoted in Thomas Woody, *A History of Women's Education in the United States* (1929; rpt. New York, 1966), 1:132.

55. Laurel Thatcher Ulrich, *Good Wives: Image and Reality in the Lives of Women in Northern New England, 1650–1750* (New York, 1982), 43–44.

56. L. H. Butterfield, ed., *Diary and Autobiography of John Adams,* vol. 1, *Diary 1755–1770* (Cambridge, Mass., 1961), 219.

57. Shurtleff, *Records of the Governor and Company of the Massachusetts Bay*, 2:203.

58. *Watertown Records Comprising the First and Second Books*, 18, 21.

59. Lyle Koehler, *A Search for Power: The "Weaker Sex" in Seventeenth-Century New England* (Urbana, Ill., 1980).

60. See, for example, the proposal in 1682 to open a free school for the "teachinge of Children to write & Cypher": Boston, Registry Department, *Records Relating to the Early History of Boston*, vol. 7, *A Report of the Record Commissioners of the City of Boston, Containing the Boston Records from 1660 to 1701* (Boston, 1881), 158.

61. *American Journal of Education* 4 (1857): 710.

62. Small, "Girls in Colonial Schools," 532–33. Small used primary sources such as town records for his study, but did not document his sources. Where I have been able to crosscheck them, I have found them accurate.

63. Ibid., 533.

64. Ibid., 533–37; quotations, 533–34.

65. *Early New England Schools*, 168, 165.

66. Ibid., 165–70; quotations, 179, 168, 170.

67. Ibid., 169.

68. Ibid., 167.

69. Robert F. Seybolt, "Schoolmasters of Colonial Boston," *Publications of the Colonial Society of Massachusetts* 27 (1928): 137; for an example of female instruction by a writing master, see Alice Morse Earle, ed., *Diary of Anna Green Winslow: A Boston School Girl of 1771* (1894; rpt. Williamstown, Mass., 1974), 12, 92–94.

70. Seybolt, "Schoolmasters of Colonial Boston."

71. William C. Sturtevant, ed., *Handbook of North American Indians*, vol. 15, *Northeast*, ed. Bruce G. Trigger (Washington, D.C., 1978), 177.

72. For initials as marks, see, for example, Joseph Underwood's V in 1684 as his mark set to an agreement to teach his male apprentice to read and write: *Watertown Records Comprising the First and Second Books*, 129.

73. Auwers, "Reading the Marks of the Past," 204.

74. Lockridge, *Literacy in Colonial New England*, 128.

75. Auwers, "Reading the Marks of the Past," 207.

76. I am indebted to Ross W. Beales, Jr., for this insight.

77. Auwers, "Reading the Marks of the Past"; and Gilmore, *Elementary Literacy on the Eve of the Industrial Revolution*.

78. Experience Mayhew, *Indian Converts: Or, Some Account of the Lives and Dying Speeches of a Considerable Number of the Christianized Indians of Martha's Vineyard, in New-England* (London, 1727), xxiii.

79. Hall, "The Uses of Literacy," 21–24. Hall emphasizes the role played by memorization and recitation in learning to read.

80. See, for example, the complaint in 1687 about such notes: Watertown, Massachusetts, *Watertown Records Comprising the Third Book of Town Proceedings and the Second Book of Births Marriages and Deaths to End of 1737* (Watertown, Mass., 1900), 31.

81. Cathy N. Davidson, *Revolution and the Word: The Rise of the Novel in America* (New York, 1986), 59.

82. Ulrich, *Good Wives*, 9–10.

83. Charles E. Hambrick-Stowe, *The Practice of Piety: Puritan Devotional Disciplines in Seventeenth-Century New England* (Williamsburg, Va., 1982), 157–61.

84. Quoted in Carl Bridenbaugh, *Cities in the Wilderness: The First Century of Urban Life in America, 1625–1742* (1938; rpt. Oxford, 1971), 283–84.

Chapter Three

Chapbooks in America

Reconstructing the Popular
Reading of Early America

Victor Neuburg

Within the context of the American colonies, chapbooks are best defined as the cheap, ephemeral booklets that were offered for sale in the bookstores and printing offices of Boston, New York, and Philadelphia, and were also hawked around the streets by itinerant traders—often characterized as Yankee peddlers—who carried them as a regular part of their stock in trade to the small towns and settlements that lay inland beyond the eastern seaboard. Like so much in the early days of colonial America, they originated in England. There, from about the middle of the seventeenth century, they constituted a major element in popular literature, rivaling both almanacs and broadside ballads as widely selling items. Numerically this trade in popular literature was considerable, and some light is thrown upon the extent of it if we recall that during the 1660s as many as four hundred thousand almanacs were sold in a year, while Charles Tias, publisher and member of a consortium, left ninety thousand chapbooks in stock when he died in 1664.[1] Because almanacs and broadsides depended for their appeal to the purchaser very largely upon local and topical factors, they were produced by printers in the colonies long before there was any substantial production of chapbooks, and right up to the outbreak of the War of Independence in 1775 chapbooks were being imported in large numbers from England.

Before considering these aspects of the trade, we should look briefly at the content of chapbooks. According to the *Shorter Oxford English Dictionary*, the term "chapbook" did not come into general use until 1824;[2] until then most contemporaries used various terms for them, the commonest of which were "small books," "chapmen's books," "small histories," or simply "histories." Tradition was the keynote. In chapbooks were to be found abridged versions of the romances of knights and maidens that, in lengthier and rather more sophisticated versions, had delighted medieval audiences. There were tales of giants, monsters, and fairies, many of them the residue of an oral peasant culture rooted in a long-distant past. There were songs, riddles, jokes, anecdotes of pirates and highwaymen; there was fortunetelling, divination, primitive weather forecasting; there were cookbooks and household manuals; and during the eighteenth century there were versions of *Robinson Crusoe* and *Moll Flanders*. Such richly varied material was published in small books measuring roughly 8.5 centimeters by 16 centimeters, often with uncut edges, comprising twenty-four, or less usually sixteen or thirty-two pages. Many were illustrated with crude though lively woodcuts—usually relevant to the printed text, but sometimes a woodcut might be used on an ad hoc basis to fill a page when the text ran out. Printed on coarse rag paper, they were sufficiently tough to withstand much of the handling that came their way, though inevitably the majority of them were read to pieces.

This, then, was the nature of the chapbooks that found their way to America. The state of printing in the original colonies was patchy, and not until 1762, with the establishment of a press in Savannah, Georgia,[3] did all of the thirteen colonies have printing plants. Few American printers, however, were able to invest money or resources in substantial enterprises. There was a fairly restricted market in the colonies for literary products, and the publishing of books, particularly those in several volumes, involved considerable risk. It was very much easier, and more profitable to the trade in both countries, to import books from England, and there was a thriving traffic in them until the War of Independence—and even after hostilities had commenced it does not seem to have died out completely.

Charles Evans in his *American Bibliography* records, between 1639 (when Stephen Days set up the first press in America at Cambridge, Massachusetts) and 1799, thirty-six thousand separately printed items, these not including tradesmen's letterheads or the blank forms that made up a considerable part of the printer's output. In Philadelphia, for example, the printing firm of Franklin and Hall lists in its Work Book for 1755 such items as "700 Vestrey Notices," "200 Advertisements desiring Landlords to pave their Footways, &C," "1000 Way Bills," "50 Invitations on Cards," "250 Certificates for loading foreign Melasses";[4] and it is apparent that such items formed an important element in the work of many local printers well into the nineteenth century.

Among what might, in the widest possible terms, be called the "literary" productions of the early colonial press were almanacs, broadsides, newspapers, medical handbooks, letter writers, and practical manuals of all kinds. Ready reckoners were especially important in a country where not every storekeeper might be adept in adding up a column of figures; and such difficulties were compounded by the fact that the pound sterling might differ in value between neighboring colonies, and there were those in which Spanish currency was widely used. Then too, among the output of the printing offices were schoolbooks, devotional works, and chapbooks.

It is with the latter that we are concerned, and at the outset there is a problem. Because of their ephemeral nature, few chapbooks have survived, and a good deal—though by no means all—of our knowledge of them comes from booksellers' advertisements, which do not as a rule specify whether the chapbooks were printed in America or imported from England. The majority, however, almost certainly were imported until after the Revolution. A wide range of titles with woodcut illustrations was readily and cheaply available to the American book trade at wholesale prices; and because they were easy to transport and did not, unlike almanacs, go out of date, importing chapbooks was an easy option. There was, in the early days of America, one other factor that told decisively against the production of chapbooks in large numbers, and this was the endemic shortage of paper throughout the eighteenth century. There was a constant demand for rags to be turned into paper. As one poet put it, "Kind friends when thy old shift is rent / Let it to th' paper mill be sent."[5] A story is also told that in 1748 a Spanish ship sailing westward was captured by an English warship and brought into Boston, where her cargo was discharged and sold. Included in it were several bales of papal bulls or indulgences destined for the Spanish colonies, printed on one side only of small sheets of good paper. The printer Thomas Fleet bought the lot cheaply and printed popular songs and broadsides on the backs of the sheets.[6]

Despite such a windfall, the problem of paper and its manufacture continued to bedevil the book trade. A New York printer, Hugh Gaine, was offering in 1760 "Ready Money for clean Linnen Rags," and eleven years later "The highest Price for clean Linen Rags".[7] Because so many colonists lived frugally and kept their clothes as long as they held together, the chronic scarcity of rags for the papermaking mill continued. In the early years of the Revolution, up to

1777, the price paid for rags was three pence per pound; in 1778, eight pence; in 1779 twelve pence or one shilling; in 1780, three shillings; and in 1781, ten shillings. In 1787, when rags were being sold for twelve shillings a pound, paper cost six pounds per ream, and the problem of paper was not finally solved in America until William Megaw of Meadville, Pennsylvania, established in 1828 a mill that made paper from straw pulp. This process brought the price down considerably, and meant that the two hundred or so paper mills at that period were no longer competing for scarce supplies of rags.[8]

I

Initially then, for a variety of reasons, many chapbooks were imported into the colonies of North America, and nearly all of them have disappeared. This is the fate of so much ephemeral, throwaway literature. In England book collectors like Samuel Pepys and James Boswell formed important collections that ensured the survival of some chapbooks;[9] but in eighteenth-century America no bibliophile thought it worthwhile to preserve such fugitive printed items, and in the early nineteenth century only Isaiah Thomas went out of his way to buy a selection of street ballads on sale in Boston during 1813. He bound them up and presented them, in three volumes, to the American Antiquarian Society in Worcester, Massachusetts—of which he had been a principal founder—and there they still are, crisp and fresh as the day they came from the printer's shop. His gesture in buying such trifles was unique. As he wrote in the first volume, the ballads were "Bound up for Preservation, to show what kind of articles of this kind are in vogue with the vulgar at this time, 1814."[10] It is perhaps ungracious to regret the fact that Thomas did not do the same for chapbooks.

Because chapbooks are so elusive, we have to look elsewhere for evidence of their collective existence rather than search for individual copies. The problem of locating specific titles is highlighted by the fact that the earliest one that I have been able to trace turns up in the sale catalogue of the Brinley Collection.[11] Item 7165—which was bought, according to a marginal note, by Yale University Library— consisted of a volume containing six chapbooks, three of which were printed in London. The earliest, *History of Fair Rosamond and Jane Shore*, was printed by William Onley in 1716.[12] The survival of only one chapbook should come as no surprise. Most of them, as has been said, were quite simply "read to pieces"—a convenient phrase, this, but with regard to these little books in America an essentially accurate one. As an example of how virtually entire editions of ephemeral publications have disappeared, there is the case of *Cinderella*. A children's chapbook version of this famous story was published by Mathew Carey in 1800, and according to his account it consisted of an edition of a thousand copies and cost him $8.50 to have printed.[13] Today one copy survives in the Huntington Library in California.

What we can be absolutely certain about is that chapbooks were advertised widely and must have constituted a not unimportant element in the book trade of early America. The earliest advertisement that I have come across occurs at the end of *Faults on All Sides. The Case of Religion Consider'd* ("Newport, Rhode Island. Printed for the author and sold by E. Nearegress and J. Franklin 1728").[14] This is a fairly substantial publication of 150 pages, at the end of which were two unnumbered leaves of advertisements, one of them reading, "Chapmen's history books offered for sale."

Another quite early, and very much more detailed, advertisement appears in *Father Abraham's Almanac . . . For the Year of our Lord, 1760*, printed by W. Dunlop in Philadelphia, which contains at the end eight unnumbered pages listing "BOOKS and STATIONARY, just imported from London, and to be sold by the Printer hereof." Among the titles listed are several chapbooks described as "A very great variety of little History Books," and some specific titles: *Seven Champ. of Christendom; New Academy of Compliments; Pleasures of Matrimony; Valentine and Orson; Reynard the Fox; Fortunatus; Parismis; Fairy Tales; Fair Rosamond and Jane Shore;* and a *Robinson Crusoe* that is almost certainly a chapbook version.[15] In *A Catalogue of Books. Just Imported from London, and to be sold by W. Bradford, at the London-Coffee-House, Philadelphia, wholesale and retail. With good allowance to those that take a quantity*, printed by William Bradford in about 1760 and containing eight leaves, a number of chapbooks are listed under "Chapmans Books" on page 15.[16] Altogether twenty titles are offered for sale, including *Buccaniers of America, Familiar Letter Writer, Lord Anson's Voyage, Guy of Warwick*, and *Fair Rosamond*. No prices are indicated, but it is of interest to note that in the surviving copy of the catalogue the following have a line drawn through them, indicating that they were no longer available: *Female Policy Detected, Pleasures of Matrimony*, and *History of Witches*. Were these chapbooks that sold especially well, or were stocks exhausted after being kept low?

Andrew Barclay, a bookseller in Boston, issued a broadside in about 1765, *A Catalogue of Books Lately imported From Britain*.[17] It comprises three columns of titles in alphabetical order, a number of which—*Hocus Pocus, Joe Miller's Jests, Reynard the Fox, Robinson Cruso* (*sic*), and *Seven Wise Masters* among them—are chapbooks. More interesting is a smaller broadside issued in 1767 by John Mein,[18] who ran the London Book-Store in Boston. He announced that he had "just imported a Grand Assortment of the most MODERN BOOKS, in every Branch of Polite Literature, Arts and Sciences." Among them were a "Great Variety of entertaining Histories," which he distinguished quite clearly as "Pretty little entertaining Books, with Cuts, for Children." The especial interest of the broadside lies in the statement that all items are offered "AT THE VERY SAME PRICE THEY ARE SOLD IN LONDON." It is not immediately clear what conclusions about price structure and profits in the American book trade can be drawn from this, but something about the retail price of chapbooks must be said later.

At roughly the same time as the broadside, Mein brought out a fifty-two-page catalogue of *Curious and Valuable Books* that were to be had at his bookstore. Two chapbooks are readily identified, *The Whole Life and Merry Exploits of Bold Robin Hood* and *Delightful History of the Gentle Craft;* but it is puzzling, in view of the fact that the broadside distinguished between chapbooks and children's books, that these two titles are listed among "Pretty Little Books for Children, with Pictures, finely gilded." Distinctions could easily become blurred and imprecise when small, ephemeral items had to be catalogued.

A Catalogue of Books, sold by Noel and Hazard at their book and stationary store, next door to the Merchants Coffee House, issued in New York in 1771, comprised twenty leaves.[19] Page 21 lists "A variety of small Histories, commonly called Chapmen's Books," among which are some unusual titles: *Life of Dean Swift, Ben Johnson's Jests,* and *Quarles Collection of Wise Sayings.* At the end of this section is a note: "With most of Bunyan's small Pieces and a Number of others sold by the Dozen or single Book."

The firm of Cox & Berry in Boston published a forty-four-page catalogue in about 1772.[20] It described "a very large assortment of the most esteemed books" and noted that "All new Books of Merit, Magazines and Reviews, imported by every Opportunity from London," were available. On pages 39–40 there is a hint of chapbooks among the sixty-nine separate items listed as "Little Books for the Instruction and Amusement of Children." Inevitably, perhaps, *The History of Robinson Crusoe* is here; but so, more surprisingly, are *The History of Joseph Andrews, The History of Tom Jones* (both "abridg'd from the Works of Henry Fielding Esq"), together with *History of Clarissa* and

History of Sir Charles Grandison, "abridg'd from the Works of Sam. Richardson Esq."[21]

The Cox & Berry catalogue appeared a few years before the outbreak of the Revolution, when there must already have been signs that the trade with Britain in books was going to become less important—although, as has been mentioned, it is by no means certain that the trade dried up completely. In November 1783, for example, John Carter of Providence, Rhode Island, published a broadside[22] in which he announced that he had for sale "an assortment of Books" that were "Just Imported from London." It comprised 125 titles arranged in three groups, and a section contained 64 "Chapman Books" including such favorites as *Seven Wise Masters*, *Fortunatus*, and *Robinson Crusoe*.

Despite such imports—and there is no reason to suppose that Carter was unique—by the later 1780s, the 1790s, and for a decade or so beyond, more and more chapbooks were, as we shall see, being produced by American printers and publishers, even though never, it seems, in really large numbers. Before we turn to this aspect of the trade, however, there are two case studies that illustrate, each in a rather different manner, details of chapbooks imported into the colonies. The first concerns Andrew Steuart in Philadelphia, and the second some business transactions between Thomas Longman in London and Henry Knox of Boston in the years before 1775.

II

Steuart, an Irishman born in Belfast, served his apprenticeship with James Magee (sometimes spelled "MacGee") in that city, then emigrated to America where he set up a press in Laetitia Court, Philadelphia, in 1758. He left there in about 1764, set up as a printer in Wilmington, North Carolina, and was drowned at Cape Fear in 1769. As a printer he was said to have been undistinguished, and his business, according to Isaiah Thomas, was "confined to pamphlets, ballads and small jobs."[23]

Steuart maintained his links with Belfast long after he had emigrated to America, and it was to Thomas Magee (presumably James's son), who had followed him to Philadelphia, that he left the running of his business when he left the city. It is also clear that he imported many chapbooks from James Magee.[24] Magee, in fact, was a notable and largely overlooked producer of traditional chapbooks for the mass market. Something like forty of his publications are preserved among the eighty-three chapbooks that James Boswell collected,[25] and are now in the Houghton Library at Harvard.

A brief article by Thomas Ollive Mabbott published over fifty years ago throws further light upon Steuart both as a printer and as an importer of chapbooks.[26] It notes that among the chapbooks at Harvard and the New York Public Library,[27] few American imprints are to be found, and the author wonders whether "the little booklets were for some reason uncommon in the colonies." He goes on:

> A small volume in my possession for many years throws some light on the problem, and is evidence that the books were more often read than printed here, since they were obviously imported for sale, but that they were at times set up and printed here too. It consists of six chapbooks sewn together roughly without cover; and it has suffered much from being carried about in the owner's pocket, while it has been so much read that some leaves have been torn out. The first booklet was printed in Ireland, and when the little volume was last sold it was described as a miscellaneous collection printed at Belfast, etc., but actually it must have been made up in America in part from chapbooks sent over for the trade to Andrew Steuart, who I think probably occasionally reprinted those which sold out quickly. But the title pages of the little books (all of four leaves) tell the story.[28]

The chapbooks—and I have abridged the titles, some of which are very long—are listed as follows:

1. *The Blind Beggar's Garland*
Belfast: Printed by James Magee MDCCLXVI

2. *The Undutiful Daughter or, the Devonshire Wonder*
Philadelphia: Printed by Andrew Steuart MDCCLXV
[This has a witchcraft theme and probably derives from a broadside ballad (ca. 1690) in the British Library entitled *The Undutiful Daughter of Devonshire, or the father's entreaties*. There is another chapbook version, *The Undutiful Daughter; or, the Hampshire Wonder*, printed in London, listed in the Harvard catalogue (2217).]

3. A songbook lacking the first two leaves.
["I think it American," says Mabbott.]

4. *The Beggar's Wedding*
Belfast: Printed by James Magee MDCCLXX

5. *The Wandering Jew*
Belfast: Printed by James Magee MDCCLXX
[There is a woodcut on the title page.]

6. *A Royal Old Song; Containing the Life and tragical End of Fair*

Rosamond who was concubine to King Henry the Second. . . . To
which is added the Northern Lass
Philadelphia: Printed by Andrew Steuart, of whom may be had
Hundreds of different Ballads. 1763
[There is a woodcut on the title page.]

The final imprint is an interesting one, and prompts questions about
where so many ballad sheets have gone and whether Steuart printed
or imported them. There is no easy way of answering either question
and, as so often in popular literature studies, there is the inescapable
feeling that one is trying to make bricks with imaginary straw. A
search of Steuart imprints at the American Antiquarian Society, however, revealed one more indication of the chapbooks that were imported into America.

With a shrewd feeling for what would sell, Steuart published in
1763 what he described on the title page as the fifty-first edition of a
religious bestseller, *Seven Sermons* by Robert Russell.[29] What is of
interest to our present concerns is the final leaf, which is entitled
"Catalogue of Histories, Novels and other Chapmen's Books, sold
(Wholesale and Retail) by Andrew Steuart at the Bible-in-Heart."
There follows a list of sixty-nine titles, not one of which appears to
have survived even in a single copy. These are the chapbooks that
Steuart would have imported, probably from Magee in Belfast, and
more rarely might have reprinted if the demand warranted his doing
so. It is the earliest list of chapbooks available in the colonies known
to me, and it contains, as one might imagine, most of the established,
readily identifiable favorites, together with others less familiar:

Robinson Crusoe	Weeks Preparation
Don Bellianis	Valentine and Orson
Fair Rosamond and Jane Shore	Royal Assassins
Laugh and be Fat	Seven Champions
Reynard the Fox	Solomon's Temple
Secretary's Guide	Aesop's Fables
Troy's Destruction	King of Prussia
Nine Worthies	Book of Knowledge
Garden of Love	Montelion
Guy Earl of Warwick	Oliver Cromwell
Compendious School Master	Gulliver's Travels

Buccaniers of America

Sir Francis Drake

Twelve Novels

William the Third

Seven Wise Masters and
Mistresses

Chinese Tales

Charles XII

Noble Slaves

Arabian Nights

Gray's Sermons

Cynthia

Token for Mourners

Doolittle on the Sacrament

Aristotle's Masterpiece

Academy of Complements

Coffee-house Jests

Mary Queen of Scots

Capt. Robert Boyle

Fairy Tales

Duke of Marlborough

Don Quixote

Irish Rogues

Pilgrims Progress

Female Policy

Royal Novels

Anson's Voyage

Gentle Craft

Travels of True Godliness

Travels of Ungodliness

Dorastus and Fawnia

Hero and Leander

Fortunatus

Christian Thoughts for every
Day in the Month

Duty of Prayer

Guide of a Christian

Hocus Pocus

Countryman's Guide

Life of Pope

System of Geography

Saint indeed

Gouge's Walking with God

Craighead on the Sacrament

Campbell on ditto

Lilliputian Magazine

Spectator's Stories

Fables and Allegories

Triumph of Wit

Steuart, in fact, is a more interesting printer and entrepreneur than
Isaiah Thomas's rather dismissive assessment of his work, quoted
earlier, might lead us to believe. On the one hand, while he was at
Wilmington he printed a newspaper, the *North Carolina Gazette*,
from October 1764 to February 1766; on the other, he printed two
miniature books, *Verbum Sempiternum*, seventh edition, and *The
History of the New Testament*. The copies in the American Anti-

quarian Society are bound together and make an attractive little volume measuring 4.5 centimeters by 3.5 centimeters, 2.5 centimeters thick. The printing in both books is clear and entirely legible. They are undated, but there is a signature in the first book, "Elizabeth Wiggins Jur. The 20th of the 5th Month A.D. 1769." Steuart's surviving publications, most with a religious interest, reveal him as a shrewd man of business who, within a wide range of book trade[30] and printing activities, was clearly aware of the existence of a market for cheap, popular books and went some way toward satisfying it by importing into America the numerous titles that presses in Philadelphia—and, indeed, elsewhere in the colonies—were in no position to produce. In his attitude to the lower end of the market he bears a strong resemblance to William Dicey of Northampton and London, whose press dominated the English chapbook trade over several decades.[31]

The business transactions between Henry Knox in Boston and Thomas Longman in London during the years leading up to the Revolution throw into sharp relief precisely what the term "importing chapbooks" meant in terms of the numbers involved and the costs—including those of transport. In 1771 Knox opened the London Bookstore with a "large and very elegant Assortment of the most Modern Books in all Branches of Literature."[32] His career as a bookseller came to an end when hostilities began in 1775, but during those four years in the book trade Knox imported books of all kinds from Thomas Longman, publisher and bookseller, then in business at the Ship and Black Swan in Paternoster Row, London.[33] In 1772 Knox issued a forty-page catalogue of his stock, omitting the fact that he also had chapbooks for sale. Perhaps he did so because they would be easy enough to sell over the counter in his shop, and his catalogue was probably intended for his more sophisticated customers. The fact remains that he bought chapbooks in considerable numbers from Longman; but since, so far as I am aware, not one of them is known to survive in America, it must remain a matter of surmise as to where Longman obtained the chapbooks that he sent to Boston. Given the location of his London premises and the proximity of the Dicey printing office in Bow Church Yard, it seems very likely that the chapbooks were collected from Dicey—but there can be no certainty about this.

Among the surviving invoices in the Knox Papers is the following:

London August 28th 1771.
Shipt on board the "Lydia" Captn James Hall for Boston in New England by Thos. Longman Bookseller in London, Four Trunks and one Case of Merchandize on the Account & Risques of Mr Henry Knox Merchant in Boston.

The value of the books, which are itemized, was £220.16.6. Insurance cost £0.15.6. Shipping with primage (an allowance made to the master and crew for loading and care of the cargo) was £0.18.0. There are annotations to the invoice regarding titles of books ordered but not sent because they were "Reprinting," "Not published," or "Out of Print," and there is one rather despairing note: "Cannot hear of any such book as Voltaire's Temple of Taste in English."[34]

The invoice included "12 Dozen of Chap Books ass[orted] £5.10.05." This means that the average cost of each chapbook in the consignment was four pence and three farthings. To this must be added some part of the shipping and insurance charges, so the wholesale price of a chapbook might be as high as five pence. Compared with London prices this is high—and, indeed, somewhat misleading, because chapbooks were not all of the same kind. In their catalogue for 1764 Cluer Dicey and Richard Marshall make the following distinctions:

Penny History Books	104 at	£0.2.6
Small Histories Ditto	100 at	£0.6.0
Stitched in embossed paper	13 for	£0.0.9
The Dutch Fortune Teller	per Dozen	£0.13.6
Robin Hood's Garland	per Hundred	£0.16.0[35]

We do not possess sufficient data to make critical judgments about chapbook prices in Britain or in America, still less to make valid comparisons. All that can be said is that in both countries there was considerable variation in wholesale and retail prices. A delightful story is told about Sarah Sophia Banks, sister of Sir Joseph Banks, scientist and president of the Royal Society. A collector of chapbooks, she went into a shop in Shoe Lane, London, where she selected a dozen titles and offered the shopkeeper one shilling (twelve pence). To her surprise she was given three pence change and told to take two more. The bookseller, under the impression that she was a trade customer, was offering her a discount on penny histories—thirteen or fourteen to the dozen for nine pence.[36]

The next Knox invoice is dated October 12, 1771. Longman sent books to the value of £191.13.3 on the *Paoli*, commanded by Captain Isaac Cazoneau. Insurance cost five shillings and six pence, shipping with primage nineteen shillings and two pence. Among the books listed were:

375	6 penny books asstd.	£7.10.0
300	1 penny ditto	£1.0.0
125	2 penny ditto	£0.16.8
12	history of Pamela abridg'd	£0.10.0

12	ditto	Clarissa	£0.10.0
12	ditto	Grandison	£0.10.0
12	ditto	Tom Jones	£0.10.0
12	ditto	Joseph Andrews	£0.10.0

A much smaller consignment went on the *Fortune,* commanded by Captain Isaac Meyrick. It consisted of "One trunk Merchandize value £50.6.7-1/2," and insurance was only fourteen pence (one shilling and two pence), with shipping and primage ten shillings and six pence. The list of books contained no chapbooks, but there were fifty each of what must have been abridged editions of "Jo. Andrews," "Tom Jones," "Clarissa," and "Grandison" at £2.0.0 each. The invoice was dated January 15, 1772, and again the goods were purchased from Longman.

Six months later there was another consignment of chapbooks, five hundred of them "Sorted bound £10." They went on the *Hayley,* commanded by Captain James Scott, and the invoice itemizes four trunks and one case of "Merchandize." Dated July 18, 1772, it records the total of goods as £242.19.8, with insurance £5.5.6, shipping and primage eighteen shillings and six pence.

When the *Hayley* made a return voyage to Boston, the invoice dated February 15, 1773, was for "Goods £311.2.3-½." Insurance was £6.13.8, shipping and primage £1.0.9. Among the books were "9 Golden Pippin £0.8.8," and there was a note that "6 Pamela in miniature" was reprinting.

On the next voyage of the *Hayley,* the invoice dated August 10, 1773, included "225 Chap Books sorted bound £4.10.0." The total of goods exported was £111.12.8, with insurance £2.11.6, shipping and primage twelve shillings and six pence. There is an interesting note on the invoice:

		)	75 Seven Champions	)	
		)	75 Wise Masters	)	
Out of print	)	50 Wise [Mistresses]	)	Chap Books
		)	50 Don Quixote	)	
		)	50 12 Caesars	)	

The final invoice, dated July 29, 1774, lists goods to the value of £234.7.6-½, insurance £3.1.6, shipping and primage nineteen shillings and six pence. Among the Longman items carried by the *Minerva,* commanded by Captain Callahan, were:

| 150 Chap Books | sorted | £3 | — | — |
| 350 Chap Books | sorted | £7 | — | — |

This is a somewhat puzzling entry—both lots cost the same per individual item, and the possibility is that they were either different orders or purchased from two separate suppliers.

Two further invoices among the Knox Papers show that he was supplying chapbooks to other booksellers. One, without a date but probably some time in 1771, was made out to E. Battle (who had a business in Boston) and includes "2 Doz: Chapman's Books 10.0." The other, "For att of David Hopkins" (probably the owner of a country store), has an item "13 doz & 10 Chap Books £6.4.6." This makes the price of individual chapbooks five pence and nine pence respectively, at wholesale prices.

From such glimpses of his activities we can conclude that Knox was an enterprising bookseller and a notable importer of books; but his business came to an end with the outbreak of war in 1775. So too throughout the thirteen colonies did much of the dependence upon Britain for the supply of books.

III

In view of the volume of imports, coupled to some extent with a chronic shortage of paper, it is safe to assume that only a few of the chapbooks that circulated in prerevolutionary America were in fact printed there; and of this total even fewer have survived. Catalogues of the collections at Harvard and the New York Public Library record hardly any, and the same is true of "A Preliminary Check List of American Chapbooks."[37] A search among the catalogues and holdings of the American Antiquarian Society proved virtually abortive, and it is difficult to escape the conclusion that the printing of chapbooks in America belongs almost entirely to the later years of the eighteenth century and the earlier ones of the nineteenth.

As an example of this I would cite the well-known title *The Famous History of Valentine and Orson*, a romance first published in about 1510 and extremely popular in various chapbook editions throughout the eighteenth century and beyond.[38] The American Antiquarian Society has twelve different editions, the earliest printed at Haverhill in 1794. The other imprints were Wilmington, 1796; Hartford, 1800; New York, 1810; Otsego, 1811; Boston, 1811 (two versions); Boston, 1812; Boston, 1813; Boston, 1814; Philadelphia, 1813; and Philadelphia, 1817.

Other chapbook favorites were being reprinted in the last decades of the eighteenth century. There was an edition of *The World Turned Upside Down* in Boston in 1780.[39] A sixteen-page version of *The Pleasant History of the Friar and the Boy* was issued in 1793 in Keene,

New Hampshire, a town described by L. C. Wroth as "that busy center for the publication of chapbooks of the 1790s."[40] Then in 1794 Mathew Carey in Philadelphia brought out a seventeenth edition of *The Most Illustrious and Renowned History of the Seven Champions of Christendom.* Perhaps most interesting of all, however, is the record by d'Alté A. Welch[41] of no fewer than nineteen editions of *The Famous History of Whittington and His Cat* published in America between 1770 and 1818—and there may well have been more. The story of Dick Whittington, the poor English boy who achieved wealth and fame in medieval London through his own efforts, is founded substantially upon fact, and clearly it became popular in America, where it is not too fanciful to suggest that it became part of the potent myth of "rags to riches" that underlay the American dream long before the "log cabin to White House" story and the novels of Horatio Alger superseded it.[42]

Leaving aside such speculations about the role of popular literature in the formation of social attitudes, what seems to have happened in the trade at the close of the eighteenth century is that more and more printers—some in very small towns—were reissuing popular and well-established titles for local readers and for purchase by local peddlers who took them further afield. The fairly small numbers that would have been involved in each print run over so scattered a market made the survival of individual copies, perhaps in rural communities, much less likely than, for example, the very much larger numbers that came from the Dicey presses in Britain. There are indeed fairly considerable survivals of the latter, largely because of the existence of a book-collecting elite that did not feature in the early days of postcolonial America. There, as we have seen, they have virtually disappeared. There is some uncertainty about whether chapbooks printed in America were designed for adults or for children—there is, for example, some ambiguity about the readership of abridgments of *Robinson Crusoe* in chapbook form, of which very large numbers circulated.[43] What is beyond argument is that chapbooks, with whatever readership in mind, figured if not prominently then repeatedly in book trade transactions in the early days of the United States.

The chapbook trade did not rely primarily upon printers in small towns. Firms and individuals in the urban centers of Boston, New York, and Philadelphia almost certainly possessed a wider range of typefaces and equipment, and their scale of operations and their involvement with the international trade provided the material and intellectual background without which a prosperous book and printing industry at all levels of public taste and demand could not develop.

IV

Not surprisingly, Boston was the largest center of printing in pre-revolutionary America. The prominence of New York grew in the years after independence as the importance of Boston declined. The other major city of the eighteenth century was Philadelphia, where, as in the other two locations, there were many printers and booksellers.

The History of Printing in America by Isaiah Thomas, first published in 1810, remains, despite its age, an excellent and accessible starting point for surveying this early period. There was a second edition in 1874, which, edited by M. A. McCorison, was reissued in 1970. Many of the people mentioned in this book were personally known to Thomas, who describes some of them, and events in which they were concerned, with an unusual and engaging frankness. Later research has amplified and extended much of the information in its pages, and one example of such work is *Boston Printers, Publishers, and Booksellers*, edited by Benjamin Franklin V (1980); but the most important sources of material relating to early American printing known to me are the various card indexes in the American Antiquarian Society, which cover people, titles, and places, with a subsidiary card index of "authorities" for biographical information. I have drawn heavily upon all this material, and freely acknowledge my debt to it.

So far as eighteenth century Boston is concerned, it is impossible to identify several firms that made a feature of printing "pamphlets and small histories," and they were the first of a large number of American entrepreneurs who were to be engaged over the following centuries in the popular literature trade. They were the forerunners of such publishing enterprises as Beadle & Adams, Street and Smith, and Bantam Books—but we must be cautious in our assessment of these pioneers. To begin with, their business activities were on a small scale and their print runs, to the extent that we can make an educated guess at them, were rarely to be reckoned in thousands. Moreover, none was a specialist in the publishing of popular literature. Unlike their contemporaries William and Cluer Dicey in London, whose market was a much larger one and who were increasingly able to specialize in this field, for these Boston printers popular literature was only a part of their total output—even though it does seem to have been a significant one. They perceived a growing demand and went some way to meet it. It was to their shops and printing offices that peddlers, hawkers, and country traders came to buy the chapbooks and broadsides that they could cry around the streets or take to isolated farms and settlements.

Zechariah Fowle (1724–76), whose publications numbered about eighty, was prominent in the popular literature trade. When Isaiah Thomas was six years old he was, at Fowle's request, apprenticed to him, and Thomas said that during the ensuing ten years Fowle printed nothing larger than a Psalter, and describes the output of the press as "chiefly ballads and small books for pedlars."[44] From 1758 to 1761 Fowle was in partnership with Samuel Draper, but the two men did not agree and so they separated. Fowle remained in business from several addresses in Boston until 1775, when he retired to Portsmouth, New Hampshire; he died there in the following year.

Among the popular publications issued by Fowle and listed at the American Antiquarian Society is *A Pack of Cards Chang'd into a compleat Almanac and Prayer-Book*, eight pages, published about 1770 and priced at "three coppers." The theme was traditional, and a version of it appeared as a street ballad printed by Taylor in Brick Lane, Spitalfields, London, during the earlier years of the nineteenth century.[45] There are similar popular items with the Fowle or Fowle and Draper imprint, but the majority of the "small histories" offered no longer exist.

The same is true of the "pamphlets and small histories" produced by Thomas and John Fleet (1732–97 and 1734–1806), printers, publishers, and booksellers,[46] whose joint business enterprise seems to have collapsed after the outbreak of the Revolution. Despite the fact that only a few of their publications have survived, it seems highly probable that chapbooks formed some part of their output; their Richard Rum chapbook will be discussed later. A surviving copy of one traditional title that they published about 1765–70 (it is undated) may well be typical of their popular productions. This is *The Most Delightful History of the King and the Cobler*, a tale of how King Henry VIII, in disguise, visited one of his lowlier subjects.[47] It was a very popular chapbook in England, where the earliest known printed version appeared in 1680 with the title *Cobler turned Courtier*. Another traditional title published by the Fleet brothers in the 1750s was a broadside entitled *Death and the Lady*, a very popular homily on mortality that was reprinted at least twice by James Catnach of London,[48] and derives quite clearly from the medieval "dance of death" motif.

In 1793 Eziekel Russell (1743–96) published *A Dialogue between a Blind Man and Death*, a sixteen-page chapbook with woodcuts. Priced at six pence, it seems expensive; but it is difficult to draw firm conclusions about chapbook prices at this period on the basis of very sketchy information. No fewer than thirty broadsides printed by Russell are recorded,[49] but his chief claim to our attention with regard to popular literature lies in the fact that he was one of the earliest—probably the first—American printers to issue in chapbook form a collection of accounts of crimes committed in the colonies. Similar publications, usually called the *Newgate Calendar*, had been popular throughout the eighteenth century in England, and an edition published in weekly parts between 1825 and 1828 cumulated into four substantial volumes with bloodcurdling illustrations. Russell's version was less ambitious. It ran to thirty-two pages and was called *The American Bloody Register*. Published in 1784, it contained the autobiographies of several criminals, with their last words and dying confessions. There were woodcuts, and the last page showed an execution taking place. Page 16 had a reference to a second number "which we shall publish immediately," but it is by no means certain that it ever appeared. Clearly Russell had a feeling for popular demand, and several of his publications advertise the fact that he would supply "Travelling Traders" at discount prices—"cheap by the quantity," as he put it.

It is very much easier to establish the involvement with the popular market of the Coverly family: father and son, both called Nathaniel (1744?–1816; 1775?–1824), and another son called John (dates unknown). The Isaiah Thomas ballads contain 302 separate items, of which nearly half bear a Coverly imprint. By the standards of early America, this figure represents a considerable output of ballad sheets that have survived—to say nothing of those that are lost—and such a total surely hints at a vanished popular literature once available on the streets of Boston.

The Coverlys were itinerant and enterprising printers, publishers, and booksellers whose imprints show that they worked at various times from a number of addresses in Boston and elsewhere in New England.[50] Coverly *père* was in business in the late 1760s, and on one occasion collaborated with Zechariah Fowle in the production of *The Death of Abel* (1768). John's name appears on *The Remarkable History of Tom Jones* ("Salem: Printed and Sold by N. and J. Coverly 1799"). This was a twenty-nine-page abridgment of Fielding's novel measuring 7 centimeters by 10 centimeters with an alphabet printed on the verso of the title page. The "N. Coverly" referred to is the younger Nathaniel, who was in business in Salem at this time but by 1806 was in Boston. There, from the Corner of Theatre Alley, Milk Street,[51] he issued both street ballads and chapbooks, among the earliest of which was *The Comical Sayings of Paddy from Cork*—no date, but probably around 1806. It had twenty-four pages and no illustrations, and cost ten cents.[52] In 1811 there were editions of *The History of Jane Shore*, twenty-four pages, eight cents for a single copy and fifty cents for a dozen; and *The History of the Seven wise Masters*, thirty-two pages, twelve and a half cents for a single copy and one dollar for a dozen. *The Prodigal Daughter* and *The Pleasant History of the Friar and Boy*, twelve and twenty-four pages respectively, came out in 1813, both unpriced, and Coverly also published *The Naval Songster*, sixteen pages, at this time.

In addition to chapbooks, he published small books for children from his premises in Theatre Alley; but because the Coverlys, father and son, moved about on many occasions, it is difficult to be precise about their printing activities. In 1795 father and son were in partnership together at Amherst, New Hampshire, while between 1806 and 1814 they were active in Boston,[53] selling their printed wares in the popular market "by the Groze Dozen or Single. A great Allowance to Country Shop Keepers." A comparison between the Coverly premises in Boston and those of James Catnach, Monmouth Court, Seven Dials, London, who was printing ballads and chapbooks at this period, suggests itself.

So far as Philadelphia and New York were concerned, there was nothing comparable in either city to the Boston chapbook trade. Both David Hall and Hugh Gaine—respectively important booksellers in each city before the Revolution—dealt in chapbooks, but there is nothing to suggest that either printed them on a large, or even a modest, scale. "The shelves of David Hall's bookshop were stocked with general trade and reference books . . . including . . . broadsides, penny histories and other chapbooks;"[54] and Hugh Gaine advertised that he had in stock "A good Assortment of Chapman Books."[55] Since, however, both these references belong to the prerevolutionary period, it is certain that such wares would have been imported.

Chapbooks were printed in both cities,[56] but from the few surviving examples it is impossible to discover and reconstruct, even in bare outline, a thriving trade in their production. It is, however, beyond doubt that chapbooks were an element in the turnover of Mathew Carey (1760–1839),[57] a leading Philadelphia publisher and bookseller, many of whose manuscript business records are held by the American Antiquarian Society. They demonstrate that he was dealing in chapbooks, although the nature of each individual transaction is not always clear. What, for example, are we to make of this entry?

11 April 1792
Small histories assorted 3/6 £6.6.0[58]

We know from the context that this was part of a deal with Berry Rogers & Berry, booksellers in New York from 1792 to 1795. Carey was in account with them, and the probability is that he was making a purchase from them. On the other hand, Carey was selling chapbooks in largish numbers to James Wilson, who had a bookstore in Wilmington, Delaware, from 1795 to 1841. The transaction read as follows:

1795
Mathew Carey to James Wilson Dr
9 April	1094 Chapbooks in paper	$21.88
30 April	470 Chapbooks	$ 9.40
5 May	489 Chapbooks	$ 9.78
12 May	416 Chapbooks	$ 8.32
27 October	64 Chapbooks	$ 1.28[59]

One year later another invoice reads:

Mr. Mathew Carey New York 10 Oct [17]96
Bt of John Thomson
9-⅓ Dozen Small Histories (Assorted) 11/- £5.2.8[60]

I cannot identify John Thomson, from whom these chapbooks were purchased at trade prices of eleven shillings per dozen: and the fact that sterling was used in this account, as opposed to dollars as in the one quoted from a year earlier, indicates that both sterling and dollars were being used at this period—about ten years after independence.

The Carey records contain many other chapbook transactions, including several for binding, as the following example shows:

25 July [1802]
Mr M Carey to J Riddle
To binding 100 Chapbooks [illegible] £1.5.0[61]

At three pence each for binding, this would add considerably to the price of a chapbook. Indeed, at about this time prices were high compared with those in England, and there is some evidence to suggest that Carey was importing some chapbook titles from London,[62] perhaps even in sheets that he would have bound in Philadelphia. There is reference to copies of *Robin Hood* at eight cents each and to *Paddy From Cork* at fifty cents[63]—but it is impossible to say whether these came from London.

There were other towns in America where chapbooks were produced by local printers in small numbers, and one of them, Norwich in Connecticut, is of especial interest. It was here that John Trumbull (1750?–1802) had a printing office where his output, according to Isaiah Thomas, was "chiefly confined to his newspaper, and the small articles with which he supplied country chapmen."[64] Not many of these have survived, but a few can be quoted. *A Narrative of the Extraordinary Adventures of Four Russian Sailors* (1785), sixteen pages, is prefaced by a comment that readers might regard it as a piece of fiction, like the adventures of Robinson Crusoe, but it is in fact true! Another was *A Wonderful Discovery of an Old Hermit* (1786), also sixteen pages. One of his most substantial publications was *The Lover's Instructor; or, the Whole Art of Courtship rendered plain and easy &c.* This was published by Trumbull in 1796 and consisted of seventy-two pages. Hardly a chapbook—though *The Art of Courtship* or some such variation was a chapbook title—this book was designed to offer practical help in behavior and letter writing. On the final page there is an advertisement suggesting that Trumbull's business was more considerable than Thomas had indicated. It read as follows:

A GREAT VARIETY OF
Curious, Useful and Entertaining
BOOKS
Are constantly kept for sale at
JOHN TRUMBULL'S
Printing Office, a few roads west of the
Meeting House in Norwich

There is no doubt, too, that Trumbull had a shrewd eye for a topical and potentially popular title, just as both William Dicey and James Catnach in London, leaders in the mass market, were ready to exploit unusual occurrences by rushing into print with news of them. In 1799 there were noteworthy storms in Bozrab, Lebanon, and Franklin, Connecticut, and Trumbull hastened to issue *An Impartial Relation of the Hail Storm on the Fifteenth of July and the Tornado on the Second of August 1799.* It was published in the same year and ran to thirty pages, but a note at the end hints at the speed with which it was produced (Trumbull's printing was usually accurate): "The Reader is desired to correct some Typographical errors which have escaped . . . by hastily reading the Proof Sheets."

In one other respect Trumbull demonstrated his feel for the popular market. In 1786 he published a twenty-four-page chapbook entitled *The Adventures of Colonel Daniel Boon One of the first Settlers at Kentucky &c. written by the Colonel himself.* It was probably derived from John Filson, *The Discovery, Settlement and Present State of Kentucke,* which had been published at Wilmington, Delaware, in 1784 and laid the foundations of the Boone legend.[65] Trumbull's chapbook deals with the Indian wars on the Ohio River from 1769 to 1783, and provides good, dashing stories with plenty of action; but despite the title, whether Boone actually wrote it seems questionable. The narrative runs to fifteen pages, and the remainder of the chapbook is taken up with the account of how a Mrs. Francis Scott made her escape from the Indians by whom she had been held prisoner. Personal and fictional accounts of such escapes had been popular since the end of the seventeenth century. Trumbull exploited this, but in doing so he was not an innovator: he was, as we shall see, following a well-established trend.

V

There were three quite specific American contributions to the chap-book tradition. One was the Indian captivity theme; the second, Richard Rum; and the last, the career of the felicitously named Chapman Whitcomb.

Indian captivities were stories about, and almost always by, dwellers on the frontier or in the wilderness who had been captured by Indians from whom, after a lapse of years, they escaped in various ways.[66] One of the earliest of these, first published at Cambridge, Massachusetts, in 1682, was Mary Rowland's captivity. It was often reprinted. Some of the other popular titles dealt with such captives as Peter Williamson, Mary Jemison, and Benjamin Gilbert. The Indians were always ready to kidnap white settlers in these stories, and their victims were of all ages and both sexes.

Two authors who wrote captivities that were published in chapbook style were Josiah Priest (1788–1851), who combined authorship with coach trimming and harness making, and the pseudonymous Abraham Panther.[67] The latter was responsible for *A very surprising narrative of a young woman, discovered in a rocky-cave, after having been taken by the savage Indians of the wilderness in the year 1777, and seeing no human being for the space of nine years. In a letter from a gentleman to a friend.* Between about 1786 and 1816 various editions were published under this title or variations of it in a number of places. The story is simple and gives a good idea of what captivities were like. "A most beautiful young Lady sitting near the mouth of a cave" is seen by two travelers in the wilderness. When she sees them she faints, and on recovering shortly afterward exclaims, "Heavens! Where am I?" She tells the sad story of a quarrel with her father and flight to the wilderness where her lover was murdered by the Indians who captured her. She spurned the advances of one brave, and was tied up overnight so that she might ponder the choice between submission to him and death. Resourcefully she chewed through her walnut bark bonds, but realizing that she could not escape she took matters into her own hands: "I did not long deliberate but took up the hatchet he had brought and, summoning resolution I, with three blows, effectually put an end to his existence." She then cut off his head, sliced the corpse into quarters, dragged it for about half a mile, and buried it under foliage. She returned to the cave and made it her home, growing Indian corn to feed herself, for nine years until the travelers happened by. They listen to her story and eventually reunite her with her aged father, who hears her account of what has happened to her and then dies, leaving her a handsome fortune.

Narratives of this sort, with all kinds of variations, were extremely popular until the end of the eighteenth century and for several years into the nineteenth. The pattern of their publication in many different locations suggests that they became part of a common heritage, and grew to be as much a feature of the American chapbook tradition as stories of Tom Thumb and Guy of Warwick, say, were of the English one.

The Richard Rum chapbook was American in origin and, so far as I am aware, unknown in England. It is generally entitled *At a Court held at Punch-Hall, in the Colony of Bacchus. The Indictment and Trial of Sir Richard Rum. . . .* Editions with this title are recorded in 1724 (the first?), 1750, 1770, 1774, 1775, 1785, 1791, and 1793.[68] There are a few versions called *The Indictment and Tryal of Sir Richard Rum at a Court . . .* , dated 1765, 1794, and 1796; and there is a related chapbook, *A Dialogue between Sam, Sword and Richard Rum* (1794).

The subject is temperance, and the full title of an early edition— effectively a summary of its contents—is worth quoting in full:

> At a Court held at Punch-Hall in the Colony of Bacchus. The Indictment and Tryal of Sir Richard Rum a Person of noble Birth and Extraction, well known both to Rich and Poor throughout all America. Who was accused for several Misdemeanours against his Majesty's Liege people, viz. killing some, wounding others, bringing thousands to Poverty, and many good Families to utter Ruin. It is not the Use, but the Abuse of any good thing, that makes it hurtful. The Fourth Edition, with a Preface, and a Song, compos'd by Sir Richard, immediately after his Discharge, not in former Editions. Boston: Printed and sold at the Heart and Crown in Cornhill. 1750.

The publisher was Thomas Fleet, mentioned earlier, who had advertised what was probably the first edition in the *New England Courant* of March 2, 1724, at a price of six pence for a single copy or four shillings a dozen. There was a similar advertisement in the same paper on March 9, but no mention is made of a second edition, although on March 16 there is an announcement of a third edition. It appears that two editions were sold out, and a third announced, within two weeks of first publication.

The fourth edition—the title quoted in full above—was advertised in the *Boston Evening Post* of March 5 and 12, 1750. It contains a preface that reads,

TO THE

READER

The following Tract has sufficiently recommended it self to the World, by the Sale of three large Impressions, the last of which went off in a little more than a Fortnights Time, a few Years ago, and so gave Birth to this Fourth Edition.[69]

It went through several more editions, one of which was printed in Philadelphia in 1796 "for Robert Stewart, travelling Bookseller," and cost eight pence.[70] What was probably the last edition appeared in Boston in 1835.

The text recounts the trial of Sir Richard before Sir Nathan Standfast and Sir Solomon Stiffrump. Among the jurors are Timothy Tosspot, Benjamin Bumper, John Neversober, and Edward Emptypurse. The indictment is read, and Sir Richard pleads not guilty. One of the witnesses, William Shuttle the Weaver, testifies, "I can never sit at my Loom, but this wicked Companion is enticing me from my Work and is never quiet till he gets me to the Tavern." Among other witnesses are "Barbadoes With the Leeward Islands," who say that "without the Help of Sir Richard we that live in the Islands could not subsist; for he is the best Branch of our Trade." John Friend, the Quaker, speaks up for Sir Richard too, saying that "he hath many times comforted me, both at Sea and Land." In his address to the court Sir Richard claims, "I have done good Service to the Common Wealth, of which I am a good and loyal Member." He is acquitted, and the implication is very clearly that rum should be drunk in moderation. A nicely ambivalent verdict, this, which reflects the conflicting economic and social demands of colonial society. It is, moreover, one that reflects an ambiguity that has characterized North American attitudes toward alcohol well into our own time.

Sir Richard's creator is not known—the chapbook was always issued anonymously. John W. Farwell suggests rather tentatively that it might have been Matthew Adams, a minister who wrote for the *New England Courant*, had a good library, and was an early friend of Benjamin Franklin.[71] In his day Adams was a popular writer, but his claim to the authorship of this bestseller must remain uncertain.[72]

Rather less uncertainty surrounds the career of Chapman Whitcomb (1765–1833), author and traveling bookseller in Massachusetts at the turn of the eighteenth and nineteenth centuries. What we know of Whitcomb is almost entirely due to the researches of J. C. L. Clark over a period of more than twenty years. His *Notes on Chapman Whitcomb*, reprinted from a series of newspapers, was privately published in a small edition in 1911. Then, after many references to Whitcomb in a series of unpublished letters to C. S. Brigham at the American Antiquarian Society, he wrote two further articles, published in the *Clinton Courant*, December 4, 1931, and April 1, 1932, which added a few details to the material he had already published.[73]

The man revealed to us—partly, at least—by Clark was a graduate of Dartmouth College, New Hampshire, in 1785. He was something of an eccentric, and turned up, dressed in green, at the wedding of a young lady who had jilted him in favor of another. He married Rhoda Willard in 1793, but the marriage does not seem to have been altogether successful, for on one occasion, Clark reports, Whitcomb publicly disclaimed any responsibility for the debts of his wife. Clark was doubtful whether, when Mrs. Whitcomb went as a widow to look after her orphaned grandchildren, she took with her the books and papers of her late husband. "I don't imagine," he wrote, "Mrs Whitcomb was very literary, or had much sympathy with her husband's tastes."[74]

Few other details of Whitcomb's family life or personality emerge, though in one of the last letters that he wrote on the subject, Clark did speculate interestingly—and, I suspect, perceptively—about Whitcomb's set of mind: "I am 'handicapped' by very slight knowledge of Whitcomb's early manhood. A certain tone about his satirical verse leads me to a conjecture, which I have hardly touched upon in my articles, that he may have attempted the ministry and failed on account of some natural limitation, leaving him rather embittered on the subject."[75]

We are on very much more certain ground when we come to consider Whitcomb's publications, of which the American Antiquarian Society possesses what must be a virtually complete collection—it is certainly the largest. As the then librarian, R. W. G. Vail, put it in a letter to H. G. Rugg of the Dartmouth College Library,

> We have perhaps the best collection of Chapman Whitcomb material, but I do not believe that we have a single duplicate. His chap books are all exceedingly rare and some of them very important. In fact, there is no other early printing town in New England as interesting as Leominster. I notice that you speak of Whitcomb as a printer. Many items were issued with his imprint, but they were almost always described as printed for Chapman Whitcomb. I doubt whether he was himself a printer, but he must have been a very attractive and interesting character. I suspect that his Christian name describes him pretty accurately.[76]

At one time he was a teacher; at another he was engaged in ragpicking; and from these occupations he seems to have drifted into becoming a traveling bookseller whose stock in trade was the chapbooks that, with one or two exceptions, he had printed by Charles and John Prentiss, who started printing in the town in 1795.[77] The titles are generally undated and bear the imprint "Leominster: Printed for Chapman Whitcomb."

Among the twenty-four Whitcomb publications in the possession

of the American Antiquarian Society there are four captivities, including the adventures of Mary Rowland and the story by the
pseudonymous Abraham Panther. One of his most interesting titles is
*The Farmer's Daughter: Being a History of the Life and Suffering of
Miss Clarissa Dalton*, an adaptation of an English chapbook based
upon an actual robbery that took place in 1785.[78] The story was
popular in America, where it was reprinted several times.[79] Whitcomb, however, gave the characters a new set of names—the leading
one became Miss Clarissa Dalton[80]—and he also changed the name
of the author from James Pen to William Penn. The American Antiquarian Society copy has the usual imprint, but there is also a manuscript note in a contemporary hand after the author's name, which
reads, "Printed for Chapman Whitcomb the old book peddeller."

All of Whitcomb's publications were intended for the popular market. In 1795 he published at Worcester, Massachusetts, a twelve-page
chapbook of his own poetry entitled *Miscellaneous Poems*. Eight of
the pages are devoted to a poem of over three hundred lines called "A
Concise View of Antient and Modern Religion." The verse is not
great, but it is readable,[81] and his facility in prose and verse suggests
comparison with the popular English writer of the later seventeenth
century, John Taylor, the "Water Poet," who was equally at home with
prose and verse in his chapbooks. Taylor in fact had an American
namesake, Amos Taylor (1748–1813?), a traveling bookseller. Having
failed to gain entry to Dartmouth College in 1779, Amos Taylor
came a teacher, and then peddled through New England books that he
had written himself. Many of his twenty-eight recorded titles[82] were
religious, and in general his work belongs only marginally to the
chapbook tradition.

Popular religious tracts were circulated in colonial days, and in
much larger numbers during the early years of the Republic. Hannah
More's "Cheap Repository Tracts" had something of a vogue from
about 1797;[83] but religious tracts belonged only in a very marginal
sense, I believe, to the chapbook tradition. Indeed, although the
worthy men and women on both sides of the Atlantic who founded
tract societies used hawkers and peddlers to distribute their evangelical wares, they saw their endeavors as being directly opposed to
more secular popular literature. An anonymous American writer
noted with approval the efforts of the Religious Tract Society in London: "In August 1805, moved by the overwhelming influence which a
flood of infidel and other publications was exerting upon the lower
orders of society, they conceived the idea of publishing a distinct
series of Tracts, adapted to gain their attention, and to supplant the
mischievous publications with which they were furnished in great

profusion by unprincipled men, for mere purposes of gain." The author went on to say that seventy-five thousand copies of the series
were circulated, with the result that "about three hundred thousand
of the profane and immoral books, commonly sold to Hawkers, were
known to have been kept out of circulation by this series of Tracts
having been purchased instead of them."[84]

Leaving aside the enviable certainty of this conclusion, there is no
doubt that tracts circulated in large numbers in the United States.
Between May 23, 1814, and May 1, 1824, the American Tract Society
published over four million tracts, at an average cost of one dollar per
five hundred of a single title.[85] These figures are impressive—but
they are hardly firm evidence of readership. Promotional zeal on the
part of the organizers may well have outrun reality; and, more important, it would be rash to conclude that every tract distributed was read
by its recipient. What the figures do indicate, in a more general way, is
a large reading public at the bottom end of the social scale.[86]

The extent to which chapbooks helped to make and to shape the
tastes of this reading public, some of whom could afford the few
coppers charged for them,[87] is still a matter for discussion. What does
seem beyond argument is that chapbooks provide us with one of the
major threads that lead us to the common reader of the eighteenth
and early nineteenth centuries. By about 1825 they had dwindled in
popularity as adult fare, but for children they remained in demand
until the end of the century and beyond. The reason for their decline
among adult readers was almost entirely cultural, and was connected
with the new sophistication of a working class called into being by the
Industrial Revolution.

There are, however, some continuities, for we find in chapbooks
the earliest stories of the American frontier (precursors of the dime
novel western and the fiction of Zane Grey) and chronicles of crime,
both of which, in differing forms, have remained popular down to our
own times. It would not be too difficult to find other interesting, if less
immediately obvious, connections between past and present. In a
more ideological sense we should remember too the reprinting in
America of the English chapbook account of Dick Whittington.[88] The
presentation—even if somewhat inaccurate—of Whittington as a
poor boy who achieved wealth, fame, and high office through his own
efforts became a forerunner of the stream of novels written by Horatio
Alger in the nineteenth century about making good—*Struggling Upward* and *Strive and Succeed* are typical titles—that helped to perpetuate the myth that any boy (not girl!) could, if he were honest,
intelligent, and hard-working, become either a millionaire or president of the United States. The persistence of such a myth over so long

a period is a remarkable tribute to the role of popular literature, which from chapbooks onward has provided significant elements in the theoretical underpinning of a free enterprise culture.

Notes

I am grateful to the American Antiquarian Society, which made me a Simon Foster Haven Fellow in summer 1984. Its hospitality and resources made this essay possible. I dedicate this essay to Liz Reilly, in love and admiration.

1. Bernard Capp, "Popular Literature," in *Popular Culture in Seventeenth Century England*, ed. Barry Reay (London, 1985), 199.

2. But it was used before then. A Thomas Longman invoice dated August 10, 1773, among the Henry Knox Papers in the Massachusetts Historical Society, Boston, lists "Chap Books." I am deeply grateful to Liz Reilly, who drew my attention to the Knox Papers and lent me relevant photocopies.

3. L. C. Wroth, *The Colonial Printer* (1931; rpt. Charlottesville, Va., 1964), 15.

4. Ibid., 218–19.

5. John Holme, "A True Relation of the Flourishing State of Pennsylvania," quoted in L. H. Weeks, *History of Paper Manufacture in the United States* (New York, 1916), 5–6. First published in 1847, the poem is about Wm. Bradford, who was printing in Oxford, near Philadelphia, from 1685 to 1693.

6. Weeks, *History of Paper Manufacture*, 45.

7. See P. L. Ford, ed., *The Journals of Hugh Gaine, Printer*, 2 vols. (New York, 1902), 1:44.

8. See *Paper Trade Journal* (November 28, 1940), sec. 2, pp. 7–8.

9. Their collections are, respectively, housed in Magdalene College, Cambridge University, and Houghton Library, Harvard University, Cambridge, Mass.

10. W. C. Ford, ed., *The Isaiah Thomas Collection of Ballads* (Worcester, Mass., 1924), 4.

11. *Catalogue of the American Library of the late Mr George Brinley of Hartford Conn.*, pt. 4 (Hartford, Conn., 1886), 137–38.

12. Onley, who owned two presses, was a prominent printer/publisher of popular literature. See Cyprian Blagden, "Notes on the Ballad Market in the Second Half of the Seventeenth Century," *Studies in Bibliography* 6 (1953–54): 177.

13. See Mathew Carey Accounts, folio vol. 15, December 1799–August 1800, American Antiquarian Society (hereafter AAS), Worcester, Mass.

14. I am grateful to Meg Ford for this reference.

15. See Erhard Dahl, *Die Kürzungen des "Robinson Crusoe" in England zwischen 1719 und 1819* (Frankfurt am Main, 1977), 173ff., esp. 178. There

was a chapbook reprint—by no means the first—in 1759, and another by Dicey at about this time. Dahl says, tentatively, 1764, but it may well have been earlier.

16. A copy of the catalogue is held by the Historical Society of Pennsylvania, Philadelphia.

17. A copy survives in the AAS. It is beautifully reproduced in G. Bumgardner, ed., *American Broadsides* (Barre, Mass., 1971), no. 48.

18. AAS ref. BDSDS 1766.

19. Copies in the Connecticut Historical Society, Hartford, and Yale University, New Haven, Conn. Although imports are not specified in this catalogue, its range of titles suggests strongly that the material was imported from London.

20. Copy in the AAS.

21. It is, of course, not entirely certain that these can properly be called chapbooks, but the notion of contemporary popular abridgments of eighteenth-century novels is an intriguing one.

22. Copy in the Rhode Island Historical Society, Providence.

23. Isaiah Thomas, *The History of Printing in America*, ed. M. A. McCorison (New York, 1970), 385.

24. It is worth noting that Hugh Gaine, a leading member of the New York book trade who had first come to the city in late 1740, had also been apprenticed to James Magee. In the late 1750s and early 1760s Gaine was advertising "A vast variety of Chap Books fit for Country Stores." See Ford, *Journals of Hugh Gaine*, 1:27. Such chapbooks may well have been imported from James Magee in Belfast. At that period they would not have been American productions.

25. *Curious Productions*, 3 vols. See F. A. Pottle, ed., *Boswell's London Journal 1762–1763* (London, 1950), 289.

26. Thomas Ollive Mabbott, "Two Chapbooks Printed by Andrew Steuart," *American Book Collector* 3, nos. 5–6 (May–June 1933): 325–28.

27. See C. Welsh and W. H. Tillinghast, *Catalogue of English and American Chapbooks and Broadside Ballads in Harvard College Library* (1905; rpt. Detroit, 1968). H. B. Weiss, *A Catalogue of the Chapbooks in New York Public Library*, was not published until 1936.

28. Mabbott, "Two Chapbooks," 326–27. The present location of this volume is unknown to me.

29. A dissenting minister in Wadhurst, Sussex, whose *Seven Sermons* was first published in London in 1697. There was a fourth edition in Boston, 1701. See C. J. Sommerville, *Popular Religion in Restoration England* (Gainesville, Fla., 1977), 52 and ch. 3 passim. On the verso of the title page of his edition Steuart had an advertisement to inform the reader that because the book was in such demand he had "been induc'd to print a large edition of this excellent little Book, which will be sold at a low Price: that they may circulate far and wide, and be of universal Good to Mankind, is the sincere wish to the Publisher."

30. In 1761 he was running a bookstore in Lancaster, Penna.

31. See V. E. Neuburg, "The Diceys and the Chapbook Trade," *Trans-*

actions of the Bibliographical Society 5th ser., 24, no. 3 (September 1969): 219–31.

32. See "Henry Knox Bookseller," *Massachusetts Historical Society Proceedings* 61 (1927–28): 205–303. The "Note by the Editor" (pp. 227–35) gives an account of Henry Knox's business venture; the remainder consists of letters with footnotes. See also *Dictionary of American Biography* (1933), 10:475–77. Knox's papers are in the Massachusetts Historical Society.

33. This was Thomas Longman II. His father, who founded the firm in 1724, had died in 1755. See H. Cox and J. E. Chandler, *The House of Longman* (London, 1925).

34. This invoice and those that follow are from the Henry Knox Papers 47, Massachusetts Historical Society. Note that British currency at this time was in pounds, shillings, and pence.

35. Catalogue, 101 and 103. There is a copy in the University of Glasgow Library.

36. V. E. Neuburg, *The Penny Histories* (1968; rpt. New York, 1969), 30–31.

37. See H. B. Weiss, *American Chapbooks 1722–1842* (New York, 1945), rpt. from *Bulletin of the New York Public Library* (July and August 1945).

38. See Arthur Dickson, *Valentine and Orson* (New York, 1929), 284–98, for a list of the various editions through which the text of this story passed.

39. Original in Oberlin College Library, Ohio. The AAS has a photocopy.

40. Wroth, *Colonial Printer*, 213.

41. In d'Alté A. Welch, *A Bibliography of American Children's Books Printed prior to 1821* (Worcester, Mass., 1972). See also H. B. Weiss, *American Editions of Sir Richard Whittington and His Cat* (New York, 1938), rpt. from *Bulletin of the New York Public Library* (June 1938).

42. Although, curiously enough, John G. Cawelti in his study *Apostles of the Self-Made Man* (Chicago, 1965) does not mention Whittington.

43. See C. S. Brigham, *Bibliography of American Editions of Robinson Crusoe to 1830* (Worcester, Mass., 1958).

44. M. A. McCorison, ed., *Three Autobiographical Fragments by Isaiah Thomas* (Worcester, Mass., 1962), 26.

45. Reproduced in C. Hindley, *Curiosities of Street Literature* (1871), 41.

46. They used this phrase in their advertising. See, for example, p. 147 of *The Youth's Instructor* (1761), which was printed by them.

47. Described, with a facsimile of the title page, in A. S. W. Rosenbach, *Early American Children's Books* (1933; rpt. New York, 1971), 31.

48. One is in my own collection. The other was being offered for sale in 1986 and probably passed into private hands.

49. W. C. Ford, *Broadsides, Ballads &c Printed in Massachusetts 1639–1800* (Boston, 1922).

50. See Benjamin Franklin V, ed., *Boston Printers, Publishers, and Booksellers* (Boston, 1980), 76ff.; Ford, *Thomas Ballads*, 19ff.; and V. E. Neuburg, *Chapbooks: A Guide to Reference Material*, 2d ed. (London, 1972), 71–72. Oddly enough, there is no mention of the Coverly family in Thomas, *History of Printing in America*.

51. In the old city Theatre Alley ran between Milk and Franklin streets. It was destroyed in 1859 when the extension to Devonshire Street was built.

52. Broadside ballads were cheaper. Nos. 49 and 227 of the Thomas ballads, both printed by Coverly, were priced at three cents each.

53. See Ford, *Thomas Ballads*, 19–22.

54. R. D. Harlan, "David Hall's Bookshop and Its British Sources of Supply," in *Books in America's Past*, ed. D. Kaser (Charlottesville, Va., 1966), 2–23, esp. 5.

55. On a broadside dated October 14, 1754, reproduced in Ford, *Journals of Hugh Gaine*, 1:facing 188.

56. Cf. Weiss, *American Chapbooks*.

57. For Carey, see E. L. Bradsher, *Mathew Carey: Editor, Author and Publisher* (New York, 1912); and Eugene L. Schwaab, ed., *Mathew Carey Autobiography* (New York, 1942).

58. Mathew Carey Papers, folio vol. 1. The prices, of course, are in old-style British currency; thus the sums involved are three shillings and six pence and six guineas.

59. Ibid., folio vol 6. Carey exploited the mass market with skill. During the 1794 theatrical season, for example, he employed peddlers to hawk around the theaters his own reprints of current popular songs. See William Rowson to Mathew Carey, March 12, 1794, Historical Society of Pennsylvania.

60. Mathew Carey Papers, folio vol. 8 (vols. 9, 10, 11, and 12 are missing).

61. Ibid., folio vol. 16. "J Riddle" remains untraced.

62. See a letter dated March 7, 1801, from Vernor and Hood in London, together with an invoice for books dispatched by them to Carey in Philadelphia. In AAS.

63. Mathew Carey Papers, vol. 16, 1801. The full title of the second chapbook is *The Comical Sayings of Paddy From Cork*. It was a favorite title in the second half of the eighteenth century.

64. Thomas, *History of Printing in America*, 303.

65. Boone's autobiography, *Life and Adventures of Colonel Daniel Boone . . . Written by Himself* (Brooklyn, N.Y., 1823), contained a tribute to the author written by Lord Byron. Timothy Flint's biography, *The Life and Adventures of Daniel Boone*, was first published in 1833 and quickly became a bestseller. Boone had died in 1820. For a good, brief account of him, see H. N. Smith, *Virgin Land: The American West as Symbol and Myth* (1950; rpt. Cambridge, Mass., 1971).

66. The best survey of them is still R. W. G. Vail, *The Voice of the Old Frontier* (Philadelphia, 1949). See also C. A. Smith, *Narratives of Captivity among the Indians of North America* (Chicago, 1912) and *Supplement 1* (Chicago, 1928).

67. See Winthrop H. Duncan, "Josiah Priest, Historian of the American Frontier," *Proceedings of the American Antiquarian Society* (April 1934); and R. W. G. Vail, "The Abraham Panther Indian Captivity," *American Book Collector* 2 (1932).

68. C. K. Shipton and J. E. Mooney, eds., *National Index of American*

Imprints through 1800: The Short Title Evans (Worcester, Mass., 1969). See also J. A. L. Lemay, "Recent Bibliographies in Early American Literature," *Early American Literature* 8, no. 1 (Spring 1973).

69. The preface is identical to that of the third, except that in the earlier the words were "gave Birth to this Third Edition."

70. Copy in John Carter Brown Library, Providence, R.I.

71. J. W. Farwell, "Sir Richard Rum," *Publications of the Colonial Society of Massachusetts* 17 (1915): 234–44. I have drawn heavily upon this printed version of a talk given by Farwell to the society. He showed members a copy of the fourth edition, which is now in the possession of the AAS.

72. In *North American Almanack . . . 1776* (Worcester, Watertown, and Cambridge, Mass.), 17 (unnumbered), there is a plea by "Sir Richard Rum" for less drunkenness in the army.

73. In an unpublished letter to the secretary of Dartmouth College dated April 18, 1932 (now in the Dartmouth College archives, Hanover, N.H.), Clark spoke of five articles in all, the last of which was to be "as complete a bibliography as possible"; but the project was never completed.

74. J. C. L. Clark to C. S. Brigham, July 11, 1927, AAS.

75. Clark to the secretary of Dartmouth College, April 18, 1932.

76. R. W. G. Vail to H. G. Rugg, April 23, 1932, Dartmouth College archives.

77. Clark to Brigham, January 15, 1913, AAS.

78. See *Annual Register* (September 3, 1785).

79. On at least five occasions between 1797 and 1814—once in Hartford, Conn., and by three different publishers in New York.

80. See Clark to Brigham, June 18, 1927, AAS.

81. See, for example, his view of the Shakers, who had several communities in New England and elsewhere:
The Shaker thinks that all are blind but he,
And wonders at their gross stupidity;
In the old lady [Mother Anne Lee, the founder], firmly, does believe,
Devoutly pins her faith upon her sleeve,
And thinks that none true faith nor grace possess,
Till to her elders, they their sins confess.

82. See M. A. McCorison, "Amos Taylor, a Sketch and Bibliography," *Proceedings of the American Antiquarian Society* (April 1959).

83. See M. G. Jones, *Hannah More* (Cambridge, 1952), ch. 6 passim; and H. B. Weiss, *Hannah More's Cheap Repository Tracts in America* (New York, 1946), rpt. from *Bulletin of the New York Public Library* (July and August 1946).

84. *Proceedings of the First Ten Years of the American Tract Society Instituted at Boston, 1814* (Boston, 1824), 181. The best account of the tract movement in America is in S. E. Slocum, Jr., "The American Tract Society: 1825–1975. An Evangelical Effort to Influence the Religious and Moral Life of the United States," diss., New York University, 1975. It is very good on the early years.

85. *Proceedings of the First Ten Years,* 178 (unnumbered).

86. See, for example, W. J. Gilmore, *Elementary Literacy on the Eve of the Industrial Revolution: Trends in Rural New England, 1760–1830* (Worcester, Mass., 1982).

87. The economics of chapbook production, in both Britain and the United States, are impossible to reconstruct. Such publications were cheap—whatever that description may mean—and were designed for as many readers as could afford them. How many could? How long were print runs? To the former question there are some partial answers in U.S. Department of Labor, *History of Wages in the United States from Colonial Times to 1928* (Washington, D.C., 1929). So far as chapbook print numbers are concerned, it is hazardous even to guess at totals.

88. The real Richard Whittington (who died in 1423) became Lord Mayor of London on several occasions. See *Dictionary of National Biography;* also S. Lysons, *The Model Merchant of the Middle Ages* (London, 1860); and W. Besant and J. Rice, *Sir Richard Whittington,* new ed. (London, 1902).

Chapter Four

A Republican Literature

Magazine Reading and Readers in Late-Eighteenth-Century New York

David Paul Nord

President George Washington was a subscriber. So were Vice President John Adams, Chief Justice John Jay, and New York Mayor Richard Varick. With such a distinguished readership, it is little wonder that the publishers of the *New-York Magazine; or, Literary Repository* decided to publish a list of subscribers to their first volume in 1790. Like other eighteenth-century magazine publishers, Thomas and James Swords were proud of their association with gentlemen of character, stature, and literary taste.[1] Yet men such as Washington and Adams were not the only readers of the *New-York Magazine*, as the standard magazine histories seem to suggest.[2] There were women on the list, and barbers, bakers, butchers, and boarding house proprietors. These are the forgotten readers of the *New-York Magazine*, and of late-eighteenth-century magazines in general. Who were these people? How did they make a living? Where did they live? What were they like? Were they different from nonsubscribers? What kinds of material did they read? This essay seeks answers to these questions.

As Carl Kaestle has recently pointed out, we have learned a great deal in the past twenty years about the demographics of simple literacy in the past, but we have only begun to develop a genuine social history of reading—that is, a history of the *uses* of literacy. This is hardly surprising, for as Kaestle says, it "is very difficult to trace printed works to their readers and still more difficult to trace meaning from the text to the reader."[3] This paper tries to do both, though with more confidence about the former than the latter. It is a study of both the subscribers and the content of the *New-York Magazine* in 1790.

The main argument is that magazine reading in this era seems to have been a more broadly democratic activity than has usually been supposed. At first glance, the magazine's content would seem to be evidence of a rather elite audience; and this has been the supposition of most historians. Yet the subscriber list shows a more varied readership. Considered together, the subscriber list and the content may offer some insight into the social function of reading in this era. They suggest the importance of reading as a form of participation in the new social order of postrevolutionary America. Edward Countryman has recently argued that "radical politics and nascent class consciousness foundered on electoral participation and on the spirit of voluntary association" in the 1780s.[4] In other words, the radicalism of the small shopkeepers and urban artisans lost its urgency as those groups began to participate more fully in a political culture that had once been closed to them. Similarly, the magazine might be viewed as another arena for popular participation, in this case participation in the formerly elite culture of science and education, arts and letters, virtue and honor, cultivation and character. The values of the magazine were traditional; it was the participation of the working class that was new. In short, this was a republican readership and a republican literature.

The Setting

"Republican" was a commonplace term in the American political vocabulary of 1790, yet its ubiquity was matched by its ambiguity. Historians still disagree over what Americans in the late eighteenth century meant when they talked about republicanism. One group of scholars, influenced by the pathbreaking work of Bernard Bailyn and J. G. A. Pocock, emphasizes the classical republican tradition—that is, the tradition of Aristotle and Cicero, filtered through Italian Renaissance humanism and the radical Whig thought of the English "country" politicians of the late seventeenth and early eighteenth centuries. In this tradition, the basis for republican government was civic virtue, the sacrifice of individual interests to the common good.[5] Other scholars emphasize the liberal dimension of American republicanism. Though current historians such as Joyce Appleby have rejected the one-dimensional Lockean perspective of Louis Hartz, they still argue that the mainstream of American political thought in the late eighteenth century was liberal—that is, committed to private property and individualism. In this tradition, virtue and the sources of human happiness lay largely outside government in a natural economy and self-regulating society.[6] A third group of scholars owes much to the classical republican perspective, in that it finds even among the common people of the revolutionary era a devotion to the ideas of civic virtue and commonwealth. But there are differences of emphasis. Growing more from social history than from the history of political thought, this literature stresses the equal rights or radical egalitarian aspects of American republicanism. These historians are usually more interested in the actual political participation of working-class Americans than they are in abstract political theory.[7]

Of course, all of these (and still other) meanings of "republicanism" were current in American thought of the 1790s. As Joyce Appleby says, "It would be surprising if scholars were able to agree upon the meaning of a word that contemporaries themselves used in such disparate contexts." People clearly used the vocabulary of republicanism, but they used new vocabularies as well, and they used the old words in new ways, as circumstances changed.[8] Linda Kerber has recently suggested that the language and values of classical republicanism remained more meaningful and vital for some Americans than others, depending upon their place in the rapidly emerging liberal order. Historians must be alert to how real people shaped political ideas to make sense of their own lives in a complex, modern world.[9]

New York City in 1790, for example, was an intricate social, political, and economic universe. At one extreme, the city was still the domain of the Livingstons, the Schuylers, and the Stuyvesants—a traditional aristocracy that continued to influence public life in the postrevolutionary era. Furthermore, New York was the American capital in 1789–90, the gathering place for a new aristocracy of founding fathers and federal officials, who attended to the business of the country by day and to the balls, dinners, and receptions of New York high society by night. At the other extreme, New York was home to the desperately poor—cartmen, mariners, common laborers; the sick, the helpless, the chronically unemployed.[10] It would be remarkable indeed if these diverse New Yorkers shared the same notions of what it meant to be a citizen of the new Republic.

Most of the citizens of New York, however, fell between these extremes. As Table 4.1 shows, my sample from the 1790 city directory suggests that nearly two-thirds of the city's heads of household were artisans or shopkeepers. Other historians have come up with roughly comparable figures. Certainly the largest group of working people in New York and in other large cities in this era was the artisans—that is, master craftsmen and their journeymen employees.[11]

What it meant to be an artisan (or even a shopkeeper) was changing in 1790. The traditional relationships among master, journeyman, and apprentice had begun to break down. Some masters were becoming retailers, manufacturers, or incipient capitalists. Some journeymen were becoming wage workers, with little hope of achieving the traditional status of independent master. Many shops were hiring untrained boys, without any commitment to the obligations of apprenticeship. The artisan system was shifting, very gradually, with the rise of laissez-faire capitalism.[12]

But though the economic world was changing, many of the values of the eighteenth-century artisan culture remained strong. In fact, some of these values were reinforced by the experience of the Revolution. During the Revolution and the decade of crisis that preceded it, the artisans and shopkeepers had become active participants in the political culture—first in crowd action, then in electoral politics. That commitment to politics would not subside.[13] Yet political equality and political participation were not the only components of "artisan republicanism," as Sean Wilentz has recently described it. The tradesmen of New York and other American cities also embraced an older ideology that tied together a devotion to craft and to commonwealth. The artisans believed in equality and independence, but not as ends in themselves, for independence should free men "to exercise virtue, to subordinate private ends to the legislation of the public good."[14] Certainly, the artisans and small shopkeepers of New York City stood for individual initiative, for economic progress, and for the rights of private property. In this sense they were liberals. Yet, as Wilentz puts it, they also stood for something else:

> With a rhetoric rich in the republican language of corruption, equality, and independence, they remained committed to a benevolent hierarchy of skill and the cooperative workshop. Artisan independence conjured up, not a vision of ceaseless, self-interested industry, but a moral order in which all craftsmen would eventually become self-governing, independent, competent masters. . . . Men's energies would be devoted, not to personal ambition or profit alone, but to the commonwealth; in the workshop, mutual obligation and respect—"the strongest ties of the heart"—would prevail; in more public spheres, the craftsmen would insist on their equal rights and exercise their citizenship with a view to preserving the rule of virtue as well as to protecting their collective interests against an eminently corruptible mercantile and financial elite.[15]

Gordon Wood has argued that the grand achievement of the founders in the 1780s was to move political thought from a classical to a romantic or liberal conception of republicanism. In the classical republican vocabulary, "virtue" and "commonwealth" were the key terms. For a republic to survive, individual aspirations must be wedded to the common good. This was the language of 1776. By 1787, the old words had taken on new meanings. The republic devised by Madison and his colleagues was a system that would not depend upon the virtue of the people. In the Federalist scheme, the traditional vices of republican government—individualism and self-interest—became strengths. The commonweal would emerge automatically in the competition of private interests.[16] While Wood's study brilliantly illuminates the changing political thought of the founding elites, it obscures the continuity, the complexity, and the contradictory nature of the political thought of those men and women of the "middling classes." Urban artisans, especially, felt the steady pull of liberalism, yet they also harbored great misgivings about the new economic order that seemed to lie ahead. For them, the commitment to classical republican values remained strong, well into the nineteenth century. Just what sort of commonwealth or republican order they envisioned was not always clear or consistent. What was unmistakably clear, however, was their insistence that they be recognized as full-fledged participants in that order, whatever it might be.[17] The most obvious arena of participation was politics. Another was reading.

The Magazine

It was into this milieu that the *New-York Magazine* was born in 1790. It wasn't the first attempt to start a magazine in New York in the postwar era. Just three years earlier, in 1787, Noah Webster had brought out the *American Magazine.* After only a year, however, he abandoned the project, mainly for financial reasons. "I will now leave writing and do more lucrative business," Webster said. "I am happy to quit New York."[18] Thomas and James Swords hoped for a better fate as they offered to the public the first issue of the *New-York Magazine* in January of 1790. Though New York had been devastated economically by the war, the city was bustling again by 1790. The population passed thirty thousand in 1789, and during the 1790s the city climbed to first rank as the commercial metropolis of America.[19] The Swords brothers often complained that the city's prosperity never trickled down to them ("the horizon remains dark and gloomy," they liked to report to their readers). But they did manage to stay in business eight full years—the longest run of any eighteenth-century American magazine.[20]

Part of the reason for the magazine's early success was its association with "a society of gentlemen," a local group of patrons of the arts and would-be "literary men," who began to work with the Swords brothers on the March issue. Their aim was to provide the magazine with "literary support" and editorial direction, and to promote "the pen of virtue and morality, science and taste." Clearly, the *New-York Magazine* represented the aspirations for culture and refinement of the American elite. The magazine's price was somewhat aristocratic as well—$2.25 a year, at a time when $0.50 a day was a common wage for a New York working man.[21] In this sense, the *New-York Magazine* was not unlike similar magazines in the United States and Britain. Its model undoubtedly was the *Gentleman's Magazine* of London, the pioneer of the general interest magazine in English. Like the *Gentleman's*, the *New-York Magazine* was impartial, restrained, stolid—not in the least critical of the culture of "the rich, the well-born, and the able," as subscriber John Adams described the new social elite of New York.[22]

Yet neither the editors nor the "society of gentlemen" viewed the enterprise as elitist. In an "Introductory Essay" published with the April issue, they proclaimed their commitment to the republican ideal of "equal liberty," especially equal access to knowledge. Following a eulogy to the democratic science of Benjamin Franklin, the editors described their vision of the purpose of a magazine:

> A well conducted magazine, we conceive must, from its nature, contribute greatly to diffuse knowledge throughout a community, and to create in that community a taste for literature. The universality of the subjects which it treats of will give to every profession, and every occupation, some information, while its variety holds out to every taste some gratification. From its conciseness, it will not require more time for its perusal than the most busy can well spare; and its cheapness brings it within the convenient purchase of every class of society.[23]

Was the *New-York Magazine* the province of the elite, as the magazine's tone suggests, or of "every class of society," as its editors declared? Fortunately, the answer to that question need not be pure guesswork, for the subscribers were listed by name in the 1790 volume.

The Readers

In 1790, the *New-York Magazine* had 370 subscribers, a small but respectable number for that time.[24] (Historians have generally assumed that each copy of a newspaper or magazine in this era was read by quite a few people.) About 80 percent of the subscribers lived in New York City (Manhattan). About 5 percent lived in Albany; another 5 percent lived in other New York State towns; and the rest were scattered from Nova Scotia to Antigua. The vast majority of subscribers were men (98 percent), though surely many of their subscriptions

were intended for wives and children as well. Seven women subscribed in their own names. I located 90 percent (269 of 298) of the
New York readers in city directories or other biographical sources. For
265 of these I was able to secure information on occupations and
street addresses. For comparison, I also drew a random sample of 400
entries from the 1790 city directory. (The nature and limitations of
the city directory are discussed in Appendix A.)

   A glance at Table 4.1 confirms that the readership of the *New-York
Magazine* was indeed more upscale than the general population of the
city. While nearly 50 percent of the readers were professionals or
merchants, only 15 percent of the random sample fell into these two
categories. Moreover, the most common professional occupation
among the readers was lawyer, while among the general population
the most common professional occupations were somewhat lower in
prestige: local government official and schoolteacher. The difference
between the two groups at the bottom of the scale is even more
striking. In the random sample, 17 percent fell into the nonskilled
category. Most of these were cartmen, laborers, and mariners. In the
subscriber group, only four individuals were classified as nonskilled: a
gardener, a nurseryman, a washer, and a widow. The first two would
certainly fall higher on a measure of skill than laborers or cartmen,
and they may not even belong in this category. The same might be said
of widows. The one widow subscriber, for example, was a Beekman,
one of the leading families of the city. The washer also was a woman;
and she too may have been a member of a social class higher than her
occupation suggests. (The other two women subscribers that I was
able to trace were a teacher and a glover.) In short, it might be said that
virtually no one from the very bottom of the socioeconomic scale—
the truly poor—subscribed to the *New-York Magazine.*[25]

Table 4.1 Occupational Status of Subscribers to the *New-York Magazine* and
a Random Sample from the *New York City Directory*, 1790

Occupation Category	Subscriber %	Random Sample %
1. Professional	20.0	6.6
2. Merchant	29.1	8.5
3. Shopkeeper	21.5	26.5
4. Artisan	27.9	41.4
5. Nonskilled	1.5	17.0
TOTAL % (N)	100.0 (265)	100.0 (377)
Occupation information missing (N)	(33)	(23)

Though the proportions at the top and bottom of the occupational scale for the two groups look quite different, the middle-range proportions are much less disparate. About half of the subscribers were shopkeepers or artisans, compared with two-thirds of the random sample. While this is a significant difference, of course, 50 percent is still a substantial proportion. If it is important that half the readers of the *New-York Magazine* were merchants and professionals, it is equally important that the other half were artisans and shopkeepers. Both groups deserve a closer look.

Who were the elite readers? Most were merchants. More than one-quarter of the total list of subscribers identified themselves simply as merchants. The range of wealth and income within this category was large. Some "merchants" were doubtless no more than hopeful or pretentious shopkeepers; others were the leading commercial operators of the city and of the nation. Whether large or small, most merchants of that era were somewhat unspecialized, working on commission and handling a variety of goods. For example, one of the *New-York Magazine* subscribers advertised in a local newspaper a stock of Madeira wine, Carolina indigo and rice, China tea, a house and lot on Queen Street, thirteen acres near Harlem, and "a neat post chaise with harness." Another subscriber advertised imported cloth, buttons, buckles, glass, and "continental certificates"—and he was willing to barter for "country produce."[26]

If the prestige of an address reflects status, the merchants in the subscriber group may not have been much more well-to-do than merchants generally. Forty-two percent of the merchant readers had addresses on the most important business streets of the city: Queen (now Pearl), Water, and Hanover Square. But 37 percent of the merchants in the random sample also had addresses on these same streets. In both samples, only a scattering of individual merchants lived in the more distant sections of the city—that is, north of what is now Fulton Street or west of Broadway.

Though many of the merchant readers were small-scale operators, some were the leaders of the mercantile elite. The names of Beekman, Kip, Livingston, Roosevelt, Van Rensselaer, and Verplank—old families and old money—dot the list.[27] Another subscriber, William Duer, is an example of a new-money man who read the *New-York Magazine*. Duer was perhaps the leading speculator of the day in land, securities, government contracts, and manufacturing ventures. He had made one fortune during the war, and he was hard at work on another in 1790. Besides the big merchants, some of the most prominent lawyers and politicians of the city were subscribers. Egbert Benson, one of the leading conservative assemblymen of New York in the 1780s, was on the list. So was James Duane, former congressman and mayor of New York. And, of course, Washington and Adams. Little wonder that the Swords brothers had such high hopes for their little magazine.[28]

But half the readers were not so wealthy or so prominent. Half were shopkeepers and artisans. Most of the shopkeepers, about 60 percent of them in both the subscriber group and the random sample, were listed simply as shopkeepers, storekeepers, or grocers. The others represented a variety of specialties: taverns, livery stables, bookstores, paint stores, hardware stores, tobacco shops, and so on. The main street for shopkeeper subscribers was Broadway, an up-and-coming business and residential street in New York in 1790. Others lived throughout the city. The artisans were a larger and even more varied group. Altogether, thirty-nine different trades were represented on the subscription list, compared with forty-eight trades in the random sample.

What kinds of artisans were likely to read the *New-York Magazine?* The quick answer seems to be, all kinds. The range of trades is strik-ing, with many crafts represented by a single subscriber. (See Appen-dix B. The only woman artisan subscriber, for example, was also the only glover on the list.) Yet some patterns may be discerned. Table 4.2,

Table 4.2 Ten Leading Occupations of Artisan Subscribers to the *New-York Magazine* and Artisans in a Random Sample from the *New York City Directory*, 1790

Subscribers		Random Sample	
Occupation	% of Artisans	Occupation	% of Artisans
1. Carpenter	9.5	1. Shoemaker	14.7
2. Printer*	9.5	2. Carpenter	11.5
3. Sea Captain*	6.8	3. Tailor	10.3
4. Barber	5.4	4. Cooper	5.8
5. Cabinetmaker	5.4	5. Ship Carpenter	3.8
6. Shoemaker	5.4	6. Hatter	3.2
7. Baker	4.1	7. Blacksmith**	2.6
8. Clock/Watchmaker	4.1	8. Blockmaker**	2.6
9. Cooper	4.1	9. Chairmaker	2.6
10. Tailor	4.1	10. Gold/Silversmith	2.6
TOP TEN TOTAL % (N)	58.1 (43)		59.6 (93)
ALL ARTISANS % (N)	100.0 (74)		100.0 (156)

*These trades do not appear at all in the random sample.
**These trades do not appear at all on the subscriber list.

for example, shows the leading ten artisan occupations for the subscribers and for the random sample. By far the three leading trades in
the general population were shoemaker, carpenter, and tailor, which
account for nearly 37 percent of the artisans in the random sample.
These three trades were not the leading trades among the artisan
subscribers, however, though they were well represented, as Table 4.2
shows. The top three trades among the subscribers were carpenter,
printer, and sea captain. This is an interesting comparison, for no
printers or sea captains turned up at all in the random sample. Obviously, these were not common artisan occupations; yet they were
relatively common on the *New-York Magazine*'s subscription list.
Conversely, two crafts—blacksmith and blockmaker—appear in the
top ten artisan occupations in the random sample, but not at all on
the subscription list.

Why printers and sea captains (but not blacksmiths and block-
makers) would subscribe to a magazine seems fairly obvious. Their
trades and their lifestyles were clearly more associated with reading.
The same might be said for the barbers, whose customers loitered
around the shops then just as they do today. But what of the cop-
persmiths and cutlers, the saddlers and sailmakers? The street addresses of the artisans provide a clue. The magazine subscribers were
somewhat more likely than other artisans to live and work in the
commercial heart of the city. This difference should not be exaggerated, however; the artisan subscribers were spread out among thirty-
four different streets in the city. Yet the artisans in the random sample
were spread out even more widely on sixty-seven different streets,
including some of the newer and less built-up areas around Bowery
Lane on what was then the far northeast side of town.

Table 4.3 shows the difference. The artisan subscribers were more
concentrated on the same streets as the merchant subscribers:
Queen, Hanover Square, and Water. King Street (now Pine) was another prominent street in this same area. Again, this concentration
should not be overstated; the artisans from the random sample were
also heavily represented on Queen and Water. But the other main
streets for them—Fair (now Fulton), Ann, and Chatham (now Park
Row)—were several blocks farther north on the outskirts of the commercial center of the city in 1790.

Because little is known about most of the individual artisan subscribers, it is difficult to say what sort of people they were. But at least
some of them were clearly men of stature and influence, both within
their crafts and in the larger public culture. Some were on their way to
becoming manufacturers and capitalists. For example, White Mat-

Table 4.3 Five Leading Street Addresses of Artisan Subscribers to the *New-York Magazine* and Artisans in a Random Sample from the *New York City Directory*, 1790

	Subscribers		Random Sample	
Street	% of Artisans		Street	% of Artisans
1. Queen	13.5		1. Queen	12.8
2. Hanover Square	8.1		2. Fair	5.1
3. Water	8.1		3. Water	4.5
4. Broadway	5.4		4. Chatham	3.8
5. King	5.4		5. Ann	3.2
TOP FIVE TOTAL % (N)	40.5 (30)			29.5 (46)
ALL ARTISANS % (N)	100.0 (74)			100.0 (156)

lock, a brewer on Chatham Street, was vice president of the New York Manufacturing Society, which was headed by the well-known merchant-politician Melancthon Smith. The aim of this society was precisely to move manufacturing from handicraft to factory.[29] Other artisan subscribers, on the other hand, were just as clearly devoted to the craft tradition. The chairman and deputy chairman of the General Society of Mechanics and Tradesmen were both readers of the *New-York Magazine*. Anthony Post was a carpenter; James Bramble was a whitesmith (a worker in tinned or galvanized iron). The General Society, founded in 1785, was a revival of the radical mechanics' committee of the 1770s, which had been instrumental in recruiting the city's working class to revolutionary politics. It was an organization of substantial, ambitious, and politically active master tradesmen. By 1796, for example, Anthony Post owned property valued at thirty-five hundred pounds. But it was also a group devoted to the traditions of craftwork and to the values of artisan republicanism.[30]

The Content

The content of the *New-York Magazine* did not impress William Loring Andrews, one of the earliest of the few historians who have written about the magazine. His enthusiasm was expended on the copperplate engravings that formed the frontispiece of each issue. Of the rest of the content, he wrote, "Aside from the record of marriages and deaths and a few local items of some slight historical importance, there is nothing in the literature of *The New-York Magazine* that, if it had been totally destroyed, would have proved a serious loss to posterity or to the world of letters."[31] In a sense, Andrews was right. Except for some early poetry by William Dunlap, the literature of the *New-York Magazine* is of little interest to "the world of letters."[32] But it is of great interest to the social historian of reading, for here we can see what the merchants, shopkeepers, and artisans described above actually read in 1790.

Through a content analysis and a close reading of the 1790 volume, one can see that many of the conventional notions about late-eighteenth-century American magazines are true of the *New-York Magazine.*[33] The magazine was highly eclectic—in subject matter, in style, and in source of material. In this sense, American magazines were like their English counterparts. The prototypical and highly successful English magazine the *Gentleman's Magazine* was perhaps most famous for its orderly but miscellaneous character. In fact, largely because of the influence of the *Gentleman's,* "magazine" became almost synonymous with "miscellany."[34] An article on the history of magazines that appeared in the *New-York Magazine* in 1790 was almost exclusively about the *Gentleman's.* A proper magazine, the article declared, should have two characteristics: it should be "very various and extensive" in its coverage and commentary, and it should unite "utility with entertainment, . . . instruction with pleasure."[35]

Certainly the *New-York Magazine* took the idea of instruction very seriously. Though few of its articles and essays dealt directly with government or politics, many were highly didactic on the subject of public virtue. In many ways, the content of the *New-York Magazine* was very much devoted to what have been called the "didactic arts," those arts and sciences considered useful to the cultivation of virtue and character, the essential ingredients of republican men and women.[36]

Table 4.4 suggests the range of material in the *New-York Magazine.* While a good deal of the content was given over to discussions of specific topics in politics, religion, or science, the largest proportion of the articles fell into a more nebulous area of "manners and morals." As Table 4.5 shows, many of these pieces were romances—usually sentimental stories of love lost or found, seduction resisted or embraced. Many were simple expositions on virtue—with titles such as "Vanity," "Avarice," "On Idleness," "The Benefits of Temperance," or simply "On Virtue." Many were purely descriptive pieces—travelogues, anecdotes on manners and customs, sundry tales of exotica. Counting all the prose pieces for 1790, about two-thirds were written in descriptive or expository style; one-third were narratives. About

Table 4.4 Proportions of Items Devoted to Various Subject Categories in the *New-York Magazine,* 1790

Content Category	% of Items
1. Politics and Government	15.3
2. Manners and Morals	46.8
3. Religion	4.9
4. Science and Health	3.9
5. Household Advice	1.0
6. Humor	4.2
7. Commentary on Art, Music, and Letters	3.9
8. "American Muse" (poetry)	3.9
9. "Intelligence" (news briefs)	3.6
10. "Marriages," "Deaths," and Other Vital Statistics	12.6
ALL ITEMS TOTAL % (N)	100.1 (308)

one-eighth were set in New York City; seven-eighths were set elsewhere or had no specific locale.

What were these stories and articles like? A closer look at some of the regular features and some of the long-running serials provides some insight. Three of the most frequent contributors to the *New-York Magazine* in 1790 were "Philobiblicus," "Juvenis," and "The Scribbler." They represent the range of material in the magazine, from the arcane to the mundane.

"Philobiblicus" falls into the arcane category. He contributed a piece each month on scriptural matters, especially issues in biblical translation. The more subtle the philology, the more complex the etymology, the better "Philobiblicus" liked it. His aim, he said in his first piece, was to be "both instructing and entertaining," particularly through the use of "fine language and elegance of expression."[37]

Table 4.5 Proportions of Items Devoted to Various "Manners and Morals" Subcategories in the *New-York Magazine,* 1790

"Manners and Morals" Subcategory	% of Items
1. Romance (love, seduction, etc.)	24.3
2. Education	9.7
3. Virtue (morality, wisdom, etc.)	29.2
4. Description (travel, exotica, slice of life, etc.)	36.8
ALL "MANNERS AND MORALS" ITEMS % (N)	100.0 (144)

"Juvenis" was more practical. Virtually all of his many pieces were homilies on virtue. In a variety of ways, he preached a simple sermon, "that happiness results from the constant practice of virtue." On his list of the important virtues were the traditional ones. "The very ideas of justice, truth, benevolence, modesty, humility, mildness, and temperance please and beautify the mind," he wrote.[38]

"The Scribbler" was considerably more down to earth than either "Philobiblicus" or "Juvenis." Writing was his avocation; he was an artisan by occupation, though in what craft he doesn't say. In his first contribution he tells the story of how excited he had been as a young man to see his first piece of writing appear in a newspaper. He began to daydream and to imagine himself a great writer and a great man:

> In my reflections upon it next day, I beheld myself wielding a pen with all the force of a furious and animated combatant, until reaching to supply it with ink, I overturned one of the implements of my profession. The noise brought me to my proper recollection, and, strange metamorphosis! I found myself in my master's workshop, busied in the execution of a design which my extraordinary avocation had destroyed, and surrounded by my fellow apprentices, who were looking at my actions with astonishment, and picking up the remains of the valuable instrument which I had thrown down, and which was broken to pieces. For this piece of mischief I was severely corrected by my master, but the disaster did not prevent me in the prosecution of my favorite hobby horse. I continued to wield the goose-quill, and I every day saw myself rising into consequence by the respectable figure Mr. Scribbler made in the newspapers.[39]

"The Scribbler"'s contributions continued to touch on the lives of the "middling classes" of New York City.

The long-running serials in 1790 also reflect the range of material in the *New-York Magazine*. In this category, the most arcane may have been the series called "Observations on the Utility of the Latin and Greek Languages," which ran for eight months beginning in April. In this series, "T.Q.C." summarized in copious detail all the various arguments supporting the study of the ancient languages—ranging from the needs of Christianity to physiology.[40] Another prominent monthly feature was the serialization of John Adams's *Defense of the Constitutions of Government of the United States*, a book that explored and promoted English constitutional theory as much as American.[41] A third serial that ran for many months was "The History of the Dutchess de C____," a romance of passion, power, intrigue, confinement, cruelty, terror, outrage, and calamity among the rich and well-born of Europe.[42]

The other material in the magazine shows a similar diversity. For example, many of the articles and stories were aimed at women.

Though only seven women were subscribers in their own names, it is clear that the readership was heavily female. The first issue, for example, carried a letter from a local woman praising the editors for launching such an important literary enterprise. She promised that she and all her friends would subscribe, and she hinted that Noah Webster's *American Magazine* had perished largely because the *men* of the city had failed to support it. About 11 percent of the articles in 1790 either had a woman as the main character or had a clearly identified female author, and many more were obviously aimed at and probably written by women. This is clearly true of the romances and sentimental fiction, generally considered at the time, as Linda Kerber has pointed out, to be the province of the woman reader.[43]

Some of the pieces aimed at women were simply conventional reflections on traditional feminine virtues: "How much more pure, tender, delicate, irritable, affectionate, flexible, and patient is woman than man?" Or, "The female thinks not profoundly; profound thought is the power of the man. Women feel more. Sensibility is the power of woman."[44] In their "Introductory Essay," the editors said that they expected their women readers to submit "many a poetic wreath," for poetry "seems peculiarly the province of that sex, whose sweetest ornament is the mild tear that trembles in the eye of sensibility."[45] The magazine also carried advice pieces for women: "On the Choice of a Husband," or "On the Virtue of Acorn Coffee" ("to cure the slimy obstructions in the viscera"), or on how to behave in company (no "sitting cross-legged, straddling, spitting, blowing noses, etc., etc.").[46] Some were parables of seduction and lost virtue, such as the sad story of Frivola, who became so obsessed with luxury that she ended her wasted life in Europe, the slave of "every species of polite dissipation."[47] The emphasis on the supposed sensibility and sentimentality of the woman reader was characteristic of popular thought in England as well as in America.[48]

But some of the articles directed toward women were less conventional. These included tales of women's heroism, calls for women's education, and articles by women sensitive to women's concerns. An example of the latter was a piece criticizing men for always talking about women's vanity.[49] In this, the *New-York Magazine* seems to have been similar to other American magazines of the time. Mary Beth Norton has found that magazines were often in the forefront of a new approach to women, an approach that emphasized a more active and equal participation of women in family life, household management, and the education of children. This new approach still placed woman's sphere within the home and family. But home and family had now taken on a somewhat larger and more political role in the nurture of the new Republic.[50]

Despite all the diversity, however, several important themes recur. Virtue, for example, was commonly portrayed as *public* virtue. The golden rule was taken very seriously by the contributors to the *New-York Magazine*. "Amongst the number of public virtues we may note love to our country, zeal in promoting the good of society, seeking the good of our neighbor in all our conduct," wrote the author of a piece called "On Virtue." Similarly, even the deeply religious "Juvenis" stopped far short of arguing that virtue is a private matter between a man and God. If a man is virtuous, he wrote, "he has sacrificed his own interest rather than wrong his neighbor. He has been benevolent to his fellow men. The children of poverty and affliction he has assisted and consoled."[51] Women's virtue was usually portrayed as a more private matter of "morality and piety," but the relationship between women's virtue and the welfare of the community was sometimes suggested—for example, in an essay on women's education by a Philadelphia schoolgirl in the magazine's first issue.[52] In short, the connection between virtue and commonwealth was vividly clear in the pages of the *New-York Magazine*.

Another recurrent theme was suspicion of luxury. On this theme, the aphorisms abounded: "Luxury and idleness are similar in their effects—By the former, families are reduced to indigence, and are involved in misery and ruin; by means of the latter, they are prevented from arriving at a comfortable situation in life." The parables and allegories were equally common. In one, Wealth and Poverty meet each other on life's road at the end of their journeys. In a piece called "On Avarice," the author argued that "the avaricious man regards nothing but his purse; the welfare and prosperity of his country never much employs his thoughts. . . . He is a stranger to public spiritedness." The theme was always that luxury is self-defeating because it is self-serving.[53] "Juvenis" perhaps expressed it most clearly: the virtuous man "has never indulged himself in luxury or any kind of excess, and used every exertion to promote the welfare of society."[54]

A third recurrent theme was the power and democracy of knowledge. In America, everyone had a right and a duty to participate in the life of the mind. Some writers put this theme rather bluntly. In a paean to science, one writer declared,

It is indeed questionable whether an ignorant people can be happy, or even exist, under what Americans call a free government. It may be also doubted, whether a truly enlightened people were ever enslaved. Science is so meliorating in its influence upon the human mind, that even he who holds the reins of power, and hath felt its rays, loses the desire of a tyrant, and is best gratified in the sense of public love and admiration. Liberty is a plant which as naturally flourishes under this genial light, as despotism is engendered by the horrors of intellectual darkness.[55]

In more subtle form, this theme ran through many of the articles in the *New-York Magazine* in 1790. Women, for example, were urged "to attend to the cultivation of letters"—and not simply because of the obligations of "republican motherhood." One writer advocated education for women partly for their own "happiness." In old age, when their traditional feminine pleasures had faded, they could take "refuge in the bosom of knowledge."[56] Even "Philobiblicus," the master of erudition, argued that instruction in Latin and Greek should be central to a "republican education," for in a republic everyone should be and could be a scholar.[57]

In this, the magazine reflected a widespread American belief that diffusion of knowledge was beneficial for republican government and for the virtue of the people. Though classical republican thinkers were sometimes rather skeptical of education for the masses, Americans were almost wholly for it.[58] Benjamin Rush, Noah Webster, Thomas Jefferson, and many others argued passionately that education must be the foundation of republican government. But they went farther than simply praising education. They stressed the broadest possible diffusion of knowledge through universal participation in public schools. As Rush put it, "A free government can only exist in an equal diffusion of literature." To this end, Rush proposed not only public schools and state universities, but also a wider diffusion of libraries and newspapers. "I consider it possible to convert men into republican machines," he declared in a now-famous quotation. "This must be done if we expect them to perform their parts properly in the great machine of the government of the state."[59] Of course, these men supported the diffusion of education and knowledge precisely because they believed it would have a conservative influence on the nation. The fear of mass education per se, which was widespread in England, never took root in America.[60] In American republican ideology, everyone had the right and the duty to participate in the life of the mind.

Public virtue, suspicion of luxury, and the power and democracy of knowledge—these were republican themes, and they were freighted with meaning for eighteenth-century Americans, perhaps especially American artisans. Of course, these themes did not appear in every story and article in the *New-York Magazine*. But they were common enough to run like brightly colored threads through the great diversity of material, from heavy political discourse to ethereal romance. This,

then, was what the readers of the *New-York Magazine*—the shopkeepers and artisans, as well as the merchants and politicians—were
reading in 1790.

Conclusion

In its first issue in January 1790, the *New-York Magazine* published an
article entitled "On the Means of Preserving Public Liberty." It provides a summary of what might be called a republican ideology of
magazine reading. "Information," the article said, had been the main-
spring of the Revolution, and it must now be the wellspring of the new
Republic. The author continued:

> A few enlightened citizens may be dangerous; let all be enlightened, and
> oppression must cease, by the influence of a ruling majority; for it can
> never be their interest to indulge a system incompatible with the rights of
> freemen. Those institutions are the most effectual guards to public liberty
> which diffuse the rudiments of literature among a people. . . . A few
> incautious expressions in our constitution, or a few salaries of office too
> great for the contracted feelings of those who do not know the worth of
> merit and integrity, can never injure the United States, while literature is
> generally diffused, and the plain citizen and planter reads and judges for
> himself. . . . Disseminate science through all grades of people, and it will
> forever vindicate your rights.[61]

This sentiment, of course, was not confined to America. The claim
to equal access to knowledge, as well as to political power, was central
to the new revolutionary spirit of Europe. The old regimes of both
France and England were notoriously fearful of the power of information and reading, as Richard Altick and Robert Darnton have made
clear.[62] The American elites were likewise impressed by the power of
information, but they tended to be less fearful of reading—perhaps
because so much reading matter remained fundamentally supportive
of the values of American republicanism. The literature of the *New-
York Magazine*, for example, was not a popular, democratic literature
produced by or even directed toward the lower classes. This kind of
modern mass media would not emerge in the United States until the
nineteenth century.[63] Yet neither was this an aristocratic literature,
accessible only to the elite. The readership was broader than this. It
was instead a kind of republican literature with a republican purpose.
It affirmed the traditional values, while inviting all (except the truly
poor) to take part. Like politics, it was an arena in which artisans and
shopkeepers could participate in public life—in this case the cultural
life—of the new nation. And participation, not social revolution, was
what artisan republicanism was all about.

Appendix A: Notes on Method

As far as I have been able to determine, this study is the first readership research based upon the subscription list of an eighteenth-century magazine. The methods that I used were fairly simple. I started with the list of 370 subscribers published in the *New-York Magazine; or, Literary Repository* 1 (1790): iii–vi. The list itself identified 298 of these as residents of New York City. I located information on 265 of these New Yorkers in city directories or, in a few cases, in the biographical sources cited in the notes. The directories I used were the *New-York Directory and Register* (New York, 1789 and 1790) and the *New-York Directory and Register* (New York, 1791 and 1792). I also drew a random sample of 400 entries from the 1790 directory. These two groups—the subscriber census and the random sample—provided the data for the reader analysis.

Of course, some people do not appear in these directories. Women, for instance, appear only if they were heads of households. In my random sample, only 7.8 percent were women, and almost all of them were identified by occupation (58 percent) or listed as widows (35 percent). Furthermore, historians have usually assumed that common laborers, especially mariners, were substantially underrepresented and that vagrants and transients were not listed at all. Yet I also found the opposite to be true as well—that is, a few of the wealthy merchants on the subscription list did not appear in the city directories. I identified them from other biographical sources. Since I was able to trace only well-to-do people, not poor people, in these other sources, my survey of subscribers may be even more upwardly biased. On the other hand, because some of the incipient manufacturers in New York in 1790 still sometimes listed themselves as artisans, there is a countervailing downward bias in the survey as well. Overall, I tend to agree with Carl Kaestle that the New York directories from the 1790s probably provide a fairly reliable representation of the range of occupations in the city. See Carl F. Kaestle, *The Evolution of an Urban School System: New York City, 1750–1850* (Cambridge, Mass., 1973), 31–32. I'm confident partly because I was able to trace all but thirty-three of the New York subscribers. Moreover, if there is an upper-class bias in my survey, that would, of course, have a conservative effect upon the conclusions of the study, undercounting those at the lower end of the economic scale. This also gives me some confidence in my suggestion that shopkeepers and artisans made up about 50 percent of the readers of the magazine.

The classification of occupations in Table 4.1 and Appendix B is based largely upon my own understanding of late-eighteenth-century employment, but it does not differ radically from the schemes used by other historians, such as Carl Kaestle and Howard Rock. See also Michael B. Katz, "Occupational Classification in History," *Journal of Interdisciplinary History* 3 (Summer 1972): 63–88. Several of the occupations in the professional category (such as clerk and local government official) are perhaps out of place there. Similarly, gardener, nurseryman, and widow may not belong in the nonskilled category. But these involve so few individuals that I don't believe the argument is distorted. Furthermore, the identical classification scheme was used for both the subscriber census and the random sample, so the comparative statements should be fairly reliable.

For the content analysis, I simply classified articles by topic. The unit of analysis was the individual article or story, though certain standard groupings of items were counted only once per issue. These included "American Muse," a collection of poems in each issue; "Intelligence," a monthly collection of short news items; "Marriages" and "Deaths"; and "Congressional Affairs," excerpts from the proceedings of Congress (coded as "politics"). I did not code the copperplate engravings at the beginning of each issue. I did not code advertisements, because in 1790 there were none. Fine distinctions among categories are not important for the argument. The aim was simply to get a general idea of the manifest content of the editorial matter in the magazine. The simple intercoder reliability coefficient for the content analysis was approximately .85, with most of the ambiguity within the "manners and morals" category (Table 4.5).

Appendix B: Occupation List of Subscribers

1. Professional:
   - attorney
   - benevolent society
   - clerk
   - college (institutional subscriber)
   - federal government official
   - local government official
   - military officer
   - minister
   - physician
   - student (college)
   - teacher

2. Merchant:
   - banker
   - broker
   - insurer
   - merchant

3. Shopkeeper:
   - boarding house
   - bookstore
   - grocer
   - porter house
   - ship chandler
   - store or shopkeeper

ironmonger
jewelry store
livery stable
paint and glass store

tavern
tobacco store
vendue master

4. Artisan:

baker
barber
bookbinder
brewer
butcher
cabinetmaker
carpenter
carver and gilder
chairmaker
chandler
clock and watchmaker
coach painter
cooper
copperplate printer
coppersmith
cutler
dancing master
distiller
furrier
glover

gold- and silversmith
hatter
mason
mathematical
  instrument maker
nail maker
pewterer
pilot
printer
saddler
sailmaker
sea captain
ship carpenter
ship joiner
shoemaker
tailor or mantua maker
tanner or currier
type founder
upholsterer
weaver
whitesmith

5. Nonskilled:

gardener
nurseryman

washer
widow

Notes

Reprinted from *American Quarterly* 40, no. 1 (March 1988).

1. Preface, *New-York Magazine; or, Literary Repository* 1 (1790): viii. Mathew Carey, proprietor of the *American Museum* magazine in Philadelphia, was similarly proud of the respectability and character of his subscribers. See preface, *American Museum* 2 (1787).

2. Frank Luther Mott, *A History of American Magazines, 1741–1850* (Cambridge, Mass., 1930), 115–16; and James Playsted Wood, *Magazines in the United States,* 3d ed. (New York, 1971), 26.

3. Carl F. Kaestle, "The History of Literacy and the History of Readers," in

Review of Research in Education, vol. 12, ed. Edmund W. Gordon (Washington, D.C., 1985).

4. Edward Countryman. *A People in Revolution: The American Revolution and Political Society in New York, 1760–1790* (Baltimore, Md., 1981), 294.

5. Bernard Bailyn, *The Ideological Origins of the American Revolution* (Cambridge, Mass., 1967); J. G. A. Pocock, *The Machiavellian Moment: Florentine Political Thought and the Atlantic Republican Tradition* (Princeton, N.J., 1975). For recent reviews of this literature, see Linda Kerber, "The Republican Ideology of the Revolutionary Generation," *American Quarterly* 37 (Fall 1985): 474–95; Robert E. Shalhope, "Republicanism and Early American Historiography," *William and Mary Quarterly* 39 (April 1982); 334–56; Lance Banning, "Jeffersonian Ideology Revisited: Liberal and Classical Ideas in the New American Republic," *William and Mary Quarterly* 43 (January 1986): 3–19; and James T. Kloppenberg, "The Virtues of Liberalism: Christianity, Republicanism, and Ethics in Early American Political Discourse," *Journal of American History* 74 (June 1987): 9–33.

6. Louis Hartz, *The Liberal Tradition in America* (New York, 1955); Joyce Appleby, *Capitalism and a New Social Order: The Republican Vision of the 1790s* (New York, 1984); and John Patrick Diggins, *The Lost Soul of American Politics: Virtue, Self-Interest, and the Foundations of Liberalism* (New York, 1984). For a recent review of this literature, see Joyce Appleby, "Republicanism in Old and New Contexts," *William and Mary Quarterly*, 43 (January, 1986): 20–34. See also Joyce Appleby, "Introduction: Republicanism and Ideology," *American Quarterly*, 37 (Fall 1985): 461–73.

7. Eric Foner, *Tom Paine and Revolutionary America* (New York, 1976); Gary B. Nash, *The Urban Crucible: Social Change, Political Consciousness, and the Origins of the American Revolution* (Cambridge, Mass., 1979); Dirk Hoerder, *Crowd Action in Revolutionary Massachusetts, 1765–1780* (New York, 1977); and Edward Countryman, *The American Revolution* (New York, 1985). See also Alfred F. Young, ed., *The American Revolution: Explorations in the History of American Radicalism* (DeKalb, Ill., 1976); and Dorothy Ross, "The Liberal Tradition Revisited and the Republican Tradition Addressed," in *New Directions in American Intellectual History*, ed. John Higham and Paul K. Conkin (Baltimore, Md., 1979).

8. Appleby, "Republicanism," 21; and Appleby, "Introduction," 469. See also Shalhope, "Republicanism," 337.

9. Kerber, "Republican Ideology," 492–95.

10. Sidney I. Pomerantz, *New York: An American City, 1783–1803* (New York, 1938), 24–25, 460–61; Frank Monaghan and Marvin Lowenthal, *This Was New York: The Nation's Capital in 1789* (Garden City, N.Y., 1943), 33–34; and Martha J. Lamb and [Mrs.] Burton Harrison, *History of the City of New York: Its Origins, Rise, and Progress* (New York, 1896), 3:11. The most detailed account of day-to-day events in New York City during this era is I. N. Phelps Stokes, *The Iconography of Manhattan Island*, vol. 5 (New York, 1926).

11. See Table 4.1. See also Sean Wilentz, *Chants Democratic: New York City and the Rise of the American Working Class, 1788–1850* (New York, 1984), 27; and Carl F. Kaestle, *The Evolution of an Urban School System: New York City, 1750–1850* (Cambridge, Mass., 1973), 31. For a discussion of my sampling and classification methods, see Appendix A.

12. Pomerantz, *New York*, 209–25; and Wilentz, *Chants Democratic*, 24–35. See also David Montgomery, "The Working Classes of the Pre-Industrial American City, 1780–1830," *Labor History* 9 (Winter 1968): 3–22.

13. Countryman, *People in Revolution*, 292–94. See also Staughton Lynd, "The Mechanics in New York Politics, 1774–1785," in *Class Conflict, Slavery, and the United States Constitution: Ten Essays* (Indianapolis, Ind., 1967).

14. Wilentz, *Chants Democratic*, 14.

15. Ibid., 102. See also Foner, *Tom Paine*.

16. Gordon S. Wood, *The Creation of the American Republic, 1776–1787* (New York, 1972), 606–15. See also Kerber, "Republican Ideology," 494; and *"The Creation of the American Republic, 1776–1787:* A Symposium of Views and Reviews," *William and Mary Quarterly* 44 (July 1987): 549–640.

17. Wilentz, *Chants Democratic*, 95. See also Howard B. Rock, *Artisans of the New Republic: The Tradesmen of New York City in the Age of Jefferson* (New York, 1979).

18. Webster quoted in Monaghan and Lowenthal, *This Was New York*, 147. See also Gary Coll, "Noah Webster, Magazine Editor and Publisher," *Journalism History* 11 (Spring/Summer 1984): 26–31.

19. Pomerantz, *New York*, 19–21, 155–59, 199–200; and Thomas E. V. Smith, *The City of New York in the Year of Washington's Inauguration, 1789* (New York, 1889), 5–7.

20. Quotation from preface, *New-York Magazine* 2 (1791): iv. Little has been written about the *New-York Magazine*. For brief sketches, see Mott, *History of American Magazines*, 114–16; William Loring Andrews, "The First Illustrated Magazine Published in New York," in *The Old Booksellers of New York, and Other Papers* (New York, 1895); Kenneth Scott and Kristin L. Gibbons, eds., *The New-York Magazine Marriages and Deaths, 1790–1797* (New Orleans, La., 1975); and Mary Rives Bowman, "Dunlap and 'The Theatrical Register' of the *New-York Magazine*," *Studies in Philology* 24 (July 1927): 413–25. Incidentally, Isaiah Thomas's *Massachusetts Magazine* also survived eight years.

21. Editorial announcement, *New-York Magazine* 1 (March 1790): n.p. See also Mott, *History of American Magazines*, 34; and Pomerantz, *New York*, 216.

22. *New-York Magazine* 1 (May 1790): 256–58; and C. Lennart Carlson, *The First Magazine: A History of the Gentleman's Magazine* (Providence, R. I., 1938). Adams quoted in Monaghan and Lowenthal, *This Was New York*, 34.

23. *New-York Magazine* 1 (April 1790): 197. I have modernized eighteenth-century spelling and capitalization.

24. By comparison, the new nation's largest-circulation magazine, the

American Museum, had about twelve hundred and fifty subscribers. See the subscription list published with the *American Museum* 2 (1787). See also Mott, *History of American Magazines,* 101.

25. Of course, some of the thirty-three subscribers that I couldn't trace may have been from the bottom occupational groups. If Table 4.1 is biased, it seems likely that it is biased upward. See Appendix A for a discussion of this issue. For a complete list of subscriber occupations, see Appendix B.

26. Smith, *City of New York,* 99. The ads are from Monaghan and Lowenthal, *This Was New York,* 52–53, 71. See also Pomerantz, *New York,* ch. 4.

27. Information on prominent individuals came from several biographical sources, including Margherita Arlina Hamm, *Famous Families of New York,* 2 vols. (New York, 1901); Lyman Horace Weeks, ed., *Prominent Families of New York,* rev. ed. (New York, 1898); and James Grant Wilson, ed., *Memorial History of the City of New York,* vol. 5 (New York, 1893).

28. On Duer, see Pomerantz, *New York,* 181. On Benson and Duane, see Countryman, *People in Revolution,* passim.

29. Smith, *City of New York,* 108; and Pomerantz, *New York,* 197.

30. *New-York Directory and Register* (New York, 1789), 117; and Smith, *City of New York,* 107. On the General Society, see Wilentz, *Chants Democratic,* 38–39 and passim. On Anthony Post, see Lynd, "Mechanics," 82, 107–8.

31. Andrews, "First Illustrated Magazine," 60.

32. L. Leary, "Unrecorded Early Verse by William Dunlap," *American Literature* 39 (March 1967): 87–88.

33. For notes on the content analysis method, see Appendix A. For a general description of the content of eighteenth-century magazines, see Mott, *History of American Magazines,* ch. 2.

34. Carlson, *First Magazine,* vii, 58. The passion for a wide variety of factual, scientific information in magazines had its counterpart in eighteenth-century European book publishing, most notably the success of the *Encyclopédie* in France. See Robert Darnton, *The Business of Enlightenment: A Publishing History of the Encyclopédie, 1775–1800* (Cambridge, Mass., 1979).

35. *New-York Magazine* 1 (May 1790): 257–58.

36. Wood, *Creation of the American Republic,* 104. See also Neil Harris, *The Artist in American Society: The Formative Years, 1790–1860* (New York, 1966).

37. *New-York Magazine* 1 (January 1790): 4.

38. Ibid. 1 (August 1790): 442. See also ibid. 1 (February 1790): 104–6.

39. Ibid. 1 (January 1790): 21. See also ibid. 1 (February 1790): 104–6.

40. Ibid. 1 (April 1790): 212–18; 1 (August 1790): 467–69.

41. The first segment is explicitly on the British constitution. See ibid. 1 (January 1790): 41–47. On Adams and this book, see Wood, *Creation of the American Republic,* ch. 14; and Diggins, *Lost Soul,* ch. 3.

42. This tale begins in *New-York Magazine* 1 (January 1790): 10–15; it ends in ibid. 1 (July 1790): 385–87. This is a translation of a romance by

Madame la Comptesse de Genlis, a popular French writer of sentiment and sensation.

43. Ibid. 1 (January 1790): 9; and Linda K. Kerber, *Women of the Republic: Intellect and Ideology in Revolutionary America* (Chapel Hill, N.C., 1980), 235–36.

44. *New-York Magazine* 1 (June 1790): 335–36.

45. Ibid. 1 (April 1790): 198.

46. Ibid. 1 (January 1790): 16–17, 51; 1 (March 1790): 160.

47. Ibid. 1 (January 1790): 22–23; 1 (March 1790): 160–61; 1 (November 1790): 646–48.

48. Richard D. Altick, *The English Common Reader: A Social History of the Mass Reading Public, 1800–1900* (Chicago, 1957), 45.

49. *New-York Magazine* 1 (September 1790): 515–16; 1 (October 1790): 563–65; 1 (February 1790): 90; 1 (December 1790): 694–95.

50. Mary Beth Norton, *Liberty's Daughters: The Revolutionary Experience of American Women, 1750–1800* (Boston, 1980), 246–50. See also Kerber, "Republican Ideology," 484–85, and *Women of the Republic*, 11–12; and Karen K. List, "Magazine Portrayals of Women's Role in the New Republic," *Journalism History* 13 (Spring 1986): 64–70.

51. *New-York Magazine* 1 (March 1790): 152–53; 1 (August 1790): 442.

52. Ibid. 1 (January 1790): 40–41.

53. Ibid. 1 (January 1790): 28–29; 1 (March 1790): 159, 162; 1 (January 1790): 18; 1 (February 1790): 113.

54. Ibid. 1 (August 1790): 442.

55. Ibid. 1 (May 1790): 295.

56. Ibid. 1 (February 1790): 90.

57. Ibid. 1 (February 1790): 89–90; 1 (October 1790): 585–86.

58. Eugene F. Miller, "On the American Founders' Defense of Liberal Education in a Republic," *Review of Politics* 46 (January 1984): 65–90. See also Eva Brann, *Paradoxes of Education in a Republic* (Chicago, 1979).

59. Benjamin Rush, "A Plan for the Establishment of Public Schools and the Diffusion of Knowledge in Pennsylvania" (1786), rpt. in *Essays on Education in the Early Republic*, ed. Frederick Rudolph (Cambridge, Mass., 1965), 3, 8, 17. See also Daniel Calhoun, *The Intelligence of a People* (Princeton, N.J., 1973), ch. 2; and Wilson Smith, ed., *Theories of Education in Early American, 1655–1819* (Indianapolis, Ind., 1973).

60. Altick, *English Common Reader*, ch. 3; Carl F. Kaestle, *Pillars of the Republic: Common Schools and American Society, 1780–1860* (New York, 1983), 33–34.

61. *New-York Magazine* 1 (January 1790): 24–25.

62. Altick, *English Common Reader*, ch. 3; Robert Darnton, "Reading, Writing, and Publishing in Eighteenth-Century France: A Case Study in the Sociology of Literature," *Daedalus* 100 (Winter 1971): 243–44.

63. David D. Hall, "Introduction: The Uses of Literacy in New England, 1600–1850," in *Printing and Society in Early America*, ed. William L. Joyce et al. (Worcester, Mass., 1983); David Paul Nord, "The Evangelical Origins of

Mass Media in America, 1815–1835," *Journalism Monographs* no. 88 (May 1984); and Michael Schudon, *Discovering the News: A Social History of American Newspapers* (New York, 1978), ch. 1. The same might be said of England, France, and Germany. See Altick, *English Common Reader;* and Darnton, "What Is the History of Books?" *Daedalus* 111 (Summer 1982): 78–79 (reprinted in this volume). See also Paul J. Korshin, ed., *The Widening Circle: Essays on the Circulation of Literature in Eighteenth-Century Europe* (Philadelphia, 1976).

Chapter Five

The Word in Black and White

Ideologies of Race and
Literacy in Antebellum
America

Dana Nelson Salvino

Mistress, in teaching me the alphabet,
had given me the *inch*, and no
precaution could prevent me from
taking the *ell*.
Frederick Douglass

In a class on early black American literature, students reading Frederick Douglass's *Narrative* decide that the most important message in the work is that literacy leads to freedom, that literacy *constitutes* freedom. And at my further questioning, they unanimously agree that the same holds true today: literacy and education are the avenue to social and economic advancement.

In their consensus, these students reflect a powerful view held throughout the Western world, and especially in America: knowledge is freedom. Particularly, knowledge begins with literacy, and freedom is constituted by the possibility of moral, economic, and social advancement. America has prided itself from the first on its liberal and liberating attitude toward literacy and education. Noah Webster exhorts the young nation in 1790: "Americans, unshackle your minds and act like independent beings. You have been children long enough, subject to the control and subservient to the interest of a haughty parent. You have now an interest of your own to augment and defend: you have an empire to raise and support. . . . To effect these great objects, it is necessary to frame a liberal plan of policy and build it on a broad system of education."[1] During the following century, America developed a system of education that was "common"—public—to all, established to disseminate literacy and knowledge and to promote the freedoms upheld in the American Constitution. Early educators like Samuel Harrison Smith hoped to foster a worldwide recognition and experience of the benefits of literacy.[2] His high aspirations are reflected in programs like those of UNESCO (United Nations Educational, Scientific, and Cultural Organization), which sponsors major efforts to boost literacy rates in so-called "underdeveloped" nations. And only recently, as Harvey Graff reminds us, the U.S. Postal Service designed a stamp that reflected this same ethic in its motto: "The ability to write. The root of democracy."[3]

What we see is a particular belief elevated throughout the history of our nation to a moral plane. The belief in the efficacy of literacy holds powerful currency. Students of literacy—linguists, psychologists, historians, anthropologists, sociologists, and ethnographers— have traditionally assumed this belief as a fact, finding direct correlations between the acquisition of literacy, on the one hand, and economic and technological progress, on the other, as well as advancement in the intellectual and cognitive skills of individuals and societies. Brian Street, in his excellent *Literacy in Theory and Practice*, proposes that studies of this type represent the "autonomous" model of literacy. Researchers such as Angela Hildyard and David Olson, and Patricia Greenfield, as Street summarizes, support efforts in compulsory schooling by arguing that the acquisition of literacy marks the cognitive difference between "the intellectual resources of Savage and Modern minds."[4] The general tendency in professional studies of literacy has been, as Bernard Bailyn observed many years ago, to view education and literacy as the "last and highest form of evolution," a view that has served as much to justify the life of the profession as to explicate its origins. Thus studies of American educational history have proliferated, yet "we have almost no historical leverage on the problems of American education."[5]

In recent years, however, scholars have begun to qualify findings based on assumptions of the supreme efficacy of literacy. Kenneth Lockridge, in his 1974 study of literacy in colonial New England, delivers an early warning against overestimating the functional powers of literacy.[6] William Gilmore closely examines the limitations of data-collecting procedures. He questions the validity of conclusions based on literacy signing rates, arguing for "multiple-moment research" as a possible corrective.[7] Patricia Herman aptly reminds us that the definition and measures of literacy have changed through time, which must limit our use of early educators' statements and statistics[8]; and Cathy N. Davidson, in her study of the rise of the American novel, observes that we should be skeptical of any definition of literacy, which will always "serve the interest of some larger argument."[9] As studies continue to suggest careful qualification, many have begun to urge us to reconsider our very attitudes toward literacy, to examine the ideological construct of literacy and its cultural roots. In this view, the power of literacy results not directly from learning the ABC's (which Harvey Graff designates the "literacy myth"), but rather from a powerful set of beliefs that accompanies the act of learning to read and write. Brian Street proposes an "ideological" model to counter the blind spots he perceives in the "autonomous" model of literacy. Street argues that the formal model has erred in viewing literacy as merely a tool or technology: "Literacy, of course, is more than just the 'technology' in which it is manifest. . . . It is a social process, in which particular socially constructed technologies are used within particular institutional frameworks for specific social purposes."[10]

These studies and others insist that any account of a given system of literacy must consider the reciprocal relation of literacy and culture. Accordingly, the present study examines the ideological contexts of literacy in America during the antebellum period, specifically as those contexts concerned the acquisition (or nonacquisition) of literacy among Afro-Americans. It will posit and explore an elemental relationship between the ways in which white citizens conceived of white literacy, and the ways in which they conceived of black (particularly slave) literacy. The relationship between these two apparently opposed concepts is crucial: the white concept of white literacy in early America can be said to have shaped white institutional stances toward black literacy during the antebellum period. To dismiss the contradiction apparent between the two with an "of course" is to oversimplify the complex ways in which the first predicts the second, and to gloss over the social context that guarantees the latter from the former. Rather than conceive of the ideology of literacy in early America as hypocritical or "falsifying," we should explore it as a "cultural imperative."[11] Examining the ideology of early American literacy as "part of a cultural system in which it is seen as a link between the mandates (or prerogatives) of the culture and individual behavior"[12] also enables us to begin to understand how slaves were able to turn the ideology of literacy to their own uses in gaining freedom, but how the fundamentally white ideological formation kept them socially segregated once free.

I

In any consideration of the institutional ideology of literacy in early America, Davidson and Gilmore urge us to account for levels of literacy; Lee Soltow and Edward Stevens ask us to place "particular literacy" in perspective. Since the colonial period, literacy has been attached to socializing functions, and what we must remember is that along with learning *how* to read, students also learned *what* to read.

Literacy was functional only in terms of a "moral imperative and proper socialization." It was a tool for democratization in the sense of integration, as well as a tool for stratification or differentiation.[13]

We can see in the early models projected for education an emphasis on students learning a proper subordination in the course of their democratic education. Says Benjamin Rush in his "Plan for the Establishment of Public Schools" (1786), "In the education of youth, let the authority of our masters be as *absolute* as possible. The government of schools like the government of private families should be *arbitrary*, that it may not be *severe*. By this mode of education, we prepare our youth for the subordination of laws and thereby qualify them for becoming good citizens of the republic."[14] Rush continues, a "reinforcement of *prejudice*" is educationally necessary to ensure the continuation of the current political system.[15] The primary goal of education, then, is to produce "one general and uniform system of education, [which] will render the mass of people more homogeneous and thereby fit them more easily for uniform and peaceable government."[16]

As Shirley Brice Heath observes in an essay on nineteenth-century concepts of writing and education, concepts of literacy were closely linked with ideals of "citizenry"[17]—including attendant valuations of morality and place. When Noah Webster urges that "classing is necessary,"[18] he perhaps means to class by academic achievement; however, he does not clearly specify, and it was commonplace for early American academic institutions to class by the student's social status. And while Robert Coram deplores the link he discerns between the arbitrary distribution of property and the degraded social position of certain classes of people, he proposes a system of education that will provide equality "without disturbing the established rules of property."[19] According to Coram's own analysis, it is impossible for the system to provide complete equality without upsetting those very "established rules." Many early American statesmen and educators acted out this paradox: while supporting equal education, they also endorsed hierarchy and stratification.

Educators also emphasized notions of utility, in education and in the nation's citizenry. The ideal established by many was an education suitable to the student: students should not be required to learn what they would never use in their material life. Farmers had no need to learn Latin to transact business efficiently; girls had no need for metaphysics or political science. Further, educators endorsed educational utility at a national level as well: education should include what citizens need to know to keep the nation running smoothly.

Hand in hand with notions of utility came notions of propriety, the ways in which students could properly exercise their literacy. In promoting a certain formation of literacy, as a means to certain kinds of ideals in a certain kind of society, educators, Soltow and Stevens point out, "were clearly aware of the possibility that, in the absence of control over reading habits, literacy might not achieve its intended goal. . . . Thus it was imperative that an ideology of literacy speak directly to the moral consequences of literacy and that pedagogues carefully select that reading most suited to their perceptions of proper socialization."[20] Educators sought to control not only what was read, but how one wrote. As Robert Pattison observes, "In the context of . . . [American civilization], it is not enough to know how to read and write; the state insists that one know how to do these according to a uniform standard of correct form."[21] These notions of correctness—from Webster's American usages to exhortations against novel reading—are as important to our understanding of the ideology of literacy in early America as the concepts of liberty and democracy that they also encourage.

This is not to suggest any lack of good will and high ideals among early American educators and statesmen, but to propose that we see the ways in which their own acceptance of social stratification played into their plans for education. Putting it most bluntly, we might say that the educational system established in early America did not encourage students to create their own possibilities as much as it enumerated and defined those possibilities in a way that taught the student his (or her[22]) social place. While early educators recognized the right to an education of many who had not traditionally been accorded that right, they also put in place an educational system that would not radically alter the existing social balance. Hence, elementary education was "common" to all, but not higher education. The rhetoric that often surrounded justifications for educating the lower class most often addressed "making them acceptable to us"; teaching the lower classes order and decency provides greater stability for the community (they won't steal from us) and the nation (they won't overthrow us). Similarly, alternative industrial or vocational schools sprang up during the nineteenth century, promising an education useful to the student, but also useful to a capitalist class system.[23]

As the flip side of the coin, early Americans constructed a view of literacy and education as powerfully enabling[24]—literacy as currency in the New World. The Puritans had constituted literacy as a sort of moral specie, a means to proper virtue and knowledge. Wider literacy was read by the community as a sign of greater moral accumulation—recall the elite status of Puritan erudition. By the late eighteenth and early nineteenth centuries, as Harvey Graff observes, "the moral bases of literacy accompanied a shift from a *moral* economy to a *political* economy."[25] The new political economy, which incorporated nationalism into the ideology of literacy, also introduced new notions of literacy as a means to individual and national progress—a concept with distinctly pecuniary associations. Notably, the early moral concept of literacy did not clash with the newer vision of literacy as a means to financial advancement. Rather, as Soltow and Stevens observe, "the moral function of literacy and its value for worldly success were mutually reinforcing."[26] Literacy continued in a tradition of evangelical Protestantism, combining notions of proper allegiance to American ideals with the inculcation of piety and virtue. That financial advantage could assimilate easily into the earlier ideology is not incongruous when considered in view of Puritan concepts of Visible Saints—accumulation of physical wealth was seen as a fairly good indication of eternal election.

Recent scholars have noted an arresting relation between Western concepts of literacy and economic interests. Even commonly accepted connections between literacy and economic status have come into question, and consequently the entire process of collecting data from documents of property has been disputed. As many have pointed out, the degree of literacy that any individual may have been able to attain in early America may have been dependent upon his or her access to books—a scarce commodity. In this way, material possession in some ways arguably precedes literacy, rather than, as Kenneth Lockridge suggests, vice versa.[27] (Relying on property documents to assess literacy rates becomes especially problematic when we begin to consider slave literacy. If we depend upon this method of estimating literacy rates and levels, slaves can only be an index to the literacy of their masters, their own bondage determined by their masters' literacy as embodied in a bill of sale.)

If we recall that books and newspapers were commodities in early America, then we must also consider the economic interest of those whose job it was to distribute the "tools of literacy"—books, paper, writing utensils. Printers and editors had a crucial role in the dissemination of the literacy ideology; while they played a publicly acknowledged moral function, they also had a fundamentally economic interest in the enterprise of literacy.[28] These editors and printers—along with educational reformers like Stephen Simpson, Charles Fenton Mercer, and Horace Mann—widely advertised the specifically economic advantages of increased literacy to their consumer audience.

While many extolled the monetary rewards of literacy, perhaps none spoke so persuasively as Horace Mann. This nineteenth-century educator, as Graff observes, went further than his colleagues and actually sought to document the "productive contribution of common-school training."[29] In his now-famous 1842 *Annual Report of the Secretary of the Board of Education*, Mann asserts an indisputable correlation between literacy and schooling, on the one hand, and occupation, production, and wage earning, on the other. As Maris Vinovskis and Graff both observe, Mann used a dubious method to obtain his information—biased questionnaires sent to friends already polled for agreement.[30] His consequent calculations and conclusions are probably radically overstated. Vinovskis's own findings on the relation between schooling and wage rates virtually negate Mann's conclusions.[31] Yet without tangible proof, early Americans manifested a general belief in the positive link between literacy and financial gain.

II

Culturally, then, literacy carried important currency. We must be careful here to remember the cautions of various studies that those who were not literate in early America do not seem to have been seriously deprived of any important rights and were able to participate fully in the economic, social, and political realms. We should observe, as Soltow and Stevens point out, that illiterates were able to participate in a literate society by making use of the skills of those who were literate.[32] Further, we might speculate that those who were most easily able to "borrow" another's literacy skills had mastered other social codes—acquired different social currency—that compensated for their lack of "literacy capital."[33] In fact, we might generalize that their physical, monetary capital paid for their deficiency in literacy skills. The point we must make here is that it was *white* illiterates who were allowed to participate by borrowing, even buying, the skills of other whites—a privilege completely denied to the black slave and often the free black. Therefore, even this caution about the social participation of illiterates must be set within a larger caution about the role of race in the ideology of literacy in nineteenth-century America.

It was only after the Civil War that white educators began to focus significant energies on black education. Given their apparent awareness of the extent of the social control encouraged by the educational system, it is perhaps surprising that the majority of white statesmen and educators ignored these avenues to controlling blacks before the war. But if we follow the socioeconomic model for education proposed by Pierre Bourdieu and Jean-Claude Passeron, the answer quickly becomes apparent. While the model indicates the relative difficulty of a lower-class member (and a woman, as *feme covert*) in obtaining the linguistic capital necessary for social advancement in antebellum America, it also indicates the near impossibility of a black even being *represented* in the model. A form of capital themselves, slaves were strictly debarred—almost always at the legislative level, perhaps less frequently at a personal level—from acquiring any cultural or monetary capital of their own.[34]

It is important too to note the shifts in attitude among whites toward black education between the Revolution and the Civil War. As Carter G. Woodson summarizes in *The Education of the Negro prior to 1861*, postrevolutionary liberalism led to a more permissive spirit, and to a real interest in educating blacks, free and slave. As the nation became more and more involved in an industrial economy, however, the permissive spirit quickly faded and was replaced by overt antipathy, both in the South, where state after state enacted antiliteracy laws aimed at blacks and at anyone (mostly free blacks or Northerners) who was teaching them, and in the North, where the prejudice manifested itself at the community level as local citizens protested and impeded black schooling efforts.[35]

The ideology of literacy became much more powerfully discriminating during this period. At a time when literacy had become "secularized" and magnified in its cultural efficacy—literacy as a means to morality, citizenship, and prosperity—and when the nation was investing avidly in its own economic prosperity, then especially were blacks denied access to literacy. Literacy had by then been made into a very real enslaving weapon against blacks: legislated into illiteracy, they were held chattel by the power of words in the form of laws legalizing their bondage and tracts confirming their inherent inferiority to whites.

Not surprisingly, white legislators revealed an uneasy awareness of blacks' humanity and intellectual capability in the very rhetoric of the laws passed to prevent those features from being manifested. As a Virginia House delegate summarized after the successful passage of an antieducation bill, "We have, as far as possible, closed every avenue by which light may enter their minds. If we could extinguish their capacity to see the light, our work would be completed; they would then be on a level with the beasts of the field and we should be safe! I am not certain that we would not do it, if we could find out the process, and that on the plea of necessity."[36] The whites who depended so completely upon the transforming effects of their own literacy counted upon legislation against slave literacy to make the slaves into what they clearly were not. By depriving blacks of literacy, whites held their own power to words over blacks. These laws guaranteed white superiority and the security of the white economic system.

But of note as well was the white inability to imagine that slaves might be able to communicate in ways other than those the white community recognized. To say that blacks were denied written literacy is not to say that they were *il*literate. While it is important that we carefully qualify comments about the differences between "literacy" and "orality," Ben Sidran's observations on the general inability of literate culture to perceive the communicative acts of oral culture are to the point.[37] Sidran argues that because oral culture communicates not only through different media but with different styles and emphases, black culture was able work efficiently in the white literate society's blind spot, communicating messages in ways that whites could not begin to understand, especially music—its rhythms, tones, and lyrics. It seems plausible to argue that while whites asserted their literacy as not only the manifestation but the creation of their supremacy, that constructed supremacy also functioned as an Achilles heel.

III

Working within the gap in whites' understanding, many slaves sought an alternative education. They recognized the duplicity of their owners' religious and secular teaching and countered its demeaning message with an affirmation of Afro-American communal values, pride, and "true Christianity."[38] Further, Janet Cornelius marks slave attentiveness to white beliefs about literacy: "Slaves were well aware of the promise of literacy as a path to mobility and increased self-worth. Claims about literacy's intrinsic practical value, espoused by educational reformers in England and the northern U.S., had an impact even in the South."[39] Attitudes about the power of education were persuasive and pervasive, and while many whites tried to teach blacks that literacy was not important for them, whites' own beliefs about its power belied their message.

We must not assume for a moment that literacy was ever easily disseminated among slaves. As Cornelius observes, because of the punishment for offenses, "it may be possible that the [slave] children themselves did not know how many people in a single plantation community might actually possess reading and writing skills."[40] But, as Thomas Webber notes, slaves who did possess those skills were highly valued in the slave community. "Not only could such persons keep the other slaves abreast of the news, write them passes, and read to them straight from the Bible, but they disproved the racist notion promulgated by whites that blacks were incapable of such learning. Stories of literate slaves traveled quickly from plantation to plantation and were a source of great satisfaction within the quarters."[41] Black slaves transmitted among themselves the white belief in the power of literacy, as their post–Civil War enthusiasm for education attested.[42] Notably too, Cornelius's study documents a steady increase in literacy among slaves through the antebellum period, with each decade seeing a rise in the percentage of slaves who were able somehow to acquire some literacy skills.[43]

For white Americans, basic literacy at least was a "free" commodity;[44] for blacks, literacy was something to barter for, even to steal. This metaphor became literal action for the black slave, who traded and finagled his or her way into literacy. For example, nursery attendants sometimes secretly learned to spell by helping white children play with their alphabet blocks. Frederick Douglass recounts his method of challenging white street boys to outperform his printing abilities. Once gained, literacy was a guarded treasure: literacy was what blacks were not supposed to have; literacy, by law, was what enslaved them. The mere fact of blacks' possession of literacy skills turned those skills against white purposes.

It may even be possible, as some have tentatively suggested, to see a direct link between the acquisition of literacy and access to freedom. Harvey Graff's study of three Ontario towns during the nineteenth century documents an average literacy rate for (free) Canadian blacks of over 50 percent in 1861. While we cannot account for the exact number of escaped slaves in Canada, it is well known that many blacks found their way to freedom there. As Graff notes, the figure of 50 percent roughly corresponds with an 1850 census figure for free blacks in the United States. By contrast, various estimates place slave literacy somewhere around 5 percent in 1861.[45] Janet Cornelius suggests an even stronger correlation. She asserts that "slaves who learned to read and write were exceptional people who used their skills in literacy in exceptional ways."[46] Her study finds that a significant portion of those who acquired literacy skills testified to using these skills to escape, and to help others escape; further, a large proportion of those same ex-slaves assumed leadership positions in community, religious, or abolitionist causes. Cornelius concludes, "Some of these community leaders were taught by whites, but the connection between slaves who seized learning for themselves and their subsequent public leadership careers suggests that the belief by slaves in the liberating aspects of literacy as a form of resistance was not unfounded."[47]

What seems important to point up in Cornelius's somewhat broad assertion is that it is not merely the literacy skills alone that were liberating: it is also the underlying belief about the purposes for which those skills can be used. We must be careful to qualify the belief that literacy in and of itself is a liberating force. Pattison argues pointedly against this as the "prisoner phenomenon." For example, Pattison asserts that Malcolm X became "liberated" not by reading, but by the belief that reading was a means to liberation.[48] The ideology of literacy becomes the determining factor. And certainly, access to print provides an informational system not available to the illiterate. It is possible that the acquisition of literacy—supported by the belief that literacy is a means to freedom—led to an increased awareness of the possibilities of escape or resistance to slavery, *and* provided an effective weapon in implementing escape plans.

The very act of publishing a slave narrative subverts white literacy practices and provides the black ex-slave with precisely the weapon that the whites feared: access to the power of the word. Frederick Douglass recounts his dawning awareness of the force of literacy in the epigraph set at the beginning of this essay. From the moment of his recognition, we see how fully he has imbibed the set of beliefs surrounding the concept of literacy in early America. His first actions emphasize the pecuniary nature of literacy. He barters, swapping bread with (presumably white) street urchins, in exchange for spelling skills. Further, Douglass is able to exploit the social economy of literacy by boasting and challenging other boys to show up his writing ability, thereby secretly enabling his own learning process. Douglass wins access to literacy and portrays this process as liberation itself, however painful, pointing the way to knowledge and freedom: "As I read and contemplated the subject, behold! that very discontentment which Master Hugh had predicted would follow my learning to read had already come, to torment and sting my soul to unutterable anguish."[49] Yet it is his belief in the power of his mental skills that guides him to freedom.

Notably, as he uses words to strike out against slavery in the act of narrating his experiences, Douglass refuses to report on the one experience that made possible the writing of his narrative: his escape. And while he apologizes for his lapse from candor, he refuses to tell about any of the means by which slaves escape, hinting instead at a huge communication network among slaves that the white slaveholder cannot access:

I would keep the merciless slaveholder profoundly ignorant of the means of flight adopted by the slave. I would leave him to imagine himself surrounded by myriads of invisible tormentors, ever ready to snatch from his infernal grasp his trembling prey. Let him be left to feel his way in the dark; let darkness commensurate with his crime hover over him; and let him feel that at every step he takes, in pursuit of the flying bondman, he is running the frightful risk of having his hot brains dashed out by an invisible agency.[50]

Here Douglass evokes a vision of the white slaveholder as "illiterate"—victim to a system of knowledge from which he is barred. Douglass's description of the unknowing slaveholder captures the very experience of illiteracy in a literate society, one of fear and powerlessness. In his choice *not* to write of his escape, Douglass manages with fine irony to turn the ideological power of literacy against his captors.

Harriet Ann Jacobs, in her *Incidents in the Life of a Slave Girl* (1861), provides further explicit and striking testimony to the ways in which literacy could be subverted for use against the white master.[51] As a girl, Linda Brent, Jacobs's autobiographical protagonist, was instructed in reading and writing by a kind mistress, who later willed Linda to her three-year-old niece, Emily Flint. Emily's father, the community doctor, is cruel and licentious, and when Linda reaches adolescence, he stalks her relentlessly. When Dr. Flint discovers that Linda can read, he begins to send her suggestive, even pornographic, letters (Jacobs herself preserved none of the actual letters, and her novel only hints at their contents). When Linda escapes from Flint, literally "holing up" in a cranny in her grandmother's cabin roof for seven years, she manages to turn her tormentor's trick against him. By slipping letters addressed to Flint to a fellow slave accompanying his master on a trip to the North, Linda tricks the doctor into believing he can capture her. Ironically, he goes into debt over futile expeditions to retrieve his lost slave. Linda Brent turns Flint's cagey employment of "letters" literally against him.

Occasionally, even slaves who did not have literacy skills were able to use literacy against whites. H. C. Bruce tells how illiterate slaves took advantage of illiterate white slave patrollers. These slaves "would take a portion of a letter picked up and palm it off on them as a pass" when stopped for questioning.[52] The use of literacy as a weapon against whites attests to black beliefs about its pragmatic value.

Slaves also turned white educational practices to their own purposes. For example, they harkened to the notion of self-education promulgated among whites. The little study group that Douglass established on the farm of Mr. Freeland is reminiscent of Benjamin

Franklin's *junta*—even down to the pooling of printed resources: the other slaves on the farm "very soon mustered up some old spelling-books, and nothing would do but that I must keep a Sabbath school."[53]

IV

While blacks embraced and subverted the white ideology of literacy for the freedom it could provide from physical bondage, their hard-earned literacy skills did not mean very much in terms of social and economic acceptance among whites. As Genovese dryly notes, "In that day as in this, an ideology, to triumph, must appeal across class lines even while it justifies the hegemony of that particular class which has the wherewithal to rule."[54] If the ideology of literacy explicitly promised liberty and social integration, implicitly it contained mechanisms for differentiation and selection. Literacy had little or no direct advantage in social and economic terms for free blacks. As Graff points out in his study of blacks in nineteenth-century Ontario, "Illiteracy could be a handicap, especially in its ascriptive associations," but "literacy by itself was no advantage." Among the ethnic groups he surveys, Graff finds that "significantly, the only group able to improve its relative position when illiterate was the blacks. To them, illiteracy was hardly a material handicap when added to that of racial status and discrimination." His conclusion is striking: "To a racial minority, faced with racial discrimination, education brought no discernible benefits, and illiteracy no detriments; race carried an independent influence."[55]

As many ex-slaves painfully testified, a black might be able to read Aeschylus and Homer, yet be able to procure a job no better than one as domestic help or dockworker. Segregated schooling was a two-edged sword. Many black historians have observed that, left alone, black educators were able to pass on black values and culture to their students. However, as Bourdieu and Passeron observe, the most important object of education in a class/capitalistic society is not the content of the education, but the "status authority" conferred by those in power. They argue that

> to reduce the pedagogic relation to a purely communicative relation would make it impossible to account for the specific characteristics it owes to the authority of the pedagogic institution. The mere fact of transmitting a message within a relation of pedagogic communication implies and imposes a social definition . . . of what merits transmission, the code in which the message is to be transmitted, the persons entitled to transmit it, or better, impose its reception, the persons worthy of receiving it

and consequently obliged to receive it, and finally, the mode of imposition and inculcation of the message which confers on the information transmitted its legitimacy and thereby its full meaning.[56]

By dissociating themselves from black educational efforts, whites refused to confer "status authority" and so negated the worth of black education within the white social economy.

V

Literacy could lead blacks out of physical, but not cultural and economic, bondage. They could use their literacy to cease *being* capital but faced even greater difficulty in *accruing* capital and being included in the social economy. As Abdul JanMohamed notes, "The black . . . can never be the subject of (white) culture, only its object."[57] Ultimately, the hegemony of the white ideology of literacy prevailed.

It is imperative that we explore the intricacies of the ideology of literacy for the impact that historical ideologies bequeath to the present. To dismiss apparently contradictory phenomena is to trivialize them, and possibly to pave the way for predictable if slightly different repetitions of the harsh inequalities of antebellum America. It is important also to consider the "economy of literacy" in the context of capitalist societies, to account for the stratification and exclusion that such an economy implies, and how it ensures its own reproduction. While some slaves were able to turn literacy to their own purposes in acquiring physical freedom, whites continued to assert their superiority over both slaves and free blacks. The overt text, if we may speak of it thus, in the ideology of literacy was "freedom," "equality," and "opportunity." But the covert text—a text of stratification and discrimination—was able largely to subvert the social promises that accompanied black acquisition of literacy. Power and knowledge, as Michel Foucault has so extensively detailed in numerous studies, exist in a complex, symbiotic relationship. And it is precisely this relationship that we have been examining here: American beliefs about literacy have historically been about the interplay of power and knowledge, deified, reified. Probing the historical legacy of the ideology of literacy in order to resist it may be a crucial step toward dealing with the educational disparities of our own systems today.

Notes

Epigraph: Frederick Douglass, *Narrative of the Life of Frederick Douglass, an American Slave* (New York, 1982), 82.

1. Noah Webster, "On the Education of Youth in America," in *Essays on Education in the Early Republic*, ed. Frederick Rudolph (Cambridge, Mass., 1965), 77.

2. Samuel Harrison Smith, "Remarks on Education," in ibid, esp. 221–23.

3. Harvey Graff, *The Literacy Myth: Literacy and Social Structure in the Nineteenth-Century City* (New York, 1979), xxi.

4. Brian Street, *Literacy in Theory and Practice* (Cambridge, 1984), 19.

5. See Bernard Bailyn, *Education in the Forming of American Society: Needs and Opportunities for Study* (New York, 1960), 5–16.

6. Kenneth A. Lockridge, *Literacy in Colonial New England: An Enquiry into the Social Context of Literacy in the Early Modern West* (New York, 1974), passim.

7. William J. Gilmore, *Elementary Literacy on the Eve of the Industrial Revolution: Trends in Rural New England, 1760–1830* (Worcester, Mass., 1982).

8. See Patricia Herman, *Southern Blacks: Accounts of Learning to Read before 1861*, Reading Education Report no. 53 (Urbana, Ill., 1985).

9. Cathy N. Davidson, *Revolution and the Word: The Rise of the Novel in America* (New York, 1986), 59.

10. Street, *Literacy,* 97. For other incisive discussions of the ideological underpinnings of literacy, see Robert Pattison, *On Literacy: The Politics of the Word from Homer to the Age of Rock* (New York, 1982); Sylvia Scribner and Michael Cole, *The Psychology of Literacy* (Cambridge, Mass., 1981); and Lee Soltow and Edward Stevens, *The Rise of Literacy and the Common School in the United States: A Socioeconomic Analysis to 1870* (Chicago, 1981).

11. Soltow and Stevens, *Rise of Literacy,* 60.

12. Ibid.

13. Ibid, 19–22.

14. Benjamin Rush, "A Plan for the Establishment of Public Schools," in *Essays on Education,* 16.

15. "Prejudice" had, of course, in the eighteenth-century lexicon, a somewhat more positive inflection than in its current usage.

16. Rush, "Plan for the Establishment," 10.

17. Shirley Brice Heath, "Toward an Ethnohistory of Writing in American Education," in *Writing: The Nature, Development, and Teaching of Written Communication*, ed. Marcia Farr Whiteman (Hillsdale, N.J., 1981), 29.

18. Webster, "Education of Youth," 54.

19. Robert Coram, "Political Inquiries," *Essays on Education,* 112.

20. Soltow and Stevens, *Rise of Literacy,* 61.

21. Pattison, *On Literacy,* 65.

22. For an excellent study of the socializing impact of early American

education on women, see Kathleen Geissler's "The Social Meaning of Women's Literacy in Nineteenth Century America," diss., UCLA, 1986.

23. See, for instance, in a somewhat later context, Donald Spivey's *Schooling for the New Slavery: Black Industrial Education, 1868–1915* (Westport, Conn., 1978).

24. It seems methodologically impossible to discuss literacy in early American ideology separately from notions of education: as Gilmore, Cremin, Soltow and Stevens, and others note, formal education began with literacy (of some sort). Put another way, education was not only accessed through literacy; literacy itself represented that education in many ways.

25. Graff, *Literacy Myth*, 25.

26. Soltow and Stevens, *Rise of Literacy*, 86.

27. See Lockridge, *Literacy in Colonial New England*, 55. "For what it is worth, an elementary analysis indicates that literacy had more to do with access to occupation and so to wealth than wealth had to do with causing individual literacy."

28. See Soltow and Stevens, *Rise of Literacy*, 62. For further discussion, see also Lawrence A. Cremin, *American Education: The Colonial Experience, 1607–1783* (New York, 1970); and Heath, "Ethnohistory of Writing."

29. Graff, *Literacy Myth*, 204.

30. Maris A. Vinovskis, "Horace Mann on the Economic Productivity of Education," *New England Quarterly* 43, no. 3 (1970): 550–71.

31. See ibid., 566–68.

32. Soltow and Stevens, *Rise of Literacy*, 45–46.

33. For a discussion of this term, see Pierre Bourdieu and Jean-Claude Passeron's provocative *Reproduction in Education, Society, and Culture*, trans. Richard Nice (London and Beverly Hills, Calif., 1977).

34. Ibid., 70–106.

35. See Carter G. Woodson, *The Education of the Negro prior to 1861* (New York, 1986), for a more detailed account.

36. Quoted in ibid., 170–71.

37. Ben Sidran, *Black Talk* (New York, 1971), 1–29.

38. See Thomas Webber, *Deep Like the Rivers: Education in the Slave Quarter Community, 1831–1865* (New York, 1978), esp. p. 2, "Black Learning: The Cultural Themes of the Quarter Community," for an excellent discussion of the education transmitted among the slaves themselves.

39. Janet Cornelius, "We Slipped and Learned to Read: Slave Accounts of the Literacy Process, 1830–1865," *Phylon* 44, no. 3 (1983): 181.

40. Ibid., 174.

41. Webber, *Deep Like the Rivers*, 136.

42. See John Hope Franklin, *From Slavery to Freedom: A History of Negro Americans* (New York, 1980), 196–209.

43. Cornelius, "We Slipped and Learned to Read," a study of 272 testimonies of ex-slaves, documents a phenomenal increase in the percentage of slaves who gained some degree of literacy during the period 1800–65. For her study, Cornelius divides the years into four periods, from 1800 to 1835, then

by decade. Markedly, the highest percentages of slaves acquiring literacy occurs during the final period, 1856–65.

44. While I am of course ready to acknowledge the qualifications recently added by literacy studies to the term "free"—that is, farmers may not have been able to afford giving up their sons for "free" education during work hours—relatively speaking, white access to literacy instruction was much freer than slave.

45. Graff, *Literacy Myth,* 68; Cornelius, "We Slipped and Learned to Read," 172.

46. Cornelius, "We Slipped and Learned to Read," 183.

47. Ibid.

48. Pattison, *On Literacy,* 134–37.

49. Douglass, *Narrative,* 84.

50. Ibid., 138.

51. Jean Fagin Yellin, who after exhaustive research calls this work a "well-documented, pseudonymous autobiography," summarizes the parallel experiences of Jacobs and Linda. See Yellin's excellent introduction to Harriet Ann Jacobs's *Incidents in the Life of a Slave Girl* (Cambridge, Mass., 1987).

52. H. C. Bruce, quoted in Webber, *Deep Like the Rivers,* 94.

53. Douglass, *Narrative,* 120.

54. Eugene Genovese, *Roll, Jordan, Roll: The World the Slaves Made* (New York, 1972), 164.

55. Graff, *Literacy Myth,* 76, 77, 81.

56. Bourdieu and Passeron, *Reproduction in Education,* 108–9.

57. Abdul JanMohamed, "Negating the Negation as a Form of Affirmation in Minority Discourse: The Construction of Richard Wright as Subject," *Cultural Critique* 7 (Fall 1987): 261.

Chapter Six

The Life and Times of *Charlotte Temple*

The Biography of a Book

Cathy N. Davidson

One summer day in 1984, while in residence at the American Antiquarian Society, I called for all copies of all editions of America's first best-selling novel, Susanna Haswell Rowson's *Charlotte, a Tale of Truth* (1791), more commonly known as *Charlotte Temple*. Arranged before me were literally dozens and dozens of *Charlotte Temple*s, each one different, each one embodying/reflecting/creating its own history of the book in American culture. For even a quick glance at the assembled volumes affirmed that Charlotte looked different—*was* different—depending upon the dress, the covers and bindings, that she wore. The calf-bound duodecimo destined for the circulating library, the child's size toy book bound for the nursery, the gilt-edged gift book designed for ostentatious display in the middle-class sitting room, the ten-cent story paper marketed for the factory girl, and the contemporary paperback with the scholarly apparatus that signified a university text: each version of Charlotte's story contained its own story about authorship, readership, and publishing in America.

Moreover, the longer I studied the books before me—large and small, ornate and plain—the more I became convinced that what I saw was not just a history of *a* novel but a history of *the* novel as a genre. Concretized by the volumes on the book carts was a new kind of literary history, one that acknowledges that novels are not just texts (as a semiotician might say), not just variant forms of a text (as a bibliographer would use the term), not just plots, characters, metaphors, and images (as the New Critic could point out), not just changing book morphology (as would interest the bibliophile), and not just evolving publishing practices (which should intrigue the historian). On the contrary, the history of the book—and, in this case, the history of the novel—entails a combination of all of these diverse elements and requires dialogue among disciplines that do not always speak the same language.

For illustrative purposes, I am focusing on *Charlotte Temple* precisely because it is a text that could be dismissed as "simple," if analyzed by conventional literary methods, but that becomes far more intriguing when viewed as a novel that, more than any other, signaled a new era in the history of the book in America. How was the novel first published, by what methods, and at what expense (to the author, the publisher, the reader)? How did it make its way across the Atlantic to become America's most enduring bestseller? Like the Marquis de Lafayette, who is a hero in America but simply an obscure French soldier buried in an untended grave in Paris and in the footnotes of French history textbooks, *Charlotte Temple* cut a more impressive figure in the land of her adoption than in the land of her birth. One might even ask if *Charlotte Temple* is the same book after a transatlantic crossing. Did success spoil Charlotte Temple? These are provocative questions (not all of them answerable) from which we can begin to see that literature is not just a matter of words but is a complex form of cultural production that has as much to do with national identities, changing economies, new technologies, and developing patterns of work and leisure as it does with symbols and metaphors. As I shall argue in this paper, an overt and covert cultural agenda, an ideological subtext, is encoded in the writing, publishing, reprinting, binding, titling, retitling, pictorializing, advertising, distributing, marketing, selling, buying, reading, interpreting, and, finally, institutionalizing (within literary criticism and historiography) of any text, even (maybe especially) a seemingly simple allegory of female crime and punishment.

I

A comparison of the original American edition of the novel with the first British edition from which it was copied reveals much about the origins of Anglo-American mass publishing.[1] The first American edition, like its English predecessor, is a simple, unassuming, unillustrated, inexpensive duodecimo volume entitled *Charlotte, a Tale of Truth*. It was published in 1794 in Philadelphia by Mathew Carey, former Irish revolutionary turned American Democrat and an ardent champion of social causes ranging from equitable taxation for farmers and the working class to public charity for the poor, Irish independence, and improved wages for exploited government seamstresses in Philadelphia who were forced to live and work in horrific conditions.[2] It was singularly appropriate that Mathew Carey should be the first American publisher of Susanna Rowson's allegory of the treachery of a British soldier and the subsequent abandonment of a naive fifteen-year-old schoolgirl in America during the Revolutionary War, for Carey had immigrated to America in September of 1784, partly to avoid further imprisonment and prosecution by the British for publishing an Irish nationalist newspaper, the *Volunteer's Journal*. No less a personage than the Marquis de Lafayette lent the twenty-four-year-old immigrant four hundred dollars to set up his printing operation in the capital of a new nation where he would be rewarded (not jailed) for his anti-British nationalism.[3]

Mathew Carey went on to become one of the most prosperous and sagacious publishers of the new Republic. Yet not even Carey predicted that the novel he printed in a run of a thousand copies (a typical size for a first edition of a late-eighteenth-century American novel) would go through over two hundred subsequent editions and become one of his, and America's, all-time bestsellers.[4] As he wrote to the author in 1812, "It may afford you great gratification to know that the sales of *Charlotte Temple* exceed those of any of the most celebrated novels that ever appeared in England. I think the number disposed of must far exceed 50,000 copies; & the sale still continues. . . . I have an edition in press of 3000, which I shall sell at 50 or 60-½ cents each."[5] I hope Susanna Rowson was gratified at this news of her novel's success, for, with no international copyright laws to protect her work, she received little direct material reward from the American editions of her novel.

But then Susanna Rowson probably did not earn much for the original English edition of the novel either. In 1790, William Lane advertised that he would pay "a sum, from Five to One Hundred Guineas," for "Manuscripts of Merit." Surviving book contracts suggest that most authors received payments at the lower end of this scale, and many reportedly worked for a mere half-guinea a novel. At such wages, it is small wonder that a number of Lane's authors often wrote mechanically, merely filling out the details of the publisher's outline or else plagiarized from someone else's novel by substituting a new title page and changing the names and a few situations in the plot. Indeed, Rowson's *Mary, or the Test of Honour* (1789), one of only two books to which she never appended her name and a work she never publicly claimed as her own, seems to have been one of Lane's formula novels.[6]

Susanna Rowson, we must remember, wrote before what Michel

Foucault has called "the birth of the author," the romantic era's glorification of individual genius and creativity in the service of art. Nor did she write under an older (and primarily European) patronage system. The late eighteenth century, in England and even more so in America, was a time of transition in the publishing world, a time when, as Martha Woodmansee has documented, none of the "requisite legal, economic, and political arrangements and institutions were yet in place to support the large number of writers who came forward."[7] Like most novelists in late-eighteenth-century England and every novelist in America before 1820, Rowson was never able to support herself solely by writing novels. That hard economic fact had a tremendous impact on who could afford to write novels, an impact that has not yet been investigated fully by literary historians.[8]

In Rowson's case, the harsh economics of authorship were further exacerbated by her personal situation. She was the breadwinner for herself, her husband, his sister, his sister's children, his illegitimate son, and two adopted children of her own. She managed financially in part because of her prodigious output as a novelist, poet, playwright, essayist, songwriter, and anthologist. Moreover, because the legal and economic rights of eighteenth-century married women were subsumed within their husband's rights, the irresponsible William Rowson received the wages of Susanna's labors, wages, it must be noted, smaller than he (as a male author) would have been likely to receive had he written the books himself. The literary economics of gender, as numerous feminist scholars have noted, further complicate literary history: Susanna Rowson had to supplement her "avocation" as a writer (by social definition, "women writers" were amateurs, even when they wrote to support themselves) with "real" work—as an actress, lecturer, teacher, and founding proprietor of one of early America's foremost women's academies, her Young Ladies' Academy in Massachusetts, an institution over whose operations she exerted full control.[9]

Mathew Carey's edition of Susanna Rowson's *Charlotte, a Tale of Truth* was, considering the liberties taken with many English novels in their translation to America, a remarkably accurate redaction of the original English version that had been published by William Lane at his famous (or infamous) Minerva Press. Here too we can read a story behind the story, for although Carey (unlike his son) was not a major publisher of fiction, he understood the status value of English books for many American readers. Until well into the nineteenth century American publishers pirated popular British novels with great frequency, and often works of American authorship were passed off as English novels and even as Lane novels.[10] Not everyone was impressed by what might be called the Minervizing of early American culture. Reporting to his countrymen on his 1819 journey through America, Englishman Henry Bradshaw Fearon noted,

> The *reading* of Americans (for I have not seen in [American] society an approach to what can be called *study*) is English; there being few native writers, and but a small number of these who possess the respect of even their own countrymen. Our novels and poetry, not excepting those which proceed from the Minerva press, meet with an immediate reprint, and constitute practically the entire American library. . . . Notwithstanding this voluntary national dependence, there are, perhaps, no people, not even excepting the French, who are so vain as the Americans.[11]

The main aspersion here, of course, is directed at American culture (or the lack thereof), the secondary slur at the Minerva Press. With that second slur, Fearon merely echoed the sentiments of many elitist Englishmen. For despite his astonishing success—or because of it— William Lane, with his Minerva Press in Leadenhall Street, was frequently castigated from the pulpit and in the press as a purveyor of cheap (in both senses of that word) books and often blamed for the decline in morals, if not the collapse of civilized society, in the Western world. What most alarmed Lane's detractors was how skillfully he catered to and fostered a new audience for literature, primarily novels. In the derisive summation of one traditionalist, Lane was "a leaden-*headed* dealer in books for the *cheesemongers*."[12]

Viewed from our contemporary vantage point, the extensive and apocalyptic denunciations of fiction in the eighteenth and early nineteenth centuries have a distinctly comical ring. One regularly encounters rampant metaphors of serpents, slavery, seduction, and satanic possession used to dramatize the ostensibly sinister powers of the insidious but increasingly popular literary form. The novel was seen to "mesmerize," "capture," and "tyrannize" a reader's attention and volition. But the contemporary reader can hardly take seriously a denunciation such as the essay "Novel Reading, a Cause of Female Depravity," which describes the sexual fall of a young woman, the "premature graves" to which her parents are brought through her disgrace, and the corollary destruction of "several relative families," all of which disasters follow, as the night the day, from reading fiction.[13] Yet the apprehensions of the eighteenth century—however baroque their metaphors—may well reflect the magnitude of the cultural changes that social authorities feared and that book entrepreneurs such as Lane in England and Carey in America early anticipated.

What does it *mean* if there is suddenly a massive demand for a literature that is linguistically simple enough to be apprehended by cheesemongers or serving girls, those readers who may have only a minimal education and a low level of literacy? Lane and Carey too understood as keenly as their detractors did that once the publishing industry shifts its primary attention and economy from a limited supply of nonfiction books intended for a specialized (and often elite) audience to a plethora of novels about and for middle- and working-class readers, we have a major shift in the social and political functions of culture. Entertainment, as Raymond Williams has argued, is never a frivolous matter but itself reiterates, in a variety of forms, the hegemonies of the culture.[14] If a hierarchical model of learning (the patriarchal Puritan family presided over by the father reading aloud to his family each night around the dinner table; the same hegemonies reinforced from the pulpit by the minister translating texts for his audience) is replaced by the mostly individualistic activity of perusing novels, the concomitant ideological implications will be as radical as the redistribution of reading power.

Furthermore, as Mikhail Bakhtin has argued, literary styles and genres in themselves embody ideologies. Bakhtin also notes, by way of example, that the novel was initially deemed subversive in every country into which it was introduced, largely because the complex intellectual and emotional activity of reading fiction empowers the hitherto powerless individual, at least imaginatively, by authorizing necessarily private responses to texts that function primarily as repositories for those responses. The distinctive feature of the novel as a genre may not be its formal qualities, its verbal artistry, its realistic or sensational plot lines, nor even its paraphrasable content, but rather the "dialogue" that it enters into with the reader, who in a literal sense is required to "complete" the textual transaction. This active apprehension of text can be psychically liberating for the individual reader in ways that are threatening to those who perceive themselves as the arbiters (or former arbiters) of cultural work. To return to Bakhtin's formulations, "In a novel the individual acquires the ideological and linguistic initiative necessary to change the nature of his own image." Moreover, the novel "has no canon of its own. It is, by its nature, not canonic. It is plasticity itself. It is a genre that is ever questing, ever examining itself and subjecting its established forms to review," an enterprise that can also encourage the reader to subject other or all established forms of authority to review.[15]

The noncanonical, the plastic, the self-reflexive, and the anti-authoritarian novel (embodying and reflecting its readers) *must* be threatening to the status quo, and it is small wonder that William Lane was vilified by one segment of English society for disseminating, with dazzling efficiency, precisely those kinds of books that seemed to undermine traditional literary and social hegemonies. Lane specialized in "Novels, Tales, Romances, Adventures, &c.," which he distributed through a network of urban and provincial circulating libraries. He not only founded these libraries but supplied their proprietors with a stock of books and "instructions and directions how to plan, systemize, and conduct" an efficient enterprise, a forerunner of the contemporary franchise business venture.[16] Lane also saw novels, his primary stock in trade, as literary peanuts: he knew that it was hard to stop at just one. Leigh Hunt, for example, confessed himself to be a "glutton of novels," and sated his appetite, early in the nineteenth century, on many of the more than seventeen thousand titles available from the Minerva Library on Leadenhall Street.[17] Equally important, by offering annual, semiannual, monthly, weekly, or even book-by-book subscription rates, Lane accommodated those who did not have large disposable incomes—women of all classes, lower- and working-class men, students, and even Romantic poets.

Lane succeeded as a publisher largely by making novels available to a new segment of the reading public that could not afford to buy those books that they wanted to read, but who, through the Minerva Library system, could happily borrow books at a fraction of their purchase price. He also perceived that occasionally his readers became so attached to a particular work that they wanted to own it, to possess it, to make it part of their lives (all that can be implied by book ownership in a society where books are still prized possessions). That too could be arranged, since every Minerva Library doubled as a bookshop. Finally, Lane made his books not only affordable but accessible, often setting up his libraries in such varied establishments as general stores (as was typical also in America), curio shops in seaside resort towns, jewelry shops, fishing-tackle suppliers, hardware stores, tobacconists, and apothecary stores.[18]

In 1794, no American publisher had yet worked out such an efficient system for disseminating books to all classes of American readers and to various regions of the nation, although Mathew Carey, employing itinerant book peddlers and arranging exchanges with other publishers, certainly had one of the country's most extensive book exchange networks. One of those itinerant book peddlers, the indomitable Mason Locke ("Parson") Weems, was able to get his books out to even small towns in distant parts of the nation. But the differences between the Lane and Carey operations in the 1790s are revealing. For example, bound with the 1791 British edition of *Charlotte* is an advertisement for Lane's "LITERARY MUSEUM, or NOVEL REPOSITORY," which was described as a "Museum of En-

tertainment, and a Repository of Sciences, Arts, and Polite Literature." Despite that claim, nearly all of the ten thousand books Lane
had in stock in 1791 were either novels or novelistic accounts of
captivity, travel, or adventure. In contrast, Carey's stock (some imported, some published by Carey) was both considerably smaller and
considerably less specialized than Lane's. Carey too bound an advertisement for his shop into his edition of *Charlotte*. Although in-
complete, this list is illustrative of Carey's interests as a publisher. It
includes just over 280 titles. Among them are tracts by philosophers
as diverse as James Beattie, Edmund Burke, and William Godwin;
evangelical religious testimonials; sermons; law books; scientific
treatises; pedagogical works; advice books; almanacs; feminist books
such as Mary Wollstonecraft's *A Vindication of the Rights of Woman*;
poetry; classics; biographies; and numerous novels, tales, romances,
and adventures on the Minerva model.[19]

One might argue that America was yet too new, too vast, and the
population too scattered for a single-minded novel-producing "factory" such as Lane's to be successful here. Or one might argue that
Carey felt intimidated by the extensive American censure of fiction,
more virulent and persistent here even than in England. But I am
inclined to think Carey's varied stock reflected more his personal
predilections than the economic and social limitations under which
he labored. Consider, for example, that when, in 1804, Hocquet Caritat published the catalogue for his library of fiction in New York City,
he could list nearly fifteen hundred titles. Caritat's library, not coinci-
dentally, had direct and reciprocal (if unequal)trade agreements with
Lane's Minerva Press.[20] Moreover, as Robert B. Winans has succinctly
observed, "The increase in the number of circulating libraries [in
America] was largely the result of the increasing demand for novels;
the general growth of the reading public was caused primarily by the
novel."[21] Although my research on this subject is still preliminary, I
might also here note that I have located over forty American libraries
that stocked *Charlotte Temple* before 1830. I have found the book
listed on surviving library rosters or, more typically, have discovered a
library bookplate within an extant copy of the novel. Some libraries,
especially institutional or social libraries that catered to a more elite
audience, did not stock novels at all. But thus far, every library roster I
have found that includes novels also lists *Charlotte Temple*.

Mathew Carey published books that could appeal to all classes of
American readers, from the poorest to the most elite, and, like most
urban publishers, he freely mixed in novels or novelistic books with
various nonfictional works. His different social agenda, however, did
not preclude him from copying closely Lane's edition of *Charlotte*.

But although he produced a remarkably similar text, Carey made significant additions to the title page of his original American edition. First, unlike Lane, he included the author's name on the title page. Second, by adding a brief attribution, he implies that the now-identified author is an American: "By Mrs. Rowson, of the New Theatre, Philadelphia." The author, like the publisher, was a new immigrant to the new nation, but Rowson's arrival in 1793 preceded the American imprint of her novel by only one year. Carey nevertheless grants Rowson de facto literary citizenship. He had no way of knowing that he was publishing a potential bestseller, yet by his designation he asserted that what he was publishing was an *American* novel.

II

By alluding to Rowson's Philadelphia theater career on its title page, Carey's edition implicitly raises two theoretical issues worth considering at some length: the historical question of a book-buying public and the historiographic issue of what constitutes a national literature. Since these are complex issues, I will address them separately, beginning with the matter of who in the early Republic could afford to buy books, which were, comparatively speaking, very expensive in the years before machine-made paper and horse- or steam-powered presses. Carey sold *Charlotte* for between fifty cents and a dollar (depending partly on the bindings and other factors relating to the material condition of the individual book). To put the novel's cost in perspective, it should be remembered that a laborer in Philadelphia in 1794 would be fortunate to earn that much in a day, a serving girl in a week.[22] But by alluding to Rowson's theatrical career, Carey cleverly "target marketed" (to use contemporary advertising jargon) the book for an audience that could afford it. Rowson was a popular character actress and playwright, well known to those upper-class and upper-middle-class Americans who paid as much for a night at the New Theatre as they might pay for a copy of Rowson's novel.[23] Citizens with enough disposable income to spend on culture and entertainment were potential book buyers, something the author-actress, an exceptionally astute businesswoman, also understood.

By describing Mrs. Rowson as "of the New Theatre, Philadelphia," Carey also raised the ideological question of nationality—implicitly supplying an egalitarian answer to Crèvecoeur's famous (and persistent) question, "What is an American?" Crèvecoeur's classic formulation of American identity, published in England by a French immigrant, was reprinted in America by immigrant Mathew Carey in 1793, three years after Crèvecoeur had returned to his native France, where he died, in 1813, at the home of his daughter, America-Frances.[24] As even this ambiguous biographical summation suggests, the whole issue of a national literature has been particularly troubling to American literary historians precisely because it affords no ready answer.[25] Except for the Native Americans, who certainly have not profited by their indigenous status, we are a nation of immigrants exuberantly eager to melt into the homogeneous ideal "American." But what that label means has been a source of anxiety almost since the nation's founding. Indeed, literary historiography has, since the time of the Revolution, been marked by an implicit ideological demand for "national purity," what Moses Coit Tyler, writing in 1878, called a "common national accent," in conflict with—if not in outright contradiction to—America's rampant heterogeneity.[26]

Nationalist ideologies have especially distinguished the historiography of the novel's rise to cultural respectability and prominence. In the years after the Civil War, literary historians began searching for that mythical creature, the Great American Novel. The very terms of the search acknowledged that, as Nina Baym has demonstrated, the novel had become a relatively respectable literary genre by the mid-nineteenth century.[27] While the new Republic strove for a Great American Epic to embody its aspirations, a hundred years later the Gilded Age sought the Great American Novel. The culture perceived its best fiction to be an apt measure of and metaphor for its status as a nation that was even then beginning to assume international political and economic power.[28] Moreover, one cannot have a Great American Novel without a proper genealogy, and, especially in the 1880s and 1890s, numerous candidates were set forth as the "first American novel." After considerable debate (especially about the notion of national purity), the award was finally conferred on a book of impeccable pedigree, *The Power of Sympathy*, published by the patriot Isaiah Thomas in 1789. This work was written by the native-born William Hill Brown and centered on a quintessentially American seduction story that included, as a subplot, a realistic recounting of a notorious scandal among Boston's aristocracy, with the names only slightly changed to pretend to protect the guilty. It is hard to be more American than that.[29]

But in his edition of Susanna Rowson's novel, Mathew Carey, in one phrase, effectively trivializes any preoccupation with national purity. Unlike subsequent literary genealogists, Carey simply sidestepped the whole question by stating that Rowson was "*of* . . . Philadelphia.*"* However, at least one of Carey's contemporaries was unwilling to accept this ascription. William Cobbett, writing as "Peter Porcupine," denounced Susanna Rowson in a pamphlet entitled *A Kick for a Bite* (1795). A scathing attack on all of her work, but mostly on her play *Slaves in Algiers* (1794), Cobbett's diatribe descends into an ad hominem attack on Rowson's feminism, her Democratic politics, *and* her Johnny-come-lately status as an American. That Cobbett himself was an immigrant who later returned to England did not keep him from offering up an exclusionary and, I would suggest, perniciously narrow definition of nationality, a subject that Mathew Carey took up in two notably harsh rebuttals of Cobbett (both published in 1799), *A Plumb Pudding for the Humane, Chaste, Valiant, Enlightened Peter Porcupine* and *The Porcupiniad. A Hudibrastic Poem.* Lest it be inferred that Susanna could not speak for herself against such a prickly critic, I hasten to add that in the preface to her *Trials of the Human Heart* (1795), Rowson noted how her "literary world [was] infested with a kind of loathsome reptile," one of which has "crawled over the volumes, which I have had the temerity to submit to the public eye. I say *crawled* because I am certain it has never penetrated beyond the title of any."[30]

Was Susanna Haswell Rowson American? A bare biography equivocates on that question. Born in England in 1762, she lived in America from 1766 until 1778 and attributed much of her literary education to a family friend, the patriot James Otis, who referred to her as his "little Scholar" and who encouraged her to read Shakespeare and Spenser, Dryden's Virgil, and Pope's Homer before she was ten. With the outbreak of the Revolution, Lieutenant Haswell and his family were returned to England in a prisoner exchange. Yet Susanna retained enough happy memories of those Americans who aided the family in their worst distress to decide, at the age of thirty-one, to return to the country from which she had been exiled at the age of fifteen (the age, of course, at which Charlotte Temple came to America). In 1804, with the naturalization of her husband, Susanna too became legally a citizen of the country that she had psychologically claimed for a decade and to which she referred as "my dear adopted country, America."[31] Four of the novels written after her immigration to America—*Trials of the Human Heart* (1795), *Reuben and Rachel* (1798), *Sarah* (1813), and the posthumously published *Charlotte's Daughter* (1828)—were printed first in America, as were her five pedagogical works, a collection of her poetry, and numerous songs, including "America, Commerce & Freedom," one of the most popular patriotic songs of the new Republic.[32]

Charlotte Temple's national provenance is equally ambiguous. The novel was not a bestseller in England. Lane did not include it in his 1798 prospectus of the most popular works from his press, nor was it even reprinted in England before 1819.[33] In contrast, Americans read, bought, and loved the book for over a century with an enduring ardor unsurpassed in American literary history. The usual pulpit pronouncement of the nineteenth century was that *Charlotte Temple* had managed to displace the Bible from the bedtables of America.

It was as an American novel that *Charlotte Temple* was read. By the first decade of the nineteenth century, Americans had even created, in Trinity Churchyard in New York City, a "grave" for Charlotte Temple. Until well into the twentieth century, this real grave of a fictional character received far more visitors than the neighboring graves of Alexander Hamilton or Robert Fulton.[34] Despite repeated allegations by historians that the tomb was not authentic, tens of thousands of visitors continued to make a pilgrimage to it for a hundred years. For them, the grave contained the last remains of another immigrant, an English girl seduced by a lieutenant in the British army who promised to marry her once they arrived on American soil. After an arduous ocean crossing (during which, presumably, she lost her virginity), Charlotte was rewarded not with marriage but with abandonment and subsequent death in childbirth while Lieutenant Montraville married a wealthy woman and went off to fight in the Revolutionary War. Is this really an American novel? Perhaps not. But it was printed as one by Carey and read as one by hundreds of thousands of American readers who also, I suspect, read in the devastating denouement of Charlotte's betrayal one of the first and paradigmatic failures of an American dream.

Susanna Rowson never disputed the authenticity of the tombstone erected during her lifetime in a graveyard in New York. Until her death she insisted that *Charlotte, a Tale of Truth* was true, despite the fact that no historical prototype has ever been substantiated.[35] But I would still suggest that the literalization of the novel by myriad American readers has made Charlotte Temple real, just as it had made *Charlotte Temple* American.

Mass culture is often dismissed as commodity, inflicted by a ruling class upon a mindless proletariat, but the ritualistic mourning for Charlotte indicates both the individual intensity of the identification with the heroine for myriad readers as well as the folkloric, communal nature of this experience—the cultural presence of Charlotte Temple is revitalized and concretized by shared, communal, crossgenerational rituals over a symbolic tomb. Readers flocked to her grave like pilgrims searching for the One True Cross. Readers further signaled their cultural participation in Rowson's novel by leaving (again ritualistically) tokens of themselves: bouquets of flowers, locks of hair, ashes of love letters.

Another indication of the force of *Charlotte Temple* is the misreading it has sustained. Many nineteenth-century descriptions of the novel create a plot that does not appear in Susanna Rowson's originating text. In the familiar misreading (sustained even in present-day accounts), Charlotte sets out, alone and pregnant, in a snowstorm to find Montraville, the faithless lover. The snow whirling madly about her, she collapses only to be saved from certain death by a poor servant who takes her into his hovel where she gives birth to a daughter and then dies among America's underclass, who welcome her with a sympathy and a friendship not found elsewhere in the revolutionary-era America vaguely symbolized in the novel. This popular redaction of Rowson's plot elides events to create a more graphic class allegory than the one Rowson "actually" wrote. More to the point, this invigorated class allegory was ritualistically reenacted (with the culminating snowstorm scene) in a melodrama version popular among the itinerant acting companies that performed in dingy nineteenth-century factory towns.

What I am suggesting is that this novel became a kind of cultural legend with significance beyond that usually ascribed to mass cultural products. This is evident in both the ritual transfiguration of the symbolic, textual Charlotte into the "real" corpse lying in Trinity Churchyard, and at the same time (and this is the classic process in oral, folk culture) the allegorical significance reenacted in readers' everyday lives. This same dual tendency toward literalization and symbolization persists. Even today, at the New-York Historical Society, one can find, filed under Rowson's name, two letters written by Margaret M. Coghlan "who *may* have been the original for Mrs. Rowson's 'Charlotte Temple.'" Margaret Coghlan's diction and her tragic story make a tale as pathetic as the one Rowson tells: "I was married during the American War in Obedience to the Commands of my father ere I had seen fifteen years, to a Captain in the Army, whose barbarous ill usage and abandonment has plunged me into an Abbess [*sic*] of Woe. . . . I have no means of Support and am struggling with more real misery, than I have power to describe."[36] In no objective, historical sense is this Charlotte Temple, who eloped with Montraville without ever consulting the loving parents who could have saved her. A number of other details in the letter (the political affiliations of the principals, the death of both parents) also suggest a disparity between historical and fictional character.

Nevertheless, the anonymous librarian who cross-listed Margaret Coghlan's letters under "Susanna Rowson" read the truth of her story on a level that transcends mere facticity. For what is essential in the Coghlan "novella" is its quintessential injustice, its disappointed promises, its sense of being betrayed by the liberal and republican ideal that posited a correlation between merit (in a woman, read "virtue") and reward. Charlotte was recognized as just such a victim by even the first reviewer of the novel, who, in London's *Critical Review,* proclaimed her a "martyr" and protested the severity of the punishment heaped upon her: "We should feel for Charlotte if such a person ever existed, who, for one error, scarcely, perhaps, deserved so severe a punishment. If it is a fiction, poetic justice is not, we think, properly distributed."[37] Mathew Carey felt this public exoneration of a "fallen woman" so important that he tipped it into copies of the first American edition of the novel under the heading "Of Charlotte, the Reviewers have given the following character."[38] For the second edition (published in October of 1794), Carey printed the review on the verso of the title page, a powerful reading directive for an early American interpretive community. Naive, sexually lax, even disobedient, Charlotte Temple was still pitied by reviewers, publishers, and readers who made her into an early American icon—a *figura* of the seduced female, an embodiment of the interdependent strands of sexual and economic exploitation. Margaret Coghlan becomes Charlotte Temple in the same way that several generations of deceived, distraught, or merely lonely readers—men as well as women, old as well as young, affluent as well as poor—also became Charlotte.

Perhaps because of the pervasiveness of novels (and, no doubt, the more recent incursions into the psyche made by radio and television), we now take for granted those generic and ideological features of the novel that most frightened eighteenth-century social authorities. As they clearly saw, novels encourage identification between reader and character. Moreover, emotional identification subverts moral censure, so much so that the fatal consequence of Charlotte's disobedience and illicit sexuality could be read not as justice delivered but as a tragic metaphor for human pain—for the reader's pain—in all its variety. This transvaluation of value was already present in the first review of *Charlotte Temple* in the *Critical Review,* was seconded by Mathew Carey when he reprinted it in his editions of the novel, and was echoed, resoundingly, in the hearts and minds of the readers of the novel who, for a century, left tokens of lost loves upon Charlotte's grave and who left tender inscriptions and marginalia in copies of the novel. In the words of an anonymous but representative reader, written on July 25, 1817, "unfortunate Charlotte" was "fair and sweet as the Lilly Inosentas / the young lamb folly misled."[39]

Early critics feared the novel for its power to thwart rational moralistic arguments, to subordinate logic to emotion, and to privilege the "wisdom of the human heart" over the sterner dicta of the head. The critics feared rightly. Within fictional space-time—the ahistorical, out-of-time dimension of the reading process—there occurs a transubstantiation wherein the word becomes flesh, the text becomes the reader, the reader becomes the hero. Through the intimate, transformative process of reading, *Charlotte Temple* transcends its seemingly formulaic plot to become something much more than a simple allegory of female crime and punishment.

III

Charlotte Temple enjoyed the longest popularity of any American novel and was the first fiction in America to signal the novel's rise to cultural prominence, especially among a new kind of reader whose tears, for over a century, kept the grass over Charlotte's final resting place as green as the dollars that passed through many a publisher's pocket. Mathew Carey, for example, followed his first American edition of *Charlotte, a Tale of Truth* with many subsequent and, after 1797, retitled versions. Appropriately, just as Carey had done unto Lane, many American publishers did unto Carey. By 1802, one could read *The History of Charlotte Temple* in a version by John Babcock of Hartford, Connecticut, or by William W. Morse of New Haven. One could read a Philadelphia *Charlotte Temple* published by Peter Stewart or other versions published in Alexandria, Virginia, and New York City.[40]

The way various publishers chose to print, bind, and market this novel reveals much about the increasing dominance of the novel as a genre and the many social functions the novel served within the culture. One *Charlotte Temple* could be repackaged in myriad ways in order to appeal to different kinds of readers and to perform different kinds of cultural work. Moreover, the external packaging of the novel—including illustrative front matter—served also to direct the reader as to how she or he might assess the text therein. I would therefore suggest that the text *changes* according to how it is presented or framed by book morphology. In short, although one may not be able to judge a book by its cover, one can read what a given cover signifies.

What do we make, for example, of the editions of *Charlotte Temple* apparently intended for children? In 1811 Samuel Avery produced a toy book *Charlotte Temple* (13 centimeters by 7 centimeters) in a cheap calf binding. An advertisement at the back indicates that Avery also published "School books, bibles, and testaments" as well as "a great variety of juvenile books, which he intends to sell, (wholesale and retail) as cheap as can be Purchased in the United States."[41] Rowson's story of filial disobedience, inept pedagogy, hypocrisy, dis-

honesty, misogyny, class conflict, and, especially, the tragic consequences of illicit sexuality is transmogrified into a cautionary tale
suitable for the nursery. Publishers thus profited from the republican
imperative to educate the young for citizenship in the new United
States. In keeping with a growing societal reaction against Puritan
pedagogical praxis, publishers too saw that education could be tem-
pered with (and encouraged through) entertainment. Through the
negative example of poor Charlotte, students could apprehend the
need for education not just in religious dogma but also in the ways of
the world. By thoroughly involving the reader's emotions in the sad
story of the seduction, abandonment, and subsequent death in childbirth of a schoolgirl misled partly by a despicable French teacher, the
text also illustrated that women, especially, had to learn to be cautious. Rowson, incidentally, insisted that she intended the book to
"advise" the "young and unprotected woman in her first entrance
into life" (p. 7), thus setting forth an educational agenda that goes
considerably beyond the three R's.

Elaborate mid-nineteenth-century gift book editions, sometimes
bound in morocco, often edged and lettered in gilt, made the book
suitable for display in any upstanding middle-class home, while story
paper versions masqueraded as newspapers in order to take advantage
of the low postal rates accorded to the postrevolutionary press and
partly circumvent high distribution costs. One story paper edition
called itself, on the title page, "CHEAP EDITION OF CHARLOTTE
TEMPLE, A TALE OF TRUTH" and boasted a price of twelve and a
half cents, a reduction (it claimed) of the normal fifty-cent price.[42]
What different class allegories did different readers discover in these
varied versions of the same text? Could aspiring middle-class readers
hold Charlotte's father accountable for her fall? After all, as the
"youngest son of a nobleman, whose fortune was by no means adequate to the antiquity, grandeur, and . . . pride of the family" (p. 11),
Henry Temple had the opportunity to marry the only child of a
wealthy man but chose instead to marry for love. Charlotte grew up in
a happy home, but her lack of a dowry certainly put her at a disadvantage on the marriage market. The plot device is then inverted in the
Montraville family, where the daughters have been provided with
enough of a dowry to allow them to attract good husbands, and the
sons (Montraville being the youngest of several) have been severely
warned against marrying "precipitously," before they are able to support a wife and family (pp. 39–41). Montraville thus rejects Charlotte
in favor of marriage with a woman who is both virtuous *and* rich. If
Rowson wrote a class allegory, the next question must be, *Which*
class's allegory? And how are gender and class intertwined in this

complex allegory? The case is by no means unequivocal in the text and is further confused by the novel's long history as a bestseller among poor, working-class, middle-class, and even affluent readers. In the words of one of Rowson's early biographers, the novel could be found in the "study of the divine and . . . the workshop of the mechanic," in the "parlor of the accomplished lady and the bedchamber of her waiting-maid."[43]

Robert Escarpit has noted that a book (as opposed to a manuscript) is characterized by a "multiplication of meaning," a public and changing act influenced by material considerations (book morphology and production) and nonmaterial ones (the previous experiences readers bring to their texts).[44] As if to signal their *recreation* of Rowson's text, numerous nineteenth-century publishers again changed the novel's title in ways that served as a reading directive for the book-buying public of that time. These new titles, printed at the height of the popularity of the sentimental novel, acknowledge, at least tacitly, another era in the history of the book in American culture. One now finds such titles as *The Lamentable History of the Beautiful and Accomplished Charlotte Temple, with an Account of her Elopement with Lieutenant Montroville [sic], and her Misfortunes and Painful Sufferings, are Herein Pathetically Depicted.* A version from the 1860s that bears this title also includes an "Original Portrait" of the protagonist as a quintessentially innocent young maiden, sweet and vulnerable, but rather incongruously adorned in the most fashionable couture of the day. Yet this sentimentalized rendition of Charlotte is in striking contrast to an almost simultaneous marketing of her story in highly sensational and even quasi-pornographic terms. An infamous story paper version (which resembles a contemporary tabloid newspaper) pictorializes a more mature and lascivious Charlotte. Although based on a famous Raphael Madonna, this rendition of a smoldering Charlotte is anything but virginal. And lest the reader miss the import of the cover illustration, the printer has emphasized his meaning with an unambiguous banner headline: "The Fastest Girl in New York."[45]

Charlotte, daughter of poverty and innocent victim of masculine (and bourgeois) deception; Charlotte, role model for the learning young; Charlotte, sentimental heroine; Charlotte, seductress: all these Charlotte Temples are evident in nineteenth-century editions even before we turn to the story itself. Book morphology, the title page, dedication, and frontispiece are all texts to be read, texts as significant and as subtle as those found in the pages on which literary scholars have traditionally focused their attention. Similarly, certain texts are chosen by advertisers as the appropriate vehicle from which to sell a product. Take, for example, the Seaside Library pocket edition of *Charlotte Temple* that was published by George Munro early in the 1890s. The book contains an advertisement for Colgate soaps and perfumes, as well as advertisements for Castoria, Beecham's Pills, and a Cactus Blood Cure (a patent medicine touted as a cure for, among other things, consumption). Another ad informs us, "Well Bred, Soon Wed. Girls who use Sapolio are Quickly Married." Yet in the midst of these ads (foreshadowing the contemporary soap opera) is an advertisement for "The Prose Dramas of Henrik Ibsen," the kind of juxtaposition that compromises current critical clichés about elite versus popular culture.

Twentieth-century texts give us still other versions of *Charlotte Temple*. The first scholarly edition of the novel was compiled in 1905 by Francis W. Halsey, who sought to redress the 1,265 errors that he had found in the many popular (but corrupt) versions of the text.[46] So long as textual accuracy is the explicit aim and insofar as a 262-page novel requires a 109-page introduction, we have text about the importance, function, and purpose not only of literature but of literary scholarship as both rigorous discipline and necessary endeavor. Interestingly, Halsey's scholarly edition coincided with the end of *Charlotte Temple's* popularity, and most twentieth-century editions have been aimed at a new audience, a specialized, elite audience of academics, as is confirmed by, for example, a 1964 paperback edition complete with footnotes and other scholarly apparatus. Gone are the sensational or sentimental titles, the extravagant typography, the pictorial representation of the injured—or potentially injurious—Charlotte, the advertisements proclaiming cures to the various ailments flesh (especially female flesh) is heir to. Instead, we have an unadorned cover with such descriptive headings as "Masterworks of Literature Series . . . Edited for the Modern Reader"—claims as medicinal, in their own way, as those made for, say, Mrs. Winslow's soothing syrup in many nineteenth-century editions.[47] Unmistakably a classroom text, the 1964 edition seems to proclaim that the text inside will not be much fun to read but, most assuredly, will be good for you. Finally, the most recent edition of the novel (and it happens to be my own) bears the unmistakable stamp of *l'histoire du livre*. This 1986 *Charlotte Temple* proclaims its relationship to its predecessors and views the publishing history and the history of the novel's reception as a paradigm for the evolution of mass culture in the United States.

From Charlotte's long-mourned martyrdom to her present literary "canonization," from the novel's death as a popular novel to its recent resurrection as a literary "masterwork," there is a story in all of these variations on the same story of *Charlotte, a Tale of Truth.* It is to that larger story too that students of literature and history should attend.

Notes

This essay is a revised version of *Ideology and Genre: The Rise of the Novel in America* (Worcester, Mass., 1987; rpt. from *Proceedings of the American Antiquarian Society* 96 [October 1986] and originally presented as the fourth annual James Russell Wiggins Lecture in the History of the Book in American Culture, American Antiquarian Society [AAS], October 29, 1986). I am grateful to the AAS for permission to reprint this essay in its present form. The subtitle of the essay alludes to the phrase used by Robert Darnton in his influential *The Business of Enlightenment: A Publishing History of the Encyclopédie, 1775–1800* (Cambridge, Mass., 1979).

1. The only known copy of the original British edition of *Charlotte, a Tale of Truth* is in the Barrett Collection at the Alderman Library of the University of Virginia, Charlottesville. I am grateful to the staff at the Alderman Library for making the extensive Rowson collection available to me.

2. See especially Mathew Carey, *Cursory Reflexions on the System of Taxation, Established in the City of Philadelphia; With a Brief Sketch of Its Unequal and Unjust Operation* (Philadelphia, 1806); *Wages of Female Labour* (Philadelphia, 1829); and *Address to the Wealthy of the Land, Ladies as Well as Gentlemen, on the Character, Conduct, Situation, and Prospects, of Those Whose Sole Dependence for Subsistence, is on the Labour of their Hands* (Philadelphia, 1831).

3. For discussions of Carey, see Earl L. Bradsher, *Mathew Carey: Editor, Author and Publisher* (New York, 1912); James N. Green, *Mathew Carey, Publisher and Patriot* (Philadelphia, 1985); and Kenneth Wyer Rowe, *Mathew Carey: A Study in American Economic Development* (Baltimore, Md., 1933).

4. Carey, Account Books, Manuscript Department, American Antiquarian Society, Worcester, Mass. (hereafter AAS). See also correspondence and miscellaneous memoranda of Mathew Carey, and the Lea and Febiger Records in the Edward Carey Gardiner Collection, Historical Society of Pennsylvania, Philadelphia. See also Eugene L. Schwaab, ed., *Mathew Carey Autobiography* (New York, 1942). For a description of most of the editions of the novel, see R. W. G. Vail, "Susanna Haswell Rowson, the Author of *Charlotte Temple:* A Bibliographical Study," *Proceedings of the American Antiquarian Society* 42 (1932): 47–160.

5. Quoted in Bradsher, *Mathew Carey,* 50.

6. For a discussion of author contracts and payments, see the superb

biographical-bibliographical study by Dorothy Blakey, *The Minerva Press, 1790–1820* (London, 1939), 72 and 73. See also A. S. Collins, *The Profession of Letters: A Study of the Relation of Author to Patron, Publisher, and Public* (New York, 1929), 44 and 113; and J. M. S. Tompkins, *The Popular Novel in England, 1770–1800* (London, 1932), 9. In her fine new biography, *Susanna Haswell Rowson* (Boston, 1986), Patricia L. Parker documents Rowson's career as a professional writer (see esp. ch. 2).

7. Michel Foucault, "What Is an Author?" in *The Foucault Reader*, ed. Paul Rabinow (New York, 1984), 101–20; and Martha Woodmansee, "The Genius and the Copyright: Economic and Legal Conditions of the Emergence of the 'Author,'" *Eighteenth-Century Studies* 17 (Summer 1984): 443.

8. For a discussion of the relationship between class affiliation and authorship, see William Charvat, *The Profession of Authorship in America, 1800–1870: The Papers of William Charvat*, ed. Matthew J. Bruccoli (Columbus, Ohio, 1968); Robert Escarpit, *The Book Revolution* (London, 1966); and Mary Kelley, *Private Woman, Public Stage: Literary Domesticity in Nineteenth-Century America* (New York, 1984).

9. The earliest biography of Rowson is Samuel Lorenzo Knapp's "Memoir," included as a preface to Rowson's posthumously published *Charlotte's Daughter; or, The Three Orphans* (Boston, 1828). The most recent and, all around, the best biography is Parker's *Susanna Haswell Rowson.* Perhaps the most interesting historiographically is Elias Nason's *A Memoir of Mrs. Susanna Rowson, with Elegant and Illustrative Extracts from Her Writings in Prose and Poetry* (Albany, N.Y., 1870). For an eyewitness account of Rowson's activities, see also Myra Montgomery to Mary Ann Means, November 22, 1808, Claude W. Unger Collection, Historical Society of Pennsylvania. For a summary of women's legal and economic status in the new Republic and for evidence that William Rowson collected his wife's wages, see Cathy N. Davidson, *Revolution and the Word: The Rise of the Novel in America* (New York, 1986), ch. 6 and p. 8. For a discussion of the discrepancy between royalties paid to women and men authors, see Hannah Adams's contemporaneous account in *A Memoir of Miss Hannah Adams, Written by Herself* (Boston, 1832).

10. An excellent example of an American publisher attempting to mimic British practices can be seen in George Clark's 1841 (Boston) edition of Tabitha Tenney's popular novel, *Female Quixotism*, originally published as two volumes bound as one by Isaiah Thomas and E. T. Andrews in 1801. Clark actually renumbers the chapters (with little regard to the plot structure of the novel) in order to create a three-volume book on the model of popular British novels of the era. Jay Fliegelman, in *Prodigals and Pilgrims: The American Revolution against Patriarchal Authority, 1750–1800* (New York, 1982), 67–79, recounts the various ways in which *Robinson Crusoe* was reprinted for an American audience.

11. Henry Bradshaw Fearon, *Sketches of America. A Narrative of a Journey of Five Thousand Miles Through the Eastern and Western States of America* (London, 1818), 365–68.

12. For a survey of the censure of fiction in America, see, for example,

Jean-Marie Bonnet, *La Critique Littéraire aux Etats-Unis, 1783–1837* (Lyon, 1982); and G. Harrison Orians, "Censure of Fiction in American Romances and Magazines, 1789–1810," *PMLA* 52 (1937): 195–214. The derisive judgment against Lane appeared in *Stuart's Star* (February 16, 1789) and is quoted in Blakey, *Minerva Press*, 14.

13. "Novel Reading, A Cause of Female Depravity," *New England Quarterly* 1 (1802): 172–74. A headnote indicates that this article was originally published in the (British) *Monthly Mirror* in November 1797.

14. Raymond Williams, *The Long Revolution* (New York, 1961), esp. 41–43, 113, and *Keywords: A Vocabulary of Culture and Society* (New York, 1976), 76–82, 145–48, 281–84.

15. Mikhail M. Bakhtin, "Epic and Novel," in *The Dialogic Imagination: Four Essays*, ed. and trans. Caryl Emerson and Michael Holquist (Austin, Tex., 1981), 37–39.

16. Both the advertisement and title page from the first British edition and the title page of the first American edition are reprinted in Susanna Haswell Rowson, *Charlotte Temple*, ed. Cathy N. Davidson (New York, 1986). Future references to this edition of the novel will be cited parenthetically within the text.

17. Leigh Hunt, *Autobiography of Leigh Hunt* (London, 1885), 124; and Blakey, *Minerva Press*, 114.

18. Blakey, *Minerva Press*, 122.

19. See Carey's advertisement, dated Philadelphia, April 17, 1794, bound with his first edition of *Charlotte Temple* (Philadelphia, 1794), n.p.

20. George Raddin, *An Early New York Library of Fiction, with a Checklist of the Fiction of H. Caritat's Circulating Library, No. 1, City Hotel, Broadway, New York, 1804* (New York, 1940).

21. Robert B. Winans, "Bibliography and the Cultural Historian: Notes on the Eighteenth-Century Novel," in *Printing and Society in Early America*, ed. William L. Joyce et al. (Worcester, Mass., 1983), 176.

22. U.S. Department of Labor, *History of Wages in the United States from Colonial Times to 1928* (Washington, D.C., 1929), 53, 57, 133–34, 137. These wages are corroborated by many contemporaneous cost accountings, such as those found at the end of the diary of Ethan Allen Greenwood for December 30, 1805, to February 9, 1806, in the Manuscript Department of the AAS.

23. For a discussion of the class affiliations of theatergoers, see Kenneth Silverman, *A Cultural History of the American Revolution* (New York, 1976), esp. 545–46.

24. Michel Guillaume Jean de Crèvecoeur, *Letters From an American Farmer* (London, 1782), letter 3. For a succinct assessment, see John Harmon McElroy, "Michel Guillaume Jean de Crèvecoeur," *Dictionary of Literary Biography*, vol. 3, *American Writers of the Early Republic*, ed. Emory Elliott, 103–7.

25. The inconsistencies in historical claims for an American identity have been analyzed persuasively by William C. Spengemann in "The Earliest American Novel: Aphra Behn's *Oroonoko*," *Nineteenth-Century Fiction* 38

(1984): 384–414, and "What Is American Literature?" *Centennial Review* 22 (1978): 119–38. For the ways in which women have been excluded from the definition of "American," see the perceptive essays by Nina Baym, "Melodramas of Beset Manhood: How Theories of American Fiction Exclude Women Authors," *American Quarterly* 33 (Summer 1981): 123–39; and Annette Kolodny, "The Integrity of Memory: Creating a New Literary History of the United States," *American Literature* 57 (May 1985): 291–307.

26. Moses Coit Tyler, *A History of American Literature, 1607–1765*, 2 vols. (New York, 1878), 1:v.

27. Nina Baym, *Novels, Readers, and Reviewers: Responses to Fiction in Antebellum America* (Ithaca, N.Y., 1984).

28. Herbert Ross Brown, "The Great American Novel," *American Literature* 7 (1935): 1–14.

29. The theoretical issue of literary nationalism in relation to the publication of the first American novel is discussed at length in Davidson, *Revolution and the Word*, 83–109.

30. Susanna Rowson, *Trials of the Human Heart* (Philadelphia, 1795), xiii–xiv.

31. Susanna Rowson, *Exercises in History, Chronology, and Biography* (Boston, 1822), preface.

32. For a complete list, with full bibliographical data, see Vail, "Susanna Haswell Rowson," 91–160.

33. Blakey, *Minerva Press*, appendix 4, n.p.

34. "H.S.B.", letter to *New York Evening Post* (September 12, 1903); and "Charlotte Temple's Grave," *New York Daily Tribune* (June 8, 1900). The latter clipping was preserved in a copy of *Charlotte Temple*, Special Collections, Kent State University Library, Kent, Ohio. Special thanks to Kathleen E. Noland for bringing it to my attention.

35. For a biography as fictional as anything Rowson wrote, see novelist Caroline Dall's *The Romance of the Association; or, One Last Glimpse of Charlotte Temple and Eliza Wharton* (Cambridge, Mass., 1875).

36. Margaret M. Coghlan to Edward P. Livingston, December 28, 1803, Robert R. Livingston Papers, New-York Historical Society.

37. *Critical Review* 2d ser., 1 (1791): 468–69.

38. Susanna Rowson, *Charlotte, a Tale of Truth* (Philadelphia, 1794). The review is affixed to the verso of the front flyleaf.

39. AAS copy of Carey's 1812 edition, verso of the last page of vol. 1.

40. See Vail, "Susanna Haswell Rowson," 93–94.

41. AAS copy of Samuel Avery's 1811 edition.

42. This is in the Skinner and Blanchard (Boston) edition of 1845. An 1877 edition of the novel, published in tabloid format by Norman L. Munro, was "Given Away with Number 211 of the New York Family Story Paper."

43. Nason, *Memoir of Mrs. Susanna Rowson*, 50.

44. Robert Escarpit, *Sociology of Literature*, trans. Ernest Pick, 2nd ed. (London, 1971), 55–74.

45. Francis W. Halsey, edition of *Charlotte Temple* (New York, 1905), reproduces on pp. xxxv and xxxvi the illustrations from both editions, the

first published by Barclay & Co. of Philadelphia about 1860–65 and the second published in New York about 1870, publisher unknown.

46. Ibid., vii.

47. Clara M. and Rudolf Kirk, eds., *Charlotte Temple* (New Haven, Conn., 1964). The advertisement for Mrs. Winslow's soothing syrup appears in *Charlotte Temple. A Tale of Truth. By Mrs. Susannah Rawson (sic)*, published by the F. M. Lupton Publishing Company of New York about 1894–98.

er Seven

Antebellum Reading and the Ironies of Technological Innovation

Ronald J. Zboray

"To American literature!"

The toast rang through the north nave of the New York Crystal Palace, where the Association of New York Publishers convened on September 27, 1855, to honor 153 of their most popular authors. The association had spent $3,787—no mean sum in 1855—to dine if not wine their authors at this teetotal event. Yet beneath the hoopla, the fustian speeches attested that the publishers, more than honoring authors, congratulated themselves on the dramatic growth of American publishing and the reading public they addressed.[1]

George Palmer Putnam, the secretary of the association, arose beneath a placard embossed with the motto "May Plenty crown the humblest board" to recite the impressive statistics of growth within the industry:

The records of American publications, for the twelve years ending in 1842, show an aggregate of 1,115 different works. Of these, 623 were original, and 429 were reprinted from foreign books. The full list of reprints would show nearly the same number as the originals, viz.: an average of 52 each per annum. In the year 1853, there were some 733 works published in the United States; of which 278 were reprints of English works, 35 were translations of foreign authors, and 420 (a large preponderance) were original American works—thus showing an increase of about 800 per cent in less than twenty years. As the average increase in the population of the United States in the same time,—great as it was—scarcely reached 80 per cent, it appears that literature and the bulk of the book trade advanced ten times faster than the population. If we compare the numbers printed of each edition, the growth is still greater; for 20 years ago who *imagined* editions of 100,000 or 75,000, or 30,000, or even the now common number of 10,000.

That latter number represented the smallest edition for a book to be considered a "decided hit."[2]

To what did the publishers attribute this growth in the book trade? Not to the rise of popular fiction, the extension of popular schooling, the transformation of the reading public, or the maturing of the American economy, and certainly not to the genius of authors. Instead the speakers at the Crystal Palace pointed to the industrialization of printing and, particularly, the progress of printing technology as the sole cause of the unprecedented expansion of publishing.

Such a view holds great ramifications for American cultural history, for the period of growth in the book trade celebrated by the New York publishers at their festival coincided with the maturation of American literary life. By 1855 all the masterpieces of the American Renaissance—Poe's poems and short stories, Emerson's essays, Thoreau's *Walden*, Hawthorne's and Melville's most important works, and even the first edition of Whitman's *Leaves of Grass*—had appeared. At the same time numerous domestic and sentimental writers commanded a large audience, the forerunners of the dime novel had appeared, and a host of popular literary genres, from the reform novel to the American historical romance, grew to maturity. And four years before the publishers met, that sales phenomenon of the century, *Uncle Tom's Cabin*, had been published.

The New York publishers' claim of credit for these cultural contributions could be written off as boasting if their example were not either explicitly or implicitly followed by generations of historians. In works not only on publishing but on cultural history as well, the easy equation of technological innovation in printing and the dramatic growth of the antebellum reading public emerges as a running refrain.[3] Such an equation presents a simple and attractive solution to a difficult dilemma: that of constructing causal links between infrastructural (i.e., industrial production) and superstructural (i.e., the life of the mind) phenomena. In other words, what is the relationship between, on the one hand, printing and publishing and, on the other, authorship and reading?

Addressing this complex relationship requires, at first, an analysis of the central role technological progress has played in explanations of the growth of the reading public. Publishers, as seen in their speeches at their 1855 festival, drew upon an artisan ideology that obscured the industrialization of printing. Through the public image they presented, they shared with readers a common set of values: faith in the inevitability and salutary nature of technological progress and a belief, under the banner of artisan ideology, that progress, liberal values, and the democratization of society and, by extension, the reading public were intertwined. For publishers, the antebellum reader was the creation of technological innovation.

Yet several ironies within publishing and reading history confound this simple view. As publishers claimed the artisan tradition for their own, actual artisans protested the industrialization of printing, seen most clearly in the new Harper Establishment of 1853. The preindustrial work rhythms of printing eroded before the trade felt the impact of technological innovation. Innovations in printing underwrote the emergence of the publisher not as an heir to the artisan tradition but as a capitalist, more like the Lowell factories' Nathan Appleton than the local humble printer. The capitalization of printing—seen most readily in stereotyping and electrotyping—altered the relationship of publishers to authors and, through advertising, to readers.

Nor did technological innovation only encourage the democratization of literature. Innovations in bookbinding created a market for books with elaborate bindings as expensive luxury commodities well beyond the reach of most Americans. Technological change in printing did not even lower the price of books to make them available "to the millions," as one publisher claimed (though the price of newspapers plummeted).[4]

Finally, the overconcentration on innovations in printing to explain the growth of the antebellum reading public ignores the importance of other technologies to the reading experience. Railroad development improved literary distribution, provided a new opportunity for reading, and helped to transform the nature of the reader's community life. And even more intimate with the reading experience, the strength and cost of domestic lighting and the availability of corrective eyeglasses contributed to shaping the social distribution of antebellum reading.

I

The speeches delivered at the 1855 publishers' festival give ample evidence of the issues underlying the overemphasis on printing innovation. George Putnam, who earlier had sketched the growth of the industry, turned to a defense of American literature and rested his case on printing: "In the *machinery* for this great manufacture, our artisans, I will venture to say, are not yet excelled, if equaled, elsewhere." The Reverend W. H. Milburn focused on the printing room in order to explain the increasingly wide dissemination of literature: "Gentlemen publishers, the well-heads opened in your press-rooms may send forth streams to refresh and gladden the homes of a continent." The most striking testimonial to printing innovation came from the Reverend E. H. Chapin, to whom fell the toast, "The Printing Press in the Age of Steam and Electricity."[5]

By all accounts the high point of the evening, Chapin's speech speaks volumes about the publishing industry's sense of itself. Technological innovation naturally plays a major role: "The printing press through all the stages of its improvement, may be taken as a symbol of the mechanical progress of the last four hundred years." He entreats his listeners to compare the presses of Gutenberg with those driven by steam in the new Harper Establishment. Yet Chapin's address, on the whole, endeavors not to glorify the machine, but to humanize it. It seems "more like an intelligent being than a machine," and he calls Harpers' steam engine "the best hand they have in the shop." Chapin personifies the press as a "troublesome democrat," "a revolutionist," "a prophet of free and beautiful thought," and "a working preacher." The press comes "stalking into the world among kings and priests," "tears the chained word of God from the pillars of the monasteries, and scatter[s] it all over the world, and kindle[s] a light to read it by." Having played such a crucial role in the making of the modern world out of feudalism, the press acts as the servant of the Divine Will. "The processes of His eternal righteousness and truth run in the iron grooves of the printing press."

The shaping force of the publishing industry stands revealed in Chapin's speech as nothing less than the hand of God. Having established publishing's historical mission, Chapin calls for holy war: "The rumble of the power of the press is better than the rattle of artillery." "Advance battalions!" he urges, as, according to a *Tribune* reporter, the audience cheers loudly. Under the banner of liberal ideology, Chapin integrated his audience of publishers with nature, located them in history, and allied them with God.

Chapin's speech shows how far the book trade's self-consciousness had come from craft pride. At the center of that consciousness no longer stood the nuts and bolts of mechanical progress. Progress in printing had gone public. The putative social outcomes of advances in printing technology had become more important than those advances alone. Chapin and the other speakers at the festival leaped from technological to social, even moral, progress without much concern for causation. Their speeches demonstrated more their faith in general technological progress than a true understanding of the manner in which printing innovation affected the growth of the book trade. For them and for the antebellum publishers for whom they spoke, technological innovations represented just one small tributary to the mainstream of "human progress," powered by the mighty currents of middle-class liberalism and industrial capitalism.

II

The antebellum publishers' image of themselves as heirs to the tradition of artisan printers obscured the fact that real artisan printers still existed in the form of workers in the various printing shops and factories. These workers had a very different opinion of the progressiveness of the industrialization of printing. "Speculator on the labor of printers" and "hireling editor" are only two of the milder epithets journeymen typesetters applied in the contemporary press to publishers.[6] Novice pressmen or compositors had increasingly little hope of fulfilling their former expectation of one day becoming master artisans with their own shops. With time the journeyman journeyed occupationally upward no more, as the "man" in him became a disembodied "hand" in a rationalized system of production.

The Harper Establishment, which opened in New York in 1853, worked this proletarianization into its very design. The plan of the new plant distinguished between publishing and manufacturing operations; each had its own building. Before this time, the Harpers either sent their work out to small shops they owned scattered over the city or to independent jobbers. The Great Fire of 1853, which destroyed the Harper headquarters, allowed the brothers to combine all operations in a single plant.[7]

The publishing building at the new plant housed employees responsible for management, inventory, and wholesaling. The building, as might be expected from the publisher's self-image as an organization of artisans, faced a square named after Benjamin Franklin. Over the entrance way of the elegant edifice, a full-length statue of Franklin presided, kept company on the top floor by smaller statues of Jefferson and Washington—all attesting to simple republican equality. Inside, one large counting room contained all operations except storage. No walls separated the various departments, but only low railings. Management remained flexible.

Not so labor: the factory—standing behind the Franklin Square building, facing dismal Cliff Street—had a separate floor or room for all divisions of the book production process. The basement acted as a receiving room, both for raw materials and for power from the boiler room located in the courtyard between the two buildings. The first floor constituted the great press room. Here "girls," as Jacob Abbott called them, attended and fed paper into twenty mighty steam presses—no journeymen pressmen of days of yore here. A foreman and assistant (invariably male) sat high above the presses at one end of the room in order to monitor both worker and machine. On the next floor up, boys put up for drying the newly printed sheets received from below. The sheets then renewed their ascent to where workmen flattened the warpings and twistings in hydraulic machines. On the next floor women folded the paper. On the fourth story, men operated hydraulic presses to sharpen the folds, after which more women sewed and stitched the sheets. The books were finished on the next floor: covers fitted, flyleaves pasted down, edges trimmed. On the top floor worked the compositors and electrotypists, the best-paid and most respected in the labor hierarchy.

The Harper Establishment demonstrates how much the organization of printing labor had changed from the artisan shops common but a half-century before. The printer then had to master many tasks, through six years of apprenticeship and a few more as a journeyman, to become the master of his shop. He had to educate himself in order to correct the often semiliterate manuscripts authors handed him. He disciplined his hands and eyes to master the considerable skills needed to set type. The printer required a thorough knowledge of arithmetic to conduct business and to collate page numbers on the signatures. His tasks might include stitching and binding, selling books and stationery, making contacts, picking up and delivering orders, sweeping floors, cleaning presses, and rolling the balls necessary for inking the type. He pulled the lever that brought the type into contact with the paper, a task so arduous that pressmen often displayed a characteristic gait due to the overdevelopment of the right side of the body.[8]

The variety of tasks and the educational aspects of apprenticeship should not obscure the difficulty of the life. Days stretched from sunup to sundown, and the master workman kept constant watch upon his journeymen and apprentices, most of whom lived within the master's household. The relationship between master workman and apprentice was codified in a contract signed at the beginning of the tenure. Typical clauses in such contracts stipulate that the apprentice should not engage in any outside economic activity and that "he shall not go to taverns or any other places of resort nor otherwise absent himself day or night from his master's service without his leave." In return, the master obligated himself to "teach and instruct . . . the said apprentice in the art, trade, or mastery of printing, and to find unto his said apprentice meat, drink, lodging, washing, medicine, and good and sufficient clothing."[9]

Despite the apparent absolute control of the master over his apprentices and journeymen, they actually exhibited a good deal of self-regulation within the workplace, perhaps embodied most in the institution of the "chapel." The chapel decided on the grievances between printers and imposed fines against poor workmanship—usually forcing the slacker to buy drinks for the whole house. Franklin discovered, upon being promoted from pressman to compositor in Palmer's printing house in London in 1724, that the chapel demanded "a *Bienvenu* or Sum for Drink," which he refused to pay. The journeymen disciplined Franklin in a common manner in printing houses, by invoking the chapel Ghost. Such imaginary apparitions quite literally haunted any journeyman who disobeyed the chapel. The Ghost waged an ever-escalating war of sabotage upon the recalcitrant printer's work. The printer found that he lost his composing stick or galleys and that the Ghost had transposed the type in his cases. The printer might be "smoked," the other workers surrounding him threateningly with lit matches and singing mournful songs. The final stage of bedevilment sent the contumacious printer to Coventry; no other worker would speak to him or even notice his existence. Even Franklin could not stand up to this kind of social pressure. After putting up a valiant fight for "two or three weeks" during which he reached the most serious stage of being "considered as an Excommunicate," he decided "to comply and pay the Money; convinc'd of the Folly of being on ill Terms with those one is to live with continually."[10]

The modern industrialization of printing began not with the technological innovations of the antebellum years, but with the reorganization of labor in the workplace throughout the eighteenth and early nineteenth centuries, a reorganization that for the most part destroyed traditional work rhythms and relationships. The wage system came to predominate over the apprentice-journeyman contract; the new system offered greater self-determination for the workers in exchange for job security. Work became more specialized as journeymen split into compositors and pressmen, with the latter receiving much lower wages. The ranks of pressmen, who needed only the strength to pull the press bar, overflowed with runaway apprentices, known derisively as "halfway journeymen." These relatively unskilled pressmen glutted the market and drove down wages.

Another eighteenth-century labor innovation in the workplace was the emergence of the manager. One of the key signs of the transformation of work not only in printing but in any trade occurred when the owner of a shop hired a manager or a "boss" to intensify the labor performed on the job, thus increasing production while holding wages steady. A 1795 contract between William Manning, a shop manager, and Isaiah Thomas and Ebenezer Andrews shows just how far the transformation of printing work had gone before the advent of any modern technological advances in printing. Thomas and Andrews promised the manager enough work for himself and "eight apprentices or a number of Journeymen equal to eight apprentices, that is to say, to the amount of seven hundred and fifty pounds per annum"— demonstrating both the preference for unskilled labor and the fixity of wages. Under the contract Thomas and Andrews promised to pay Manning according to how much he produced, making it in his interest to get his workers to produce more, although they would not get paid for doing so.[11]

The wage system, the manager, and the intensification of labor heralded by both had been adopted by most major printing shops by the beginning of the nineteenth century. Franklin, for example, became a manager in 1727 for Samuel Keimer, certainly not the most advanced printer of his time. As early as 1786 twenty-six Philadelphia journeymen printers went on strike against widespread wage reductions from $6.00 to $5.83 ⅓ a week. So firmly in place was the new organization of labor that by the first quarter of the nineteenth century, journeymen founded more than a dozen "typographical societies," concerned not only with wage scales but also with labor conditions, the halfway journeyman problem, and, most prominently, sickness, death, and unemployment benefits—the rudiments of security.[12]

In 1831, the newly formed Typographical Association of New York issued a circular to its employers that summarizes the laborer's response to the transformation of printing work. The document complains of "two thirds" men (halfway journeymen), "roller-boys" (pseudo-apprentices), and the "newcomers to New York" (recently arrived immigrants undercutting the wages of native workers). The association accused employers of union-busting by importing workers and avoiding union help through "a constant change of workmen." Against these and other practices, the association unsuccessfully sought in 1836 to preserve traditional shop organization by incorporating the chapel into its constitution.[13]

III

Just as the New York Typographical Association and others like it reached their peak of influence prior to the Panic of 1836, Isaac Adams perfected the steam-driven flatbed press that would serve as the culmination of antebellum innovation in fine-book printing. The wide adoption of the Adams steam press and others like it signaled the full transformation of presswork. Upon such presses, mere girls, the cheapest part of the labor force, could, as they did at the Harper Establishment, supervise all pressing operations and perform tasks that fifty years earlier could cripple grown men.

Side by side with the steam press stood stereotyping and elec-trotyping as important innovations in antebellum printing. Before the adoption of these processes, compositors redistributed the type used to print the first edition of a work. New editions required the printer to recompose and proof the type again, meaning that labor expenses for compositors remained the same for first and subsequent editions. Stereotyping (1811) and electrotyping (1841) solved this problem by allowing an impressment to be taken of the set type, fashioning from it a permanent, relatively inexpensive metal plate that could be stored away and used for subsequent editions.

Stereotyping and electrotyping dramatically diminished the total work available for compositors. With more compositors looking for work, the worth of their labor in the market fell. Technologically obsolete journeymen pressmen chasing composing jobs exacerbated the problem. Typographers early on recognized the dire impact of industrialization upon them: "The business of stereotyping [has] in-creased to a great extent; and the numerous improvements in the art . . . render it every year more difficult for compositors to support themselves and their families."[14]

The stereotype and electrotype plates that threatened the live-lihood of the workman underwrote the emergence of the publisher as capitalist. The plates represented capital investment; they could be used over long periods of time, rented out to other publishers, or sold outright. Longfellow, for example, escaped the impecunious fate of so many of his fellow authors by owning his own plates. Not so fortunate was Herman Melville. His contract with Harpers for *Moby-Dick* stipulated that after seven years of publication, he "shall have the right to the purchase and complete ownership of the stereotype plates of said work on paying to the said Harper and Brothers one-half of their original cost." Melville, like most American authors of the peri-od, could hardly afford to purchase his plates even at half their cost. As publishing capitalized, the financial relations between authors and publishers underwent transformation. The Harpers, for example, went from commonly granting authors "½ net profits or proceedings" in the 1830s to their usual practice of the 1850s of stipulating royalties on 10 percent on the trade list price after the sale of the first one thousand or two thousand copies. Such royalties signaled a great departure from the eighteenth-century practice in which authors helped to underwrite the costs of publication.[15]

Stereotyping and electrotyping also changed the way publishers marketed their books and their authors. Prior to these innovations, publishers had to guess the size of first editions and hope that if they underestimated, the type would still be composed to allow them to get out a second edition easily. Stereotyping and electrotyping encouraged publishers to engage in in-depth, long-term advertising campaigns to boost not only the sales of the particular work but also the author's celebrity, in the hopes that previous works by that author might be sold. Authors more than ever came before the public eye, and publishers gave substantial emoluments to reviewers in numerous periodicals for sterling reviews—reviews used extensively in advertising copy. "The mere announcement of a book may not create a desire to read it," the trade paper *American Publishers' Circular* advised in 1856, "while, if a large number of testimonials to its merits are presented, this may be accomplished." J. C. Derby's advertisement for Elizabeth Oakes Smith's *Newsboy,* for example, followed this wisdom and listed fourteen extensive critical testimonials with the announcement of "Tenth Thousand Sold!" Whatever the truth of such claims, stereotyping and electrotyping made the size of editions very flexible, so that large numbers of books could be printed throughout the year or beyond if a book suddenly became popular.[16]

Alongside the steam press, stereotyping, and electrotyping, technological innovations in other crafts supported the industrialization of printing. Two papermaking machines competed during the antebellum period, the belt-based one of Foudrinier (1799) and the cylinder of Thomas Gilpin (1816). Both took until the 1830s to come into widespread use. On both, paper for the first time could be produced in large widths on a continuous roll—a big step from the time-consuming, sheet-by-sheet hand process common from the sixteenth century on. The cost of raw material for paper remained high until the mid-1850s, when wood and pulp replaced always rare cotton and linen rags. The bookbindery too felt the impact of industrialization. The hand-operated stabbing machine (ca. 1820), the rolling press (1840), the folding machine (1843), the rounder and backer (1854), and various gilding, marbling, cutting, and trimming machines eased the process of bookbinding, although they left untouched laborious hand sewing.[17]

The resulting variety of bindings forces a distinction between book purchase and reading. How many people bought books and never intended that they or anyone else would read them? That the publisher of a successful novelist seldom issued his work in a single type of binding suggests the importance of the book as commodity. George Putnam, for example, offered a fifteen-volume duodecimo version of Irving's works in cloth ($19.00), sheep ($20.00), half-calf ($30.00), half-morocco, gilt tops ($33.00), calf, extra ($37.50), calf, antique ($40.00), and morocco, super extra ($48.00).[18] A number of books in ornately gilded morocco upon the mantelpiece or in a sideboard bookcase testified to the owner's expensive taste in selecting fine commodities. The contents of the book mattered very little; the same book sold in standard bindings for a fraction of the cost. A fine binding, of course, hardly indicated that the book went unread. Such bindings could enhance the experience of reading a much-beloved book. Nevertheless, the profusion of bindings negated the old adage that one cannot judge a book by its cover. The conspicuous consumption of books during the era meant that some readers preferred owning books over reading them.

IV

Finely bound books by their very price stood in reach of only the well-to-do few. Did the same technology that permitted the widescale production of such luxury items "democratize" the reading experience in America as publishers and other commentators so commonly claimed? For example, Frances Trollope noted that Americans "are great novel readers." And James Fenimore Cooper could "scarcely remember ever to have entered an American dwelling however humble, without finding fewer or more books."[19]

Despite glowing accounts of book readership in the antebellum United States, innovations in printing technology by no means caused such a drop in the price of books as to make them widely available. The price of hardcover books during the antebellum years ranged between $0.75 and $1.25. Technology and the widescale book market had thus cut the average cost of books to about 50 percent of the cost in the late eighteenth century. However, economically secure, skilled white male antebellum workers made only about a dollar a day, and women workers commonly made only a quarter of that. The one-dollar price of books represented a full one-sixth of the male's weekly wages and well over half the woman's wages—equivalent today to anywhere between fifty and a hundred fifty dollars, a price few, then and now, would be willing to pay for books. "In the family of the working man," James Waddel Alexander wrote, "books cannot in all cases be very numerous."[20]

Even paperbacks stood outside the reach of workers. While a handful of paperbacks sold for as low as twelve and a half cents, the usual minimum price was thirty-eight cents, the most common price was fifty cents, and the maximum was about sixty-three cents. The most inexpensively priced paperbacks from American authors came not from the most famous such as Cooper and Irving, but rather from Emerson Bennett, whose works U. P. James brought out in 1854 for twenty-five cents a copy, and George M. Foster, whose New York exposés appeared only at the end of the period. Only a little more common were thirty-eight cent editions of American novels; Timothy Shay Arthur, Cooper, and Irving did sometimes appear in this format. By far, most American authors appeared in fifty-cent editions, still out of reach to most working-class readers.[21]

So the increased productive power of American publishing did not make books more available to the masses in any significant way. Those few books that could be bought—those appearing in twelve-cent editions—were usually novels by foreign authors. For example, a cabinetmaker's apprentice in the mid-1840s, Edward Jenner Carpenter, recorded in his diary that he read such foreign novels as *Jacob Faithful, Arrah Neil, The Life and Adventures of Jack of the Mill, The Story of the Jilted Doctor*, and *Attila the King*. Although he read some American fiction in the newspapers, the only American novel he read was *Easy Nat; or, Boston Bars and Boston Boys*, perhaps because he was interested in the temperance issue and it was one of the few American novels appearing in a very inexpensive edition. The high price for American-authored books suggests that contrary to what the speakers at the 1855 publishers' festival proclaimed, technological innovation hardly brought American literature in book form to the masses.[22]

V

The attention given to technological innovations in printing as explanations for the growth of the antebellum reading public too often obscures changes in other technologies that influenced reading. The technologies of publishing and of reading, though obviously similar, do not exactly coincide.

Of these less obvious technological innovations, perhaps none was as great as that of the railroad. Of course, historians of publishing have long recognized that the railroad greatly improved literary distribution and contributed to the dramatic increase in the sales of antebellum books. Usually, however, these historians have contented themselves with chronicling the increase rather than attempting to trace the patterns of dissemination.[23]

The early transportation revolution, dominated by roads and waterways, encouraged the decentralization of publishing in scattered urban centers, whereas during the Age of Rail, production centralized in New York, Boston, and Philadelphia. Because of the intensification of the reading public in the Northeast, relatively fewer imprints reached the Old Northwest and, especially, the South. Rather than distributing literature evenly throughout the country, the coming of the railroad created geographical biases in literary distribution and, by extension, in the experiences of readers. That railroad development tended to take place in areas of industrial development with higher literacy rates reinforced these spatial biases.[24]

Authors and publishers, aware that the Northeast constituted the primary market for literature and that the distribution of literature by rail left most of the South untouched, could afford to ignore the South altogether. The phenomenal sales of *Uncle Tom's Cabin*, its numerous imitators, and other liberal reform novels of the 1850s demonstrated that "American" literature could get along very well without the South, where these novels, if allowed through the mails, were certain to alienate readers. Even fiction writers, usually hungry for the widest public, could contemplate cutting out the South as a potential market. The novelist Henry Peterson suggested this approach in a cover letter for a manuscript he submitted in 1844 to James Munroe and Company: "I should have sent it first to the Harper's who last year published a tale for me, had I not feared that from their extensive connection with the South it would be time thrown away."[25]

The railroad, besides shaping the avenues of antebellum book distribution, also provided a new opportunity for reading. Traveling on an American railroad, Charles Dickens noted that "a great many newspapers are pulled out, and a few of them are read." On the Boston and Maine line, Hawthorne saw passenger cars "each perhaps with fifty people in it, reading newspapers, reading pamphlet novels." Rail passengers could purchase books as well as read them. Charles Lyell observed "that railway cars are everywhere attended by news-boys." Publishers supplied reading matter particularly suited to rail travel, as in the case of George Putnam, who brought out in the 1850s a series of "Railroad Classics," which Putnam claimed to be "small enough to be put into a pocket" with "print . . . large enough to be read without damaging the eyes."[26]

Perhaps the greatest impact of rail upon the antebellum reader concerned the nature of American community life. Areas well served by rail, such as the Northeast, experienced a veritable flood of printed information, a new nationally oriented mass culture to compete with the standing local culture. Low postage rates for newspapers encouraged this flood. The *Universal Yankee Nation* pointed out in 1843, "There is scarcely a hamlet in New England which the Daily Mail does not reach . . . , dispensing information, instruction and amusement, almost as cheaply as free gifts amongst every class in society."[27]

Local interests hardly stood idle in the face of this inundation. For example, in 1842 publishers in Portland, Maine, made "a concerted attack upon the practice of carrying papers in bundles by railroads, out of the mail" (i.e., mass shipments with special, low, nonpostal railroad rates to be distributed by local agents). By forcing all newspapers, including penny papers, to pay full mail postage as single items, the Portland publishers hoped to limit the local circulation of papers published in Boston. Fortunately for Boston publishers, the campaign of their counterparts in Portland failed.[28]

The shift from a local to a national print culture presented readers with very different literary content. "Literary papers who[se] circulation are confined to one locality, usually succeed in suiting the tastes of their readers," William R. Hayden editorialized in 1852 in the *Star Spangled Banner*, "for matters of local interest are sufficiently abundant to furnish material for most of the articles required." Nationally oriented papers had to look elsewhere for material: for "a paper that is read all over the Union, and by those of every variety of taste and judgment, the task of writing to please all, and yet remain true to nature and progress becomes indeed a hard one." In fact most of the stridently nationalistic Boston and New York papers—the *Star Spangled Banner*, the *Universal Yankee Nation*, the *Yankee Blade, Flag of Our Union*, and *Uncle Sam*, among others—eschewed news (aside from short, tabloidlike human-interest stories) for sensational, romantic fiction, usually American-authored and often with American settings. American fiction in newspaper form thus helped to unite the still-heterogeneous national reading public created by rail.[29]

Railroad development transformed the nature of community life for readers and oriented them outward to the national culture and away from local exigencies. Local institutions had to be ever-more aware of the national context of their existence and had to make peace with the emerging national mass culture. The railroad presented the individual with more books and newspapers than ever before and promulgated, at first, fiction as preferred reading matter. In fiction the reader found nationally validated role models, modes of sentimental expression, and a community of reading interests stretching across the country. The print culture brought to communities by rail encouraged the individual to think, act, and feel nationally.[30]

VI

Other often-overlooked technologies also influenced antebellum reading. In a time of sunup to sundown labor, readers required adequate illumination for reading during the few moments of leisure at night. Like many other facets of antebellum life, illumination was socially distributed. The whale oil lamps of the period gave but an inferior light; camphene, which came into use in the 1830s, gave a more brilliant light, but the fluid cost so much for working people that it could be used only for special occasions, if at all. Even whale oil was so expensive that the most popular glass lamps became miniature sized, giving off less light than a modern 60-watt bulb and making the reading of book-length materials impossibly trying.[31]

Poorer readers could, of course, find ways to deal with inadequate illumination. The old story about the young Abraham Lincoln studying by the light of the family hearth probably did have its counterparts in many poorer homes, although one questions how long the eyes could stand the dim flicker of firelight. The apprentice mentioned earlier, Edward Jenner Carpenter, stayed on late at his cabinetmaking shop to read books and newspapers in order to take advantage of the lighting offered gratis by his employer. Some workers, such as seamen under sail, did have abundant daylight leisure time and were able to read so much that reformers spoke out, with a vehemence usually reserved for the temperance crusade, against the practice of reading cheap novels at sea. And it was a common practice in shops still tied to preindustrial work rhythms for someone to be hired to read the newspaper aloud while workers performed their tasks. Nevertheless, for most workers, inadequate illumination seriously discouraged prolonged reading during leisure hours.[32]

The quality of eyesight also had an obvious impact on reading. No historian has yet described the epidemiological dimensions of ocular problems in antebellum America; with the population's general ill-health and poor diet, the size of the problem must have been formidable. Working people in particular seemed susceptible to eye problems, according to Jules Sichel, an optometrist: "Born among the working classes, the child . . . is placed in apprenticeship, and not only is often constrained to exercise his sight upon minute details of form, but the

fatigue of his arms forces him to hold objects nearer his eyes." "Habit-
uated continually to adjust his sight to these limited distances, he
finally ends, necessarily," Sichel concluded, "by losing the faculty of
accommodation to distant objects and becomes myopic." No matter
in what class eye problems occurred, they were thought to be exacerbated by novel reading, as J. Henry Clark observed:

> The practice of incessant novel-reading, so common among our young
> people, is believed to result in injury to the sight. The power of vision is
> often bartered away for a very small price, to very little purpose. Novels
> are printed upon very poor paper and in small type. The imagination is
> heated, the eyes are constantly riveted upon the page, curiosity is excited,
> and no attention paid to position or to light; and thus this fruitless,
> profitless, pernicious habit, while it poisons the imagination, dissipates
> the mind, and wastes precious time; often deprives the reader of the
> opportunity for acquirements afterwards in a better direction, by leaving
> him with enfeebled eyesight.

Clark's dim view of fiction did not prevent his publisher from insert-
ing at the end of the book an advertisement for a novel by T. S.
Arthur.[33]

Corrective eyeglasses during the period cost too much for common
people. The large-scale manufacture of spectacles began only in 1833;
steel spectacles, which replaced the more expensive eyeglasses made
previously of precious metals, first appeared in 1843, but would take
decades to reach the masses. Nevertheless, steel spectacles probably
did open the world of print to many lower-middle-class people who
could previously ill-afford glasses.[34]

VII

No one can argue against the great impact of technological innovation
upon antebellum reading. The industrialization of publishing presented readers with more books of diverse sorts, heralding an era
dubbed by one historian as one of "promiscuous reading."[35] The price
of books also fell, thus widening the base of book purchasers. Penny
papers put reading material in reach of even poorer farmers and the
working class. The extension of rail lines and the completion of the
northeastern rail network in the 1850s assured that books and periodicals, in one way or another, could reach just about anywhere. And
the advent of better illumination and less expensive corrective eye-
wear removed some of the obstacles to reading some individuals
faced.

Yet ironies abound in this story of the transformation of the antebellum reading public. The era of promiscuous reading brought forth, from the perspective of the eighteenth century, an information glut. Even booksellers found themselves "at a loss in the absence of reliable critical information, [as to] what recent publications [to] order."[36] While the increase in new titles may have, arguably, lowered critical standards, it also provided new opportunities for talented and even experimental writers.

Nor did technological innovation democratize the reading public as much as publishers and the press claimed. Books, even most paperbacks, remained too expensive for working-class people. The less expensive books continued to be the province of a distinctly urban institution, the periodical depot. The vast majority of Americans still living in rural areas had little access to such outlets and, by extension, to such literature. Country booksellers simply could not afford to stock even a representative variety of the numerous books published in the major northeastern cities. And the distribution of literature followed closely the development of rail lines, leaving much of the West and the South outside the main channels of dissemination. Even within the highly cultivated markets of the Northeast, the reading public became fragmented by sex, class, and religion in the face of the onslaught of new titles. In short, if the democratization of literature means the equal participation of all in a unified print culture, the antebellum years witnessed a distinctly undemocratic trend.[37]

Yet the very idea of literary democracy must be called into question. In a time of capitalist takeoff, such as the antebellum years, who can expect the distribution of knowledge and economic power *not* to conform? To do so makes literary dissemination independent of economic life. Books, magazines, and newspapers had to follow the same geographical and social patterns of dissemination as other luxury commodities. The vigorous urban middle class produced by rampant industrialism had, because of greater leisure time and a higher disposable income, simply more access to a wider selection of literature than workers and most rural dwellers.

Nor does it elucidate much about the antebellum years to look back longingly at the more homogeneous print culture of colonial New England. Those colonists may have shared in common fewer texts, known them better, and have seen such knowledge more equitably distributed, but their literature was founded on a much less complex socioeconomic base than that of antebellum America.

Perhaps the dream of a simpler society such as the Puritans' inspired antebellum publishers to see themselves as artisan printers. The printer's important place in society had been established since the Protestant Reformation. The image of the artisan printer gave the publisher, emerging out of unprecedented conditions of growth and capitalization, an immediately apprehendable social position. Of course, the publishers' expropriation of the image weakened the claim to social recognition of real artisan printers protesting the industrialization of their trade. But publishers also inherited the age-old, fervent Protestant belief in the democratization of knowledge through print. This belief, perhaps more than anything else, caused them to engage in the democratic cant that they spoke for an undifferentiated nation of readers. However, the publishers' accomplishments in disseminating literature, though real, did not conform to the democratizing ideal of the Protestant printer. Instead, the social distribution of literature followed quite closely the march of American economic development—a different and much more complex sense of "democracy."[38]

The ultimate irony of antebellum technological innovation belonged to readers. As economic development disrupted local community life, the publisher presided over the partial transference of community spirit to the world of literature. Wearing the familiar, comforting mask of the humble artisan printer, the publisher offered through print a new national community. Beneath the mask lay the very same force that threatened local exigencies and necessitated the redefinition of the readers' community life: the reality of nascent industrial capitalism and the innovations in labor and technology it wrought.

Notes

Reprinted from *American Quarterly* 40, no. 1 (March 1988).

The author wishes to express his gratitude to Kenneth Silverman, John Tebbel, Thomas H. Bender, Richard Sennett, and Paul R. Baker for reading and commenting upon the portions of the material presented here that appeared in the original dissertation. Research for this work was performed in part under the Albert S. Boni Fellowship of the American Antiquarian Society.

1. For reports on the event, see "Publishers' Association, Banquet at the Crystal Palace," *New York Daily Tribune* (September 28, 1855); "Authors among Fruits," *New York Daily Times* (September 28, 1855). The Publishers' Association account book in the Booktrades Collection at the American Antiquarian Society, Worcester, Mass., shows the cost of the festival. See also Warren G. French, "Honor to Genius: The Complimentary Festival to Au-

thors, 1855," *New-York Historical Society Quarterly* 24 (1955): 357–67; John Tebbel, *A History of Book Publishing in the United States,* vol. 1, *The Creation of an Industry: 1630–1865* (New York, 1972), 225–27; and Madeleine B. Stern, *Books and Book People in Nineteenth Century America* (New York, 1978), 145–50.

2. "Publishers' Association." The phrase "decided hits" belongs to James Cephas Derby, *Fifty Years among Authors, Books, and Publishers* (New York, 1884), 185.

3. See, for example, Hellmut Lehmann-Haupt, *The Book in America: A History of the Making, the Selling, and the Collecting of Books in the United States* (New York, 1939), 121–45; Daniel Boorstin, *The Americans: The Colonial Experience* (New York, 1958), bk. 3, pts. 11–12; and Elizabeth L. Eisenstein, *The Printing Press as an Agent of Change,* 2 vols. (Cambridge, 1979), pt. 3.

4. The phrase belongs to Frederick Gleason, who from 1837 to 1860 published over one hundred and fifty American-authored novels, far more than any other publisher. Gleason is discussed throughout Mary Noel, *Villains Galore . . . : The Heyday of the Popular Story Weekly* (New York, 1954).

5. "Publishers' Association." Milburn quoted in Derby, *Fifty Years,* 38. The best account of Chapin's speech can be found in "Complimentary Fruit Festival of the New York Book Publishers Association to Authors and Booksellers," *American Publishers' Circular and Literary Gazette* 1 (1855): 65–79.

6. Ethelbert Stewart, *A Documentary History of Early Labor Organizations of Printers, 1786–1853* (Washington, D. C., 1907), 912.

7. This and the following two paragraphs are based upon Jacob Abbott, *The Harper Establishment; On How the Story Books Are Made* (New York, 1855), passim.

8. Rollo G. Silver, *The American Printer, 1787–1825* (Charlottesville, Va., 1967), 10, 137. On the complexities of coordinating type and page, see Joseph Katz, "Analytical Bibliography and Literary History: The Writing and Printing of *Wieland,*" *Proof* 1 (1971): 8–25.

9. Contract between J. D. Bemis, Canandaigua, New York, printer, and Charles Loomis, quoted in Charles James Smith, "Our Missionaries," *Centennial Celebration of the Congregational Church of Rushville, New York* (Rushville, N.Y., 1902), 27.

10. Benjamin Franklin, *The Autobiography of Benjamin Franklin: A Genetic Text,* ed. J. A. Leo LeMay and P. M. Zall (Knoxville, Tenn., 1981), 46, canceled passages deleted. For an in-depth description of the chapel and its Ghost, see George A. Stevens, *New York Typographical Union No. 6: A Study of a Modern Trade Union and Its Predecessors* (Albany, N.Y., 1913), 127.

11. Contract between William Manning and Isaiah Thomas and Ebenezer Andrews, May 15, 1795, Isaiah Thomas Papers, box 3, folder 3, American Antiquarian Society, Worcester, Mass.

12. Franklin, *Autobiography,* 53–57; Henry P. Rosemont, "Benjamin

Franklin and the Philadelphia Typographical Strike of 1786," *Labor History* 22 (1981): 398–421.

13. Quoted in Stewart, *Early Labor Organizations*, 894–98.

14. Ibid.

15. William Charvat, "Longfellow's Income from His Writings, 1840–1852," *Publications of the Bibliographical Society of America* 38 (1944): 9–21; the Melville contract appears in Contract Book no. 2, 1832–67, Harper and Brothers Papers, Rare Book and Manuscript Library, Columbia University, New York. For the different Harper's contract arrangements, compare in the same source the April 1835 agreement for Catherine Maria Sedgwick's *The Linwoods* with the one for Melville's *Typee*, dated December 7, 1850.

16. On publisher-financed reviewing, see William Charvat, "James T. Fields and the Beginnings of Book Promotion," *Huntington Library Quarterly* 8 (1944–45): 82–94; "Where, When, and How to Advertise," *American Publishers' Circular and Literary Gazette* 2 (March 22, 1856): 157–58; and "The Newsboy" (advertisement), *Norton's Literary Gazette and Publishers' Circular* 5 (1855): 632.

17. Frank Comparato, *Books for the Million: A History of the Men Whose Methods and Machines Packaged the Printed Word* (Harrisburg, Penna., 1971), 11, 31, 107–9, 131–33.

18. M. Thomas, *Forty-Second Philadelphia Trade Sale Catalogue* (Philadelphia, 1854), 279.

19. Frances Trollope, *Domestic Manners of Americans*, ed. Donald Smalley (New York, 1949), 93, 313; and James Fenimore Cooper, *Notions of Americans Picked Up by a Traveling Bachelor* (New York, 1963), 2; 94.

20. Trade sale catalogues are the best sources for prices; the average prices presented here derive from a reading of all trade sale catalogues in the American Antiquarian Society (1837–57) including all holdings listed for that location in George L. McKay, *American Book Auction Catalogues, 1713–1934* (New York, 1937). Charles Quill [James Waddel Alexander], *The Workingman* (Philadelphia, 1843), 55.

21. Thomas, *Forty-Second Philadelphia Trade Sale*, 307; M. Thomas and Sons, *Forty-Fourth Philadelphia Trade Sale Catalogue* (Philadelphia, 1856), 81. Cf. Frank L. Schick, *The Paperbound Book in America: The History of Paperbacks and Their European Antecedents* (New York, 1958).

22. Edward Jenner Carpenter, Journal, 1844–45, American Antiquarian Society, passim; a biographical sketch of Jenner appears in Winifred C. Gates, "Journal of a Cabinet-Maker's Apprentice," *Chronicle of the Early American Industries Association* 15 (1962): 22–23.

23. Two of the best of these studies are Warren S. Tryon, "The Publications of Ticknor and Fields in the South, 1840–1865," *Journal of Southern History* 14 (1948): 305–30, and "Ticknor and Fields' Publications in the Old Northwest," *Mississippi Valley Historical Review* 34 (1947): 589–610. For a thoughtful overview, see James Gilreath, "American Book Distribution," *Proceedings of the American Antiquarian Society* 95 (1985): 501–83.

24. Ronald J. Zboray, "The Transportation Revolution and Antebellum Book Distribution Reconsidered," *American Quarterly* 38 (1986): 53–71.

25. Henry Peterson to James Munro and Company, February 8, 1844, James Munroe and Company, Correspondence, 1833–66, folder 2, American Antiquarian Society.

26. Charles Dickens, *American Notes* (Gloucester, Mass., 1966), 79–80; Nathaniel Hawthorne, *The American Notebooks*, ed. Claude M. Simpson (Columbus, Ohio, 1972), 488; Charles Lyell, *A Second Visit to the United States of North America* (New York, 1849), 2;40–41; and advertisement, *American Publishers' Circular and Literary Gazette* 3 (1857): 258.

27. Ronald J. Zboray, "The Railroad, the Community, and the Book," *Southwest Review* 71 (1986): 474–87; and "Editorial," *Universal Yankee Nation* 3 (April 8, 1843): 759.

28. "Carrying Papers by Railroad," *Universal Yankee Nation* (December 17, 1842), 504.

29. William R. Hayden, "Editorial," *Star Spangled Banner* 4 (April 2, 1852): 2. On the Boston papers and other fiction-bearing newspapers of the period, see Noel, *Villains Galore*.

30. See Zboray, "The Railroad, the Community, and the Book" and, for the intersection of literacy, fiction, and community life, "The Letter and the Antebellum Fiction Reading Public," *Journal of American Culture* 10 (1987): 27–34.

31. Lawrence S. Cook, *Lighting in America: From Colonial Rushlight to Victorian Chandeliers* (New York, 1975), 52, 67, 76–80.

32. Carpenter Diary, passim; and Harry R. Skallerup, *Books Afloat and Ashore: A History of Books, Libraries, and Reading during the Age of Sail* (Hamden, Conn., 1974), 209.

33. Jules Sichel, *Spectacles: Their Uses and Abuses in Long and Short Sightedness* (Boston, 1850), 13; and J. Henry Clark, *Sight and Hearing* (New York, 1856), 70.

34. E. E. Arrington, *The History of Optometry* (Chicago, 1929), 119.

35. David Hall, "Introduction: The Uses of Literacy in New England, 1600–1850," in *Printing and Society in Early America*, ed. William L. Joyce et al. (Worcester, Mass., 1983), 45.

36. "Newspaper Criticism," *American Publishers' Circular and Literary Gazette* 2 (1856): 29–30.

37. See "Fetridge's Periodical Depot," *Gleason's Pictorial Drawing Room Companion* 3 (1853): 80; and Michael H. Harris, "The Availability of Books and the Nature of Book Ownership on the Southern Indiana Frontier, 1800–1850," diss., Indiana University, 1971, 55; on the emergence of a differentiated reading public, William Charvat, "Melville and the Common Reader," *Studies in Bibliography* 12 (1958): 41.

38. For a fuller discussion, see Ronald J. Zboray, "A Fictive People: Antebellum Economic Development and the Reading Public for American Novels, 1837–1857," diss., New York University, 1984.

Chapter Eight   **Sense and Sensibility**

A Case Study of Women's
Reading in Late-Victorian
America

Barbara Sicherman

The influence of the printed word may well have been at its peak in
late-Victorian America. It was a time of rapidly expanding education
and literacy, book and magazine production, and opportunities for
self-improvement. The profusion of print, and the evident hunger for
it among the working as well as the middle classes, prompted official
and self-appointed guardians of culture to proffer advice on how and
what to read.[1] Women were integral to the culture of reading. Besides
participating in self-study programs like the Society to Encourage
Studies at Home, they established reading clubs and literary societies
in hundreds of communities across the nation. Taking their cultural
mission seriously, clubwomen and other community leaders gave
high priority to establishing libraries; indeed, one source estimates
that women founded 75 percent of all American public libraries.[2]
     As yet we know little about the import of these activities or how
women decoded what they read. Scholars who have examined the
domestic novels of American antebellum women writers have variously found in them feminist messages of subversion or conservative
reinforcement of the cult of domesticity.[3] While interesting as exegesis, these studies rarely consider actual reading experiences, which
we know included the work of English as well as male writers; nor do
they tell us how readers engaged with texts at the time.[4] Moreover, as
Janice Radway has demonstrated in her study of twentieth-century
romance reading, critics have been too quick to impose their own
views on texts and to assume they have a universal and controlling
power over readers.[5]

A study of a late-Victorian upper-middle-class, mainly female family permits us to explore how reading functioned as a cultural style and how it affected women's sense of self (subjectivity) in the past. Historians have noted the puzzling aspects of the Progressive generation of women, in particular their ability—despite growing up at the height of Victorianism, when images of "true womanhood" and the sanctity of the home still dominated popular culture—to move out into the world in daring ways. A study of women's intense engagement with books suggests that many found in reading a way of apprehending the world that enabled them to overcome some of the confines of gender and class. Reading provided space—physical, temporal, and psychological—that permitted women to exempt themselves from traditional gender expectations, whether imposed by formal society or by family obligation. The freedom of imagination women found in books encouraged new self-definitions and, ultimately, the innovative behavior associated with the Progressive generation.

This study has been influenced by reader-response criticism, an approach that changes the locus of literary study from texts to readers and that emphasizes readers' ability to find their own meanings in texts.[6] Applied to historical subjects, this approach enables us to reconstruct the situational aspects of reading (the what, where, when, and how), while also casting light on individual "stories of reading" and reading as a social system. In this particular case, the Hamilton family constituted an "interpretive community," one that privileged certain texts and interpreted them according to its own codes. Within this common framework, individuals singled out books to which they attached special importance and meaning.

What follows is not a full-scale analysis of reading in the Hamilton family.[7] Rather I have attempted to identify the varied uses of reading in a highly cultured family and to suggest ways in which evidence about reading can be utilized not only in writing individual and family biography but also in understanding shared generational values and changing female subjectivity. The study suggests the need to modify assessments of how women read fictional texts. It also casts doubt on current generalizations about late-nineteenth-century reading and suggests that women's reading behavior may have diverged from that of men.[8]

I

The Hamiltons of Fort Wayne, Indiana, were an intensely and self-consciously literary family. The fortune acquired by the patriarch, a

Scotch-Irish immigrant who came to the city in 1823, provided his five surviving children and eighteen grandchildren with the accouterments of the good life, including education, books, and travel. One of the city's most prominent families, Hamiltons of three generations were distinguished by their literary interests. The oldest members of the third generation, seven women and one man all born between 1862 and 1873, belonged to three nuclear families; in childhood the cousins were each others' only playmates. Two of them attained international renown: Edith Hamilton as a popular interpreter of classical civilizations, her younger sister Alice Hamilton as a pioneer in industrial medicine and Harvard's first woman professor. All had serious aspirations. Margaret and Norah had careers in education and art, respectively. Their cousin Agnes, who hoped at first to become an architect, later entered settlement work, while as young women her older sisters Katherine and Jessie studied languages and art. Allen Hamilton Williams became a physician.[9]

The family's literary tradition descended from their paternal grandmother, Emerine Holman Hamilton, a member of a prominent Indiana political family and a supporter of temperance and woman suffrage. Alice remembered her chiefly as a woman who "lost herself" in books: "She loved reading passionately. I can remember often seeing her in the library of the Old House, crouched over the fireplace where the soft-coal fire had gone out without her knowing it, so deep had she been in her book." Emerine "enthralled" her grandchildren with Scott's poems, which she rendered mainly in prose, sometimes dropping into poetry.[10] With her three daughters Emerine established a Free Reading Room for Women in 1887, which contained, in addition to magazines, newspapers, and reference books, about four hundred volumes, mainly works of "general literature and art and the best fiction." After Emerine's death in 1889, the reading room was renamed for her and became a circulating library, with an enlarged collection that included history and biography as well as children's books. In 1896, after the founding of a public library, the collection, then numbering more than four thousand volumes, went to the Young Women's Christian Association, headed by Emerine's granddaughter Agnes.[11] It is significant that although everyone in this family read passionately, it was the women who extended reading from a private pleasure to an occasion for community service. Emerine's two sons, for their part, ensconced themselves in their libraries—well stocked with port and cigars as well as books. The collection of Edith and Alice's uncle was, at six thousand or more volumes, the largest in Fort Wayne.[12]

Edith once exclaimed that she wished "people did not think us quite so terribly bookish."[13] It is difficult to see how it could have been otherwise. The cousins were inducted into the family's literary culture at an early age, their lives and happiness closely bound up with books. When the Hamiltons thought of each other, they thought of each other reading. Edith away at school wished she could fly home and watch her closest cousin Jessie reading (Sunday books on Sunday), while Jessie later recalled Edith at thirteen reading a book in Greek while combing her hair.[14] Alice claimed that she and her youngest sister Norah were not "born" readers, but "family pressure made us too into bookworms finally."[15] A father's return from business was an occasion for gift books to children, as were holidays; in her early teens, Agnes received a volume of Scott each vacation. The young women also had access to their fathers' ample libraries—except for a few "forbidden" books, of which Alice later recalled only *The Decameron,* the *Heptaméron* of Marguerite of Navarre, and Eugène Sue's *The Wandering Jew.*[16] Bookstores constituted a central focus of interest on shopping sprees in New York City with their unmarried aunt, Margaret Vance Hamilton. After 1889, the young women borrowed books from the reading room.

Reading constituted the core of the Hamiltons' education, indeed was barely distinguished from it. Edith, Alice, and their younger sisters were educated entirely at home until sixteen or seventeen, when they went to Miss Porter's School in Farmington, Connecticut (as did the cousins and the aunts). They received formal instruction only in languages, and even these were largely self-taught. Otherwise their father proceeded by having them read his favorites and by setting them research tasks in his ample reference library. He had Edith and Alice memorize all of *The Lady of the Lake;* and, in their early teens, he gave them a page of the *Spectator* to read over three times and then write out from memory. They also learned the Bible, which Alice claimed she knew better than any other book. Religion was a serious matter in this household, at least for the women, who attended the First Presbyterian Church and taught sabbath school. But Montgomery Hamilton, more interested in theology than devotional practice, taught religious texts like any others: he had Edith and Alice do research in the Bible and memorize the Westminster Catechism.[17]

Both the method of learning—reading, memorizing, and reciting—and the subject matter obviously formed an important substrate of the Hamilton women's mental landscape.[18] Exposure to the classic works of male writers connected them to an important tradition of historical writing. In his fiction and poetry, Scott opened up the imaginative possibilities of the past, while Addison explicitly sought to bring philosophical discourse to the "tea-tables," that is, to women.

Edith responded to the *Spectator* exercise by humorously announcing a literary vocation to her closest cousin, Jessie: "I flatter myself my style is getting quite Addisonian. I hope you keep all my letters; some day, you know, they will be all treasured up as the works of 'Miss Hamilton, the American Addison, Scott & Shakespeare'!"[19] Alice perceived the gender symbolism of this education, contrasting her parents' reading tastes along with differences in their temperaments and religions as markers of character. Her father, who had a passion for "clarity and definiteness," favored Macaulay, Froude, Addison, and Pope, while her mother, Gertrude Pond Hamilton, preferred *The Mill on the Floss, Adam Bede,* and Gray's *Elegy.* While noting that her father's hatred of sentimentality sometimes included his wife's "generous enthusiasms," Alice concluded that his attitude was "probably a wholesome factor in a household of women."[20]

The young Hamiltons read widely in books the Victorians designated "the best."[21] These included numerous works of history and biography—Knight's as well as Macaulay's history of England, but evidently not the American historians Bancroft and Hildreth. Fiction, which had only recently become approved intellectual fare, played a major part in their upbringing.[22] The Hamiltons were familiar with the full range of English middle-class fiction, not only George Eliot, Dickens, and Thackeray, but those they considered "old novelish," like Maria Edgeworth.[23] Scott was a favorite with three generations— Emerine and her second son, Montgomery, as well as Edith and Jessie.[24] Two points about the Hamiltons' reading preferences deserve special mention: their bypassing of the New England literary tradition so important to many intellectual families, and their penchant for British fiction; although British fiction dominated the American literary scene until the 1890s, the Hamiltons probably represent an extreme.[25] They were, however, avid readers of the magazines of Gilded-Age America, of which *Harper's* seems to have been a special favorite.

In addition to the books one expects serious Victorians to have read, a wide range of works, popular in their day but no longer in the canon, were central to the Hamiltons. These included books read in childhood and adolescence, including the Katy books by "Susan Coolidge" (which they preferred to Louisa May Alcott's) and the works of Mrs. (Juliana) Ewing and Charlotte Yonge.[26] Religious novels also absorbed them, as did the devotional literature that constituted suitable Sunday reading in this very Presbyterian family.[27] There was also an array of now-forgotten books read mainly for diversion, some verging on "trash," a designation that probably included excessively romantic or sentimental as well as lurid works. The Hamiltons accepted the category without always agreeing on its boundaries: one person's trash was evidently another's sensibility. Thus Edith noted of a book her younger sister's college friends considered trashy, "It seems to me an earnest, thoughtful book, with a high tone through it all. I do like it very much."[28]

II

There was, then, considerable freedom in the Hamiltons' choice of reading and in the range of books that mattered. There was also greater diversity in reading behavior than has been assumed. The conventional wisdom among historians of the book is that by the late nineteenth century reading had become a private rather than public activity (one that promoted individualism and isolated individuals from one another) and that there had been a shift from a pattern of intensive reading of a few books to one of extensive and presumably more passive reading.[29] Yet a number of the reading customs in the Hamilton family suggest that these interpretations have been too monolithic in general and that reading had a different context, and therefore meaning, for women. Chief among these practices was reading aloud, which for the Hamiltons was a pleasurable and a lifelong habit.[30] Most such occasions were informal and structured by circumstance. There might be two participants or several; texts as well as readers might alternate. At times reading aloud was a duty as well as a pleasure: parents read to children, older siblings to younger ones, adult daughters to their mothers, women to invalids. Above all, reading aloud was social.

Hamiltons of two generations for a time constituted themselves into "a sort of a reading club."[31] In richly detailed letters, Jessie described the group and other reading occasions to her younger sister Agnes, away at school between 1886 and 1888. Daily at half past four, the Hamilton cousins "went over to Gibbon" (also known as "Gibbonhour") at their Aunt Mary Williams's:

> You don't know what fun it is to go into her rooms where the dark red curtains are pulled across the windows and the lamps and wax candles are lit and spend an hour reading. Gibbon is becoming quite interesting[,] it is no longer an effort to listen. After dinner at seven we went to Aunt Marg's room to read Carlyle's French Revolution, it is splendidly written and wonderfully powerful when you can tell exactly what he is driving at. Of course the mind was not the only part refreshed, the fruit, oranges, bananas, green, purple and pink grapes made a lovely picture in a straw basket. And what do you think we did there, something that seemed to

make one of my dreams suddenly to become substance—we hemmed the dish towels for the Farmington House.[32]

When someone had to be absent, the group switched to *A Bachelor's Blunder*, of which Jessie observed, "I read parts of it aloud to mamma and though it is not anything you care about as you do Thackeray or George Eliot still it is very interesting." On another occasion, *A Bachelor's Blunder* followed *King Lear*.[33] Carlyle was resumed the following winter, but on at least one occasion Jessie reported that "somehow it did not work and we rambled off to other things."[34]

The letters suggest that for Jessie, as aspiring artist, the sensuous and social aspects of the reading sessions were central to her enjoyment—the physical accompaniments, the food, the alluring rooms with their beauty and hint of mystery. A range of family business was transacted at the sessions, including sewing (in this case for the cottage in Farmington that Margaret Vance Hamilton was fixing up for her nieces), planning their vocational futures, and gossiping about absent members. Altogether there is a fluidity about this reading circle: several books are kept going at the same time, there is no rush to finish, at times the sessions even break down. Jessie's comments further suggest a receptive attitude to all sorts of books, and a lack of self-consciousness, even in this very proper family, about reading "light" fiction. Although differentiated from the classics, *A Bachelor's Blunder* is mentioned in the same breath with, and deemed worthy of substituting for, Carlyle or Shakespeare. Jessie's description of social reading reveals the playful side of Hamilton family life, a quality seen as well in their love of word games. Such playfulness can be afforded only by those who are both seriously committed to literature and secure in their position as members of a cultured class.

The multiple possibilities of reading are most fully revealed in the diaries and letters of Agnes Hamilton. The most morally earnest of the Hamiltons, Agnes was the only one inclined to worry that she spent too much time reading novels, particularly the sort designated trash. She likened her "insane passion" for reading to an addiction and attributed her indulgence to a desire to escape unpleasant family situations, a trait she thought she shared with her paternal grandmother. After completing *Our Mutual Friend* and Bulwer-Lytton's *My Novel*, she wrote, "I have resolved not to read another novel for a week, at least, and consequently I feel like a reformed drunkard."[35] But Agnes's investment in books was more than a matter of escape or obsession. At twenty-one she wrote, "I live in the world of novels all the time[.] Half the time I am in Europe, half in different parts of

America; I am sober and sensible, gay and frivolous, happy or sor-
rowful just as my present heroine happens to be or rather as the tone
of the book happens to be. I never heard of a person more easily
influenced. Sunday I read Stepping Heavenward. I had not read it for
years and for two weeks I could not keep it out of my mind."[36] In
addition to articulating the appeal of literature to fantasy and imagination, Agnes's comment suggests that reading could be an experience of considerable intensity. After completing Kingsley's *Hypatia*,
which she liked "almost as well as any book I ever read," she observed,
"I cannot enjoy these books I am reading now as much as I ought for I
hurry so from one to another. All the enjoyment is while I am in the
midst of it. Usually when I read a splendid novel I don't touch another
for months so that I go all over it again in my mind."[37] Thus, in
contrast to the rather offhand character of the group sessions, the
Hamiltons invested a great deal of themselves in certain books, some
of which they undoubtedly approached expecting to be overwhelmed.
Jessie wanted to be well before she and Agnes started reading Kingsley's reform novel, *Alton Locke*, so she could "enjoy" it fully.[38] Clearly different styles of reading coexisted, dictated in part by the nature of
the book, by the occasion, and by readers' expectations.

Among the books that acquired intense emotional meaning were
those read in childhood and adolescence.[39] These continued to be the
stuff of Hamilton family life well into adulthood. Reading has long
been recognized as a topic of absorbing interest to adolescents, especially adolescent girls.[40] For girls books have represented an important arena for shared friendship as well as a means of creating a world
more satisfying than the one ordinarily inhabited, a world in which to
formulate aspirations and try out different identities. The Hamiltons'
continued intense preoccupation with books, including children's
books, well into adulthood suggests the prolonging of behavior that
would be considered adolescent today.[41] In this family at least, such
deferred maturity—what Erik Erikson has called a moratorium—
prolonged the period in which the women, encouraged by one another, formulated and often reformulated their vocational plans.

For the Hamilton women, reading offered the occasion for a relatively unmediated experience, exemption from artificial social conventions, and an invitation to fantasy and imaginative play. Although
they rejected Society and looked down on women whose sole interest
was finding a husband, they nonetheless—especially in Jessie and
Agnes's family—experienced the restrictions of Victorian gentility. In
a world full of social constraints, the Hamiltons associated reading
with freedom and possibility. Edith once observed, "Alice and I are out
of humour, because at four o'clock we must get into something stiff

and go down to Mrs. Brown's to meet some people and drink some tea. What I want to do, is to take *Wuthering Heights* and go and sit down on the shore below Arch Rock. I can feel how sweet and still and cool it would be there, how smooth and misty and pale blue the water would be, and how the little ripples would break at my feet with a soft splash."[42] In less poetic vein, reading gave the Hamiltons access to people and situations they would normally neither encounter nor countenance. Thus Agnes noted her eagerness to read *The Old Mam'selle's Secret*, "utter stuff as it is, and full of the nastiest people I should not speak to in real life."[43]

Books also gave the Hamiltons a way of ordering, and understanding, their lives. They provided a common language and a medium of intellectual and social exchange that helped the women define themselves and formulate responses to the larger world. The process started early. When Jessie went off to Miss Porter's, seven younger Hamiltons ranging in age from fourteen to six wrote a joint letter addressed to "Dear boarding school girl." Agnes and Alice, thirteen and twelve respectively, elaborated: "Do you find boarding school as nice as it was in 'Gypsy's Year at the Golden Crescent', or in 'What Katy Did at School'? or are you homesick like the story Mrs. Stanton told in one of the 'Bessie's'?"[44] Here the Hamiltons are not only relating life to fiction, but behaving like fictional characters: the boarding school story, a staple of preadolescent fiction, often included letters from at-home relatives. In this case fiction provided both a rehearsal for future experience (for those who had not yet gone to school) and a reference point for those who had.

Books gave the Hamiltons a symbolic code and a shorthand for experience that continued throughout their lives. When cousins or sisters were geographically distant, a literary allusion captured experience in relatively few words. Thus Alice could describe a rector as "a delicious mixture of Trollope and Mrs. Oliphant and Miss Yonge" and expect to be understood precisely.[45] Only occasionally did literature fail. Edith had difficulty in fathoming Bonté Amos, an audacious but intriguing Englishwoman who belonged to the advanced Bertrand Russell set: "She is a kind of girl I have never even read of before." They took these comparisons seriously. Edith reread a novel whose heroine had been suggested as a possible model for Miss Amos, but thought the parallel inexact.[46]

As the boarding school letter indicates, reading did not foreclose experience for the Hamiltons but offered them a range of possible responses. When Agnes began her diary shortly after her fifteenth birthday, she cited three fictional models from which to choose: "There are so many different ways of commencing journals that I did not know how to commence mine, whether to do as Else did and commence by telling about every member of the family or as Kate in Stepping Heavenward did and describe myself, but I think I will do as Olive Drayton and go right into the middle of it with out any commencement."[47] Such explicit formulation of the possibility of choice suggests both the open-ended quality of reading in this family and the degree to which the Hamiltons maintained control over their reading experiences.

The Hamiltons' world was peopled with fictional characters. It was not just that as readers they were "admitted into the company and present at the conversation."[48] The fictional company was very real to them. Allen Williams at twenty-one exclaimed, "I never can get over a feeling of personal injury in never having known the Abbottsmuir children; don't you think that, after Ellen Daly and Norah, they and Polly and Reginald seem to belong especially to us?"[49] To Agnes too, characters in a favorite book "seem dear friends and I get a homesicky feeling if I cannot get hold of the book not for anything especially fine in it but just for the people."[50] Alice Hamilton in her seventies observed, "Since we saw so little of any children outside our own family, the people we met in books became real to us . . . [among them] Charlotte Yonge's May and Underwood families, who still are more vivid to me than any real people I met in those years."[51] For the Hamiltons, then, there was a reciprocal relation—a continuum—between fiction and life.[52] If fiction was a referent for people one encountered in real life, life also cast light on fiction: Alice claimed she understood Howells's women "much better" through knowing a real-life stand-in.[53] In view of the fluidity of the boundaries it is not surprising that the Hamiltons fictionalized their own lives. After being absorbed for weeks in the story of a romance between the art teacher and a student at Miss Porter's, Edith wrote Jessie, "Don't you feel as if you had got into a story book? And with Susy Sage of all people for the heroine."[54]

The tendency to fictionalize their lives was most evident at the time of Allen Williams's engagement. His fiancée, Marian Walker, a Radcliffe student preparing for a medical career, reminded Allen not only of his closest cousins, Alice and Agnes, but also of the heroines of two novels beloved by the young Hamiltons, Nora Nixon in *Quits* (1857) by Baroness Tautphoeus, a popular English writer of the 1850s and a distant relative, and Ellen Daly in Annie Keary's *Castle Daly* (1875). As Allen informed Agnes, "[Marian] is very fond of Quits! I have told her she cannot meet any of the family until she has read Castle Daly. Can you forgive her for not having done that?" To Alice he exclaimed, "Of course she is like Nora, otherwise I could not have fallen in love. And of course *Quits* is one of her favorite books."[55] The use of such preferences as a means of establishing boundaries for group membership may strike us as quintessentially adolescent, but Allen was in his late twenties. Though professing greater maturity, Alice responded in kind:

> And it just warms my heart and fills me with gladness to have the boy turning into the sort of a man that I wanted him to be, to have him doing an impulsive, unpractical, youthful thing. . . . Why he talks like the heroes in Black's novels, like Willy Fitzgerald and George Brand and Frank King. I am so glad. . . . Agnes it mustn't pass over, it is too sweet and dear and fresh and cunning. . . . Would anybody believe that that introspective, slightly cynical, critical, over-cultured fellow could be so naive, so unconsciously trite, so deliciously young! . . . I think almost the funniest part is his account of the effect the announcement had on the two mothers. It is just like poor Traddles and his Sophie in "David Copperfield" and these poor children seem to take it just as seriously.[56]

Although Alice Hamilton cast Allen as a hero, there is no evidence, then or later, that she was interested in the marriage plot for herself. Allen called her an "unconscious hypocrite" for suggesting that Marian give up her medical career, since he believed his cousin cared only for her work.[57] At forty-nine Alice still gushed about a book in words similar to those she had deployed for Allen's romance: "It is just as cunning as can be and so romantic, you can't believe any hero could be so noble."[58] But her life history, like that of the other Hamilton women, makes it clear that she preferred her heroes in the covers of a book rather than at first hand; in this one case at least, the boundaries between fiction and life remained fixed. Given their assumption that women must choose between marriage and career, for the Hamiltons and other ambitious women of the era, heroes in books were safer than men encountered in life. Indeed, there was a potent antimarriage sentiment in this family. Of the eleven women of the third generation, only the youngest married; a generation younger than her oldest cousins, she did so as an act of rebellion.[59]

III

The Hamiltons' experiences of reading suggest a need to reconsider traditional assumptions about how fiction works on readers. It is usually assumed that women respond to fiction principally through the mechanism of identification with heroines, especially the heroines of "romantic" plots. Among the Hamiltons, however, it was the men who seem to have been fascinated by heroines and who took them as models of womanhood. Montgomery, for example, wrote an essay on the subject for the Princeton literary magazine and, like his nephew Allen Williams thirty years later, alluded to Baroness Tautphoeus's novels during his romance with Gertrude Pond.[60] It was other sorts of plots, plots of adventure and social responsibility, that appealed to the Hamilton women.[61] Favorite novels—even those that end with an impending marriage—provided models of socially conscious and independent womanhood. In reading *Quits*, for example, the women probably responded more to the character of the heroine than to her fate. Nora Nixon, the unaffected and generous heroine of *Quits*, is a natural woman who loves the outdoors, orders her life rationally, and does exactly what she pleases, which happens also to be socially useful. Active, worldly, and independent, she provides a striking contrast to the stereotyped domestic and submissive "true woman." Ellen Daly, the Irish heroine of *Castle Daly*, is less able to control her surroundings than Nora, but she too is unselfconscious, generous, and independent.[62]

The heroine of Charlotte Yonge's paradigmatic *The Daisy Chain* (1856) may have provided the model for real family projects as well as fantasy. In much the same manner as Jo March in *Little Women*, Ethel May is transformed from a helter-skelter tomboy and prospective bluestocking into a thoughtful and family-centered woman. In Ethel's case this is her family of origin, for she resists marriage in order to care for her father and siblings. But Ethel has a public as well as private mission and succeeds in carrying out her resolve to found a church in a poor neighborhood. Her passion for Cocksmoor had its counterpart in the Hamiltons' involvement in Nebraska, a poor section of Fort Wayne where the women and some of the men taught sabbath school. Agnes, who later worked at a religious settlement, was instrumental in persuading her own First Presbyterian Church to establish a regular church there. Ethel May's deepest commitments—her loyalty to family and religion—were also major preoccupations of Agnes's, and it is likely that she found in Ethel a model, as she did in similarly inclined women she encountered in novels and biographies.

If the Hamiltons had a penchant for socially conscious heroines, an analysis of their reading also suggests that the traditional emphasis on identification with one character is far too restrictive an approach to an experience as complex as reading.[63] Recent work reveals the possibilities of more varied interactions between readers and texts. Norman Holland insists on the organic unity of a literary work, including plot, form, and language as well as characters, each of which can influence a reader's response. Starting from the premise that what readers bring to texts is themselves, he further suggests that the reader

identifies not so much with a particular character as with the total
interaction of characters, some satisfying the need for pleasure, others
the need to avoid anxiety. Holland's concept of "identity themes,"
characteristic modes of response that influence reading as well as
other behaviors, is useful for historians since it provides a key to
individual reading preferences that can be applied to the past.[64] Within an explicitly feminist framework, Cora Kaplan emphasizes the
possibilities of multiple identifications by women readers, with heroes as well as heroines.[65]

Certainly for the Hamiltons, the continuum between fiction and
reality gave considerable play to the imagination. Reading provided
both the occasion for self-creation and the narrative form from which
they might reconstruct themselves. Given the way they peopled their
lives with fictional characters and the intensity of their interactions
with books, they were quite capable of reading themselves into fiction or other forms of adventure without a strong identification with
a particular heroine.

Alice Hamilton offers a striking example in claiming a literary
inspiration for her decision to become a physician: "I meant to be a
medical missionary to Teheran, having been fascinated by the description of Persia in [Edmond] O'Donovan's *The Merv Oasis.* I doubted if I could ever be good enough to be a real missionary; but if I could
care for the sick, that would do instead, and it would enable me to
explore far countries and meet strange people."[66] Since *The Merv
Oasis* (1882) is a work of travels and adventure, over a thousand pages
in length and with no discernible missionary focus, Alice clearly drew
from it what she would. The message she found there is consistent
with her early preferences in fiction, among them Charlotte Yonge's
novels which highlight conflicts between individual achievement
and the family claim. This was a matter that deeply troubled her as a
young woman, and she resolved it only when she found work that
enabled her to combine science and service, thereby effecting a balance between individualism and self-sacrifice as she saw it.[67]

Edith's aspirations and literary preferences were of a different kind.
There is no mention in her letters of doing good, a frequent theme of
Alice's; rather there is a longing to "live" and to do great things. Often
moody as a young woman, in reading she found a lifeline, a way of
getting out of herself. At sixteen her favorites were Scott's *Rob Roy*
(1818) and *Lorna Doone* (1869) by R. D. Blackmore.[68] The heroine of
Rob Roy, Diana Vernon, is one of Scott's most appealing—she is an
outdoorswoman, well read, outspoken, and fearless. But the characterization is unlikely to account for the novel's appeal. (Diana fades
away, becoming first an obedient daughter then, in a hastily contrived

ending, wife.) It is more likely that Edith responded to the settings and
plots: her favorites were tales of derring-do in wild places (the Scottish
highlands, the Devonshire moors) and historical settings. They might
well have cast a spell on one who was herself "a natural storyteller"
and who later captured the imagination of millions with her retell-
ings of classic myths and her romantic vision of ancient Greece.[69]

In suggesting that for the Hamiltons reading reinforced a family
culture that promoted personal aspiration and achievement, I am not
claiming a direct cause-and-effect relationship between reading and
behavior. The late nineteenth century was a time of expanding opportunities for women, without which the aspirations of various Hamiltons could not have been enacted in the way they were. What I am
suggesting is that a reading culture such as the one maintained by the
Hamiltons provided a means for accustoming and encouraging wom-
en to imagine new possibilities for themselves. In a supportive environment, such possibilities had a greater chance of becoming
realities.

How typical were the Hamiltons? In the intensity of their involvement with books, in the degree to which their reading activity was
family-centered, and perhaps too in their bypassing of the New England literary tradition they may have been somewhat idiosyncratic.
But they were at the extreme end of a continuum rather than the
oddities they might at first appear to be.

Testimony to the importance of reading comes from the autobiographies of prominent women who came to maturity in the 1880s
and 1890s. For many, books acquired an almost magical status, books
in general as well as particular books; among the consequences attributed to specific works are religious conversion, loss of faith,
choice of vocation, and the breakup of a marriage.[70] By contrast,
formal schooling received little attention, an omission that is not
surprising at a time when self-study was common, when the early
education of even those who attended college was often informal and
erratic, and when most formal learning was by recitation. The invoca-
tion of books was no doubt a convention of a cultural elite. But its
frequency is itself significant and contrasts with the lack of attention
to peers and formal education, both staples of more recent autobiographical narrative. The diminished religiosity of educated Victorians undoubtedly contributed to this new veneration of literature
as a source of cultural authority and models of selfhood.

Books were also markers of "taste" and, therefore, ultimately of
class.[71] What one read, how much, even how one read, not to mention
the size of the paternal library, were important markers of cultural
style in middle- and upper-middle-class homes. But love of books was

not the prerogative of the wealthy alone; indeed, for many individuals raised in a religious tradition suspicious of display, a reverence for books was a way of distancing themselves from those with merely social aspirations. For women in particular, the level of a family's intellectual aspirations was more important than its bank account or social pedigree in encouraging ambition.[72]

Of course, a passion for books and other cultural artifacts could become the means by which the cultured classes insulated themselves from unpleasant realities. In a memorable passage in her autobiography Jane Addams warns against the dangers of self-culture, in particular the habit of her class of "lumbering our minds with literature," an epiphany that followed the intrusion of a literary reflection when she confronted extreme poverty. Yet Addams too fell back on the literary culture of her youth and tried to pass it on to her immigrant neighbors: one of the first public activities at Hull House was a reading group that began with George Eliot's *Romola*, a work set in Renaissance Florence.[73] In so doing, she was continuing a tradition of women's reading that had social as well as private dimensions.

Growing up in an era when the printed word was venerated, women like the Hamiltons found in books not just the messages of official purveyors of culture, though they found these too. For some, engagement with books in childhood and adolescence permitted entry into a world of fantasy that helped them formulate aspirations for themselves different from those traditional to women, and ultimately to act on them as well. Although many of the pejorative connotations of the old association of women and fiction had disappeared by the late nineteenth century, when "good" fiction had attained the status of a cultural icon, reading was still a gender-marked activity, no doubt because it seemed a relatively passive form of intellectual exercise and one that had no practical outcome. This study has tried to demonstrate that reading had more practical and positive consequences for women than has been assumed. Many found in reading an occasion that, by removing them from their usual activities, permitted the formulation of future plans or, more generally, encouraged vital engagement with the world, a world many thought would be transformed by women's special sensibilities. Women's passion for reading must then be viewed as more than simple escapism, as absorption in books has often been designated.

IV

What generalizations may be drawn from a case study such as this one? In the matter of method, a contextual study of groups of real readers permits historians to adapt the approach of ethnographers to the past. If one looks at groups of readers, it becomes clear that reading was not restricted to writers of one genre, sex, or nationality, and that both occasions for reading and particular texts developed complex symbolic meanings for specific reading communities. Further, by studying reading as behavior rather than as textual analysis, historians can peel back later layers of interpretation and come nearer to the contemporary meaning of a work. A study of past readings also permits a deeper understanding of aspirations and emotional preferences as distinct from ideology—what Raymond Williams calls "structures of feeling" or sensibilities.[74] These are often difficult to get at, particularly in an era when sentimentality and self-revelation were suspect, as they were in the late nineteenth century.

Substantively, a case study of this sort can cast light not only on the impact of books and the nature of reading experiences in the past, but on our understanding of these processes. The emphasis on the escapist aspects of certain kinds of fiction, indeed on the distinction between "light" and "serious" reading, seems misplaced in view of the varied and complex sorts of reading behavior that existed in the past. Reading theorists have argued that reading is not simply a passive form of cultural consumption, that something happens to readers that becomes imperative for them to understand, and that reading stimulates desire rather than simply pacifying it. The spectator role permits readers to remove themselves temporarily from the necessity to act, enabling them to use this freedom "to *evaluate* more broadly, more amply" and thus to "modify categories according to 'the way I feel about things.'"[75] There were different sorts of reading in the Hamilton family, but their experiences of reading, both social and individual, were of the sort that encouraged them to extend the range of the possible. In their interpretive community, children's books, "light" fiction, and devotional literature (fiction or nonfiction) could all play a part in the formation of one's sense of self. From this study, it is also apparent that generalizations based on assumed oppositions between modes of reading (intensive/extensive) and loci of reading (public/private) cannot be sustained.

Evidence of the sort provided by the Hamiltons makes it possible to discover how reading behavior and self-consciousness changed over time. This study suggests a link between reading and the formation of female subjectivity in a particular historical period. By so doing, I do not wish to minimize the importance of reading for women in other times and places: adolescent girls seem to have exhibited consistently greater passion for reading than their male counterparts. Nevertheless, a number of factors seem to have contributed to the empowering nature of women's reading experiences in the late nineteenth century. Books were then especially revered cultural artifacts (without serious competition from nonprint forms of entertainment) and, at a time of rapidly expanding educational opportunity, women also had freer access to them than in earlier generations. The lesser importance of formal education in children's early years may have fostered a greater degree of self-invention compared with later, more routinized educational patterns. It is likely too that the relatively informal mode of transmitting cultural values played a part in the open and playful approach to reading exhibited by the Hamiltons.[76]

Finally, the literature of the era was especially conducive to dreams of female heroism outside family life. The downplaying of sexuality in Victorian fiction and the lesser concentration on the marriage plot in girls' adventure stories encouraged women to fantasize about other sources of fulfillment, including those that gave women a large public role.[77] Novels like Charlotte Yonge's, while telling stories about the taming of tomboys, nevertheless afforded scope for female agency, albeit within a separate sphere. Books could not create a desire for female heroism where none existed in the reader. But, in conjunction with a family culture that encouraged female aspiration and education, reading could provide the occasion for perceiving one's inmost needs and wants—desires that could later be acted upon. Like earlier critics who viewed women's reading as suspect, though for different reasons, some feminist critics have recently emphasized the dangers of reading for women.[78] In the context of late-Victorian American life, however, the impact of reading was more likely to be liberating than confining.

Notes

This paper was presented at the Berkshire Conference on Women's History, June 20, 1987; comments by the other participants, Joan Jacobs Brumberg, Janice Radway, and Martha Vicinus, were extremely helpful. I also want to thank Cathy Davidson, Marlene Fisher, Martin Green, David D. Hall, and Mary Kelley for their comments; Ann Brown, Tammy J. Banks-Spooner, and Elizabeth Young for research assistance; and W. Rush G. Hamilton for permission to quote from the Hamilton Family Papers, Schlesinger Library, Radcliffe College, Cambridge, Mass.

1. On working-class reading, see Michael Denning, *Mechanic Accents:*

Dime Novels and Working-Class Culture in America (London and New York, 1987). Two diverse examples of the how-and-what genre are Noah Porter, *Books and Reading, or What Books Shall I Read and How Shall I Read Them?* (1870; rpt. New York, 1883); and *List of Books for Girls and Women and Their Clubs; with Descriptive and Critical Notes and a List of Periodicals and Hints for Girls' and Women's Clubs,* ed. Augusta H. Leypoldt and George Iles (Boston, 1895).

2. On women's literary and voluntary activities, see Karen J. Blair, *The Clubwoman as Feminist: True Womanhood Redefined, 1868–1914* (New York, 1980), esp. 57–71; Anne Firor Scott, "Women and Libraries," *Journal of Library History* 21 (Spring 1986): 400–405, and "On Seeing and Not Seeing—A Case of Historical Invisibility," *Journal of American History* 71 (June 1984): 7–21; and Theodora Penny Martin, *The Sound of Our Own Voices: Women's Study Clubs, 1860–1940* (Boston, 1987).

3. Cf. Ann Douglas, *The Feminization of American Culture* (New York, 1977); Nina Baym, *Woman's Fiction: A Guide to Novels by and about Women in America, 1820–1870* (Ithaca, N.Y., 1978); and Mary Kelley, *Private Woman, Public Stage: Literary Domesticity in Nineteenth-Century America* (New York, 1984). Kelley also analyzes diverse interpretations of the genre. See also Linda K. Kerber, *Women of the Republic: Intellect and Ideology in Revolutionary America* (Chapel Hill, N.C., 1980), 233–64; Dee Garrison, *Apostles of Culture: The Public Librarian and American Society, 1876–1920* (New York, 1979), 67–101; and Elizabeth A. Flynn and Patrocinio P. Schweickart, eds., *Gender and Reading: Essays on Readers, Texts, and Contexts* (Baltimore, Md., 1986).

4. An exception is Nina Baym, *Novels, Readers, and Reviewers: Responses to Fiction in Antebellum America* (Ithaca, N.Y., 1984), who analyzes contemporary periodical reviews and includes British as well as American fiction.

5. Janice A. Radway, *Reading the Romance: Women, Patriarchy, and Popular Literature* (Chapel Hill, N.C., 1984). Engaging the debate over the impact of popular cultural forms, in particular the degree to which female subjectivity is controlled by such a formulaic genre as the romance, Radway finds a restricted but authentic self-assertion both in the circumstances under which romances are read and in the meanings attached to them. Cathy N. Davidson, *Revolution and the Word: The Rise of the Novel in America* (New York, 1986), has also pioneered in developing a reader-centered approach. See also Elizabeth Long, "Women, Reading, and Cultural Authority: Some Implications of the Audience Perspective in Cultural Studies," *American Quarterly* 38 (Fall 1986): 591–612.

6. Susan R. Suleiman and Inge Crosman, eds., *The Reader in the Text: Essays on Audience and Interpretation* (Princeton, N.J., 1980), and Jane P. Tompkins, ed., *Reader-Response Criticism: From Formalism to Post-Structuralism* (Baltimore, Md., 1980), are useful introductions to reader-response theory. One of the most influential statements is Stanley Fish, *Is There a Text in This Class? The Authority of Interpretive Communities* (Cambridge,

Mass., 1980). Wolfgang Iser, "Interaction between Text and Reader," in *Reader in the Text*, 106–19, and Hans Robert Jauss, "Literary History as a Challenge to Literary Theory," in *New Directions in Literary History*, ed. Ralph Cohen (Baltimore, Md., 1974), 11–41, were also helpful.

7. I am currently engaged in a study of three generations of Hamiltons as part of a larger project on reading and gender in nineteenth-century America.

8. The work of David D. Hall provides the best point of entry into the literature on the "history of the book" in America; see especially "Introduction: The Uses of Literacy in New England, 1600–1850," in *Printing and Society in Early America*, ed. William L. Joyce et al. (Worcester, Mass., 1983), 1–47, and "The World of Print and Collective Mentality in Seventeenth-Century New England," in *New Directions in American Intellectual History*, ed. John Higham and Paul K. Conkin (Baltimore, Md., 1979), 166–80. See also Carl F. Kaestle, "The History of Literacy and the History of Readers," in *Review of Research in Education*, vol. 12, ed. Edmund W. Gordon (Washington, D.C., 1985), 11–53.

9. The younger brothers in the cousins' families were considered "children" by the others. There was also a fourth and much younger group of cousins. On the family, see Alice Hamilton, *Exploring the Dangerous Trades* (Boston, 1943), hereafter cited as *EDT*; Barbara Sicherman, *Alice Hamilton: A Life in Letters* (Cambridge, Mass., 1984), esp. 11–32 and genealogy; and Mina J. Carson, "Agnes Hamilton of Fort Wayne: The Education of a Christian Settlement Worker, *Indiana Magazine of History* 80 (March 1984): 1–34. The representativeness of the Hamiltons is considered below.

10. *EDT*, 23–24. Emerine was evidently named for a character in *The Prisoners of Niagara, or Errors of Education* (Frankfort, Ky., 1810), a sentimental novel written by her father. Jesse Lynch Holman, a judge and ordained Baptist clergyman, later tried to buy up and destroy the work, because he thought its morals were unsound. Israel George Blake, *The Holmans of Veraestau* (Oxford, Ohio, 1943), 5–6.

11. Robert S. Robertson, *History of the Maumee River Basin* (Allen County, Ind., 1905), 2:337–40; and library file in the Indiana Collection, Vertical File, Allen County Public Library, Fort Wayne, Ind. The reading room remained a family activity: the Hamiltons donated books, and some of the young women dispensed books to patrons. It was women's space: the intrusion of a man upset Emerine's youngest daughter, Margaret Vance Hamilton, and led the librarian to fear she would be dismissed. Katherine Hamilton to Jessie Hamilton, Sunday, September 22 [1889?]. Folder 133, Hamilton Family Papers, Schlesinger Library, Radcliffe College, Cambridge, Mass. (All references to archival sources not otherwise identified are from this collection.) Margaret Vance Hamilton was also active in establishing the Fort Wayne Public Library, an outgrowth of activities of the Woman's Club League.

12. Montgomery Hamilton, Alice and Edith's father, had a library of about a thousand books, many of them reference works. The collection of his older brother, A. Holman Hamilton, specialized in English, Irish, and Scottish folklore. It also included books on witchcraft, rare medieval works, tales

of "low life" as well as "good" fiction for adults and young people, numerous magazines (some for children), and books on subjects like architecture that accorded with his daughters' vocational interests. The collections of various Hamiltons are described in Robertson, *History of the Maumee River Basin,* 350–58. There are numerous book orders in the A. Holman Hamilton Papers, Indiana State Library, Indianapolis. Marybelle Burch generously provided materials from this collection.

13. Edith Hamilton to Jessie Hamilton, August 3, 1892.

14. Doris Fielding Reid, *Edith Hamilton: An Intimate Portrait* (New York, 1967), 30.

15. *EDT,* 19.

16. Ibid., 18–19. The same "forbidden" books turn up regularly in autobiographies of Progressives, along with dime novels (the latter mainly boys' reading). The term "French novel" was almost generic for racy, with Sue, Dumas, and George Sand often singled out. See Baym, *Novels, Readers, Reviewers,* 178–80, 184–86, 213. The category may have included some pornography, the most costly books ordered by A. Holman Hamilton for which prices are available; at least one was ordered by Alice's father. A. Holman Hamilton Papers, Indiana State Library.

17. *EDT,* 27–31.

18. The impact of memorization deserves study. On Miss Porter's, where a similar mode of reading and recitation prevailed, see Louise L. Stevenson, "Sarah Porter Educates Useful Ladies, 1847–1900," *Winterthur Portfolio* 18 (Spring 1983): 39–59.

19. Edith Hamilton to Jessie Hamilton, Tuesday evening [early 1882?].

20. *EDT,* 30–32.

21. Agnes Hamilton's Diary, the most comprehensive source of information about the Hamiltons' reading, includes lists for the years 1885–97. On Victorian culture, see Daniel Walker Howe, ed., *Victorian America* (Philadelphia, 1976), especially the essays by Howe and David D. Hall.

22. As evangelical hostility to fiction abated, even cultural conservatives praised literature for unlocking the powers of the imagination. See Porter, *Books and Reading;* and Louise L. Stevenson, *Scholarly Means to Evangelical Ends: The New Haven Scholars and the Transformation of Higher Learning in America, 1830–1890* (Baltimore, Md., 1986).

23. Agnes Hamilton to Jessie Hamilton, July 14, 1894.

24. After 1860 or so, Scott was consigned mainly to younger readers. On his popularity, see John Henry Raleigh, "What Scott Meant to the Victorians," in *Time, Place, and Idea: Essays on the Novel* (Carbondale, Ill., 1968), 96–125; and James D. Hart, *The Popular Book: A History of America's Literary Taste* (Berkeley and Los Angeles, n.d.), 68–69, 73–78.

25. Several factors may account for the family's neglect of the New England tradition. Montgomery disliked the "woolgathering of the New England school," and it is likely that other Hamiltons also disapproved of Emerson's romantic individualism. *EDT,* 31. The family's midwestern location and prominence in the Indiana Democratic party were also important. (Emerine's brother William Steele Holman served sixteen terms in Congress,

her father was a judge, and her son A. Holman Hamilton was a two-term member of Congress.) On the Holman family's political milieu, see Jean H. Baker, *Affairs of Party: The Political Culture of Northern Democrats in the Mid-Nineteenth Century* (Ithaca, N.Y., 1983), esp. 33–37. On nineteenth-century American reading patterns, see Hart, *Popular Book;* on England, Richard D. Altick, *The English Common Reader: A Social History of the Mass Reading Public, 1800–1900* (Chicago, 1957).

26. *EDT,* 19. Susan Coolidge was the pen name of Sarah Chauncy Woolsey.

27. See Robert Lee Wolff, *Gains and Losses: Novels of Faith and Doubt in Victorian England* (New York, 1977), for a discussion of religious novels, many of them read by the Hamiltons.

28. Edith Hamilton to Jessie Hamilton, July 14 [1889]. The book was *The Silence of Dean Maitland* (n.d.) by Mary Gleed Tuttiett, using the pseudonym Maxwell Gray. See also Edith Hamilton to Jessie Hamilton, September 14 [1889].

29. Burton J. Bledstein, *The Culture of Professionalism: The Middle Class and the Development of Higher Education in America* (New York, 1976), 77–78, emphasizes the isolating nature of Victorian reading. In "The World of Print and Collective Mentality," 171–72, and "Introduction: The Uses of Literacy," David D. Hall accepts the intensive-extensive dichotomy, while Davidson, *Revolution and the Word,* 72–73, and Robert Darnton, *The Great Cat Massacre and Other Episodes in French Cultural History* (New York, 1984), 249–52, criticize the claim that the intensity of the reading experience diminished.

30. Reading aloud was also a ritual at Miss Porter's. Even in their nineties Alice and Margaret Hamilton belonged to a reading club.

31. Agnes used the term for a group that met "every Saturday in Aunt Marge's room, we read Henry Esmond and while one reads the rest of us do our mending or other sewing." Agnes Hamilton Diary, April 25 [1885].

32. Jessie Hamilton to Agnes Hamilton, January 9, 1887. See also Jessie Hamilton to Agnes Hamilton, January 19 and 23, 1887; and Allen Hamilton Williams to Agnes Hamilton, June 1, 1887.

33. Jessie Hamilton to Agnes Hamilton, January 23, 1887; see also Jessie Hamilton to Agnes Hamilton, February 11, 1887. *A Bachelor's Blunder* (1886) was a contemporary English novel by William Edward Norris.

34. Jessie Hamilton to Agnes Hamilton, March 11, 1888. See also Jessie Hamilton to Agnes Hamilton, February 13, 1887.

35. Agnes Hamilton Diary, July 31 [1887]. See also Agnes Hamilton to Edith Trowbridge, August 19, 1895, folder 405.

36. Agnes Hamilton Diary, May 7 [1890]. Agnes had a penchant for works like Elizabeth Payson Prentiss's *Stepping Heavenward* (1869), a spiritual manual in the guise of a novel. Its heroine, who is depicted as ill-tempered and selfish at the outset, emerges as a paragon of Christian womanhood after intense suffering.

37. Agnes Hamilton to Jessie Hamilton, December 31, 1886.

38. Agnes Hamilton Diary, September 9 [1888].

39. Margaret Meek et al., eds., *The Cool Web: The Pattern of Children's Reading* (London, 1977), offer stimulating articles on children's reading by James Britton, D. W. Harding, C. S. Lewis, and Aidan Warlow. Useful historical works include J. S. Bratton, *The Impact of Victorian Children's Fiction* (Totowa, N.J., 1981); Elizabeth Segel, " 'As the Twig Is Bent . . .': Gender and Childhood Reading," in *Gender and Reading*, 165–86; F. J. Harvey Darton, *Children's Books in England: Five Centuries of Social Life* (1932; rpt. Cambridge, 1966); Mary Cadogan and Patricia Craig, *You're a Brick, Angela!: The Girls' Story, 1839–1985* (London, 1986); and Gillian Avery, *Nineteenth Century Children: Heroes and Heroines in English Children's Stories, 1780–1900* (London, 1965). Edward Salmon discusses girls' and boys' reading in *Juvenile Literature as It Is* (London, 1888) and "What Girls Read," *Nineteenth Century* 20 (October 1886): 515–29. On the United States, see R. Gordon Kelly, *Mother Was a Lady: Self and Society in Selected American Children's Periodicals, 1865–1890* (Westport, Conn., 1974).

40. Lewis M. Terman and Margaret Lima, *Children's Reading: A Guide for Parents and Teachers*, 2d ed. (New York, 1931), esp. 68–84; and G. Stanley Hall, *Adolescence: Its Psychology* (New York, 1905). Terman and Lima maintain that "at every age girls read more than boys" (p. 68).

41. Children's books were read frequently by adults in the nineteenth century. Six of the ten bestsellers in the United States between 1875 and 1895 were children's books. Hellmut Lehmann-Haupt, *The Book in America: A History of the Making, the Selling, and the Collecting of Books in the United States* (New York, 1939), 160–61. See also Darton, *Children's Books*, 301.

42. Edith Hamilton to Jessie Hamilton, Thursday [late 1890s], folder 604.

43. Agnes Hamilton to Edith Trowbridge, August 19, 1895. *The Old Mam'selle's Secret* (1868) was by the popular German romance writer E. Marlitt, the pen name of Eugenie John. Agnes had read and liked the book many years before. Agnes Hamilton to Alice Hamilton, August 10, 1881.

44. To Jessie Hamilton [early 1882], folder 385. The books, by Susan Coolidge, Elizabeth Stuart Phelps (Ward), and Joanna Hooe Mathews respectively, were published in the late 1860s and early 1870s.

45. Alice Hamilton to Agnes Hamilton [June? 1896].

46. Edith Hamilton to Jessie Hamilton [fall 1896 and December 18? 1896]. See also Sicherman, *Alice Hamilton*, 104–7.

47. Agnes Hamilton Diary, December 6 [1883].

48. Benjamin Franklin quoted in Davidson, *Revolution and the Word*, 52.

49. Allen Hamilton Williams to Bag [Agnes Hamilton], August 11, 1890. These characters are drawn from books read in childhood or early adolescence. See below for additional comments on Nora (sometimes spelled "Norah") and Ellen.

50. Agnes Hamilton to Edith Trowbridge, August 19, 1895.

51. *EDT*, 19.

52. Davidson, *Revolution and the Word*, emphasizes the continuity between the subject matter of early American novels and contemporary life; see esp. 112–35.

53. Alice Hamilton to Agnes Hamilton [postmarked November 9, 1896].

54. Edith Hamilton to Jessie Hamilton, January 31 [1886].

55. Allen Hamilton Williams to Bag [Agnes Hamilton], July 30, 1896, and to My dear girl [Alice Hamilton], August 15 [?], 1896.

56. Alice Hamilton to Agnes Hamilton, September 12 [1896]; the letter is reprinted in its entirety in Sicherman, *Alice Hamilton*, 101–4.

57. Allen Hamilton Williams to Dear child [Alice Hamilton], September 17, 1896.

58. Alice Hamilton to Margaret Hamilton, Sunday [July 7], 1918, Alice Hamilton Papers, Schlesinger Library. The book was *The First Violin* (1877) by Jessie Fothergill, which Agnes at nineteen had characterized as "a very trashy book but great fun." Agnes Hamilton Diary, July 29 [1888]. According to a report of the American Library Association in 1881, Fothergill was one of the authors whose works were "sometimes excluded from public libraries by reason of sensational or immoral qualities." Quoted in Garrison, *Apostles of Culture*, 74.

59. Interview with Hildegarde Wagenhals Bowen, December 30, 1976. It is possible that the type of romantic hero admired by Alice contributed to the women's penchant for singlehood, since of course no real-life hero "could be so noble." There were also more pragmatic reasons, including the fact that the marriages in their parents' generation were mainly unhappy, and the fathers and uncles "difficult" at best. Then too, sisters and cousins discouraged each other from leaving the family; and since they stuck together, it was difficult for a young man to breach the ranks.

60. Montgomery Hamilton to A. Holman Hamilton, July 30, 1864.

61. On the appeal of certain plots, see John G. Cawelti, *Adventure, Mystery, and Romance: Formula Stories as Art and Popular Culture* (Chicago, 1976), esp. 37–50. Nancy K. Miller emphasizes the differences in the plots of female and male authors; see "Emphasis Added: Plots and Plausibilities in Women's Fiction," *The New Feminist Criticism: Essays on Women, Literature, and Theory*, ed. Elaine Showalter (New York, 1985), 339–60.

62. Although there is no evidence that Nora and Ellen were as important models of heroism to the women as they were to Allen, there are numerous references to *Quits* and *Castle Daly* in their correspondence. They named their Aunt Margaret's Farmington cottage "Happy-Go-Lucky Lodge," the home of the beloved Irish aunt in *Castle Daly*. Anne O'Flaherty, the unmarried and independent fictional aunt, had a strong sense of responsibility for her Irish tenants. Even as a college student, Edith was delighted to come across a favorable reference to *Quits* by Washington Irving.

63. See, for example, Rachel M. Brownstein, *Becoming a Heroine: Reading about Women in Novels* (New York, 1984).

64. Norman Holland, *The Dynamics of Literary Response* (New York, 1975), esp. 262–80. See also his *Poems in Persons: An Introduction to the Psychoanalysis of Literature* (New York, 1973) and *5 Readers Reading* (New Haven, Conn., 1975). One need not accept Holland's exact psychoanalytic formulation to recognize the value of his approach in illuminating individual responses to literature.

65. Cora Kaplan, "*The Thorn Birds:* Fiction, Fantasy, Femininity," in *Sea Changes: Feminism and Culture* (London, 1986), 117–46. See also Janice Radway, *Reading the Romance* and "Reading *Reading the Romance*," introduction to the English edition (London, 1987).

66. *EDT,* 26. Alice also attributes the growing consciousness of social problems she and Agnes shared to reading Charles Kingsley and Frederick Denison Maurice. Claiming "we knew nothing about American social evils," she ignores their work at the sabbath mission school in Nebraska. Alice was interested in "slumming" by age eighteen, which was probably before she read the English social theorists. This seems to have been another case of literature seeming more real than life. *EDT,* 26–27.

67. On this conflict, see Sicherman, *Alice Hamilton.*

68. Edith Hamilton to Jessie Hamilton, Thursday, July 24 [1884]. Each book contains a sympathetic Robin Hood figure, whose dubious morality is treated ambiguously.

69. Alice called her sister "a natural storyteller." *EDT,* 19.

70. See, among others, the autobiographical accounts of Florence Kelley, Mary Richmond, Mary White Ovington, S. Josephine Baker, Mary Simkhovitch, Vida Dutton Scudder, and Charlotte Perkins Gilman. M. Carey Thomas's diary provides contemporary substantiation. Thomas Papers, Bryn Mawr College, Bryn Mawr, Penna. On nineteenth-century literary culture, see Steven Mintz, *A Prison of Expectations: The Family in Victorian Culture* (New York, 1985), esp. 21–39.

71. See Pierre Bourdieu, *Distinction: A Social Critique of the Judgement of Taste,* trans. Richard Nice (Cambridge, Mass., 1984).

72. See Barbara Sicherman, "College and Careers: Historical Perspectives on the Lives and Work Patterns of Women College Graduates," in *Women and Higher Education in American History,* ed. John Mack Faragher and Florence Howe (New York, 1988), 130–64.

73. Jane Addams, *Twenty Years at Hull-House* (1910; rpt. New York, 1960), 63–64.

74. Raymond Williams, *Marxism and Literature* (Oxford, 1977), 128–35.

75. James Britton, *Language and Learning* (London, 1970), 97–125; quotation, 109–10. See also Iser, "Interaction between Text and Reader," 106–19, and Jauss, "Literary History as a Challenge to Literary Theory," 35–37.

76. Paul Lauter, "Race and Gender in the Shaping of the American Literary Canon: A Case Study from the Twenties," *Feminist Studies* 9 (Fall 1983): 435–63, and Joan Shelley Rubin, "Self, Culture, and Self-Culture in Modern America: The Early History of the Book-of-the-Month Club," *Journal of American History* 71 (March 1985): 782–806, discuss the standardization of cultural fare in the twentieth century. See also Christopher P. Wilson, "The Rhetoric of Consumption: Mass-Market Magazines and the Demise of the Gentle Reader, 1880–1920," in *The Culture of Consumption: Critical Essays in American History, 1880–1980,* ed. Richard Wightman Fox and T. J. Jackson Lears (New York, 1983), 39–64.

77. On female heroism and sexuality, see Martha Vicinus, "What Makes a Heroine?: Nineteenth-Century Girls' Biographies," *Genre* 20 (Summer 1987): 171–88.

78. See, for example, Patrocinio P. Schweickart, "Reading Ourselves: Toward a Feminist Theory of Reading," in *Gender and Reading*, 31–62; quotation, 41.

Chapter Nine

Reflections on the Changing Publishing Objectives of Secular Black Book Publishers, 1900–1986

Donald Franklin Joyce

This essay explores what has happened to the objectives of black-owned secular book publishing enterprises during the course of the twentieth century. Conclusions are based on three sets of data:

1. A study conducted in 1976 that focused on sixty-six black-owned book publishing firms in the United States from 1900 to 1976;

2. a survey conducted in 1982 that focused on black-owned book publishing firms active in the early 1980s; and

3. responses to a questionnaire sent to black-owned publishing houses active since 1982.[1]

Identification of several of the book publishers originally studied was made by examining main entries in *The Catalog of the Arthur B. Spingarn Collection of Negro Authors* (Boston, 1971), and some by reading imprints of citations for 1900–49 in Geraldine O. Matthews et al., *Black American Writers, 1773–1949: A Bibliography and Union List* (Boston, 1975). To identify additional black-owned book publishers active between 1900 and 1974, book advertisements in the following periodicals and journals were examined: *Colored American Magazine*, 1900–1909; *Crisis*, 1910–88; *Half-Century Magazine*, 1916–25; *The Messenger*, 1917–28; *Voice of the Negro*, 1946–47; *Black World* (formerly *Negro Digest*), 1942–51, 1961–77; *Opportunity, Journal of Negro Life*, 1923–49; *Negro History Bulletin*, 1940–88; and *Journal of Negro History*, 1916–88. Other black publishers were identified through the following journal articles: Carole A. Parks, "An Annotated Directory: The Black Book Publishers," *Black World* (March 1975); Dudley Randall, "Negro Publishers from Black Readers," *Publishers Weekly* (October 22, 1972); and Bradford Chambers, "Book Publishing: A Racist Club?" and "Why Minority Publishing? New Voices Are Heard," *Publishers Weekly* (March 15, 1971). Three more publishers that came into existence after the Spingarn Collection *Catalog* and Matthews *Bibliography* were completed were identified serendipitously.

To gather information on currently active black book publishers, a questionnaire was sent to ten publishers identified from book listings in *Books in Print, 1985–86*. The questionnaire contained the following questions:

1. As a black book publisher, primarily publishing books detailing the black experience, what are your book publishing objectives?
2. Would you describe your editorial policies?
3. What distinctive editorial practices do you employ in editing manuscripts for books that you publish on black experience?
4. In what year was your firm established?
5. Would you describe the marketing channels used by your firm to market its books?
6. For what audience are your books aimed?
7. Under what type of business structure is your firm operating: privately held corporation, publicly held corporation, nonprofit corporation, proprietorship, partnership?

Only three active publishers responded to the questionnaire. A fourth publisher, Winston-Derek Publishers, Inc., located in Nashville, Tennessee, agreed to an interview.

The discussion that follows will focus on selected black book publishers founded in the early years of this century and on four publishers that were active in 1986.

Black Book Publishers of the Past

Black-owned book publishing has always been a purposive endeavor. Unlike some of their white colleagues, black book publishers have seldom published books that might be classified as escape reading. Books published by black publishers have been and continue to be utilitarian, in the sense that they foster moral, social, or practical values.

Since the early years of the twentieth century, when black secular book publishing began to flourish in a meager way, the objectives of black secular publishers have involved satisfying definite intellectual and cultural needs within the black community. Often these needs reflected the reaction of blacks to the larger society's hostility or indifference toward the black community. In other instances the needs arose from changes within the black community. The following publishers provide examples.

Orion Publishing Company.   The Reverend Sutton E. Griggs established the Orion Publishing Company in Nashville in 1901 to publish his own writings. Through Orion, Griggs released his protest novels, which depicted the injustices blacks were suffering at the hands of white Southerners. In one of his novels, *The Hindered Hand; or, the Reign of the Repressionist* (1905), Griggs included a chapter on miscegenation that was his public answer to a vicious attack on Afro-Americans in Thomas Dixon's novel *The Leopard's Spots: A Romance of the White Man's Burden* (New York, 1902).[2]

As illustrated through the books he wrote and published, Griggs's publishing objectives were well defined. He wanted to publish books to articulate the black community's response to racial injustices and to vindicate black Americans whose social, moral, and intellectual sensibilities had been attacked by white writers.

The Colored Cooperative Publishing Company.   The Colored Cooperative Publishing Company, a publishing cooperative, was established in Boston in 1900 to publish the monthly *Colored American Magazine*. The publishers stated their objectives in one of the early issues of the magazine: "To the encouragement of those who are faint, or would slavishly bend under the weight of a mistaken popular prejudice; and to the inspiration and the aid of our noble men and women who are fearlessly and successfully vindicating themselves and our people, the *Colored American Magazine* is published."[3]

One book was published by the Colored Cooperative, Pauline Hopkins's *Contending Forces* (1900).[4] A novel depicting the struggles against prejudice and indifference of a middle-class Afro-American family living in post–Civil War Boston, this work is a romance in the traditional fashion of the period. In her preface, Hopkins discusses her views about the value of fiction to Afro-Americans, views that are consistent with those of the publishers of the *Colored American Magazine:* "Fiction is of great value to many people as a preserver of manners and customs—religious, political and social. It is a record of growth and development from generation to generation. No one will do this for us; we must ourselves develop the men and women who will faithfully portray the innermost thoughts and feelings of the Negro with all the fire and romance which lie dormant in our history and, as yet, unrecognized by writers of the Anglo-Saxon race."[5] The goal of publishing books to lift the Afro-American morally, spiritually, and intellectually, as expressed by Pauline Hopkins and her publishers, was one shared by many Afro-American publishers of the period as well as today.

McGirt Publishing Company.   Another Afro-American magazine publisher that also published a book was the McGirt Publishing Company. Founded in Philadelphia in 1903 by poet James Ephraim McGirt to publish *McGirt's Magazine, An Illustrated Monthly Devoted to Art, Science and Literature,* the company released one book in 1907, James Ephraim McGirt's own *The Triumphs of Ephraim: A Collection of Short Stories.*[6] This collection is illustrative of McGirt's attempt to publish books that, like those of the Reverend Sutton E. Griggs, protested the injustices suffered by Afro-Americans at the hands of the larger society. Afro-American literary critic John Parker commented on this characteristic in assessing *The Triumphs of Ephraim:* "This group of stories, everywhere indicative of the limited locale, stems from the problem of the Negro's juxtaposition with the white majority in America— color prejudice, exploitation, the operation of restrictive covenants and the frustration-aggression phenomenon."[7]

J. A. Rogers Publications.   Established in 1917 by Joel Augustus Rogers, J. A. Rogers Publications was an active black book publishing firm until Rogers's death in 1960. Like the Reverend Sutton E. Griggs, Rogers published books with the aim of vindicating the Afro-American. Rogers, however, was a skillful researcher and presented his findings in treatises instead of protest novels. Writing in 1946, Rogers outlined his publishing objectives: "I noticed that books alleging inherent Negro inferiority continued to appear. And Dixon's *Clansman* now had been made into a flaming attack on Negroes in a motion picture, 'The Birth of a Nation.' All of these, I felt should be answered not with sentiment, as I noticed certain white friends of the Negro and Negroes themselves were doing in the Chicago Press, but with facts."[8]

Two of Rogers's publications that realized these objectives were *World's Great Men of Color* (1946), a collective biography of outstanding personalities of African descent who had made major contributions to the history of Western civilization;[9] and *Nature*

Knows No Color Line (1952), a work that traces African ancestry among whites from the early Greeks to contemporary America.

Negro Yearbook Publishing Company.   While most of the early twentieth-century Afro-American secular book publishers were based in the North or in urban centers in the South, sociologist Monroe N. Work and his business partners, Robert E. Park and Emmett J. Scott, established the *Negro Yearbook* Publishing Company in rural Alabama at Tuskegee Institute in 1910. From 1912 to 1952, eleven editions of the *Negro Yearbook* appeared. This well-edited serial monograph of facts and statistics reported on many aspects of Afro-American life, such as "Negro Progress; the Race Problem; the Negro World Distribution; Governments; Chronology in America; Slavery; Abolition; Education; Music; Fine Arts."[10]

The objectives of the *Negro Yearbook* Publishing Company were discussed by Monroe N. Work in 1940 in an autobiographical sketch:

> When I came to Tuskegee, educators and others seeking to advance the interest of the Negro were confronted with such questions as: What had the Negro accomplished? What can he do? Does it pay to educate him? Morally is he deteriorating? Has his emancipation been justified? The publication by Hoffman in 1896 of *Race Traits and Tendencies of the Negro* presented a more or less hopeless view. To the indictment by this publication there was at hand no effective answer. From 1908 on I was compiling a day by day record of what was taking place with reference to the Negro. Thus, it became possible to answer in a factual manner questions relating to all matters concerning him.[11]

The *Negro Yearbook* was frequently used by research departments of the NAACP (National Association for the Advancement of Colored People) and the National Urban League in compiling statistics of the Afro-American. Sections of the work appeared in many Afro-American newspapers. For many years it was regarded as the most comprehensive authority on Afro-American life.

Association for the Study of Negro Life and History.   Founded in 1915 by Carter G. Woodson and associates, the Association for the Study of Negro Life and History (now known as the Association for the Study of Afro-American Life and History), based in Washington, D.C., inaugurated its book publishing program in 1918 with the publication of Carter G. Woodson's *A Century of Migration* and Eugene McDougle's *Slavery in Kentucky*. The association was established to promote research in black history by publishing the findings of trained researchers, both black and white. Speaking in 1940, Dr. Woodson discussed the significance of the association and its publishing program: "This undertaking was the first systematic effort of the Negro to treat the records of the race systematically and to publish the findings to the world. Up to that time [1915] no organization with this scientific objective and a program to attain this end had been able to function efficiently along these lines in the United States."[12]

Between 1918 and 1940, the association published twenty-eight monographs. Most of these works were groundbreaking studies in areas of Afro-American and African history neglected by most scholars. Among them were Alrutheus Ambush Taylor, *The Negro in South Carolina during Reconstruction* (1924); Herbert Aptheker, *Negro Casualties in the Civil War* (1939); Henry Noble Sherwood, *Paul Cuffee* (1923); Ruth A. Fisher, *Extracts from the Records of the African Companies* (1930); and George F. Zook, *The Company of Royal Adventurers Trading into Africa* (1919). Many of the books originally published by the association are available today in reprint editions.

Associated Publishers, Inc.   In 1921, when the incorporators of Associated Publishers, Inc., announced the founding of this black book publishing enterprise in Washington, D.C., they boldly proclaimed the firm's goals:

> This firm will publish books of all kinds, but will direct its attention primarily to works bearing on Negroes so as to supply all kinds of information concerning the Negro race and those who have been interested in its uplift. . . . During the recent years the Negro race has been seeking to learn more about itself and especially since the social upheaval of the World War. The Negro reading public has been largely increased and the number of persons interested in the Negro have so multiplied that any creditable publication giving important facts about the race now finds a ready market throughout the United States and even abroad. To supply this demand these gentlemen have launched the enterprise, The Associated Publishers, Incorporated.[13]

This statement illustrates the concern of the firm's incorporators with publishing books that would document past and present Afro-American culture for blacks and for others interested in the cultural and intellectual uplift of black Americans. From 1921 to the present, Associated Publishers has issued a host of books that reflect these objectives. Notable among them have been Carter G. Woodson's *The History of the Negro Church* (1921), a classic treatise on the black church; Frederick Bond's *The Negro in Drama* (1940), an early history of blacks in the American theater; and James Dallas Parks's *Robert S. Duncanson, 19th Century Black Romantic Painter* (1980), the first book-length study of a little-known artist who was one of America's finest nineteenth-century landscape painters.

Associates in Negro Folk Education.   Another black-owned book publishing enterprise based in Washington, D.C., was the Associates in Negro Folk Education. Headed by Howard University philosophy professor Alain LeRoy Locke, this firm was an active book publisher between 1935 and 1940. The Associates in Negro Folk Education was composed of Afro-American scholars from various disciplines who wrote nine books in the firm's Bronze Booklet series. To underwrite the publishing venture, Dr. Locke secured a grant from the Adult Education Association that covered publishing costs and a small honorarium for each author.

Robert Martin, one of Locke's assistants and a professor of political science at Howard University, described the publishing objectives of the firm: "Dr. Locke's basic objective was to provide authentic information on major aspects of American Negro life written by recognized, highly qualified authors for a wide spectrum of readers, especially Afro-Americans, at a low cost, so that the books could be afforded by the masses."[14] These objectives were reflected in Locke's editorial foreword to Sterling Brown's *The Negro in American Fiction*, Bronze Booklet no. 7 (1937): "This Bronze Booklet aims at a survey of the Negro in American fiction, both as character and author. It is the first full-length presentation of this subject, but differs from the usual academic survey by giving a penetrating analysis of the social factors and attitudes behind the various schools and periods considered."[15]

Among the other titles in the Bronze Booklet series are Ralph J. Bunche, *A World's View of Race* (1936); T. Arnold Hill, *The Negro in Economic Reconstruction* (1937); and Ira DeAugustine Reid, *Adult Education among Negroes* (1935). Many of the books in the Bronze Booklet series have been reprinted and are available today.

Freelance Press.   In 1950 two Afro-American poets in Cleveland, Casper LeRoy Jordan and Russell Atkins, organized the Freelance Poetry and Prose Workshop of Cleveland. The workshop was an interracial group of writers, mostly Afro-American, who met to read and discuss their works. In the same year, the workshop established the Freelance Press to publish *Freelance Magazine*, in which the works of members of the workshop were to appear.

With the publication of Conrad Kent Rivers's book of poems

Perchance to Dream, Othello in 1959, Freelance Press became an active book publisher. The objectives, unique among Afro-American book publishers considered so far, were, as indicated by one of the editors of Freelance, to publish books that articulated and portrayed through literature various aspects of both the black and the white American experience.[16] Illustrative titles released by this publisher are *The Mantu Poets of Cleveland* by Russell Atkins (1968); and *Permit Me Voyage* (1968), a book of poems by Adelaide Simon, a white poet in the workshop. Between 1959 and 1971, nine titles were published by Freelance. After 1971, Freelance ceased releasing books but continued publishing *Freelance Magazine* until 1980.

Thus, black book publishing enterprises established before 1960 had objectives that were for the most part defined by the intellectual needs of the black community. Only as the period ended do we see one of these publishers releasing a work depicting the white American experience.

Contemporary Black Book Publishers

Today many black publishers are publishing books to meet definite intellectual and cultural needs within the black community, as their predecessors did. However, some are also publishing books that reflect the intellectual aspirations of blacks and other minorities.

Broadside Press.   Located in Detroit, Broadside Press has changed ownership three times since its founding in 1966 by poet-librarian Dudley Randall. From 1966 to 1977, Randall was at its helm. In 1977, because of financial losses, Randall sold Broadside to the Alexander Crummell Memorial Center in Highland Park, Michigan. The firm's name was changed to Broadside/Crummell Press. Today its owner is Hilda Vest, and once again it is known as Broadside Press.

Publishing black poetry primarily, Broadside has issued the works of some of the leading black poets in the United States. Among its volumes are Gwendolyn Brooks's *Beckonings* (1975); Nikki Giovanni's *Black Feelings, Black Talk* (1970); and Aneb Kgositsile's *Blood River* (1983).

Broadside markets its books through direct-mail advertising to bookstores, libraries, and educational institutions. The firm distributes its books through national book distribution jobbers and sells direct to bookstores and individuals. It also sends out a newsletter describing recent publications.

The objectives of Broadside are, according to Hilda Vest, "to publish works that depict those aspects of Black life that make us human, but not the stereotypes that many of the major publishing houses choose to present as Black topics."[17] Like most black publishing enterprises, Broadside, aiming its publications at the average black American, has developed a distinctive editorial policy. Publisher Vest expressed it succinctly: "I want poetry that is not extremely difficult to understand, but exhibits a creative edge. I am looking for poems that will help the Black man's image of himself."[18]

Directionscope: Selected and New Poems (1971), by Haki Madhabuti (Don L. Lee), contains poetry illustrative of Broadside's current editorial policy, as an excerpt from one of these poems, "We Walk the Way of the New World," shows:

we run the dangercourse
the way of the stocking caps and murray's grease
(if u is modern u used duke greaseless hair pomade
jo jo was modern/an international nigger
      born: jan 1, 1863 in New York, Mississippi.
his momma was no more militant than he was/is
jo jo bes no instant negro
his development took all of 106 years.[19]

Lotus Press.   Like Broadside, Lotus Press is based in Detroit and specializes in publishing poetry. A nonprofit and federal-tax-exempt literary publisher, Lotus was established by poet-educator Naomi Long Madgett in 1972. Since its founding, Lotus has released more than fifty volumes of poetry. This firm markets its books through mail advertising to libraries and educational institutions. Lotus books are also advertised in national book trade journals.

The current Lotus catalogue lists such titles as Satisfa's *For Dark Women and Others* (1983), a book of poems on the strengths and burdens of black women; Gary Smith's *Songs for My Father* (1984), a collection of poems celebrating poetry by several black and white poets from Jupiter Hammon to Gwendolyn Brooks; and Paulette Childress White's *The Watermelon Dress: Portrait of a Woman* (1984), a long poem depicting the emotional odyssey of a young girl into womanhood.

Publisher Naomi Long Madgett, when queried about the publishing objectives of Lotus, responded substantively:

To keep the best of black poetry alive by making inexpensive, attractive paperbound volumes available to the bookstores and libraries of the world. To provide a worldwide audience to black poets of excellence, regardless of their ideology, subject matter, or style. Our goal is literary excellence. We are not interested in work that is political without being technically sound; nor are we interested in beginners who have not studied the fundamentals of their craft.[20]

The editorial policies that guide Lotus are, Madgett asserts, aimed at ensuring the publication of quality poetry unbound by racial considerations:

We are interested in literary excellence. We do not believe there is a white standard and a black standard. Good literature transcends such artificial divisions. But we do not dictate to the author; we are not looking for anything in particular except in terms of excellence. The poet may be angry, as revolutionary as he/she is conditioned to be—or as ostensibly nonracial in subject matter (and I say "ostensibly" because I do not believe any black poet's work is nonracial, regardless of appearances and superficial observances)—the ultimate questions concerning good and enduring values in art must be answered positively.[21]

In 1981 Lotus released Dudley Randall's *A Litany of Friends: New and Selected Poems*. The following excerpt from one of the poems in this volume, "The Happy Painter (for Leroy Roster)," is an example of the technical mastery publisher Madgett expects in manuscripts her firm publishes:

In the clear beam of the skylight
he stands before a heroic canvas
of the young Frederick Douglass
striking his first blow for freedom
Paintings light the studio
a soft nude
for a bachelor's bedroom
glows on a portrait of a lovely woman.[22]

Winston-Derek Publishers, Inc.   Established in 1976 in Nashville by Dr. James Peoples, a former schoolteacher, Winston-Derek Publishers, Inc., is one of the leading black-owned book publishers in the United States today. The firm now has 140 titles in print.

With its main office in Nashville and a branch office in New York City, Winston-Derek has participated with major white publishing houses in several co-publishing ventures, much to its advantage. In 1978, for example, this publisher formed a three-way distributorship with Abingdon Press and Nelson Publishers. The three firms produced a joint catalogue listing all their publications, and Winston-Derek utilized the established distribution system its older partners had developed. "This really gave us national exposure," Peoples stated in an interview.[23]

Books published by Winston-Derek are marketed through the joint catalogue, which is mailed to libraries, bookstores, and educational institutions. The firm also advertises in book trade journals. Most of Winston-Derek's books are distributed through jobbers, although it makes some direct sales to bookstores. And the publisher operates its own bookstore.

Although it is black-owned, Winston-Derek has broad publishing objectives. As Peoples discussed in an interview, the firm does not restrict itself to publishing books about the black experience; it also issues books about other minorities as well:

> Winston-Derek books are designed primarily to reach the literary world with a reservoir of wholesome and factual information in regard to the culture of all peoples. We primarily wish to concentrate on enlarging the focus of many ethnic groups in America who have been left void on the printed page for over two hundred years. These are not only Blacks, but Hispanics and other smaller Caucasian groups. Therefore, we find ourselves interested in those materials that deal with Americana from 1600 to the present, regardless of what ethnic group it may be, if they are materials that can present a heritage and legacy of a people. However, we understand ourselves to be primarily Black involved, because we are the ones who have suffered the most.[24]

Winston-Derek's aim to publish books documenting the Afro-American heritage is evident in Sandra Smithson's *To Be the Bridge: A Commentary on Black/White Catholicism in America* (1984). Written by a black Catholic nun, this work discusses the nonresponsive attitude of the Catholic Church toward its black communicants in the nineteenth century. Smithson boldly asserts, "The history of the Catholic Church in this country points to racist practices that completely comprised its mission. True, there have been, are, and always will be individual Catholics who may plead innocent. Unfortunately, this will not prove to be a saving grace, for it is not the individual but the community which is to be a sign."[25]

A title published in 1983, David R. Collins and Evelyn Witter's *The Golden Circle*, illustrates the firm's attempt to release books on the Native American heritage. Written for children, this is the story of a Native American trapper who showed several white families who had arrived on the *Mayflower* how to survive their first winter in the New World.

An example of the wholesome religious literature produced by Winston-Derek is James A. Jones III's *Conversations with Children* (1985). An excellent teaching volume, this work is a compilation of sermons and conversations for children.

Wild Trees Press.   In February 1984, Wild Trees Press was founded as a publishing partnership by prizewinning novelist Alice Walker and writer Robert Allen in Anderson Valley, California, where Walker wrote her Pulitzer Prize–winning novel *The Color Purple.* Alice Walker described the beginnings of this feminist press: "We loved the valley, it reminded me a little of Georgia. We had also made lots of friends. The valley is incredibly rich and all sorts of things are grown. We decided to grow books."[26] In response to a questionnaire about their objectives as a black publishing firm, the publishers acknowledged that they were black-owned but said they were mainly interested in literature of quality by writers of diverse races: "We are a Black-owned publishing company, but we publish works by writers of various races. We seek to publish books which we find moving and significant and of high literary quality and special insight."[27]

The first book published by Wild Trees appeared in December 1984. It was J. California Cooper's *A Piece of Mine,* a collection of twelve short stories about the misfortunes and struggles of black men and women in a small town. One story in this collection, "$100 and Nothing," indicates the exceptional literary quality and insight these publishers expect in the manuscripts they publish. "$100 and Nothing" is the story of a hard-working black woman named Mary. Abandoned by her parents, Mary was reared in an orphanage until she came of age. Through her own efforts, she acquired and developed a thriving grocery store, but she also acquired a lazy, abusive, and ungrateful husband whom she unfortunately loved. The narrator relates one episode of abuse that Mary experienced at the hands of her husband:

> I went home to lunch with Mary once and he got mad cause we woke him up as we was talking and eating. Lord, did he talk about Mary! Talk about her skinny legs and under her clothes and her kinky hair. She tried to keep it but she worked and weeped too hard, for him! She just dropped her head deeper down in her plate and I could see she has a hard time swallowing her food.[28]

This book, which has gone through three printings, has ten thousand copies in print and has been widely reviewed.

The current Wild Trees catalogue lists three other titles. Jo Anne Brasil's *Escape from Billy's Bar-B-Cue* (1985) is a humorous novel about a Southern white woman coming of age in the 1960s. This work had an initial press run of three thousand copies, which sold out three weeks prior to its publication date. Charlotte Mendiz's *Condor and Hummingbird* (1986) is a novel about the relationship among three women in Bogotá, Colombia. Septima Clark's *Ready from Within: Septima Clark and the Civil Rights Movement* (1986) is the first-person narrative of a civil rights fighter's quest for racial equality for blacks in the South.

Wild Trees aims its books at the general adult audience, selling through bookstores and such distributors as Bookpeople, Publishers Group West, Bookslinger, the Red Sea Press, and Inland. The publishers described other marketing channels: "We publish an annual catalogue, and attend the American Booksellers Association annual convention as our main marketing activities. We also seek reviews for each title and have had some success with this."[29]

Conclusion

The objectives of black book publishers have changed since 1900. These changes have reflected the changing racial attitudes of the larger American society toward black Americans, changes in the intellectual needs of the black community, and a concern among black book publishers for the history and culture of other minorities. The racist writings attacking black Americans that flooded the market in the early decades of the twentieth century prompted black publishers to issue books that vindicated the Afro-American or articulated the black response to racial injustices. Although some racist-inspired writings are on the market today, their number and influence are negligible compared with early in the century. To be sure, black publishers are still publishing books to vindicate the Afro-American, but this objective is not as dominant with these publishers as it had been with their predecessors. As the literacy rate among Afro-Americans rose, black publishers began publishing books to uplift American blacks by documenting their history, celebrating their culture, and portraying their experience. Today, because of the growing literary sophistication of the black community, many black book publishers are dedicated to publishing black literature of excellent quality. Others, although publishing books to depict the black experience, have broadened their aims to include documenting and portraying the culture and history of other minorities.

Notes

1. The original study, entitled "A Chance to Speak for Ourselves: The Growth and Development of Afro-American-Owned Book Publishing in the

United States, 1900 through 1974," was accepted as a dissertation by the faculty of the Graduate Library School of the University of Chicago. Findings from it and the 1982 survey were reported in the monograph *Gatekeepers of Black Culture: Black-Owned Book Publishing in the United States, 1817–1981* (Westport, Conn., 1983).

2. *The Hindered Hand; or, the Reign of the Repressionist* was reprinted by Mnemosyne Publishing Company in 1969.

3. R. S. Elliot, "The Story of Our Magazine," *Colored American Magazine* (May 1901), 43.

4. *Contending Forces* was reprinted by Southern Illinois University Press in 1982.

5. Pauline Hopkins, *Contending Forces* (Boston, 1900), 13–14.

6. This work was reprinted by the Books for Libraries Press in 1972.

7. John W. Parker, "James Ephraim McGirt: Poet of 'Hope Deferred,'" *North Carolina Historical Review* 16 (July 1954): 322.

8. J. A. Rogers, *World's Great Men of Color*, 2 vols. (New York, 1946), 1:6.

9. *World's Great Men of Color* was reprinted in 1972.

10. Monroe N. Work, ed., *The Negro Yearbook* (Tuskegee, Ala., 1912), 1.

11. Monroe N. Work, "An Autobiographical Sketch, February 7, 1940," Monroe Nathan Work Papers, Tuskegee Institute Historical Collection, Tuskegee, Ala.

12. Carter G. Woodson, "An Accounting for Twenty-Five Years," *Journal of Negro History* 25 (July 1940): 422.

13. "Notes," ibid. 6 (July 1921): 380.

14. Robert Martin to the author, May 31, 1976.

15. Alain Locke, "Editorial Foreword," in Sterling Brown, *The Negro in American Fiction* (Washington, D.C., 1937).

16. Interview with Caspar L. Jordan, January 10, 1976.

17. Hilda Vest, questionnaire, February 8, 1986.

18. Ibid.

19. Haki Madhabuti (Don L. Lee), *Directionscope: Selected and New Poems* (Detroit, 1971), 188.

20. Naomi Long Madgett, questionnaire, February 6, 1986.

21. Ibid.

22. Dudley Randall, *A Litany of Friends: New and Selected Poems* (Detroit, 1981), 15.

23. Interview with James Peoples, February 27, 1986.

24. Ibid.

25. Sandra Smithson, *To Be the Bridge: A Commentary on Black/White Catholicism in America* (Nashville, Tenn., 1984), 8.

26. "Wild Trees Press," *Bookpaper* (February 1986), 10.

27. Alice Walker and Robert L. Allen, questionnaire, June 11, 1986.

28. J. California Cooper, *A Piece of Mine* (Navarro, Calif., 1984), 3.

29. Walker and Allen, questionnaire, June 11, 1986.

Chapter Ten **Becoming Noncanonical**

The Case against
Willa Cather

Sharon O'Brien

In the 1920s Willa Cather achieved both critical acclaim and popular success. So confident was she of her ability to attract contemporary and future readers that in 1927 she asked her publisher Alfred A. Knopf for a 1 percent increase in her royalties for *Death Comes for the Archbishop*. Believing that this novel's reputation—and sales—would outlast her lifetime, she prophesied that someday Knopf's son would be paying royalties to her niece.[1]

Cather's literary and economic faith in *Death Comes for the Archbishop* has been vindicated: considered one of her finest novels, the book continues to sell in paperback. But her literary reputation has not been maintained at the height it attained in the 1920s, when critics and reviewers deemed her a major American novelist. During the 1930s and 1940s, she was increasingly subjected to attacks by reviewers who not only disliked novels like *Shadows on the Rock* (1931) and *Lucy Gayheart* (1935) but also questioned her literary stature, arguing that she was a minor, not a major, writer. As Clifton Fadiman phrased it in a typical commentary that appeared in the *Nation* in 1932, Cather's intensifying preoccupation with the historical past might "permanently transport her to regions where minor works of art may be created, but major ones never," an unfortunate fate since the author of *The Song of the Lark* (1915) and *My Ántonia* (1918) had been not a "minor writer, but a major one."[2] Fadiman's assessment was prophetic. Although Cather has won a place in the American literary canon, it is not a high one; she has been considered an important writer and yet somehow not a "major" one, somehow not an equal colleague of Hawthorne, James, or Faulkner, and perhaps not even in the same realm as Fitzgerald, Hemingway, or Dreiser.

Fadiman assumed that he and his fellow reviewers were merely recording, not constructing, Cather's decline. But recent developments in literary theory have questioned traditional assumptions of literary value and evaluation, requiring that we cease to regard the American literary canon as an objective, impartial list of those classic writers whose works have simply withstood the test of time. Several critics and writers have challenged the view that literary value arises from timeless, universal qualities inherent in the work, qualities most effectively seen and described by trained literary scholars. Reader-response criticism has called our attention to the ways in which meaning and value, as well as the aesthetic criteria used to determine these, are the products of the social, political, and ideological assumptions that readers bring to texts, which are thus not stable or fixed entities. Other studies of canon formation have pointed out that the assessment of literary value and the selection of certain texts and writers as "classic" or "major" are not based solely on aesthetic criteria; rather, the construction of a literary canon results from a complex process of cultural production and transmission in which publishers, reviewers, editors, literary critics, and teachers structure the interaction between the text and the reader.[3]

Understanding the ways in which the literary canon is shaped and perpetuated—a process requiring the inclusion of some writers and the exclusion or marginalization of others—thus can help us to see the role of professional readers in determining literary value, and so give us insight into the "interests, institutional practices, and social arrangements that sustain the canon of classic works."[4] Examining Willa Cather's varying reputation offers particularly fruitful insights into the complex dynamics of literary evaluation and preservation. Unlike Hawthorne, whose reputation grew steadily (although for historically changing reasons) from the publication of his first stories, and unlike Kate Chopin, Sarah Orne Jewett, or Harriet Beecher Stowe, women writers who have never been considered "major," Willa Cather possessed canonical status during the 1920s only to lose it in the 1930s. If we attribute a writer's literary reputation not to the inherent value and stable meaning of his or her work but to the historical circumstances in which that work is published, read, interpreted, and evaluated, then Willa Cather's ascent and decline is a case study in the politics of canon formation.

Cather's unmaking did not result merely from the political and social climate of the 1930s, even though the nation's economic plight led some left-wing reviewers and critics to attack what they considered her conservatism and escapism. Cather's literary decline coincided with, and was in part a product of, the self-conscious attempt of reviewers, critics, and academics to create an American literary canon. Although this endeavor began in the 1920s, it flowered during the 1930s and 1940s—the years when college professors and men of letters were struggling to establish American literature as a respectable field of professional inquiry within English departments. In doing so, they felt the need, as Perry Miller later phrased it, to "make clear which are the few peaks and which the many low-lying hills."[5] For the most part, the literary men who defined the canon during this period placed Willa Cather in the foothills of American literature—the appropriate landscape, many critics assumed, for a woman writer.

To situate Cather's decanonization historically, I will first review the social and literary circumstances that led to her establishment as a major writer in the 1920s. Then I will turn to the historical, ideological, and institutional forces that contributed to her demotion from "major" to "minor" writer in the 1930s and 1940s; finally, I will explore Cather's creative (and human) response to her literary decline—an increasing reliance upon nonprofessional readers as the professional readers became more hostile. By examining the making and the unmaking of a major writer, I hope to illuminate the social, political, and ideological dynamics of canon formation in twentieth-century America.

I

Cather's first novel, *Alexander's Bridge* (1912), was politely praised by reviewers impressed by the beginning writer's command of style and characterization even as they noted her apprenticeship to Henry James and Edith Wharton. In his review in the *Smart Set*, H. L. Mencken observed that most novice writers in America chose to model themselves either after E. Phillips Oppenheim or Marie Corelli, allying themselves with either the "School of Plot" or the "School of Piffle." Cather had aimed higher, however, and despite a "certain triteness" she was, Mencken thought, a "promising" writer.[6] Although not proclaiming Cather a major novelist, Mencken thus made an important distinction; here was a serious, not a popular, writer.

After Cather left the drawing room for the prairies and turned to her Nebraska past in *O Pioneers!* and *The Song of the Lark*, she began to draw increased attention from reviewers who saw emerging an authentic American voice, a challenge to both a meretricious popular taste and a decaying genteel tradition. With the publication of *My Ántonia* in 1918, critics who took it as their mission to define and to encourage an indigenous and vigorous American literature promoted Cather from a promising to a major American novelist. Eager to displace the waning influence of New England literary culture, to challenge middle-class pieties, to establish an American literary tradition separate from (and perhaps equal to) that of England, and to solidify their own roles as cultural arbiters, critics like H. L. Mencken, Randolph Bourne, Heywood Broun, and Carl Van Doren linked Willa Cather with Theodore Dreiser and Sherwood Anderson as writers bringing a new realism to American letters. Bourne praised Cather's breaking of "stiff moral molds" and leaving the ranks of "provincial" writers with *My Ántonia;* meanwhile, delighted with the "extraordinary reality" he found in the novel, Mencken became Cather's particular champion.[7] Hoping to wean American teachers and readers from their servile worship of England's literature, such critics found Cather's progress from the London of *Alexander's Bridge* to the Nebraska of *My Ántonia* a paradigmatic, and exemplary, journey.

Cather's first supporters were, by and large, journalists and men of letters who waged their campaign for a national literature with a "distinctively American spirit" outside the academy.[8] Indeed, professors of English who preferred philological dissections of Chaucer to the vitality of American authors were anathema to these literary radicals; Bourne, for example, characterized his English courses at Columbia as "dead rituals in which academic priests mumbled their trite commentary."[9] Among Cather's first advocates, only Carl Van Doren was an academic; during the 1910s he was teaching American literature at Columbia. But he, like Mencken and Bourne, was a literary maverick whose devotion to the study and promotion of American literature led to his editorship of the *Cambridge History of American Literature* (1917–21). Although continuing to teach at Columbia, Van Doren soon moved into the literary world outside the academy, becoming literary editor of the *Nation* in 1919 and of the *Century* in 1922.

In the first major assessment of Cather in a literary history, *Contemporary American Novelists: 1900–1920* (1922), Van Doren compared her favorably with her mentor Sarah Orne Jewett (to whom *O Pioneers!* was dedicated), claiming that the "thin, fine gentility" of Jewett's world faded beside the "rich vigor" of Cather's pioneer fiction, whose "spaciousness" and epic sweep owed more to Whitman than to Jewett. Noting that Cather's epics featured female heroes, Van Doren nevertheless found them able to represent what he considered a universal American story: "The struggle of some elected individual to outgrow the restrictions . . . of numbing circumstances."[10] Dedicated to challenging "numbing" social and literary conventions themselves, the critics and reviewers who defined Cather as a major writer in the late 1910s and early 1920s saw in her work an analogue to their own critical enterprise, the struggle of elected individuals to challenge and regenerate a native American culture.

Endorsed by these important cultural arbiters, Cather enjoyed a remarkably prolific and creative period in the 1920s. Six books appeared in seven years: *Youth and the Bright Medusa* (1921), *One of Ours* (1922), *A Lost Lady* (1923), *The Professor's House* (1925), *My Mortal Enemy* (1926), and *Death Comes for the Archbishop* (1927). Although some of these novels received mixed reviews, Cather's literary reputation continued to ascend throughout the decade as she gained the external signs of literary esteem: she won the Pulitzer Prize for *One of Ours;* she was granted honorary degrees from Yale, Columbia, and the University of Michigan; she was invited to Breadloaf and the McDowell colony; she was elected to the National Institute of Arts and Letters; and she was awarded the American Academy of Arts and Letters Howells Medal for *Death Comes for the Archbishop.* Further evidence of Cather's firm position as a major contemporary writer was the selection of *Death Comes for the Archbishop* by the College Entrance Board as a text for high school students to prepare: this was sound cause for congratulation, Houghton Mifflin editor Ferris Greenslet informed Cather, because selection meant that a book had been established as an American classic.[11]

During these years Cather enjoyed the American writer's dream of uniting critical approval with popular success as her aesthetic and financial worth increased: she was given high rankings in several literary polls; she hired an agent; she moved from Houghton Mifflin to Knopf, largely because she thought that her Boston publisher did not sufficiently appreciate, and promote, her novels; her sales increased along with her reputation; her novels began to interest Hollywood producers, and *A Lost Lady* was made into a movie.[12]

By the end of the 1920s, then, Cather seemed to be firmly established as a major writer whose works had attracted both critical and popular acclaim. Yet premonitions of the attacks to come can be seen in the negative, even hostile reviews of *One of Ours,* Cather's novel of World War I. The book was generally dismissed by male reviewers as a woman writer's romanticized, outmoded view of combat. It was, Mencken charged—evidently using the worst epithet he could imagine—very like the work of a "lady novelist."[13] For the first time, Cather was explicitly judged as limited because of her gender. Trespassing on the preserve of masculine fiction in the last section of the novel, in which her hero Claude Wheeler enters the war in France, Cather had trod on forbidden ground and so, many reviewers agreed, exposed the limitations of the female imagination.[14]

That Cather had feared and anticipated such criticism is evident in an important letter she sent to H. L. Mencken shortly before he reviewed the novel. Cather began by reminding Mencken of their common ground: they were both enemies of a debased, popular American literature, she wrote, both committed to overturning Booth Tarkington platitudes and raising American literature to a higher plane. She went on to reveal many anxieties: that her gender might have prevented her from making a soldier's story seem authentic and powerful; that male critics might assess her novel more accurately than she could, simply because their gender gave them privileged access to a war story, whether or not they had ever seen combat; and that she might deserve punishment for having attempted such an unfeminine design. Please read the novel soon, Cather asked Mencken, because she might be hit by a taxicab if he delayed. The novel might be a complete mistake, she confided, but he would be a good man to smell out falsity. If, despite her best efforts, she had told her soldier's story in a sentimental, old-maid way, Mencken should tell her so loudly, like a man: he should rub it in, because she would deserve it.[15] Mencken gave her the pounding she had feared she deserved. The last half of *One of Ours*, he charged, degenerated to the "level of a serial in the *Ladies' Home Journal*.".[16]

Mencken's and other attacks on *One of Ours* suggest that Cather, the supposed realist, might not be able to deal adequately with contemporary social and political issues; at the same time, they equate such issues with masculine experience and claim that a woman writer's imagination could not encompass this expansive territory. During the 1930s and 1940s, the politics of gender evident in the negative reviews of *One of Ours* became more prominent as a small but influential group of reviewers and academic critics decided to take on Willa Cather.

II

In some ways Cather's reputation continued to rise during the 1930s. She was reviewed well in journals like the *Saturday Review* and *Commonweal*, she gained more prizes and honorary degrees, and *Shadows on the Rock* was an immediate bestseller.[17] But with this novel, set in seventeenth-century Quebec, she began to anger a new generation of critics and reviewers who, influenced by the economic and social collapse of the Depression as well as by Marxist political thought, believed that art should grapple with the stern social, political, and economic realities of its time. Although their reviews and articles did not dominate in numbers, this rising generation of Marxist and liberal critics and reviewers—including Granville Hicks, Newton Arvin, Louis Kronenberg, Edmund Wilson, Lionel Trilling, Maxwell Geismar, and Alfred Kazin—were highly influential, taking over from Mencken and Van Doren as cultural arbiters and shapers of the canon. As Cather seemed to retreat further and further into the past in search of an orderly and harmonious world, traveling first to the nineteenth-century Southwest and then to seventeenth-century Quebec, the pages of new left-wing journals like the *New Republic* and the *Nation* as well as those of the *New York Times Book Review* began to fill with criticism of Cather as a romantic, nostalgic writer who could not cope with the present. Cather wrote, contended Newton Arvin in a typical commentary in the *New Republic*, as if "mass production and technological unemployment and cyclical depressions and the struggle between the classes did not exist," and so she failed to "come to grips with the real life of her time."[18]

By 1933 the attack had infiltrated even the staid pages of the *English Journal*, the publication of the National Council of Teachers of English, which hosted Granville Hicks's now famous essay "The Case against Willa Cather." Hicks equated Cather's literary decline with her growing political conservatism. Cather had "never once tried to see contemporary life as it is," he charged. Fleeing to an idealized conception of a heroic past, she had been "barred from the task that has occupied most of the world's great artists, the expression of what is central and fundamental in her own age." Having surrendered to a "supine romanticism," Hicks argued, Cather could no longer examine "life as it is."[19] What had seemed like the individual's rebellion against mediocrity to Carl Van Doren struck reviewers in the 1930s as bourgeois humanism and disdain for the masses: Cather and her literary reputation were caught in the midst of a generational and ideological shift in American literary culture as a new cohort of critics began to apply different standards to determine literary merit. A writer whose reputation rested on the estimation of the previous generation of reviewers, as well as one who invited rebuttal by openly declaring in 1936 that "economics and art are strangers," Willa Cather was a tempting target for socially conscious critics.[20]

At first glance, the attack on Cather in the 1930s and later arose from the politics of class rather than of gender. Indeed the left-wing attacks on Thornton Wilder—viewed, like Cather, as an old-fashioned humanist—were, if anything, more vicious than the dismissals of Cather.[21] Hence this was not simply, or exclusively, an attempt to exclude a woman writer from the company of great writers. Yet a subtext in the attacks suggests that gender may have been the dominant, if unacknowledged, variable in shaping the case against Willa Cather. In his influential literary history, *The Last of the Provincials* (1947), Maxwell Geismar introduced his discussion of Willa Cather by saying, "In approaching our first feminine writer among the dozen or so contemporary American novelists who deserve a full literary consideration, it is essential, of course, not to consider her as a 'feminine' writer."[22] But Geismar and his colleagues throughout the 1930s and 1940s invariably did consider Cather as a "feminine" writer as they set up a set of metaphoric equivalences: "feminine," "romantic," "sentimental," "soft," and "small," a circle of associations that led them, seemingly inevitably, from "woman" to "minor writer."

Granville Hicks concluded his review of *Shadows on the Rock* by stating that "today, perhaps even more than in the past, it takes stern stuff to make a novelist. Miss Cather, one is forced to conclude, has always been soft; and now she has abandoned herself to softness."[23] Hicks's implicit assumption—that the world of contemporary social and economic issues realistically described is "masculine," and that a failure to demonstrate "stern stuff" in writing of this world is "feminine," and therefore inferior—becomes explicit in Lionel Trilling's seemingly more judicious, and certainly more influential, essay in Malcolm Cowley's important literary history, *After the Genteel Tradition* (1937). Trilling linked Cather's decision to write historical fiction with a "defiant" rejection of her own time, which he in turn associated with her fondness for limited female interests. Commenting on *Shadows on the Rock* (in which Cather uses food preparation and preservation to explore women's contributions to the establishment and preservation of culture and society), Trilling found that her "mystical concern with pots and pans" did not seem more than an "oblique defense of gentility or very far from the gaudy domesticity of bourgeois accumulation glorified in the Woman's Home Companion."[24] Seemingly kinder, in *On Native Grounds* (1942) Alfred Kazin continued this association of "female" and "minor" when he concluded that if Cather's "world became increasingly elegiac and soft, it was riches in a little room."[25]

And so Cather's demotion from major to minor writer in the reviews of the 1930s and the literary histories that followed was connected not only with the left-wing critics' explicit application of aesthetic criteria that demanded social relevance from all writers, male as well as female, but also with their implicit application of aesthetic criteria that equated social and literary relevance with masculinity. The question remains, however, why the male critics and reviewers of the 1930s sought to unmake a major writer who had been made by the male critics and reviewers of the 1910s and 1920s. Why was gender any more a factor in the reviewing process in 1930 than in 1920?

That gender became the underlying, and arguably the most important, source of the attacks on Cather has to do not simply with individual male-biased readings of texts by women writers but with the social, political, and institutional situation of Cather's 1930s reviewers. The 1920s critics who established Cather's reputation could play a paternal role in relation to a young woman writer, but the young critics seeking to establish themselves in the 1930s were sons seeking to displace their fathers, professionally and ideologically— Mencken, for example, came under fire from the new liberal establishment for his reactionary political stance. At the same time, they were sons confronting a maternal presence their fathers had left as a literary legacy, a woman writer of the first rank. In attacking Willa Cather, the leftist critics who came of age in the 1930s were thus engaged in a complex oedipal drama, seeking both to replace the older generation of male critics and to repudiate a powerful maternal literary figure by defining her as limited.

The emphasis in the 1930s reviews on Cather's weakness, softness, and smallness likely arose, at least in part, from a covert acknowledgment of the strength and expanse of Cather's heroines, of her literary imagination, and of her previous literary reputation. Cather's "dominant and increasingly inaccessible women" seem to be "'always surrounded by little men,'" complained Maxwell Geismar, and this observation characterizes the relationship between Cather and the new generation of critics at the beginning of the decade: a dominant and increasingly inaccessible woman surrounded by men concerned with the issue of size.[26]

Several members of this new generation of critics and reviewers were playing a new professional and institutional role that also contributed to Cather's displacement as a major writer. Whereas most of Cather's early critics were journalists, professional reviewers, and editors who combated gentility and philistinism from outside the academy, the majority of Cather's critics in later decades were, for all or part of their professional careers, teachers of literature within English departments as well as book reviewers and authors of literary histories: Newton Arvin (Smith College), Alfred Kazin (City College of New York), Granville Hicks (Rensselaer), Maxwell Geismar (Sarah Lawrence), Henry Seidel Canby (Yale), and Lionel Trilling (Columbia).

Those who attended college or graduate school in the 1960s and 1970s—when American literature and American studies held firm, if not always highly respected, positions within the academy—may need to be reminded of the ideological and institutional pressures faced by scholars and teachers of American literature in the decades before World War II. "To those of us who had a special interest in American literature," remembers Jay B. Hubbell, "it seemed that, as Vernon L. Parrington once phrased it in a letter to me, 'There are too many Anglo-Saxon hounds guarding the sacred degree.' . . . It seems clear to me now that some of us who were interested in American literature were suffering from feelings of inferiority."[27] Such feelings are easy to understand. Not only were pioneers of American literary study like Hubbell surrounded by critics and colleagues who doubted that their native literature was worthy of serious study, but there was almost no institutional recognition of American literature in the 1910s and 1920s: very few courses in colleges and universities, little encouragement of graduate studies, no journals, and no sessions devoted to American literature at the convention of the Modern Language Association.[28]

By the end of the 1920s and throughout the 1930s and 1940s, however, important changes took place as the study of American literature became increasingly professionalized. These decades were marked by the increasing presence of American literature in curricula and the development of graduate programs in American civilization; the founding of professional journals (*New England Quarterly* in 1928 and *American Literature* in 1929); sessions on American literature at the Modern Language Association convention, beginning in 1928; and the publication of literary histories and studies of individual American writers.[29] Seeking to stake out the new territory of American literature as an important field of scholarly inquiry, surrounded by Shakespeareans and Miltonists who questioned whether Americans had produced a worthy national literature, after 1930 scholars, critics, and reviewers were increasingly concerned with defining and codifying an American literary canon, the establishment of which could both reflect and justify their own professional enterprise.

In so doing, they systematically overlooked or excluded women writers from the highest reaches of the newly emerging canon, defining their work either as minor or as major but second rank: if Americans were to have a first-rate canon to compete with that of the British, it would have to be male.[30] Hence from the late 1920s through the 1940s we have the phenomenon of academic critics simultaneously defining American women writers as minor and promoting American male writers as major, as if these were yoked, interdependent aspects of the same project: F. O. Matthiesson praising Sarah Orne Jewett in his 1929 biography, even as he defined her art as regional and limited and went on to exclude her and other women writers from his *American Renaissance* (1941); Newton Arvin dismissing Cather at the same time that he was elevating Hawthorne

and Whitman; Granville Hicks demoting Cather and Wharton while
he promoted Dreiser and Anderson in *The Great Tradition* (1933);
Henry Seidel Canby comparing Cather unfavorably with Sinclair
Lewis in Robert Spiller's *Literary History of the United States* (1948).
Canby's assessment of Cather summarizes and preserves her literary
decline, at the same time revealing the important role the ideology of
gender had played in her diminishment:

> Her art was not a big art. It does not respond to the troubled sense of
> American might and magnitude realized but not directed, and felt so
> strongly by such men as Sinclair Lewis in the same decades. It is national
> in significance, but not in scope. Her colleagues among the men "sweated
> sore" over that job, whereas her books rise free and are far more creative
> than critical. She is preservative, almost antiquarian, content with much
> space in little room—feminine in this, and in her passionate revelation of
> the values which conserve the life of the emotions.[31]

The equation Canby makes between gender and literary size (feminine = little) raises an important issue. It is possible that the same
pattern that social historians see characterizing the establishment of
the medical profession in America also informs the professionalization of American literature in the 1930s and 1940s: during the informal, uncodified beginnings of a profession women may play powerful
roles, but the process of professionalization is also one of mas-
culinization. Hence—just as midwives were exiled as the American
Medical Association became established—women writers were required to leave the highest reaches of the canon, as if their presence
there would somehow make it questionable that the American literary canon and the work of those who sought to establish it were
serious enterprises.[32]

III

Willa Cather was aware that a male-dominated publishing and critical establishment was attempting to reduce her stature, an awareness that informs her changing literary relationship with Sarah Orne
Jewett during the 1920s and 1930s. Jewett had been an important
influence in Cather's personal and professional life, and when Cather
dedicated *O Pioneers!* to Jewett she was acknowledging her mentor's
role in her literary emergence. By the mid-1920s Cather was the
established writer and Jewett the diminished one, however, and when
she edited her collection of Jewett's fiction in 1925 for Houghton
Mifflin, Cather was determined to increase Jewett's size, literally and
figuratively. She told editor Ferris Greenslet that the existing editions

of Jewett's fiction were simply too small—people would refuse to take them out of libraries, she explained, because they would assume they were children's books.[33] Greenslet promised her an edition in a larger format, and in her introduction Cather addressed her real aim—increasing Jewett's literary stature—by grouping *The Country of the Pointed Firs* with *Huckleberry Finn* and *The Scarlet Letter* as three American texts that would, in her view, withstand time and change.

By the mid-1930s, however, Cather had less confidence in her ability to guarantee Jewett, and herself, a place in the American canon. Just as her own literary value was beginning to be questioned, so was Jewett being relegated to a footnote in American literary history by the shapers of the canon. Granville Hicks's assessment of Jewett is typical of the more generous evaluations: although declaring her "only a minor writer," he acknowledged that she was "master" of delicate insights, and so a "master of a tiny realm," a "little world." But Hicks undercut even this faint praise (which echoes the metaphors of size used to limit Cather's significance), indulging in an ad feminam attack: after granting Jewett "powers of perception," he went on to say that "in other respects she was merely a New England old maid, who had a private income, traveled abroad, read the *Atlantic Monthly*, and believed in piety, progress. and propriety."[34]

Distressed by such dismissals of Jewett as a minor writer whose spinsterish eccentricity and genteel prudishness prevented her from addressing important subjects, Cather revised her 1925 preface to *The Country of the Pointed Firs* in her essay, "Miss Jewett," published in *Not under Forty* (1936). She removed her prediction of Jewett's longevity and classic status, attributing Jewett's "limited audience" to the development of a new class of unsympathetic readers: young urbanites, born in New York City and educated at New York universities, "violently inoculated with Freud," and most likely of foreign descent, perhaps Jewish or German.[35] In "Miss Jewett" Cather describes these unpleasant people as readers, not as critics, but a letter she wrote to Zoë Akins shortly after *Not under Forty* was published reveals that she had in mind professional readers: those reviewers and critics whom she termed her "haters," among them Trilling and Geismar. In a 1945 letter to Ferris Greenslet, she referred to Hicks as one of her tormenters.[36] Nowhere does Cather suggest that she was changing her own estimation of Jewett's work or that her own fiction was declining in quality; rather, her essays and letters throughout the 1930s suggest her recognition that the social, political, and institutional structures defining the production and the reception of literary texts were changing, relegating both Jewett's and her own fiction to marginality. She sensed that the politics of gender might have something to do with this decline: the critics cursed her, she wrote to Sinclair Lewis, because she did not write like a man.[37]

The essays Cather included in *Not under Forty* reflect her one attempt to fight the power of professional readers and critics on their own terms, by seizing power herself and publishing her own book of literary and cultural criticism. Her essays on the "novel démeublé," on Mrs. Fields, on Sarah Orne Jewett, and on Katherine Mansfield show her distaste for a contemporary society that dishonors the past; they also show a woman writer's attempt to claim and to preserve a female literary heritage. *Not under Forty* itself received negative reviews from critics who saw only more evidence of Cather's escapism and marginality, and she was so distressed by the attacks that she resolved never to express her critical opinions in print again. She realized that she had revealed herself particularly in her essay on Jewett, she told Zoë Akins, and although the criticism made her angry she had learned her lesson: she would be silent.[38]

Unable to silence reviewers and critics or to affect the cultural climate, Cather sought to control the way her books would be read and interpreted by refusing to let them be shaped and organized by literary and academic institutions. She limited the excerpts from her fiction that could appear in anthologies and refused permission to include any of her work in anthologies intended for use in high schools or colleges; she also successfully prevented the publication of cheaper editions of her books. As Alfred A. Knopf recalls, Cather did not want her books to be read in the classroom, because if readers were exposed to her in a coercive environment they might "grow up hating her."[39]

Cather refused such dissemination of her fiction because her view of the relationship between writer and reader was based on the private model of friendship. "When we find ourselves on shipboard, among hundreds of strangers," she wrote in "Miss Jewett," "we very soon recognize those who are sympathetic to us. We like a writer much as we like individuals; for what he is, simply, underneath his accomplishments."[40] Since the act of reading, ideally, was like striking up a friendship—with the same qualities of freedom, choice, and sympathy—Cather did not want readers to be forced to read her. So strongly did she wish readers to discover her novels independently that throughout the 1920s she even refused to allow her books to be adopted by book clubs. She relented only with *Shadows on the Rock*, in part responding to the private claims of friendship: her good friend Dorothy Canfield Fisher, then one of the judges of the Book-of-the-Month Club, wrote her a long letter defending the club's policies.

Paradoxically, Cather's attempts to ensure that readers would approach her work freely and sympathetically were cutting off institutional means for ensuring the accessibility of her novels and for solidifying her literary reputation. So to us it may seem that Cather was limiting her readership by restricting the ways in which people could encounter her books (and so revealing literary and social elitism), but from her perspective she was trying to preserve her novels from the cultural and literary institutions that were seeking to define, interpret, and limit her work. In a sense, she was trying to preserve the independence and autonomy she valued in the writer/reader bond from the social and institutional forces that were increasingly structuring it in the 1930s and 1940s—reviews, scholarly articles, anthologies, book clubs, high school and college curricula. Cather could have faith in the endurance of this bond, separated from the power of professional readers and critics, because during the period of her literary decline she was receiving hundreds of letters from readers who reaffirmed her faith in herself and in her work. Some of these she included in her own letters to old friends and supporters, thus creating an informal, supportive network of readers through her correspondence.

The links Cather maintained with readers through letter writing became particularly important during World War II, years of pain, isolation, and depression that were occasionally lightened by the hundreds of letters she received from soldiers who were reading her books in Armed Services Editions—a form of cultural transmission that she did not find coercive. During the last years of her life, Edith Lewis tells us, Cather took increasing pleasure in her correspondence with readers from all over the world: "Letters that were truly from 'the people,' not from any particular class of people, bringing to her their gratitude, their homage, their affection, in the kind of language she most appreciated—the language art cannot invent—were a sort of giving back to her, a return in kind, of the qualities of feeling she had herself expended in her writing career." Although, sadly, we do not have these letters, Lewis selects some quotations to suggest their range and quality: "'I would love to count myself your friend.' . . . 'Your books have somehow helped me, a boy from Wisconsin, to take heart again in my effort to rebuild my health and life' . . . 'I am glad you are alive, and have written so many splendid books.' " Finding a "great anonymous affirmation of her art" in these private voices, Cather tried to answer each one personally.[41]

So Cather found in these letters evidence that the writer/reader relationship could resemble the private bonds of affection and friendship; her letters from readers doubtless helped her to keep writing by offsetting the criticisms of her professional readers. Perhaps she found some assurance in them that her work would continue to be read and appreciated, even if not considered "major" by scholars and critics. In a sense she has been right; although not placed among the peaks of the American literary canon, Cather has continued to have a wide popular readership, a readership that preceded (and may be independent from) the recent revival of interest in her work in the academy.

Although Cather would have wanted to attribute this continuing readership to the same private, intuitive sympathies that create friendship, literary and cultural institutions have played a central role in keeping Cather's work alive—paradoxically by modifying the restrictions she sought to place on them. After her death Cather's executors negotiated an agreement with Houghton Mifflin, publisher of Cather's first four novels, that allowed the publication of *My Ántonia* and *O Pioneers!* in educational editions for high schools and the inclusion of *My Ántonia* in college anthologies. Twenty years later, seeing that Cather's sales were declining (in part because hardback editions were becoming too expensive for classroom use), Alfred Knopf persuaded Edith Lewis to agree that Cather's novels should be brought out in paperback.[42] Currently all of Cather's novels and most of her short stories are available in this format. Thus, even though individual readers may regard discovering a Cather novel as comparable to beginning a friendship, her continuing readership must be connected with the social, economic, and institutional structures that have kept her work in print and available to readers.

Over the last fifteen years Cather's stock in the academy and the canon has also been slowly rising, judging from the increasing appearance of her fiction in college curricula, the number of sessions at the Modern Language Association convention devoted to her work, and the publication of numerous articles in professional journals, biographies, and book-length studies of her fiction. A new consensus about her literary value has still not emerged, however, in part because past evaluations like "her art was not a big art" still have shaping power, and in part because many of the feminist scholars and critics who are focusing new attention on her work are simultaneously questioning the politics of canon formation.[43] What is clear is that a new generation of professional readers—looking at Willa Cather through different interpretive frameworks from those of her 1930s reviewers—is seeing a more significant, complex, and interesting writer than the conservative, "antiquarian" novelist described by Trilling, Hicks, and Canby.

Since Cather valued the nonacademic over the professional reader (no matter how sympathetic), she might not be entirely pleased by this development. For a student to encounter *O Pioneers!* in a course on American women writers rather than in a high school anthology might not strike her as an improvement, since she valued only acts of reading arising from choice and affinity. Yet Cather herself did not fully recognize that the seemingly private act of reading is itself structured by public forces and power relationships: we simply do not read writers whose work has not been published, evaluated, preserved, and transmitted by social, economic, and literary institutions of some sort. In fact, Cather could imagine the act of reading as private and intuitive only because she had attained at least a minimal place in the canon and a secure place in the structure of publishing as one of Alfred Knopf's most important authors.

Her relatively privileged position allowed Cather to ignore the social and institutional forces that had granted her a certain amount of literary power. Had she been even more disenfranchised during the 1930s and 1940s, as was a writer like Zora Neale Hurston, she might not have been able to compare reading with friendship, because she would have seen more clearly the powerful forces that limited her ability to attract friendly readers. In fact, Cather's metaphor of the shipboard friendship—based on her experience as a passenger on the luxurious ocean liners of the 1920s—reveals this paradox, suggesting that she could envision the writer/reader bond as private precisely because of the public forces that placed her at least in the foothills of the American literary canon. To develop such a shipboard friendship, one must be already a member of an elite, privileged group of travelers that includes a few people while excluding many more, much the way a literary canon exalts some writers and eliminates others.

Notes

Reprinted from *American Quarterly* 40, no. 1 (March 1988).

I want to thank Jane Tompkins for reading the first draft of this essay, and Bob Winston for some last-minute editorial advice.

1. Alfred A. Knopf, "Miss Cather," in *The Art of Willa Cather,* ed. Bernice Slote and Virginia Faulkner (Lincoln, Nebr., 1974), 210.

2. Clifton Fadiman, "Willa Cather: The Past Recaptured," *Nation* (December 7, 1932), 563.

3. Important book-length studies of the politics of canon formation in the United States are Jane Tompkins, *Sensational Designs: The Cultural Work of American Fiction, 1790–1860* (New York, 1985) esp. 186–201; and Cathy N. Davidson, *Revolution and the Word: The Rise of the Novel in America* (New

York, 1986), esp. 254–62. See also Nina Baym, "Melodramas of Beset Manhood: How Theories of American Fiction Exclude Women Authors," *American Quarterly* 33 (Summer 1981): 123–39; Annette Kolodny, "The Integrity of Memory: Creating a New Literary History of the United States," *American Literature* 57 (May 1985): 291–307; and Paul Lauter, "Race and Gender in the Shaping of the American Literary Canon: A Case Study from the Twenties," *Feminist Studies* 9 (Fall 1983): 435–63. For a study of the links among literary theory, pedagogy, and canonization, see William E. Cain, *The Crisis in Criticism: Theory, Literature, and Reform in English Studies* (Baltimore, Md., 1984). I have been helped in my understanding of canon formation by Barbara Herrnstein Smith's theoretical essay "Contingencies of Value," in *Canons*, ed. Robert von Hallberg (Chicago, 1984), 5–40.

4. Tompkins, *Sensational Designs*, 37.

5. Perry Miller, ed., *Major Writers of America* (New York, 1962), xvii; quoted in Kolodny, "Integrity of Memory," 295. See David Stineback, "No Stone Unturned: Popular Versus Professional Evaluations of Willa Cather," *Prospects* 7 (1982): 167–76, for a different view of Cather's reviewers and critics.

6. H. L. Mencken, review of *Alexander's Bridge*, in *Critical Essays on Willa Cather*, ed. John J. Murphy (Boston, 1984), 96.

7. Randolph Bourne, review of *My Ántonia*, in ibid., 96; and H. L. Mencken, review of *My Ántonia*, in *Willa Cather and Her Critics*, ed. James Schroeter (Ithaca, N.Y., 1967), 8. See "'America's Coming-of-Age' Criticism: Early Views," also in Schroeter's collection, 1–5. For a discussion of Bourne's and Mencken's roles in promoting American literature and shaping literary taste, see Kermit Vanderbilt, *American Literature and the Academy: The Roots, Growth, and Maturity of a Profession* (Philadelphia; 1986), 205–13.

8. Bourne, quoted Vanderbilt, *American Literature and the Academy*, 207.

9. Ibid., 206.

10. Carl Van Doren, "Willa Cather," in *Willa Cather and Her Critics*, 13–19.

11. Ferris Greenslet to Willa Cather, October 21, 1932, Houghton Library, Harvard University, Cambridge, Mass.

12. For a survey of the polls, see Jay. B. Hubbell, *Who Are the Major American Writers?* (Durham, N.C., 1972), 201–35.

13. Review of *One of Ours*, in *Willa Cather and Her Critics*, 10–12.

14. For a discussion of the reviews of *One of Ours*, see Barry Gross, "Willa Cather and the 'American Metaphysic,'" *Midamerica*, vol. 8, ed. David D. Anderson (East Lansing, Mich., 1981), 68–78.

15. Willa Cather to H. L. Mencken, February 6, 1922, Enoch Pratt Library, Baltimore, Md.

16. Schroeter, *Willa Cather and Her Critics*, 10.

17. For a selections of the positive reviews and assessments, see ibid. and Murphy, *Critical Essays*.

18. Newton Arvin, "Quebec, Nebraska, and Pittsburgh," *New Republic* (August 12, 1931), 345.

19. Schroeter, *Willa Cather and Her Critics*, 139–47.

20. Willa Cather, "Escapism," in *Willa Cather on Writing* (New York, 1949), 27.

21. See Daniel Aaron, *Writers on the Left: Episodes in American Literary Communism* (New York, 1961), 241–43.

22. Schroeter, *Willa Cather and Her Critics*, 171.

23. Granville Hicks, *Forum* (September 1931).

24. Schroeter, *Willa Cather and Her Critics*, 148–55. The critical attacks by Trilling and others on *Shadows on the Rock* support Nina Baym's argument that theories of American literature exclude women authors because the myth of America—the story of the untrammeled individual confronting an untamed wilderness—is in fact gender-coded (see Baym, "Melodramas of Beset Manhood"). Interestingly, *Shadows*—the novel that signified Cather's peripheral status to many reviewers—is a version of the mythic American story, the establishment of a society in the wilderness. Cather, however, was challenging the gender-coded myth of America: her protagonist is not the individual male but the collective culture, and the culture manages to inscribe itself upon the wilderness without the acts of violence and domination that in Cather's view were not as central to the story of settlement as the acts of peace and accommodation. "And really," she wrote in a letter published in the *Saturday Review* in 1931, "a new society begins with the salad dressing more than with the destruction of Indian villages" (*Willa Cather on Writing*, 16). Critics could view the novel as peripheral because although it addresses the central American story of immigration, transplanting, and resettlement, it does not tell the male version of that story.

25. Schroeter, *Willa Cather and Her Critics*, 170. The same imagery of size was used by Fred Lewis Pattee, who praised Cather's novels, which he nonetheless described as "cameo cuttings" (*The New American Literature, 1890–1930* [New York, 1930], 265).

26. Schroeter, *Willa Cather and Her Critics*, 187.

27. Jay B. Hubbell, *South and Southwest: Literary Essays and Reminiscences* (Durham, N.C., 1965), 22–23.

28. For a discussion of this period in the history of American literary study, see ibid., 3–48, and Vanderbilt, *American Literature and the Academy*, 243–70.

29. For an institutional history of the development of American studies that traces some of these developments, see Gene Wise, "'Paradigm Dramas' in American Studies: A Cultural and Institutional History of the Movement," *American Quarterly* 31, bibliography issue (1979): 293–337. See also Gene Wise, "An American Studies Calendar" in the same issue, 407–47.

30. See Lauter, "Race and Gender," for a fuller analysis of the role played by the politics of gender in the shaping of the canon.

31. *Literary History of the United States*, vol. 2, ed. Robert E. Spiller et. al. (New York, 1948), 1216.

32. see Barbara Ehrenreich and Deirdre English, *For Her Own Good: One Hundred and Fifty Years of the Experts' Advice to Women* (New York, 1979); and Margaret W. Rossiter, *Women Scientists in America: Struggles and*

Strategies to 1940 (Baltimore, Md., 1982). Lauter also correlates the establishment of the canon with professionalization and the consequent marginalization of women writers ("Race and Gender," 446–48).

33. Willa Cather to Ferris Greenslet, February 17, 1924, Houghton Library, Harvard University.

34. Granville Hicks, *The Great Tradition: An Interpretation of American Literature since the Civil War* (New York, 1933), 104–5. Waldo Frank was even more contemptuous in a 1925 review of Cather's edition of Jewett's stories: "We must all snatch from our coming days the nodding wish to turn from the rot of our world into a sweet-scented realm of senile wishes, in order to enjoy Miss Jewett" (*New Republic* 44 [October 14, 1925]: 204). Van Wyck Brooks's assessment makes clear the role played by gender in Jewett's decline: "Her vision was certainly limited. It scarcely embraced the world of men, and vigorous, masculine life of towns like Gloucester, astir with Yankee enterprise and bustle, lay quite outside her province" (*New England: Indian Summer* [New York, 1940], 347–48).

35. Willa Cather, "Miss Jewett," in *Not under Forty* (New York, 1936), 92–93.

36. Willa Cather to Zoë Akins, October 28, 1937, Huntington Library, San Marino, Calif.; and Willa Cather to Ferris Greenslet, January 31, 1945, Houghton Library, Harvard University.

37. Willa Cather to Sinclair Lewis, n.d., Beineke Library, Yale University, New Haven, Conn.

38. Willa Cather to Zoë Akins, October 28, 1937, Huntington Library.

39. Knopf, "Miss Cather," 211.

40. Cather, "Miss Jewett," 94.

41. Edith Lewis, *Willa Cather Living: A Personal Record* (New York, 1953), 186–88.

42. For an account of these negotiations, see Knopf, "Miss Cather," 222–24.

43. I include myself among such critics. My biography of Willa Cather (*Willa Cather: The Emerging Voice* [New York, 1987]), which draws on feminist and psychoanalytic theory, describes Cather's attainment of literary identity and authority but does not argue that her fiction deserves a higher rank in the literary canon.

Chapter Eleven

The Book-of-the-Month Club and the General Reader

The Uses of "Serious" Fiction

Janice A. Radway

In 1986, the Book-of-the-Month Club (BOMC) celebrated its sixtieth anniversary with special promotions and publicity campaigns. Club officials offered their members a company-sponsored history of the institution, special editions of "BOMC Classics," including J. D. Salinger's *The Catcher in the Rye* and Isak Dinesen's *Seven Gothic Tales*, and two commemorative posters proclaiming "The Joys of Reading." In addition, the club mounted an elaborate exhibition at the New York Public Library celebrating "America's coming of age in literature, culture and the arts."[1] Designed to chronicle significant cultural events both high and popular from 1926 to 1986, the exhibition nevertheless entwined club history with the high culture tradition by prominently featuring books selected by the club that have since been recognized as major artistic achievements.

Although these activities were designed in part to garner publicity and thus to help in the club's membership drive, they were also the creation of editors who are cognizant of the company's past and self-conscious about its cultural role as "an American institution." Its editors often characterize the company as "the book club of record" where "serious book readers" can find "the best new books" in every field imaginable.[2] In fact, the Book-of-the-Month Club is well regarded within the publishing industry as an institution that manages to combine commercial goals with a concern for "quality."[3] The company is attended to, of course, because a club bid can be an important source of revenue for publishers. But industry executives also respect the skill with which its editors sift through more than five thousand manuscripts annually to choose approximately two hundred and fifty books that the club eventually offers to its membership.

In spite of the esteem it now enjoys within the publishing world, the club's reputation in what might be called the literary world remains that of the quintessentially "middlebrow" forum.[4] This placement is assigned to the club's selections by those who define literary culture in America, the critics of the literary press, and scholars in the academic world. The Book-of-the-Month Club offers, in such a view, neither the best works of contemporary literature nor the worst examples of mindless trash. Its books, rather, fall into that large, amorphous middle ground of the unremarkable but respectable. It is worth keeping in mind, however, that this linear arrangement is conceived of as a hierarchy and that midrange books are seen by such commentators not simply as different from those occupying higher positions but as failed attempts to approximate the achievement of the best books.

This should come as no surprise given recent discussions of the social construction of taste by Pierre Bourdieu, Barbara Herrnstein Smith, and Richard Ohmann, among others.[5] As Smith has reminded us, "Like its price in the marketplace, the value of an entity to an individual subject is *also* the product of the dynamics of an economic system, specifically the personal economy constituted by the subject's needs, interests, and resources—biological, psychological, material, and experiential."[6] To dismiss the middle range as products of a fundamental insufficiency, therefore, as the result of a certain incompetence, is to accomplish several other goals simultaneously, all of which have relevance to the self-interest of those making the distinction. It is to state, first, that there is a single hierarchy of value within which all verbal products are ranged and that all such works aspire to the highest position. It is also to affirm the validity and preeminence of that single set of criteria against which all works are measured, and thus to insist that there is only one appropriate way to read. Finally, it is to value reflexively and in a hierarchical way those individuals who are able to recognize such value and to appreciate it by reading properly. To label the club middlebrow, therefore, is to damn it with faint praise and to legitimate the social role of the intellectual who has not only the ability but the authority to make such distinctions and to dictate them to others.[7]

If one accepts the social hierarchy that this taste structure masks, it is easy to accept the validity of the particular criteria that serve as the working test of excellence. In fact, the high value placed on rationality, complexity, irony, reflexivity, linguistic innovation, and the "disinterested" contemplation of the well-wrought artifact makes sense within cultural institutions devoted to the improvement of the individuality, autonomy, and productive competence of the already privileged individuals who come to these institutions for instruction and advice.[8] Appreciation for the technical fine points of aesthetic achievement is also understandable among people whose daily work centers on the business of discrimination. But it is worth keeping in mind that the critical dismissal of literary works and institutions that do not embody these values *as failures* is an exercise of power that rules out the possibility of recognizing that such works and institutions might be valuable to others because they perform functions more in keeping with their own somewhat different social position, its material constraints, and its ideological concerns. The easy critical dismissal of the club and other "popularizers" is an act of exclusion that banishes those who might mount even the most minimal of challenges to the culture and role of the contemporary intellectual by proclaiming their own right to create, use, and value books for different purposes.

My preoccupation with the Book-of-the-Month Club arises, then, out of a prior interest in the way books are variously written, produced, marketed, read, and evaluated in contemporary American culture. My subjects might best be described as ways of writing (rather than Literature), ways of reading (rather than texts).[9] I have begun to examine the club's editorial operation with the intention of eventually comparing the manner, purpose, and substance of the editors' choice of books with the choices of actual Book-of-the-Month Club members. Such a comparison seems potentially interesting for a variety of reasons.

Although the club has only recently begun the process of compiling large quantities of information about its membership, it seems unlikely that more than a very small portion is composed of literary intellectuals, given its reputation among them as the purveyor of the middlebrow and the mediocre.[10] It seems probable, therefore, that for a significant number of club members, books play a quite different role in their lives and serve other purposes than they do for people who make their living producing, analyzing, and distinguishing among cultural products. Furthermore, because Book-of-the-Month Club editors know from long experience that they can sell a fairly predictable number of books in any one of several informally defined categories, it also seems likely that their membership is not homogeneous. They may in fact be serving different kinds of readers who use books for different purposes and thus judge them according to divergent criteria.

The editors themselves also occupy an interesting social position.

It is not well known that the heart of the Book-of-the-Month Club's operation is located in midtown Manhattan. In fact, if they are familiar with the club at all, most Americans place it somewhere in middle America and attribute its selections to a small group of judges. Although all distribution and membership correspondence originates in Mechanicsburg (near Harrisburg), Pennsylvania, and a group of six judges chooses the monthly main selection, the editorial process is actually initiated, overseen, and carried out by a group of twenty or so individuals who live in and around New York City. Those "editors" are responsible for reading most of the five thousand yearly submissions, for writing the readers' reports that are generated for every book the club receives, and for the selection of alternates offered to the membership as supplements to the actual book of the month. Like most people who work in the publishing industry, they are well educated, overwhelmingly white, and solidly middle-class. Most are former English or history majors trained in the close reading of texts. In fact, the two editors in charge of the editorial operation at the time this research was conducted had completed substantial graduate work in literature. Many of their colleagues are published authors themselves. Lunching regularly with friends and professional acquaintances from the publishing industry, the BOMC editors are well integrated into what Coser, Kadushin, and Powell have called the "culture of publishing."[11]

For the most part, Book-of-the-Month Club editors read typescripts or bound galleys six to nine months before they are published as books. Those editors, therefore, are among the first readers from outside the publishing house to encounter a book, to react to it formally, and to judge both its quality and its commercial possibilities. Indeed they see books many months before even the most prominent reviewers. In most cases, they have only a page or two of introductory material from a subsidiary rights director or the memory of a ten-minute phone call to orient their reading.[12] With little more to go on than a paragraph or two of description and a few sketchy plans for future publicity, they must "place" the book, evaluate it, and decide whether they can convey their enthusiasm to a potential reader in a description that is routinely two hundred to three hundred words long and no more than one thousand.[13] Their reading is governed finally not only by their own preferences and training but by the fact that the club is a business designed to sell books to others. They are always trying to read as they believe their members do.

A study of the editorial selection process at the Book-of-the-Month Club, therefore, should allow us to witness the complex ideological calculations and negotiations of a particular fraction of the American middle class as it attempts to define itself with respect to the already established taste hierarchy while simultaneously trying to function commercially as the servant of less culturally oriented sections of that class. By tracing the well-documented editorial deliberations of the only group that reads virtually all of the adult trade hardcover books published in contemporary America, we should be able to learn something about the taste and underlying ideological assumptions of those key individuals who are controlling the gate, deciding not only what cultural creations will be formally produced but also which among those will be distributed in "an urgent or attractive way."[14] The BOMC editors are, after all, much like the publishers, editors, and agents of the professional-managerial class discussed by Ohmann who are responsible for deciding the actual content of our literary culture.[15] It is important to note as well that like the publishers and editors they resemble, the BOMC editors are cultural workers. They possess a substantial measure of what Bourdieu has called "cultural capital," and they exercise a certain amount of power in contemporary society by helping to determine what will count as culture for others.[16] Given the relatively minor role of publishing in the larger economy and the pay scale in the industry, it also seems likely that they command somewhat less economic capital. Not unlike the academics who trained them and the literary critics whose job their own resembles, the BOMC editors' social position is a function of their economic situation, but it is also a function of their capacity and authority to discriminate and to identify artistic and cultural excellence.

At the same time, because the membership of the club is broader, more diverse and dispersed, than they are, the editors control or rein in their own preferences and attempt to read as they believe their "general" readers do. When asked whether they consider their own taste representative of their readers' taste, nearly all the editors replied that only a small segment of the membership shares their preferences. Their assumption results regularly in a winnowing process based on their perception of the nature of a "popular," though again middle-class, taste. As a consequence they are always attending to what individuals outside the cultural industry actually do with books. They have their own theories about why people buy cookbooks and diet books, for instance, and they regularly turn down books of fiction and history that they themselves appreciated but felt would be uninteresting to their membership. Therefore, their deliberations should also reveal much about variations, rifts, and even contradictions within middle-class taste and the various ideologies of which it is a product. The editors' readers' reports and decisions may permit us finally to begin to trace the interactions among the different factions of what Bourdieu calls the dominant class: among those who already possess cultural capital, those who lack confidence about their continuing mastery of it and therefore desire a continuing connection to some cultural establishment, and those willing to mediate between the two by assisting the culturally insecure to find new examples of the high tradition. The editors' deliberations should be particularly interesting, finally, because the commercial interests of the club militate against their sharing in the common assumptions of the cultural elite with whom they identify: the assumption that appreciation and understanding of art and cultural tradition can come only with long acquaintance and careful education, and the further assumption that once one has acquired such a capacity, one will not need the advisory service of expert others.

I

The New York editorial office of the Book-of-the-Month Club employs about 135 people. The warehouse, distribution, and membership operation in Mechanicsburg (or Camp Hill, as it was referred to in the past) provides work for another 600. Until recently, connections between the two units were fairly informal. As a consequence, editors rarely gauged their selections formally to sales statistics. The club functioned editorially without market research largely as a consequence of founder Harry Scherman's original decision to keep the marketing operation of the club separate from the process of book selection. Although Scherman and his managers knew a great deal about the club audience because they worked closely with George Gallup as early as the 1930s, they did not permit the editorial judges to see this data because Scherman did not believe it could predict future critical or market success, and because he wanted to demonstrate that the process of selection was unbiased. As a legacy of this decision, the club's past editorial operations have been based on surprisingly little hard data. Most of the information that was amassed was only to structure new membership drives or to design initial-offer advertising. Although the situation is changing rapidly at the moment, the editorial decisions upon which the present study are based were still grounded predominantly in hunch, intuition, and luck.[17] This is not to say that the editors knew little about their audience, only that the knowledge they had of it was not in quantifiable form but existed as the tacit, relatively unconscious product of long personal experience.

To date, my interviews with editors and my systematic review of the club's readers' reports for 1984, 1985, and 1986 suggest that while commercial concerns frequently dictate club choices, especially main selections, many alternate selections are made simply because individual editors like particular books and believe that they should be brought to the attention of other readers, even if that group potentially numbers no more than two thousand or three thousand. As a consequence, the club often seems to function as a small bookstore with an idiosyncratic backlist designed to appeal to many different readers rather than as a homogenizing, mass-market distribution operation pitched always and only to the lowest common denominator.[18] One of the justifications editors give for this sort of operation is identical to that cited by Al Silverman, the club's chairman, in a mission statement written for all company employees. Recounting that he had been asked by someone why a book that had sold poorly had been offered as a selection, he explained, "I told him that we took it because it was a wonderful book, that we knew it probably wouldn't sell much but that it was one of those silent, long-term investments that might pay off in member satisfaction for a segment of our audience." He continued, "Every year we need our Ludlums, our le Carrés, our Kings, and our sure-fire non-fiction books. But we also need the kind of books that are not sure bestsellers, and not faddish, but that delight our audience, and surprise them, a book that members buy not just to read, but also to keep."[19] Silverman's statement implicitly acknowledges the values grounding the taste hierarchy and characteristically identifies the club as an institution with the search for enduring excellence. With equal frequency, however, one also hears editors justify selections by noting that people have different tastes and that those tastes ought to be satisfied without making judgments about them.

One of the most striking things about the Book-of-the-Month Club, in fact, as a social organization, is its effort to create and maintain a nonhierarchical, nonelitest atmosphere even as it identifies itself as a cultural institution with the values associated with high culture. Indeed I think it is this atmosphere, as it is embodied in regular editorial procedures, that is largely responsible for the catholic character of the club's offerings despite its recurring nods to cultural authority. In fact, it is a remarkably collegial organization, where editors and management work hard to value each other's contributions equally. This collegiality is realized most visibly in the company's tendency to promote from within. It is not uncommon for a copywriter in the Book-of-the-Month Club to move up to an editorial chair. Indeed, Joe Savago, who was executive editor at the time this research was conducted, had begun working for the club only twelve years previously, first as an outside reader and then as a copy editor for the *BOMC News*. In 1986, Savago worked more closely with editor-in-chief Nancy Evans than almost anyone in the club and was promoted at her departure in January, 1987. Jill Sansone, a senior editor at the time these interviews were conducted, was responsible for assigning manuscripts to both outside and in-house readers. She started in the production department working on layout and copy for the *News*; Anne Close, another editor, first worked for the club as an executive secretary.

The collegial nature of the club's atmosphere is well known within the publishing industry and prized by those who work there. Indeed, I have been struck by the intensity with which its editors discuss their jobs. Every editor I have spoken with sees that job as one of reading. "What could be better," they all ask rhetorically, "than to be paid to read books?" Furthermore, every editor seems to feel supported and trusted both by his or her colleagues and by the club's top management. All are convinced that if they argue vociferously for a book, they will be listened to and, for the most part, heeded. Nothing I have seen to date contradicts that view or the following picture of the club drawn by Evans in an interview with executive editor William Zinsser, who was eliciting her opinions for the anniversary history of the club. Evans observed that "it's quite extraordinary to have this group of people who truly love books." She continued, "There's not a soul here who doesn't. We are all honest-to-God readers. Of course we have a million other things to do all day, but at bottom this is an intense group of book lovers. Sure we have to make money, and sure we make marketing decisions, but if there's passion for a book, that passion can prevail here, and if we can just get that passion through the pages of the *News* we get it back in kind."[20] Evans's view of the company as a community of book lovers is voiced independently by everyone involved in the actual editorial operation. They also repeat her emphasis on the importance of individual judgment. As Eve Tulipan, another senior editor, remarked, the spoken folk wisdom of the Club is "do what you like."

In fact, a hierarchy of taste has not developed within the club, in the sense that some editors' views or tastes are valued more than others'. Such a potentially divisive structure has been avoided by a fairly elaborate though informal scheme of horizontal specialization. Each editor reads regularly in one or two fields and is regarded as the resident expert on previous publications, genre conventions and expectations, and standards of assessment within those particular categories. Distinctions are made by individuals *within* equivalent categories, rather than among them or their champions. The need for internal social harmony, therefore, seems to foreclose any tendency toward a hierarchical ranking of the categories along a single scale of value.

This process of horizontal categorization dominates the Book-of-the-Month Club's editorial operation. From the moment a book first arrives in the manuscript room, it is treated as a particular example of any one of a number of loosely defined categories.[21] It is tacitly given its first label by Jill Sansone or one of the other senior editors when they decide upon the best readers for the book. Sansone makes the assignments on the basis of the publicity material the club has received from the publisher, on past experience with a known author, on the reputation of the publishing house itself, and on her own broad knowledge of the industry. Although she does not indicate in any formal way that a book is "military history," "self-help health," or "popular business management," when an editor receives a manuscript to read, the very fact that it has come to him or her already indicates that it is probably a particular kind of book and thus ought to be read in a certain way. In evaluating the assigned manuscript, every editor seems to judge that book primarily against other similar books published previously in the category. As Zinsser observed, the club's "basic operating principle is that we should offer the best book in the field." His view was corroborated not only by Joe Savago, who remarked that the editors are "dedicated to presenting a book as exactly what it is," but by virtually all of the club's editorial procedures: readers' reports nearly always place a book in a certain category and frequently refer to the need to fill a particular categorical slot; the weekly list of books for Thursday morning editorial conferences notes in a sentence or two just what sort of book the manuscript is; and the copy for a book in the *News* also prominently features a statement about the book's genre.

No one currently at the club can recall a moment when this categorization process was instituted. Indeed, it seems likely that it evolved over time, in part out of material necessity. As Joe Savago explained, a book is nearly always a "blind purchase" in the sense that buyers know next to nothing about the book and therefore cannot predict how it will satisfy them. Since the Book-of-the-Month Club is clearly in the business of selling books to readers who presumably come to it with already defined tastes and needs, it must find some way to indicate to its members that they are in fact likely to enjoy a certain title. Hence the need for a handle that will position the book for its members. The club must manage this categorization process, furthermore, with enough accuracy to ensure that readers will not feel "burned" by the club and thus refuse to return to it for assistance. The practice of nonhierarchical categorization, then, is also the product of the commercial desire to satisfy as many preexisting tastes as possible.

A relatively small number of operative categories dominates readers' reports, informal discussion, and the *BOMC News*. Among them are popular history, which seems to include the subfields of military history, Civil War history, and World War II history; popular biography; self-help health; popular business management; popular science; fitness; cookbooks and crafts; reference books; classic English mysteries; crime fiction and thrillers; and the final, amorphous category of general fiction, which is informally subdivided into the commercial and the serious. It is especially important to note that this last division, despite the name, is treated editorially as only one more genre or category that must be covered rather than as the apogee toward which all else aspires. The list is a varied one and it points, I think, to different uses of books and different ways of reading. Although I cannot be sure of this until I interview actual club members, it seems entirely plausible that these categories have evolved because they roughly describe discrete ways of reading and distinct functions for a varied assortment of books. If this is true, the categories would function as Fredric Jameson claims literary genres do; in *The Political Unconscious* he observes that "genres are essentially literary *institutions,* or social contracts between a writer and a specific public, whose function is to specify the proper use of a cultural artifact."[22] Categorical placement within the *BOMC News*, then, not only may serve to identify books for readers but may tell them how to read them as well.

Eventually I hope to explore just how the social contract between writers and readers varies across these categories. What, for instance, are the proper uses of the cultural artifacts biography or popular history, and how are they different from the club reader's use of serious fiction? Is a Book-of-the-Month Club member's or editor's understanding of the proper use of serious fiction the same as the understanding embodied in academic exercises in literary criticism? If all club categories prescribe uses that are related to each other in some fundamental way that is yet different from the use made of literature by intellectuals with the highest cultural authority, will an understanding of those uses tell us something more about the variations in the content of middle-class taste in contemporary America or the functions of literacy outside the academy? For that matter, will it help us to refine our understanding of middle-class ideology by specifying more clearly how actual subjects define and experience the contemporary world? As a way of initiating such an inquiry, I would like to concentrate for the rest of this paper on the editorial decisions surrounding the selection of what is usually called serious fiction at the Book-of-the-Month Club in order to explain how its editors define the category and what they think its functions ought to be.

II

The Book-of-the-Month Club has never formalized its definition of serious fiction, its characterization of what it offers within the category, or its criteria for selection. Outside readers do not receive directions about how to make judgments, nor are club editors ever formally instructed by a superior as to what exactly makes a manuscript club material. While some editors use the term "serious" frequently, others are uncomfortable with it because it connotes something that is boring. Indeed in reports on serious fiction titles, one regularly encounters a certain hostility toward the academy and the institutionalized teaching of literature, which the editors seem to believe transforms fascinating books into dry exercises in analysis. Thus, although they use the term because it is convenient, the editors are careful to insist that serious literature can still be a pleasure to read. "Serious" should not be synonymous with "dour" in their view or, for that matter, with the gratuitously obscure. The conflict we saw earlier between the public rhetoric of the club, which emphasizes cultural authority and artistic excellence, and its more catholic editorial operations, which concede the diversity of books for both social and commercial reasons, is played out here as an ambivalence about the nature of serious fiction. On the one hand, the editors seem to share the assumption of the high culture aesthetic that fiction should be technically complex and self-consciously *about* significant issues. On the other, they demand that such fiction be pleasurable to read, a stipulation that differs little from that made regularly by readers of bestsellers and genre fiction who desire always to be entertained.

In fact, when asked to discuss the category of serious fiction, Book-of-the-Month Club editors begin by opposing it to what it is not. They observe first that what they are trying to eliminate is "trash" or "junk" and proceed to the claim that they are striving to find "intelligent" novels that will "stretch" their readers. Pressed further to elaborate upon the distinction, the editors almost always settle on the issue of language and say that trash is sloppily written. Indeed, the single most common complaint in the readers' reports that eventually judge a work of fiction to be trash involves the charge of linguistic excess. Book-of-the-Month Club editors regularly exclude books whose writing they characterize as self-consciously descriptive, effusive, sentimental, or melodramatic. What they dismiss most frequently, of course, are romance novels and some historical fiction, in large part because their prose is overly "lush," a word used regularly to disparage such writing.

Furthermore, Book-of-the-Month Club editors regularly praise the writing in the serious fiction they consider and accept. For them, writing is good if it is characterized by economy, condensation, and precision. In praising Martin Cruz Smith's recent novel *Stallion Gate*, for instance, Savago characterized Smith's prose as "clean," "supple," and without cliché. Later he described elements of the book as "tight," "flawless," and "brilliantly, seamlessly melded." It would seem, then, that the categorical distinction between the worst of the commercial—"trash," in club parlance—and the "serious" is grounded first on the binary opposition lush/spare. This would seem, furthermore, a simple instance of the distinction Bourdieu has elaborated upon so extensively, the distinction between a popular aesthetic celebrating sensibility and sensation and a bourgeois aesthetic (synonymous in his view with the high culture aesthetic) recommending reflection and understanding.[23] As Bourdieu notes, "'Pure' taste and the aesthetics which provides its theory are founded on a refusal of 'impure' taste and of *aisthesis* (sensation), the simple, primitive form of pleasure reduced to a pleasure of the senses."[24] In making this initial distinction between serious fiction and trash, the BOMC editors again seem to be locating themselves along the same hierarchical continuum employed by literary critics and academics and to be associating themselves, in opposition to the taste of the masses, with the higher, more culturally respectable pole. A function, perhaps, of their training, this move also establishes their cultural authority and asserts their right to select books for others.

Having said that, however, it is important to insist again that neither the distinctions nor the categories are that simple at the Book-of-the-Month Club. The club prominently features entertainment and genre fiction and sells both by highlighting the visceral pleasures they produce. It is true that this is done for commercial reasons and that in making such selections the editors still take care to choose the best books they can find. They admit, even, to a search for "class trash." Yet it is equally important to note that the editors are also genuinely uncomfortable with arraying the categories along a simple hierarchy and prefer to view them as different sorts of books for different purposes. Al Silverman articulated this other component of the club view in his mission statement when he cautioned that the "serious book reader is not one who reads serious books only—Proust, Rilke, Dostoevsky. A serious book reader is one who buys loads of books a year, most to be educated and entertained, but sometimes to be uplifted."[25] Although the club *is* more likely to offer a commercial book as the monthly main selection, it also regularly features at least one serious fiction title as a new, featured alternate. In any given month, of the roughly twenty to thirty fiction titles listed in the two-hundred-and-fifty-book catalogue, about eight to eighteen might be considered serious fiction.

The BOMC editors believe strongly that some books can simultaneously excite the senses and stand up to aesthetic contemplation and evaluation. Savago's review of *Stallion Gate* suggests as much in a conclusion that itself challenges the familiar categorical opposition that is the object of Bourdieu's analysis. I would like to quote Savago at some length, for he demonstrates here the limits of aesthetic distancing in the BOMC version of the high culture aesthetic:

> Line for line this is the best *writing* I've read in years—Cruz Smith can do anything he wants, from dialogue to nature writing, humor to menace, in a prose that's clean and supple and contains not one single (I was waiting for one) cliché. He writes as an insider, an expert, on whatever subject's at hand—and there are many: the science and the nuts-and-bolts of the bomb and its assembly; the art and psychology of boxing; Indian mores and the New Mexican landscape; jazz music, jazz piano playing and improvisation; the war in the Pacific. The details, everywhere, seem not lifted from some hastily done "research" but to spring from vivid memory, intimate experience. The plotting and the sheer craftsmanship of the scenes, of the movement back and forth in time, is tight and flawless. This is the sort of book you'd be a fool to call commercial as opposed to literary, or vice versa. It is simply a wonderful book, period, in which story, character, prose and craft are all brilliant and brilliantly, seamlessly melded. Terrific.

In Savago's mind, carefully crafted prose could be harnessed to larger unities that themselves produce different kinds of pleasure. Serious fiction or the literary, then, was not necessarily synonymous for him with the poetic exploration of the limitations and possibilities of language itself, that which Jameson has labeled the molecular project of modernism, and which Savago himself termed "autistic."[26] While Savago appreciated deftly woven sentences and intelligent metaphors, his reports also always focused on a few of the abstract molar unities (constructions produced by the reader to create plot, personality, coherent character, and so on) cited by Jameson that have traditionally been used to recontain the molecular. In fact, his reports were dominated by a concern for "the continuity of personal identity, the organizing unity of the . . . personality," and the role the two play in the creation of a significant narrative.[27]

Savago's opinions are shared widely at the club. One of the most explicit statements I have yet seen by a Book-of-the-Month Club official about the question of aesthetics was made by Lucy Rosenthal, a former judge and senior editor, in an interview with the *Missouri Review* on literary culture in contemporary America. Discussing both her own work as a novelist and the standards she employed at the club, she discriminated between different kinds of writing in a way that seems to approximate the working definition of the "serious" used by most of the other editors. In response to the interviewer's question about whom she writes for, Rosenthal replied, "I want my writing to be accessible. I want people not to be bored. So I wrote the kind of book that would not bore me." She continued, "I'm not a snob. I don't think I write for an audience directly. I write to tell a story."[28] Storytelling, evidently, at least in Rosenthal's view, is a democratic art that must be defended because some people—"snobs," in her view—do not value it. Comments she has made elsewhere provide some insight as to what she may believe they value in its place. In discussing the writer Norma Klein, in a review of *Give Me One Good Reason*, Rosenthal observed that "Klein's novel is more lifelike than literary, a storyteller's book, not a poet's, the work of a writer engaged more with life and its possibilities than with language, and its resources for language's own sake."[29] While Rosenthal would not dismiss all poetry, it does appear that, like Savago, she is not interested solely in the refined, distanced contemplation of the aesthetic signifier but is searching for a way to attend both to the particularities of individual words *and* to the larger, more utilitarian work they can do in telling a story about coherently formed, interesting individuals.

The typical form of a club reader's report on fiction suggests that the other editors are similarly engaged. Neither an exercise in textual exegesis nor one in aesthetic connoisseurship, these reports are first and foremost records of the temporal experience of encountering characters, and only secondarily critical evaluations of a book's mastery of its materials. Although many reports begin with a sentence or two placing the author or the book itself in terms of genre, the first three-quarters of most of them are devoted to detailed descriptions of the characters, their histories, and their activities in the fiction. For most BOMC editors, the crucial molar unity seems to be the coherent, unified personality. They approach the books they read as stories about people. It is only after the editor has attempted to give an account of what it's like to read through a piece of fiction, to spend time with the characters involved, that he or she assesses its consequence or its literary skill. The criteria of significance and craft are always applied, but if a writer does not also produce an encounter with a recognizable and interesting individual of one sort or another, his or her book will likely be rejected by the club.

When reading with their members in mind, then, the editors of the Book-of-the-Month Club are not seeking the pleasures produced by a historically informed and technically sophisticated appreciation of language play itself. Although they themselves are capable of such readings and they often display fine passages for their colleagues or note literary lineages and genealogies, their reports are dominated by a preoccupation with what language brings into being. Listen, here, to the distinctions drawn by Savago in his report on the 1983 novel by Stephen Wright, *Meditations in Green: A Novel of Vietnam.*[30]

> Yes, this is easily the best writing I've read in many months, the book is a kind of masterpiece and the author a kind of genius, but No, it's probably not for us. What? Is the BOMC member beneath Good Writing? No, not per se, of course. Good Writing in the service of a fairly conventional, generic effort is certainly *not* wasted on your average literate reader. John le Carré sells almost as well as [X] and mostly, I suspect, to a class of reader which appreciates the difference—and le Carré is a primo BOMC author. But *Meditations in Green* is an essentially formless series of vignettes and scenes and surrealities and ironies with a large and shifting cast of occasional characters, not a straightforward story-novel with a plot. It doesn't try to "go anywhere," it just *goes* brilliantly.[31]

Because Wright's "novel" lacked the conventional generic structure, Savago was not at all sure it could be sold to the club's members. His reservations were echoed by another reader who judged the book's innovations "failures." "The author's experiments with form and style do not pay off," the reader wrote. "[Green] has tried to create a virtuosically-controlled chaos, but what results is merely chaos. Plainly, this novel is a mess. The first 100 pages or so are so difficult and obscure that I gave up reading about a dozen times. The lack of plot makes for a terrible predictability and repetition." "With a very strong editor and a couple of rewrites," this reader concluded, "we would probably have a good novel here. As it stands, few will get through it."

Within the category of serious fiction, it seems, the Book-of-the-Month Club is looking for works that are carefully written but manage to combine an aesthetic, formalist focus with the referential act of designation. They are not interested in those books that foreground their interest in language to such an extent that they are *about* language, its possibilities and constraints. Having said, however, that it is personality, character, and story that such language must bring

into being, I also want to add that club editors are additionally preoc-
cupied with the search for a "new voice" and have frequently selected
books that do not foreground character and plot in the traditional
nineteenth-century way. Although this may at first sound like the
reassertion of the value of style, the BOMC editors do not necessarily
equate voice with a personal, idiosyncratic language. For them, the
voice must never be disembodied. Their particular demand that the
literary voice issue from a recognizable personality and therefore
from an identifiable place provides the key, I think, to the meaning of
the molar unities in the BOMC aesthetic and ultimately to the function or use of the category of serious fiction, at least as the editors
conceive it within the parameters prescribed by the commercial goals
of the club.

III

Although the term formally refers to a publicity category of the Quality Paperback Book Club, "new voice" is also used as a general critical
term by all the editors. When I asked Savago about the term, he
explained that when he read, he was not so much interested in characters in the story as he was in listening to the author speak. His interest
in the voice, however, was neither purely aural nor stylistic, for he
added that what he listened for was "intelligence." As he said, "I hear
them as smart or not-smart, ardent or not-ardent persons, basically
giving me the inside of their heads, via a fiction." He continued,
"What I come away with from a book is not a memory of the characters . . . but a sense of who the author is and whether the author is
someone I would like to get to know . . . by reading other books of
theirs." Of Don DeLillo, whom he admired greatly and had championed successfully at the club, he said, "I want to know what DeLillo
has to say every two years about the world we live in now because I
believe he is really on top of it." He added, "And I want to know what
Kundera has to say about anything."

Indeed, of Milan Kundera's *The Unbearable Lightness of Being*,[32]
Savago wrote in his report that it was "probably the most intelligent
novel I've read in years," adding immediately, "which is to say that it's
not much of a novel—conventionally speaking—at all." Savago's report went on in the following fashion:

> The traditional imperative of the novel—to move, dammit; to absorb
> (which is to say, drown) the reader in the *motion* of other people's lives has
> never left much room for ideas. Most novels have none at all—no fresh or
> distinctive ones, in any case; others seem founded upon ideas, but ideas so
> imbedded that we must critically extract them via such formulations as

"well, what Dickens is *saying* here is that . . ." Kundera . . . has broken free of this injunction against discursive intelligence, authorial intrusion.

Savago went on to argue in the report that the essential value of Kundera's book rested on his own authorial meditations about issues raised by the actions of characters in the fiction. He claimed further that "the quantity and quality of thought which Kundera has given to these and dozens of other questions would be compromised if he put a slick, compressed version of this thought into some character's mouth, or created a character here and there to 'embody' this or that insight." Indeed it was the very brilliance of Kundera's perceptions that convinced Savago that the club ought to consider the novel. For him, voice was not an idiosyncratic mode of speech, an idiolect, as it were, but rather a linguistic embodiment of a distinctive, significant point of view of familiar problems and an identifiable world.

Given Savago's reservations about the book and the additional fact that most club fiction, even of the "serious" sort, does indeed locate the coherence of personality in its characters, it may be surprising to note that both the Wright and Kundera novels, as well as titles by DeLillo, Thomas Pynchon, Russell Banks, and E. L. Doctorow, have all been offered as club alternates.[33] Although it is impossible to reconstruct the editorial debate that led to selection in each case, Savago's final observations with respect to *The Unbearable Lightness of Being* provide a suggestive clue. He ended his report with the following summary:

> And so this novel moves with consummate grace, I think, between the intensely concrete, lyrical evocative novelistic moment in its characters' lives and the discursive analysis of what is at stake, how the characters came to be here, what they are seeking and what they, in fact, find. You can't read it fast, you can't get swept away by it, lost in it, but you can be shocked continually by all that's unexamined in your own life, turn to your own life, and do something about it, with Kundera's intellectual rigor and clarity as a model.

In his remarks, Joe Savago seems to be focusing on the aptness of Kundera's ruminations, on their relevance to the lives of contemporary readers. The book will be useful, he implies, to those people searching for suggestions, models, and directions about how to live. If an unconventional novel can still be read as "equipment for living," in Kenneth Burke's phrase, that quality can overcome the problems posed by a failure to fulfill the more common expectation that fiction must be about recognizable characters with recognizable problems.[34] Thus a book can experiment with novelistic form, and it can even foreground a unique and unusual way of using language. But if that language cannot be construed by a reader as the speech of a recognizable personality with something to say about the world he or she shares with the reader, the book will likely by judged by the BOMC editors as too distant, too obscure, or too boring. DeLillo and Kundera could be "used" because, as Savago remarked in an interview, they "are like the world, your world, as seen by DeLillo and Kundera." Perspective really is the right word here. What such writers create is a peculiarly inflected, uniquely skewed perspective on a *common* world. They do not, as in the case of Savago's "autistic" writers, "bring a world into being *sui generis.*"

In fact, when one looks at the various titles in the category of serious fiction that did make their way onto the Book-of-the-Month Club lists for 1985 and 1986, and correlates them with the relevant readers' reports, it becomes clear that most of the books were chosen because their fine prose produced either an affecting and absorbing monologue or a more traditional narrative about recognizable characters. But even the traditional narratives were always treated as recitations that bore the marks of their enunciation by an identifiable and critical intelligence speaking always to the reader about the world held in common. Thus the editors demanded always that both monologues and more traditional narratives permit readers to map the insights gained from the experience of reading onto the terrain of their own lives. The BOMC editors seem to believe, finally, that their readers purchase serious fiction because they value verbal facility but also, and perhaps more important, because they are seeking a model for contemporary living and even practical advice about appropriate behavior in a changing world.

It is interesting to note in this context that although BOMC readers' reports about commercial fiction also focus on character, virtually no attention is paid to the larger significance of the characters' fate or to the intelligence of the individual controlling their action. Although it will require more sustained research to be sure, it now appears to me that what matters in commercial fiction is not primarily the congruence between fiction and the real but rather the capacity to catch the reader up in a story that seems to propel itself forward with force. The elementary pleasures of plot are the test of achievement here, and, apparently, the more accomplished the concealment of the fact that the story has been conceived and ordered by an author, the more intense the necessary experience of transport provided for the reader.

If the editors are right about serious fiction, it may well be the case that books in that category function for club members in a way sim-

ilar to the many self-help manuals, advice books, and reference volumes that make up the majority of the club's alternate list. Indeed
literacy may still serve primarily as a tool or a technology for such
people, which is to say a device for doing something, for bringing
about change, for accomplishing some purpose. If this is true, it is
understandable why fiction would be valuable to the extent that it is
readily applicable to one's own life, problems, and concerns. No less
relevant to daily life than self-consciously didactic manuals, the
artfulness of fiction is surbordinated in this evaluative system to its
pragmatic possibilities for application.

I think it important to highlight this preoccupation with relevance
and the functionality of fiction because it is almost too easy to interpret the editors' preoccupation with character and "the illusion of
the coherent self" as evidence of a simple, conservative, middle-class
humanism.[35] In such a reading, the BOMC's interest in the individual
voice and coherent character might be read as the reactionary refusal
of the middle class to encounter the social world it has made, which is
to say a discontinuous universe produced by advanced commodifica-
tion. The BOMC aesthetic would then be seen as the product of an
earlier stage in the development of a unified ideology, a stage associated above all with a confident, nineteenth-century individualism.
But recent club selections such as DeLillo's *White Noise,* Kundera's
The Unbearable Lightness of Being, Banks's *Continental Drift,* and
Margaret Atwood's *The Handmaid's Tale* give pause about the validity of such an interpretation, since each in its own way self-consciously explores the nature of the postmodern universe and the fragmentation of the unified subject. Even if these selections are not
enough to suggest that the ideology grounding the club's decisions is
multiply constructed of historical survivals, emerging positions, and
even contradictory views, then I think the particular way books are
made to be of use should.[36]

It is clear that in their wish to distinguish their books from those
they consider trash, the BOMC editors are engaging in the familiar
move of disparaging the pleasures of the mass, the facile, and the
shallow. And yet their demand that fiction be useful is most often
articulated through the more specific requirement that if a book does
not provide a character or a voice with whom the reader can identify
completely, it must at least include one who is admirable enough to
function as the moral center of the story. This helps to explain a
characteristic feature of readers' reports on rejected novels: their insis-
tent focus on the moral and ethical failings of characters in the fictions. In many cases where books are otherwise acceptable, the editors reject them because the characters are morally reprehensible and

without redeeming virtue; the preeminent failure of such books is their failure to engage the reader's sympathy.

The reading strategies employed by the editors seem to be based in the end on a certain bedrock assumption about the congruence of art and life, the very same assumption Bourdieu identifies as the foundation of the popular aesthetic.[37] As he says of the aesthetic judgments made by working-class individuals in France, "Everything takes place as if the 'popular aesthetic' were based on the affirmation of continuity between art and life, which implies the subordination of form to function, or, one might say, on a refusal of the refusal which is the starting point of the high aesthetic, i.e., the clear-cut separation of ordinary dispositions from the specifically aesthetic disposition."[38] Bourdieu notes further that such judgments are produced by an ethos rather than an aesthetic, since contemplation is neither distanced nor disinterested but produced by ethical and moral norms that perform a systematic reduction of the things of art to things of life. Whereas Bourdieu's bourgeois aesthetic is predicated on an "elective distance from the necessities of the natural and social world," the popular aesthetic springs from "a deep-rooted demand for participation."[39]

Indeed what the Book-of-the-Month Club editors demand most of writers they are to honor as serious is an ability to make them care. A stance that might be labeled by others as one of intellectual rigor or critical distance is therefore experienced by them as one characterized only by "coldness." They complain frequently about novels that view their characters too coolly, from too much distance, or without compassion.[40] So while it seems clear that in their distaste for the lushness of trash the editors are asserting the distinctiveness of a high culture aesthetic based on the rational and the refined, they are also refusing that refusal of the world that has permitted the isolation and enshrinement of the aesthetic as something valuable in and for itself. The artistic is valuable to them only insofar as it does not declare its utter separation from the world. It must first draw the reader into its world by appearing to erase the boundaries between the book and external reality. Having thus assured communion and participation, it then must provide the occasion for moral and ethical judgments that can be turned reflexively upon the reader and later used as guidelines for behavior. The value of serious fiction, in fact, is a function of its capacity to be used as a map that, despite its status as a representation, is a tool for enabling its reader to move about more effectively in the world to which it refers.

My point, finally, is that this emphasis on functionality suggests that what we see at the Book-of-the-Month Club is not simply an earlier stage in the development of a single reified ideology but a complex and conflicted aesthetic system that shares some assumptions about the role of art with what has been called the high culture aesthetic, even while it preserves the demands and accompanying criteria associated with a more popular aesthetic. Whether the core conflict is simply the product of the editors' own ambiguous social position as well-educated and trained cultural workers charged with serving commercially those with different, less trained taste is difficult to say at this point. In fact, I think that explanation is probably too mechanical. The editors' enthusiasm for the serious fiction they choose *because* it is so deeply involving seems too intense to be entirely calculated. Rather, I suspect that the aesthetic judgments made by the club editors with respect to serious fiction are representative of an evaluative system that is their own and that works for them precisely because it is constructed of contradictory elements.

It is, first of all, an aesthetic system that in its bow to cultural authority and artistic excellence affirms the validity of the traditional hierarchy of taste. The editors' choices and their justifications for those choices regularly underscore their identification with the keepers of the dominant cultural traditions of the West. This ought not to surprise, of course, since the editors themselves are middle-class individuals possessing much in common with those of the dominant class who define and maintain the value of high culture. In associating themselves with that tradition, therefore, they reflexively assert their right to choose books for others and exercise, even if inadvertently, their power to define what will count as culture for people outside the culture industry as well.

Yet the system's emphasis on the pleasures, even passion, generated by reading and on its capacity to instruct seems carefully calibrated to the interests of people caught up in the daily round of quotidian activities and responsibilities who have little time for leisurely intellectual contemplation or meditation on the fine points of technical achievements in the arts. Neither distanced from the immediate dilemmas of their own lives nor fully confident enough to approach them without respite or advice, the editors of the Book-of-the-Month Club seem to be engaged in a quest for a literature that can operate transitively as a set of strategies to help them and their members cope with the world that surrounds and holds them. They seem to experience that world as a place that still has some unnamable power over them, as a universe they do not fully control. Their persistent preoccupation with the values associated with the popular aesthetic of the dominated classes may be a token, finally, of their own ongoing sense of domination from outside, perhaps in this case by the very institutions and material constraints their own class is responsible for calling into being. Their aesthetic system therefore seems at once to reveal their power and to perpetuate it even as it gives us evidence that they do not understand themselves to be fully in control of that power, their world, or themselves. If this is true, then the particular dilemmas returned to repeatedly in the stories they are led to select may tell us much about the particular problems of middle-class life and thus something about the utopian longings it generates in some of its subjects. Exact specification of those dilemmas will have to await a systematic analysis of the fiction offered to its members by the Book-of-the-Month Club.

Notes

This essay has also appeared in *Critical Inquiry* 14 (Spring 1988).

1. See, for instance, the September and October 1986 issues of the *Book-of-the-Month Club News,* the catalogue distributed to club members fifteen times a year, which is available at the club or at the New York Public Library. On the exhibition, which was designed by William Zinsser and Jessica Weber, see the club pamphlet "Extraordinary Years, 1926–1986" and a short description of it in "The Talk of the Town: Books," *New Yorker* (April 28, 1986), 25–26.

2. The data for this paper include interviews with Book-of-the-Month Club officials and editors as well as a systematic survey of the club's readers' reports for serious fiction during 1984, 1985, and 1986. I would like to thank Lawrence Crutcher, Nancy Evans, Lorraine Shanley, and Al Silverman for allowing me to conduct this study and for granting access to internal club documents. I would especially like to thank William Zinsser for his support and encouragement of my research, as well as all the editors who took time from their busy schedules to talk with me about their ways of reading. I am also indebted to the John Simon Guggenheim Memorial Foundation for its generous support of this project. Finally, I would like to dedicate this article to the memory of Joseph J. Savago.

3. "Quality" is an adjective used throughout the publishing industry to describe both books and publishing houses themselves. A "quality house" is one that publishes a significant number of literary titles as well as a considerable amount of serious nonfiction. "Quality books" are thus generally distinguished from those intended for the mass market. In conducting interviews with the subsidiary rights directors of major publishing houses, I have discovered that most believe that the Book-of-the-Month Club is interested in distributing "quality books" to its members. On the various sectors in the publishing industry, see Lewis A. Coser, Charles Kadushin, and Walter W.

Powell, *Books: The Culture and Commerce of Publishing* (New York, 1982), 36–69.

4. See, for example, Dwight MacDonald, "Masscult and Midcult: II," *Partisan Review* 27 (Fall 1960). See also Joan Shelley Rubin's important discussion of the early years of the club's history in "Self, Culture, and Self-Culture in Modern America: The Early History of the Book-of-the-Month Club," *Journal of American History* 71 (March 1985): 782–806. There Rubin distinguishes herself from the most negative of the club's critics, acknowledges that the BOMC has enlarged the audience for books, and develops a complex argument about the particular historical mediations the "middlebrow" has accomplished.

5. Pierre Bourdieu, *Distinction: A Social Critique of the Judgement of Taste*, trans. Richard Nice (Cambridge, Mass. 1984); Barbara Herrnstein Smith, "Contingencies of Value," *Critical Inquiry* 10 (September 1983): 1–35 (rpt. in *Canons*, ed. Robert von Hallberg [Chicago, 1984], 5–40; and Richard Ohmann, "The Shaping of a Canon: U.S. Fiction, 1960–75," *Critical Inquiry* 10 (September 1983): 199–221.

6. Smith, "Contingencies of Value," 11–12.

7. For a somewhat different formulation of this argument, ibid., 18–19.

8. For a discussion of the connections between the social position and role of literary academics and the values they promote through the process of canonization, see Jane Tompkins, *Sensational Designs: The Cultural Work of American Fiction, 1790–1860* (New York, 1985), esp. 186–201.

9. See, for instance, my earlier effort to specify how a group of women actually read and evaluate individual books in the much-maligned romance genre, *Reading the Romance: Women, Patriarchy, and Popular Literature* (Chapel Hill, N.C., 1984). I am indebted to Mary Pratt's discussion of the concept of "literariness" and the way it disciplines ideologically for this particular way of describing my own interests. See her "Towards a Critical Cultural Practice," presented at the Conference on the Agenda of Literary Studies, Marquette University, October 8–9, 1982.

10. There are some statistics available that tend to corroborate this inference. A 1958 club survey of the membership indicated that while 83 percent of its members had a college education, only 13 percent of the members were teachers of one sort or another. This may have changed recently with the club's use of the *Oxford English Dictionary* as a club premium, but the continuing difference between the club's selections and those of the Reader's Subscription Book Club, associated with the *New York Review of Books*, the literary journal read by many American intellectuals, suggests that the Book-of-the-Month Club still does not cater to this group. On the *New York Review*, see Ohmann, "Shaping of a Canon," 205; and Charles Kadushin, *The American Intellectual Elite* (New York, 1974).

11. See Coser, Kadushin, and Powell, *Books*, esp. ch. 3, "Networks, Connections, and Circles," 70–93.

12. It is the subsidiary rights director at a publishing house who is responsible for getting a manuscript to the Book-of-the-Month Club, for writing the

introductory material, for alerting individual editors to the impending arrival of the manuscript, and for the negotiation of the contract. These individuals, in fact, are responsible for the sale of all reprint and production rights to the books published by the house. According to ibid., 31, they are increasingly the key people in trade publishing. For an extremely negative view of the power of the subsidiary rights departments in contemporary publishing, see Thomas Whiteside, *The Blockbuster Complex: Conglomerates, Show Business, and Book Publishing* (Middletown, Conn., 1980).

13. These are the approximate word limits for the descriptive material for alternate and main selections in the *Book-of-the-Month Club News.* The magazine is an interesting cross between a merchandise catalogue and a literary review.

14. Ohmann uses this phrase to describe the process by which agents, editors, and reviewers together decide which books will receive special promotion and critical attention. See his discussion of publishing officials as gatekeepers, "Shaping of a Canon," 202–12.

15. Ibid., 209–10.

16. What this means in Bourdieu's universe is that they have acquired extensive familiarity with the legitimate cultural tradition through the process of familial and academic education. There is danger, of course, in an incautious mapping of Bourdieu's findings onto an American context. My goal here is not to superimpose his entire system upon American social and cultural reality but to show how suggestive his approach can be in beginning to explore the social determinants of aesthetic judgments that have heretofore been dismissed as insufficiently rigorous, lacking high seriousness, and middlebrow.

17. The Book-of-the-Month Club was a family-owned business until 1977, when it was sold to Time, Incorporated, by Axel Rosin, the son-in-law of company founder Harry Scherman. Time, Inc., did little with the Club until 1987, when major changes were instituted. Although the new president, Lawrence Crutcher, has apparently done little to affect the day-to-day editorial operation, he has recently overseen the institution of a sophisticated market research program under a new marketing manager, has called for new product initiatives, and has instituted major cost-cutting activities. Since all of this is clearly designed to increase the profits of the club, it is possible that the nature of the editorial operation may be changed at some point. This remains to be seen however. Because the readers' reports I have read in preparation for this essay were written before the results of the first market surveys began to come in, the aesthetic judgments and decisions discussed here were based largely on assumptions about the club's membership. I know from informal conversations with the editors that many of their assumptions were borne out by the research, although they were surprised by a few of the demographic findings. Their membership seems to be younger and even more conversant with "book culture" than they had supposed.

18. At one point, the club made an effort to capitalize on this feature of its operation and referred to itself as "America's Bookstore." In elaborating on

this view of the club, former editor-in-chief Nancy Evans (she left the club in January 1987 to become president and publisher of Doubleday, Inc.'s, trade division) said in an interview with William Zinsser, "Our strength is that there is no book that we stock in our store that we have not read. There is no book in our store that we can't say, 'Read this book. We put it in our store because one of us here, or two of us here, or three of us, think that it's the best book of its kind, or that it's a special book that's worth your time.' " Typescript of an interview between Nancy Evans and William Zinsser, August 2, 1985, 2. Quoted with their permission.

19. Al Silverman, "The Book-of-the-Month Club—What We Stand For: A Message from the Chief Executive Officer," 6. Quoted with the permission of Mr. Silverman.

20. Transcript of interview between Evans and Zinsser, August 2, 1985, 5. Quoted with permission.

21. It is apparently the case that the publishing houses do little preliminary screening of the material they send to the Book-of-the-Month Club. When asked, subsidiary rights directors indicate that they send 98 percent to 100 percent of the adult trade hardcover books they publish. This is not true, however, for university presses or more specialized publishing houses.

22. Fredric Jameson, *The Political Unconscious: Narrative as a Socially Symbolic Act* (Ithaca, N.Y., 1981), 106.

23. Bourdieu, *Distinction*, esp. 30–50.

24. Ibid., 486.

25. Silverman, "What We Stand For," 4.

26. Fredric Jameson, "Towards a Libidinal Economy of Three Modern Painters," *Social Text* I (Winter 1979): 193–94, and *Fables of Aggression: Wyndham Lewis, the Modernist as Fascist* (Berkeley, Calif., 1979), 7–10.

27. Jameson, *Fables of Aggression*, 8.

28. Catherine Parke, "An Interview with Lucy Rosenthal," *Missouri Review* (1984): 164–65.

29. Quoted in ibid., 168.

30. Stephen Wright, *Meditations in Green* (New York, 1983).

31. X is used here to replace the name of a popular thriller writer. Because the club must continue to work with living writers, I have offered to remove names of people who might be offended by the club's internal editorial commentary.

32. Milan Kundera, *The Unbearable Lightness of Being*, trans. Michael Henry Heim (New York, 1984).

33. Don DeLillo, *White Noise* (New York, 1985); Thomas Pynchon, *Gravity's Rainbow* (New York, 1973); Russell Banks, *Continental Drift* (New York, 1985); and E. L. Doctorow, *World's Fair* (New York, 1985).

34. Kenneth Burke, "Literature as Equipment for Living," in *The Philosophy of Literary Form*, 3d ed. (Berkeley, Calif., 1973), 293–304. I would like to thank Peter Rabinowitz for directing my attention to this essay. My findings here are remarkably similar to those of Elizabeth Long, who has been working on middle-class women's reading groups. She first reported these findings in her paper "Literary Judgment and Women's Reading Groups," presented at

the 1985 meeting of the American Studies Association, where I first reported these findings about the Book-of-the-Month Club. The congruence of our findings suggests that the patterns of reading we have detected in our separate data are widespread throughout certain segments of the middle-class reading population.

35. On this point, see Elizabeth Long's argument in "Women, Reading, and Cultural Authority: Some Implications of the Audience Perspective in Cultural Studies," *American Quarterly* 38 (Fall 1986): 606–10.

36. My own understanding of the conflicted nature of ideology has been influenced by the work of Raymond Williams and Stuart Hall. See especially Williams's *Marxism and Literature* (Oxford, 1977) and *The Sociology of Culture* (New York, 1982). For a clear formulation of Hall's argument, see "Notes on Deconstructing 'the Popular,'" in *People's History and Socialist Theory*, ed. Raphael Samuel (London, 1981), 227–40.

37. Bourdieu, *Distinction*, 4–7 and 32–34.

38. Ibid., 32.

39. Ibid.

40. In commenting, for instance, on the heroine of Reynolds Price's *Kate Vaiden* (New York, 1986), one editor observed, "She seemed cold and undisciplined in an uninteresting kind of way. Some people might find the book mesmerizing, but I found it only mildly absorbing."

Chapter Twelve   **Literacy and Mass Media**

The Political Implications

Donald Lazere

Much has been written about the effects of mass media, especially television, on literacy and learning in the United States, but the momentous political implications of these effects have not been adequately explored. I will make a case here that the restricted cognitive patterns induced by media in audiences also induce predominantly conservative attitudes, not in the sense of a reasoned conservative ideology but in the sense of an uncritical conformity that reinforces the social status quo and precludes oppositional consciousness. I will not deal systematically here with the political implications of other aspects of media such as subject matter, structural features including formats, formulas, and organization of time and space, or the makeup of producing institutions and personnel, but I have argued elsewhere, in refutation of neoconservative critics who claim to find a left-wing bias pervading American media, that in spite of some liberal elements, each of these aspects too has, on balance, a conservative complexion.[1]

My own political leanings are socialistic, and part of the agenda of this essay—by no means a hidden part of it—is a concern that media-induced illiteracy is contributing toward the kind of one-dimensional society that Herbert Marcuse warned about, in which the capacity to imagine alternatives to the status quo, especially alternatives of a socialistic nature, has been systematically destroyed. I do not expect more conservative readers to share this concern or to agree with all of my arguments in its support, but I do hope to gain their assent to the ultimate thrust of my argument, which is that the low level of cognitive development to which the discourse of American mass media and politics is presently geared is woefully inadequate for the effective functioning of a democracy, and that scholars of literature and language, whatever their own political convictions might be, have a responsibility to work toward raising our public discourse to a more reasoned level of dialogue between the ideologies of the Right and Left. Part of this responsibility lies in reorienting our theoretical concerns, research, and curricula to include the topics that are surveyed, in a very tentative way, in this essay.

My vantage point on these issues is that of a scholar in composition and literature with a collateral interest in theory of culture and politics. My explorations here begin with the striking congruence between the cognitive patterns discovered by research on the influence of television viewing on children, a concise summary of which is contained in Kate Moody's *Growing Up on Television*,[2] and by research in English on the nature of reading and writing deficiencies in college students. Direct cause-effect relationships between television viewing in childhood and reading and writing skills, especially in college students, are difficult to verify empirically, but the similarity of patterns is too obvious to ignore. Mina Shaughnessy, a pioneer researcher of college remedial writing students, found their most common cognitive traits to be the following: difficulties in concentrating and sustaining an extended line of thought in reading and writing (including thematic, symbolic, or propositional development); lack of facility in analytic and synthetic reasoning; deficiencies in reasoning back and forth from the concrete to the abstract, the personal to the impersonal, and the literal to the figurative, and in perceiving irony, ambiguity, and multiplicity of points of view.[3]

The similarity between these patterns and those induced by television viewing in children extends further to findings in several other fields of scholarship, including (1) studies by cognitive-developmental psychologists like Jean Piaget, Lawrence Kohlberg, and William Perry of the cognitive traits associated with lower stages of moral reasoning proficiency;[4] (2) historical and psychological studies of oral versus writing-oriented culture and discourse;[5] (3) studies in social psychology and political socialization dealing with the authoritarian personality;[6] (4) sociological accounts of a "culture of poverty";[7] and (5) sociolinguistic research such as that of Basil Bernstein and Claus Mueller finding "restricted" linguistic codes and cognitive operations in lower social classes, compared with the "elaborated" codes more common to the middle and upper classes.[8] (The problematic definition of class involved in the last three groups of studies will be discussed later.)

This essay will not deal directly with literature. It should be evident, however, that the issues discussed here have the highest significance for the future of literature and its study. The cognitive capacities lacking in the individuals studied by Shaughnessy and these researchers in other fields are precisely those most closely associated with literature and literary criticism. This is a powerful reaffirmation of the value of literary study at all levels of education for promoting cognitive development and critical thinking. Moreover, there are countless valuable connections to be made between literary scholarship and recent research in the above fields; our critical concerns and methods can make a distinctive contribution to studies in those fields, and such studies in turn present new avenues for literary theory and research that can contribute greatly to revitalizing our profession. For example, the methods of reader response research can be applied to studying stages of moral reasoning, linguistic codes, and political attitudes in children and adults from differing sociological control groups, both in their reading of literature and in their reception of television and other mass media.

To date, however, more studies along these lines have been done in composition than in literature, though they are still at the beginning stages in the former as well. One study, for instance, conducted by Andrea Lunsford, a follower of Shaughnessy, applied cognitive-developmental stage theories to the teaching of college remedial writers, who, according to Lunsford's research, tend to be fixed in Piaget's egocentric and Kohlberg's conventional stages of moral reasoning, with correspondingly authoritarian, good-guys-versus-bad-guys political attitudes.[9] Lunsford's study accords with many in the behavioral and social sciences finding an explicit or implicit association of low levels of literacy and cognitive development with political attitudes that are conservative in the sense of conformist and authoritarian. The remainder of this essay will examine point by point the links between such conservatism and cognitive deficiencies.

Oral versus Literate Discourse

Historians of literacy, including Eric Havelock, Walter Ong, Jack Goody, and Ian Watt, have correlated the social origins of written discourse and of analytic reasoning. According to Goody and Watt,

> In oral societies the cultural tradition is transmitted almost entirely by face-to-face communication; and changes in its content are accompanied by the homeostatic process of forgetting or transforming those parts of the tradition that cease to be either necessary or relevant. Literate societies,

on the other hand, cannot discard, absorb, or transmute the past in the same way. Instead, their members are faced with permanently recorded versions of the past and its beliefs; and because the past is thus set apart from the present, historical enquiry becomes possible. This in turn encourages scepticism; and scepticism, not only about the legendary past, but about received ideas about the universe as a whole. From here the next step is to see how to build up and to test alternative explanations; and out of this there arose the kind of logical, specialized, and cumulative intellectual tradition of sixth-century Ionia. The kinds of analysis involved in the syllogism, and in the other forms of logical procedure, are clearly dependent upon writing, indeed upon a form of writing sufficiently simple and cursive to make possible widespread and habitual recourse both to the recording of verbal statements and then to the dissecting of them. It is probable that it is only the analytic process that writing itself entails, the written formalization of sounds and syntax, which makes possible the habitual separating out into formally distinct units of the various cultural elements whose indivisible wholeness is the essential basis of the "mystical participation" which Lévy-Bruhl regards as characteristic of the thinking of non-literate peoples.[10]

Marshall McLuhan's benign, superficial predictions about the postliterate age being ushered in by electronic communication fail to consider seriously the prospect of an attendant, universal regression of reasoning capacities.

Thomas J. Farrell, finding the same traits in his college remedial English students that Shaughnessy noted, has applied to them Walter J. Ong's intriguing hypothesis that children's cognitive development recapitulates the historical development from oral to literate society.[11] According to Farrell, remedial students have been blocked in the development of reasoning capacities from those that Vygotsky associated with childhood speech to the more complex ones embodied in writing. Moody's and similar studies indicate precisely the same block in children whose language processing capacities are formed through television to the exclusion of reading and writing. Moody writes,

> Television's most successful techniques—short segments, fast action, quick cuts, fades, dissolves—break time into perceptual bits. Reading requires perceptual continuity to track line after line. Television habituates the mind to short takes, not to the continuity of thought required by reading. The pace and speed of television cause children to be easily distracted; they are inundated with too many messages and cannot stop to make sense of this confusion. Focusing and paying attention to print become an unnatural strain for the conditioned TV viewer . . . .
> When human eyes read a line of print they see letters—little black marks—one after the next in long, straight, parallel lines. To gather mean-

ing, eyes move from left to right. The image on the TV screen is produced and perceived in a completely different way. Pictures exist as a constantly moving field of winking dots in a see-through grid. It's quite possible that left-right eye habits employed in reading are unconsciously eroded by several hours a day of watching television. The eye and brain functions employed in TV viewing likely put demands on different parts of the brain than those used in reading, causing incalculably different kinds of cognitive development at the expense of reading and writing aptitudes.[12]

Oral discourse can of course be highly complex and analytic—usually when it takes place between already literate speakers and audiences. Exclusively oral-visual language acquisition in children, however, limits the probability of their later developing more adult, complex capacities in either speech or written discourse. Beyond the level of children's programming, television is obviously capable of making intellectual demands on viewers, as in televised Shakespeare or "Hill Street Blues," the rare program that requires the audience to synthesize motifs out of a mosaic of characters, events, images, and sounds. It is widely admitted in the media business, however, that most mass communication aimed at adults, both in television, radio, records, or film, and in print, is at a literacy level not much higher than that of children's programming. In order to maximize ratings and sales of advertised products, commercial media must appeal to the largest possible market, thus to the lowest common denominator of cognitive development. Having an adult populace that is fixed in an infantile mentality also conveniently happens to prevent people from becoming very critical about either advertised products, the corporations that produce them and those that own the media, or the whole sociopolitical order in which those corporations play a central role.

Similarly, American political discourse has regressed from the marathon Lincoln-Douglas debates to the glib, attenuated format of televised debates, thirty-second spot commercials, and managed press conferences. The professional consultants who developed the format of rapid-fire, "top-forty" stories for local newscasts justified it by claiming, "People who watch television the most are unread, uneducated, untraveled and unable to concentrate on single subjects more than a minute or two."[13] William Safire reports that when he was a speech writer for President Nixon, Nixon told him, "We sophisticates can listen to a speech for a half hour, but after ten minutes the average guy wants a beer."[14] And Howard Jarvis, author of California's notorious tax-cutting Proposition 13, when asked why he spent all of his advertising funds on television rather than newspapers, replied, "People who decide elections don't read."[15]

The crosscultural studies by Michael Cole and Sylvia Scribner of orality and literacy in present-day societies conclude that in African cultures that are still primarily oral, people's reasoning in oral modes becomes highly sophisticated toward meeting the needs of their particular society.[16] William Labov has reached similar conclusions in his studies of the black American language and subculture of the inner city.[17] An article by Cole and Jerome Bruner, however, argues that exclusive acquisition of language through black dialect and oral culture puts black children at a disadvantage in schools and other realms of American society dominated by Standard English and written culture.[18] This echoes Goody and Watt's thesis that since the beginnings of literate societies, access to written language within them has been a prime mark of dominant social classes, a form of what the French sociologist Pierre Bourdieu calls "cultural capital."[19] There may be somewhat of a tautology here in the fact that society's recognition of literacy, or at least standard dialect, as a sign of status in those who possess it and of inferiority in those who don't is to some extent an arbitrary matter of class bias; there is no denying, however, that in our society's sophisticated information environment, facility in reading and writing is indispensable for either social domination or effective opposition.

Ben Sidran's *Black Talk* provides an interesting sidelight on this issue.[20] American blacks, restricted since slavery days to oral discourse, were able to code oppositional messages in both the lyrics and musical structure of the blues that were indecipherable to the writing-oriented white mind. Here again, this confirms that oral discourse, or what Basil Bernstein calls restricted codes, may be highly sophisticated within a subculture though not functional in the larger culture. The significance of the complex coding in the blues is that it was the recourse of a dominated group denied access to overt political communication, especially in written form.

There is a clear correspondence in contemporary America of orality and literacy to hierarchies of social class and power, although the cause-effect relationship is problematic. Oscar Lewis identifies the traits of oral culture, such as the lack of a strong sense of past and future referred to by Goody and Watt, with those of the culture of poverty.[21] In regard to mass media, studies of the class makeup of television viewers show that, above the level of the underclass who are too poor and alienated to own televisions, poorer and less educated people watch the most and are most credulous about what they watch.[22] Thus oral culture of television is bound to reinforce the oral culture of poverty. Furthermore, as John Fiske and John Hartley's *Reading Television* points out, those who produce television usually come from the dominant, literate classes.[23] (One hears about television and advertising executives who refuse to let their children watch television lest it rot their minds.) In this segment of class relationships, then, literacy represents not just cultural capital but social control, with dangerous potential for propagandistic manipulation of viewers.

Finally, psychologists confirm that the information processing involved in watching television is a passive cognitive operation compared with the active mental effort necessary to decode written language.[24] This passivity reinforces the absence of audience interaction with broadcasters and of control over media institutions and mass-mediated politics. All these aspects of orality in media transmission and audiences, then, contribute to a mood of anomic, resigned acceptance of powerlessness and submission to the status quo.

Egocentrism and Sociocentrism

As Moody suggests, the substitution of the television world for the real world impedes cognitive development from what Piaget calls the egocentric—or "narcissistic," in psychoanalytic terms—to the reciprocal stage in which mature object-relations are established. The ever-increasing privatizing of cultural activity—plays and films (now even pornographic ones) viewed at home rather than in a theater, music heard on radio, records, or television rather than in a concert hall, televised sports, and so on—leads toward the solipsism of Jerzy Kosinski's "vidiot" in *Being There*. The resulting inhibition of normal ego formation perpetuates childlike dependency on parental and political authority. The egocentric cognitive stage is also most susceptible to ethnocentric and to what Piaget terms sociocentric biases, hence to chauvinistic propaganda.[25] Moreover, the empirical research of George Gerbner's "Cultural Indicators" project at the Annenberg School of Communications, University of Pennsylvania, indicates that heavy television viewers tend to develop exaggerated fears of violence in the streets and of foreign enemies, making them susceptible to simplistic appeals to law and order and to the official use of force by the military and police.[26]

Lack of Analytic Reasoning

Among the further cognitive deficiencies found by researchers in the language of mass media and its reception by audiences are an absence of the analytic and synthetic modes of reasoning necessary to relate the personal and the impersonal, concrete and abstract, cause and effect, or past, present, and future (compare the "present orientation" of the culture of poverty and of oral societies), as well as to view issues in sufficient complexity to resist stereotyping, either/or thinking, and demagogic emotional appeal.[27] In the present American political context these cognitive deficiencies comprise yet another factor contributing to conformity, authoritarianism, and passivity.

People suffering from immediate, intense political oppression—the situation of the proletariat in Marx's scenario for socialist revolution, of Third World colonies, of American blacks who waged the civil rights movement—need little abstract information or sophistication in reasoning to be persuaded that change is in their interest. In a society like present-day America, however, the grosser forms of injustice and conflict have been greatly reduced and the majority of the population socialized into a mood of at least passive assent. Even though major evils in the social system may persist, they tend not to be readily felt or understood through the firsthand experience of most people outside of the hapless underclass. In order for people to perceive and effectively oppose such evils, they need not only to have access to a diversity of information sources, many of which are in print and written at an advanced level of literacy, but to have the analytic reasoning capacities to evaluate distant events and abstract data. The handicap here of people at low levels of literacy is compounded by the nonanalytic traits of mass media.

The mind at advanced stages of cognitive development seeks both to relate personal, specific impressions to exterior, general truths and to ground abstract generalizations in concrete examples. American mass culture, however, tends to lurch between unrelated poles of concreteness and abstraction, in such a way as to avoid critical analysis of sociopolitical issues. On the one hand, media ceaselessly multiply, with tacit approval, concrete images of the status quo—commodity consumption, celebrities, how-to techniques, the activities of government officials, and so on. On the other hand, when media discourse deals with abstractions, it is usually not in order to question critically the value system implicit in these concrete images, but to propagate equally unexamined platitudes about the American way of life, patriotism, democracy, and the free world. These abstractions can be reasonably concretized and defended, but all too often in our public discourse they are not.

When politicians and news and dramatic media report events related to issues such as crime, racial conflict, feminism, communism, and Third World insurrection, they tend to approach such events as isolated phenomena, outside a framework of causal, historical, or class analysis. For example, conservative media critics have accused television dramatic programs of liberal bias in avoiding the portrayal of black or Hispanic criminals. A more plausible explanation is that a truthful portrayal of such criminals would have to be placed in the historical and economic context of racial and class discrimination—with the intention not of absolving individuals from responsibility, but of exploring the complexities of individual versus social responsibility. The simplistic formulas of genres like the half-hour cop show, however, preclude such complexities, so their producers' only alternative to fueling racist prejudices is to evade the issue by portraying nearly all street criminals as white. In any society, it serves the interests of the dominant classes to have volatile issues mystified by being portrayed in accounts lacking the analytic specificity that might raise questions about the intrinsic inequities of the established order. A similar mystification is accomplished when political events are reported outside of a dialectical analysis of historical action and reaction that might imply the impermanence of the status quo. For example, American politicians' and news media's discussions of the Cold War and Third World or black American uprisings tend to disregard as a possible factor the natural cycle of historical change that may be leading to the decline of world dominance by the United States, Western Europe, and the white race. Similarly, official accounts of anti-American forces in Cuba, El Salvador, or Nicaragua chronically ignore the context of a century of United States military and corporate intervention in Central America that may have made rebellion and acceptance by rebels of Communist support inevitable, disastrous though the consequences might be for all concerned.

Restricted Linguistic Codes in the Working Class

Claus Mueller sums up a growing body of research in sociolinguistics and political socialization in Europe, England, and the United States that supports Basil Bernstein's thesis about restricted codes and authoritarianism in the working class: "Conformity and allegiance to established authority as well as resistance to change were found to be political predispositions of individuals brought up in the lower classes. Empirical research also demonstrates that class-specific factors such as conformity, reception to one-sided arguments, and the absence of skepticism correlate with the susceptibility to persuasion and manipulation." Applying Bernstein's thesis to media content and audience response, Mueller cites a study of the language of the middle-class *New York Times* and working-class *New York Daily News*, which respectively embody elaborated and restricted codes, and another study of a German tabloid equivalent of the *Daily News* whose language was characterized by "concrete metaphors, dichotomized statements, simplified sentence structures, typified formulations, an undifferentiated vocabulary, and stereotypifications. The use of a restricted code by these papers results in unqualified descriptions of political reality which more often than not are conservatively slanted . . . Sensationalism, repetition, and a simplistic depiction of political reality contribute little to the readers' knowledge of society."[28]

Along lines similar to those of twentieth-century Marxists like Georg Lukács, Antonio Gramsci, and the Frankfurt School, who have argued that the working class has been deflected through false consciousness from the role Marx foresaw for it as the vanguard of the socialist movement, Bernstein and Mueller imply that the injuries of capitalistic class structure, education, and controlled media have imposed the restricted linguistic codes that prevent workers from being able to understand socialistic ideas that are in their own interest. According to Mueller,

> Today's working class symbolism has become so opaque that it is impossible for the worker to link his situation to an ideological framework with which he could understand, and more importantly, act upon the deprivation he experiences. . . . The concept of alienation, for example, can hardly be made operative politically because a semantic barrier built of a restricted language code excludes it from the worker's ideational world. This sort of difficulty was encountered by West German trade unions which tried to make the symbol "participation" a meaningful one for the workers.[29]

Richard Ohmann, commenting on Bernstein and Mueller, presents a similar hypothesis about American workers' attitudes:

> A number of studies . . . suggest that only a few people—those sharing in power or influence, by and large—have ordered and relatively abstract understandings of society. (This is not to say, of course, that their understandings are right, or that workers are not in many ways more sensible.) Workers' belief systems tend to be less conceptual, more fixed on concrete things, more centered in the local and particular. Their ideas on specific issues also tend to be more fragmented and inconsistent than the ideas of the more highly educated and privileged. Finally, the American working class as a whole lacks a consensus in beliefs and values, compared to the ruling class and the professional and managerial strata.[30]

(Ohmann's last two sentences echo Fiske and Hartley's analysis of the difference in class and power between those who program television and its primary audience.) Ohmann goes on to say that research such as Bernstein's "does imply that a totalizing system of ideas such as marxism would be uncongenial, by virtue of its form, to workers."

And he concludes, "When we try to communicate to workers a socialist understanding of things, must we think of our task as, in part, making up a cognitive and linguistic deficit? Or should we take it that the problem is more in the ways *we* talk and write, and attempt somehow to translate marxism into more concrete and immediate terms than the ones we ordinarily use?"[31]

Another illuminating perspective on this problem was provided by Armand Mattelart, a Belgian sociologist of communication working in Chile with the Allende Popular Unity government during its three years in power from 1970 to 1973. Mattelart discussed the difficulties of a socialist government, with strong working-class participation, trying to improvise alternatives to the institutions and conventions of a whole system of mass culture established for capitalistic ends and projecting a middle-class worldview, exemplified by the Disney productions Mattelart and Ariel Dorfman had previously criticized in *How to Read Donald Duck*. About the halting experiments in communicating the socialist experience through newspapers published by the *cordones industriales*, units of popular power founded by militant workers in the Santiago suburbs in 1972, "a kind of embryonic 'soviet,' " he observed with regret,

> In this partisan political press, all the normality of daily life was absent. The not-said was considerable; in other words, new social relations were implicitly redefined but few were expressed explicitly.
>
> I remember being in a *cordon* just one month before the coup d'etat, and the talk was about the changes which these men had experienced with their wives and children, during the three years of Popular Unity. Yet never, either in the press of the *cordones*, or that of the extreme Left, or in the traditional press, had this type of fundamental change inspired a theme for mass information.
>
> All the books about the Chilean experience talk about political strategy in the strict sense of the term, but they ignore, apart from a few literary flights, the richness of this popular explosion. This is the real repression: the people live another life, a more important one, and yet can't express it, except in familiar gatherings; then they go back to the factories, unable to speak of it with their workmates, their *compañera*, their children.[32]

Limited Imagination

Perhaps the most profoundly conservative force in all of the cognitive patterns discussed here is their potential for inhibiting people from being able to imagine any social order different from the established one. The present reality is concrete and immediate, alternatives abstract and distant; ability to understand an alternative is further obstructed by lack of the sustained attention span necessary for analytic reasoning, the capacity to imagine beyond the actual to the hypothetical (which semantically entails reasoning from the literal to the figurative and symbolic), and a sense of irony, necessary to question the social conditioning that endorses the status quo.

Such widespread constriction of imagination would be a conservative force blocking fundamental change in any social order—as it undoubtedly is in an ostensibly leftist country like the U.S.S.R., and as it would be to a lesser extent in a firmly entrenched liberal America under a sequence of charismatic Democrats like Roosevelt or Kennedy, or even in the most ideally realized socialist society. Nor is the point of this argument that change is always a priori beneficial; even leftists can respect, to a point, the classic conservative position that people may show good sense in preferring to bear those ills they have rather than fly to others they know not of. What *is* at issue is the hypothesis that people's loss of the capacity to imagine things other than they are could preclude their supporting changes that would in fact be strongly in their interests. Without necessarily espousing socialism, for example, can we not entertain the possibility that such a state of mind would keep socialistic policies off the American agenda no matter how demonstrably preferable they might be to capitalistic ones, in general or on particular issues?

Qualifications and Counterarguments

I want now to anticipate some objections that can be raised to the foregoing analysis. One necessary qualification of it is that mass media, and particularly television in recent years, have in some ways offered linguistic codes and a worldview that are more literate, complex, and cosmopolitan than the indigenous local culture of many segments of their audience. Hence the viewpoint of fundamentalist Christians and many other conservatives that television, Hollywood films, and "the Eastern news media" are hotbeds of liberalism. Nevertheless, while television's language, for example, may promote higher cognitive development in previously illiterate sectors of the public, studies such as those reported by Moody indicate that it leads to a regression in literacy in sectors, mainly of the middle class, whose children's cognitive development was previously structured largely through reading and writing. Furthermore, I submit that mass media have tended to replace the parochiality of local culture not with a substantially leftist alternative but merely with different modes of conservatism and conformity, in the form of nationally regimented consumer culture and patterns of cognitive formation.[33]

Second, many conservatives' perceptions of the political implications of declining literacy and the negative cognitive effects of television, rock music, and so on are quite the opposite of mine: that they undermine worker efficiency, social cohesion, and support for authority. The left- and right-wing interpretations are not mutually exclusive. It is quite possible that a decline in literacy and reasoning faculties, with resulting anomic inefficiency in workers, is simply an unforeseen by-product of a whole national culture dedicated to engineering compliant consumers and employees. In the late 1960s, a violent public reaction against a perceived excess of critical thinking by college students helped to justify the cuts in funding that have reduced American public schools to a shambles. By the 1980s, however, even big business was promoting a return to liberal education and the fostering of critical thinking skills in an attempt to correct the excess of compliancy.

The growing credibility gap undermining American institutions' authority (whether that authority was merited or not, and whatever the role of media in discrediting it) has created only in a passive sense the legitimation crisis perceived by critics on both the Left and Right. As Erich Fromm noted about the authoritarian effects of mass society in his 1941 classic *Escape from Freedom,* "The result of this kind of influence is a twofold one: one is a skepticism and cynicism towards everything which is said or printed, while the other is a childish belief in anything that a person is told with authority. This combination of cynicism and naiveté is very typical of the modern individual. Its essential result is to discourage him from doing his own thinking and deciding."[34] In other words, people (especially those whose memory span has been stunted by mass media) may voice skepticism toward authority in general, yet be gullible in each new manipulation by authorities, like Charlie Brown with hope eternally springing that Lucy won't pull the football away *this* time. Likewise, Americans today may be cynical toward the status quo, but they are equally cynical toward any alternative. The resulting apathy, then, simply leaves social control open to those powerful enough to exercise it, while the masses, like those in Dostoevsky's "The Grand Inquisitor," gratefully cede the burden of authority to those more clever, be they scrupulous or not. When I ask my composition students to write on what would go through their minds if they were drafted to fight in Central America or the Middle East, the most common responses are either that they don't know enough about the situation to evaluate it themselves, so they would have to trust the judgment of our government even though it may be unreliable, or else that they would be opposed on principle to fighting in these foreign countries but that they would go anyway, out of fear of punishment or peer pressure.

I can also anticipate a conservative rebuttal arguing that low literacy can be manipulated politically by the Left as well as the Right, that people at low levels of cognitive development cannot adequately understand supply-side economics, the theory of nuclear deterrence, the distant but real evils of communism, and so on. Similarly, conservative intellectuals chastized the New Left and counterculture of the 1960s for buying into the media-induced myths of immediate gratification in expecting instant social transformation. These lines of argument contain much validity. And demagogic emotional appeals can certainly be used for left-wing causes, as by Stalin or Mao, or to rally the masses against the status quo as well as in support of it, as Hitler did in his rise. But in order for this to succeed, either there must be massive, active discontent or else the opposition forces must be able to control communications media, education, and so on—as, for example, if Communists were able to expose American children to three hundred and fifty thousand propaganda messages by the age of eighteen, as they are now exposed to comparable propaganda for capitalism in the form of that many television commercials. The lower stages of cognitive development, basically those of children, are most susceptible to sociocentric appeals to support *our* country, *our* race and ethnic group, *our* socioeconomic system (that is, capitalism, especially in the idealized form of it packaged as "free enterprise" or supply-side economics), and to fear foreign races, nations, and ideologies. It is much less easy to rally people at this level to international cooperation and pacifism than to aggression, patriotism, and retribution against alleged atrocities by our Enemies. These low-level sociocentric appeals are reinforced by the massive socialization in Americanism, free enterprise, and religion that our children receive in the home, primary and secondary schools, and church, as well as through advertising, publicity, and governmental edicts.

The most profitable path for media, then, is clearly to reinforce this conservative socialization. The sheer weight of inertia in the established social order is a stronger conservative force than any ideological principle. It is a struggle for most people just to get by from one day to the next; social stability and the force of habit and routine ease the anxieties of daily life. For people who simply do not want to be bothered with complicated analyses of intangible social ills or reasons to change their comfortable routine, a simplistically conservative ideology provides a welcome rationalization. So although some leftist influence may be asserted, say, by college teachers and some segments of the media, and although it may indeed sometimes be manipulative, it is apt to be strongly outweighed by conservative influences.

The Question of Class

Returning now to the references to social class in several of the scholars cited here, there has been much controversy since the early 1960s over the empirical validity of Bernstein's, Oscar Lewis's, and other such studies and over the possible class biases of the researchers themselves. Much of this controversy stems from the fact that although some scholars involved, such as Bernstein and Mueller, see their studies comprising a leftist critique of class-structured society, their findings have also been appropriated by conservatives like Seymour Martin Lipset and Arthur Jensen, who see them either as a justification for "compensatory education" toward middle-class socialization or as evidence of intractable difficulties in educating the poor and racial minorities, in both of which cases blame has tended to be shifted from the discriminatory nature of capitalist society onto the victims of that discrimination.

Further confusion on this issue has resulted from the ambiguous or differing definitions of class among the various scholars involved on both the Left and Right. Correlations between political attitudes and economic status, occupation, level of education, culture, and cognitive development are often not established sufficiently. Nor have many of these scholars adequately delineated particular segments within classes, between which there are apt to be significant differences in the criteria studied. It is often unclear in studies of the working class whether their subject is only the industrial proletariat or also white-collar workers and the petit bourgeois—whether it includes both organized and unorganized labor, men and women, urban and rural laborers, the hard-core poor, whites and other races, and so on.

Crucial though it is for these disputes and ambiguities to be resolved in media scholarship, their resolution is not essential for our concerns here. The salient fact here is that none of the disputants would claim that the cognitive traits associated with restricted codes, exclusively oral culture, the culture of poverty, or the authoritarian personality are beneficial to either individuals or a progressive society in contemporary America—no matter in what social class they appear. To the extent that illiteracy and mass media perpetuate restricted cognitive capacities, these forces contribute to an impoverished, powerless mentality in millions of people who belong to diverse social classes by other criteria such as income level, race, and so on. Teachers in colleges with upper-middle-class, suburban white students have been struck by the similarity in cognitive deficiencies between many of these students and the inner-city black and Hispanic students Shaughnessy studied. C. Wright Mills and the Frankfurt School theorists plausibly suggested that mass society and culture have created a new class division in which a large percentage of the proletariat and middle classes—including millions of relatively affluent people—have become homogenized in the consciousness comprised by the authoritarian cognitive patterns described above. Conversely, Alvin Gouldner hypothesized that a "culture of critical discourse"—his term for Bernstein's elaborated codes—has become a prime determinant of membership in the dominant class in contemporary society, whose members include both the administrators of the status quo and, in smaller numbers, its most articulate critics.[35]

All other things being equal, there is no denying the liberalizing effect of higher education, elaborated language codes, and the cosmopolitan outlook bred by travel and access to high culture. (The fact that creative literature in particular is characterized by precisely the cognitive traits in Bernstein's elaborated codes—irony, ambiguity, multiplicity of viewpoints, and so on—is a powerful reaffirmation of the value of literature and its academic study.) And most empirical research confirms that the higher the class and literacy level of audience members, the more discriminating they and their children are apt to be in receiving media messages. The major exception to this rule is those at the very bottom of the social ladder, whose alienation, while not usually leading to an articulated critical consciousness, at least serves as a skeptical shield. In a study of public attitudes in America toward the Vietnam War, Bruce Andrews asserted that "lower-status groups" were the least willing to support government policy. One reason, he suggested, is that "with less formal education, political attentiveness, and media involvement, they were saved from the full brunt of Cold War appeals during the 1950s and were, as a result, inadequately socialized into the anticommunist world view." This analysis was somewhat belied, however, by Andrews's acknowledgment that much of the opposition from these groups was of the "win or get out" variety.[36]

This is not to argue that higher education or social class inevitably leads to liberal or socialist beliefs. In the contemporary American context elaborated linguistic-cognitive codes are for many people the preconditions for such beliefs, but they by no means guarantee them. Countervailing factors such as the blandishments of prosperity, power, or the elitist social milieu of high culture often make people who are born into or attain the upper social classes as conservative as, or more so than, those in lower classes. (The conservative effect of power on academic and journalistic intellectuals is the central theme of Noam Chomsky's several books attacking "the new American mandarins.") On immediate issues such as labor disputes, unionized industrial or clerical workers are likely to be more militant than, say, college professors, though the former are less likely to be capable of synthesizing militancy on concrete issues into a systematic leftist ideology. And regardless of self-interest, educated people may rationally assimilate leftist perspectives yet move beyond them to a refined conservative philosophy.

Indeed, elaborated codes are necessary for the formulation of *any* reasoned ideology—socialist, liberal, conservative, libertarian, or whatever. The implication of my entire analysis here is not that cultural critics and educators should try to impose a leftist political persuasion on the public or students. They *do* have a responsibility, however, to help deprogram public and students from the uninformed conservatism induced by illiteracy and mass media, while at the same time striving to raise American public discourse to the higher levels of unconstricted debate among all reasoned ideologies.

Notes

Reprinted from *New Literary History* 18 (1986–87).

1. See the introductory sections and readings in *American Media and Mass Culture: Left Perspectives*, ed. Donald Lazere (Berkeley, Calif., 1987).

2. Kate Moody, *Growing Up on Television* (New York, 1980).

3. Mina Shaughnessy, *Errors and Expectations* (New York, 1977), 226–74.

4. Jean Piaget, *The Language and Thought of the Child* (New York, 1955); Sarah F. Campbell, ed., *Piaget Sampler* (New York, 1976); Lawrence Kohlberg, *The Philosophy of Moral Development* (San Francisco, 1981); and William Perry, *Forms of Intellectual and Ethical Development in the College Years* (New York, 1970).

5. See Eric A. Havelock, *Preface to Plato* (Cambridge, Mass., 1963); Jack Goody and Ian Watt, "The Consequences of Literacy," in *Language and Social Context*, ed. Pier Paolo Giglioli (New York, 1972), 311–57; Walter J. Ong, *The Presence of the Word* (New Haven, Conn., 1967) and *Orality and Literacy* (New York, 1982); Marshall McLuhan, *The Gutenberg Galaxy*

(Toronto, 1962); and Lev Vygotsky, *Thought and Language* (Cambridge, Mass., 1962).

6. T. W. Adorno et al., *The Authoritarian Personality* (New York, 1950); Gordon W. Allport, *The Nature of Prejudice*, 25th anniversary ed. (Reading, Mass., 1979); Milton Rokeach, *The Open and Closed Mind* (New York, 1960); and Seymour Martin Lipset, *Political Man* (New York, 1960), 87–179.

7. Oscar Lewis, *Five Families: Mexican Case Studies in the Culture of Poverty* (New York, 1959) and *La Vida* (New York, 1965); and Eleanor Burke, ed., *The Culture of Poverty: A Critique* (New York, 1971). "The culture of poverty" was an ill-chosen phrase that provoked much controversy in the 1960s because it was interpreted in some quarters of the Left as falsely implying that poor people, especially black and Hispanic, had an impoverished culture or none at all. This was not the intended meaning of the term—perhaps "psychology of poverty" would have been a less ambiguous way of denoting the internalized patterns that often resign people to poverty regardless of what the initial, external causes of it may be.

8. Basil Bernstein, *Class, Codes, and Control* (New York, 1975) and *Class, Codes, and Control*, vol. 3 (Boston, 1977); Claus Mueller, *The Politics of Communication: A Study in the Political Sociology of Language, Socialization, and Legitimation* (New York, 1973); and Martin Deutsch, Irwin Katz, and Arthur R. Jensen, eds., *Social Class, Race, and Psychological Development* (New York, 1968).

9. Andrea Lunsford, "The Content of Basic Writers' Essays," *College Composition and Communication* 31, no. 3 (1980): 278–90.

10. Goody and Watt, "Consequences of Literacy," 352–53.

11. Thomas J. Farrell, "Developing Literacy: Walter J. Ong and Basic Writing," *Basic Writing* 2, no. 1 (Fall/Winter 1978): 30–51.

12. Moody, *Growing Up on Television*, 63, 67.

13. *San Francisco Sunday Examiner and Chronicle* (March 16, 1975), 14.

14. William Safire, *Before the Fall* (New York, 1974), 314.

15. *Los Angeles Times* (February 10, 1980), pt. 2, p. 1.

16. Michael Cole and Sylvia Scribner, *Culture and Thought: A Psychological Introduction* (New York, 1974); Scribner and Cole, *The Psychology of Literacy* (Cambridge, Mass., 1981).

17. William Labov, "The Logic of Nonstandard English," in *Language and Social Context*, 179–215.

18. Michael Cole and Jerome Bruner, "Some Preliminaries to Some Theories of Cultural Difference," in *Yearbook of the National Society for the Study of Education* (Chicago, 1972).

19. Goody and Watt, "Consequences of Literacy," 341. Pierre Bourdieu and Jean-Claude Passeron, *Reproduction in Education, Society, and Culture*, trans. Richard Nice (London and Beverly Hills, Calif., 1977).

20. Ben Sidran, *Black Talk* (New York, 1971), 2–13.

21. Lewis, *La Vida*, xlviii.

22. Among the many empirical studies confirming this point, see George Gerbner et al., "Charting the Mainstream: Television's Contributions to Political Orientations," *Journal of Communication* 32, no. 2 (1982): 100–27.

23. John Fiske and John Hartley, *Reading Television* (New York, 1978), 109–26.

24. See Moody, *Growing Up on Television*, 67.

25. Piaget, "The Development in Children of the Idea of the Homeland and of Relations with Other Countries," in *Piaget Sampler*, 37–58.

26. George Gerbner and Larry Gross, "The Violent Face of Television and Its Lessons," in *Children and the Faces of Television: Teaching, Violence, Selling* (New York, 1981), 149–62.

27. For further analysis of the conservative effects of stereotyping in the regularization of media formulas and temporal and spatial frames, see Todd Gitlin, "Television's Screens: Hegemony in Transition," in *Cultural and Economic Reproduction in Education*, ed. Michael Apple (London, 1982), 202–46, as well as T. W. Adorno's seminal essay "Television and the Patterns of Mass Culture," in *Mass Culture*, ed. Bernard Rosenberg and David Manning White (New York, 1957), 474–89. Adorno observed, "The more stereotypes become reified and rigid in the present setup of cultural industry, the less people are likely to change their preconceived ideas with the progress of their experience. The more opaque and complicated modern life becomes, the more people are tempted to cling desperately to clichés which seem to bring some order into the otherwise ununderstandable" (p. 484).

28. Mueller, *Politics of Communication*, 100, 98.

29. Ibid., 115.

30. Richard Ohmann, "Questions about Literacy and Political Education," *Radical Teacher* 8 (May 1978): 24.

31. Ibid., 25. Ohmann revised his position, in a direction more critical of Bernstein and Mueller on grounds of their definitions and methods, in "Reflections on Class and Language," *College English* 44, no. 1 (January 1982): 1–17. See also the subsequent exchange between Ohmann and two commentators in ibid. 45, no. 3 (March 1983): 301–7.

32. "Cultural Imperialism, Mass Media and Class Struggle: An Interview with Armand Mattelart," *Insurgent Sociologist* 9, no. 4 (Spring 1980): 76–77.

33. In an exchange between Christopher Lasch and Herbert Gans on this point, Gans presented a liberal-pluralist case for the broadening effects of mass culture, while Lasch's position, as in his "The Culture of Narcissism, was similar to mine here. Lasch, "Mass Culture Reconsidered," *democracy* 1, no. 4 (October 1981): 7–22; Gans, "Culture, Community, and Equality," ibid. 2, no. 2 (April 1982): 81–87; and Lasch, "Popular Culture and the Illusion of Choice," ibid., 88–92.

34. Erich Fromm, *Escape from Freedom* (New York, 1941), 250.

35. Alvin Gouldner, "The New Class as a Speech Community," in *The Future of Intellectuals and the Rise of the New Class* (New York, 1979), 28–42.

36. Bruce Andrews, *Public Constraint and American Policy in Vietnam* (London, 1976). Noam Chomsky cites Andrews as evidence that the lower classes had sounder instincts about Vietnam than many intellectuals—but he casually relegates to a footnote the key "win or get out" qualifier. Chomsky, *Towards a New Cold War* (New York, 1982), 89, 405–6.

Contributors

Robert Darnton was educated at Harvard and Oxford universities and is now Shelby Cullom Davis Professor of European History at Princeton. His books include *Mesmerism and the End of the Enlightenment in France; The Business of Enlightenment: A Publishing History of the Encyclopédie 1775–1800; The Literary Underground of the Old Regime;* and *The Great Cat Massacre and Other Episodes in French Cultural History.*

Cathy N. Davidson, professor of English at Duke University and managing editor of *American Literature,* is a recent recipient of a Guggenheim Fellowship. Among her books are *The Experimental Fictions of Ambrose Bierce, Revolution and the Word: The Rise of the Novel in America,* and editions of America's first two best-selling novels, Susanna Haswell Rowson's *Charlotte Temple* and Hannah Webster Foster's *The Coquette.*

Donald Franklin Joyce is director of the Felix G. Woodward Library, Austin Peay State University. He is the author of *Gatekeepers of Black Culture: Black-Owned Book Publishing in the United States, 1817–1981* and *Blacks in the Humanities, 1750–1984: A Selected Annotated Bibliography.* His articles have appeared in *Illinois Libraries, Journal of Library History, American Libraries, Book Research Quarterly,* and *The Library Quarterly.*

Donald Lazere is professor of English at California Polytechnic State University, San Luis Obispo. He is the editor of *American Media and*

Mass Culture: Left Perspectives and the author of *The Unique Creation of Albert Camus*. He has written on the politics of literacy, literature, and mass media for *New Literary History, College English, Humanities in Society, The New York Times Book Review,* the *Los Angeles Times,* and *Newsday.*

E. Jennifer Monaghan is an associate professor in the Department of Educational Services, Brooklyn College, City University of New York. She is the founder of the History of Reading Special Interest Group of the International Reading Association and edits the group's newsletter. She is the author of *A Common Heritage: Noah Webster's Blue-Back Speller.*

Victor Neuburg was educated at Varndean and the universities of London and Leicester. He has taught at universities in London, Buffalo, New York, and Halifax, Nova Scotia. Among his many books and articles on English and American mass education and popular literature are *Popular Education in Eighteenth-Century England; Chapbooks; Popular Literature;* and *The Batsford Companion to Popular Literature.* He is currently at work on *Gone for a Soldier,* a social history of the British army.

David Paul Nord, associate professor in the School of Journalism at Indiana University, has published extensively on the history of mass media in the life of the American city. His articles have appeared in journals such as *Communication Research, Journalism Monographs,* and *Journal of Urban History.* He is also the author of *Newspapers and New Politics: Midwestern Municipal Reform, 1890–1900.*

Sharon O'Brien is professor of English and American Studies at Dickinson College. In 1987–88 she was a Fulbright lecturer in American Studies at Trinity College, Dublin. The author of *Willa Cather: The Emerging Voice,* she is also editor of the Library of America edition of the works of Willa Cather. She is now working on a study of Three Mile Island as cultural symbol and tourist experience.

Janice A. Radway is a professor in the Program in Literature at Duke University and author of *Reading the Romance: Women, Patriarchy, and Popular Literature.* She has been editor of *American Quarterly* and a Gugghenheim Fellow. She is now working on a study of the Book-of-the-Month Club and the transformation of literary production and reading in the twentieth century.

Dana Nelson Salvino is assistant professor of English at Louisiana State University, and is working on a book tentatively titled "Problems of Knowing: Reading 'Race' in American Literature, 1630–

1870." She has published in *American Quarterly, Belles Lettres, Centennial Review,* and *Early American Literature.*

Barbara Sicherman is William R. Kenan, Jr., Professor of American Institutions and Values at Trinity College, Hartford. An American cultural historian, she specializes in women's history. She is author of *Alice Hamilton: A Life in Letters* and coeditor of *Notable American Women: The Modern Period.*

Ronald J. Zboray is assistant professor of history at the University of Texas at Arlington and microfilm editor of the Emma Goldman Papers at the University of California, Berkeley. His articles have appeared in *Film and History, Southwest Review, American Quarterly, Book Research Quarterly, American Archivist, Journal of American Culture,* and the *International Journal of Micrographics and Video Technology.*